SLICK

SLICK

The Silver and Black
Life of Al Davis

MARK RIBOWSKY

Macmillan Publishing Company   NEW YORK
Maxwell Macmillan Canada   TORONTO
Maxwell Macmillan International
NEW YORK   OXFORD   SINGAPORE   SYDNEY

Macmillan Publishing Company   Maxwell Macmillan Canada, Inc.
866 Third Avenue   1200 Eglinton Avenue East
New York, NY 10022   Suite 200
    Don Mills, Ontario M3C 3N1

Macmillan Publishing Company is part of the Maxwell Communication Group
of Companies.

Ribowsky, Mark.
    Slick: the silver and black life of Al Davis/by Mark Ribowsky.
      p. cm.
    Includes index.
    ISBN 0-02-602500-0
    1. Davis, Al, 1929-   . 2. Football—United States—Coaches—
Biography. 3. Oakland Raiders (Football team) 4. Football—United
States—Team owners—Biography.   I. Title.
GV939.D342R53 1991   91-13617 CIP
796.332'092—dc20
[B]

Macmillan books are available at special discounts for bulk purchases for sales
promotions, premiums, fund-raising, or educational use. For details, contact:

           Special Sales Director
           Macmillan Publishing Company
           866 Third Avenue
           New York, NY 10022

10 9 8 7 6 5 4 3 2 1
Printed in the United States of America

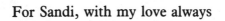

For Sandi, with my love always

ACKNOWLEDGMENTS

Because vivid men beget vivid memories, few of the more than one hundred people interviewed for this book could be termed reluctant sources, nor could their recollections about Al Davis be called vague. If there was one common thread to all of them, it was that they had not just memories but something more, something that clarified a myth, something someone needed to get off a chest, something about Al Davis's character, good or bad. Again, this is testament to what Al Davis is, but also to their longing for history to finally get the story right. In synthesizing and interpreting this mass of fact, emotion, and conjecture, I can only hope I have done justice to them and to Al Davis.

For major contributions to truth and insight, I am at once grateful to five people in particular who filled in decisive gaps in Davis's life and his psyche: Ron Mix, Tom Keating, Harry Schuh, Todd Christensen, and Pat Sarnese. Much of the perspective of this book derived from the thoughtful cues of these splendid athletes, whose vision extends way beyond the gridiron.

I would also like to express my heartfelt appreciation to Gladys Valley, John Rauch, and John Sauer for reliving days of rage and regret that they all would just as soon let die.

For a football nut, it is an indescribable high to be in the company of coaching genius. By no accident did Al Davis move into prominence through the graces and example of Sid Gillman and Weeb Ewbank, and it is with deep respect that I thank these two giants of the game for their time and perception.

On a different plane of respect and admiration, I thank George Ross, who in the world of sports journalism is an all-time great himself. This kind, direct man helped bring Al Davis to the Raiders and his closeness to the team and to the man positioned him perfectly to see both Davis's talents and his duplicity. Through George's efforts, obscure ownership documents that might have been lost in time instead arose to shed valuable light on the Raiders' operation.

From the hard concrete of Brooklyn to the soft polyturf of the Los Angeles Coliseum, many voices made this book radiate with detail and drama. For their trenchant observations, and for giving me their trust, my sincere thanks to Ernie Pugatch, Larry Krevins, Leon Cohen, Bob Wallach, Bill Label, Ben Schwartzwalder, Bill Altenberg, Dick Bergeron, Hank Lauricella, George Morris, Pug Pearman, Budgie Broome, Bob Daugherty, Barry Thomas, Jim McDaniel, Carl Wunderler, Bob Schwarze.

Also to Dan Ficca, Ben Charles, Don Voyne, Mel Hein, Marv Goux, Nick Pappas, Ray George, Marv Marinovich, Jim Sears, Dave Kocourek, Lance Alworth, Joe Madro, Jack Faulkner, Ollie Spencer, Dave Costa, Dalva Allen, Clem Daniels, Jim Otto, Dave Grayson, Daryle Lamonica, Scotty Stirling, Lee Grosscup, Pete Banaszak.

I should also like to acknowledge the dozens of college sports information offices and alumni associations across the nation that contributed key telephone numbers of football players long gone from the public stage. A special nod of appreciation goes to Luke LaPorta of Syracuse, Alan Didinger of Wittenberg, Claude Ruggian of Adelphi, Skip Richey of Ft. Belvoir, Josh Baker of The Citadel, and Melanie Neff of USC. And one more nod for archival help to Holly Haverty of *Sport*, Steven Gietscher of *The Sporting News* and Herman Masin of *Scholastic Coach* for referencing and forwarding a sheaf of back clippings.

I am thankful for, and blessed to have, a friend like Patti Stren, who told me this would be a great book so many times that I began to believe it.

And I am genuinely indebted to several people who should rightly be credited for their advice, consent, wisdom, and encouragement in the course of this work: my agent, Jay Acton, whose inspired suggestion grew by leaps and bounds into the book now before you; my editor at Macmillan, Rick Wolff, an athlete and a scholar whose judgment is matched only by his respect for good writing; and his assistant, Jeanine Bucek, whose endless supply of good cheer is like tonic to an exhausted writer.

Finally, thank you, Al Davis, for being so inscrutable and so daunting a figure that no writer dared do this book before I did.

INTRODUCTION

A story about Al Davis and gall: In 1956, Davis—the twenty-seven-year-old line coach at The Citadel, and notorious even then—was, as ever, in the eye of a storm. In two seasons at the Charleston, South Carolina, military academy, Davis had recruited something like two dozen players, had gained a national reputation as a football maven, and had managed to unnerve almost everyone at the place: John Sauer, the head coach, because he believed Al was taking bows for the ideas of Sauer and other top football men in the country (Al often intimated that he practically wrote the Citadel playbook and coined the term "Racehorse Football" for the team's attack); the players, because he had not come through on alleged recruiting promises; and, as a result, The Citadel's NCAA representative, who was eager to find out more about Al Davis's methods.

With rumors of improprieties and NCAA penalties growing around Al's feet like wild tarweed, John Sauer quit—with three years left on his contract—lest he be implicated. And yet, only days after Sauer was out of the picture, the young line coach called on The Citadel's president, the famous general Mark Clark. Seemingly oblivious to the chaos he had caused, Al Davis asked to be named head coach.

It mattered not that Mark Clark had commanded the Allied invasion of Italy and liberated Rome in World War II. To Al, he was like all the others, simply a means to advancement. Sizing up the tall, erect, five-star general, Davis was effusive in his loyalty to The Citadel—why, he had even named his infant son after Clark. Then he got down to business, with the Al Davis finesse and charm.

"General," he began, "I hear you're looking for a coach that can win games."

"Yes, Al, I am," drawled Clark.

"Well, I'm available."

Clark, whose desk was piled high with letters indignant about Al Davis from Citadel alumni and the parents of unhappy Citadel sons, answered with military directness.

"Al," he said, "I want to win football games, too. But"—now he drew out the words slowly, emphatically, pointedly—"not at any price."

Stung by the rebuff, Al Davis quickly took his leave from The Citadel—to some there, it seemed that he went in a laundry truck in the dark of night, a step ahead of the authorities—but with the satisfaction of having outflanked the great general. Soon after, he had a job as assistant coach at USC. And when Al Davis arrived in Los Angeles, the loyal son of The Citadel had taken with him several of Mark Clark's best football players.

Gall. It's the first thing that must be mentioned by way of introducing the subject of this book. Al Davis, who never played a down of college or pro football, has ridden gall like a wild steed to heights of power few in football have reached. Gall. Al Davis has always believed that he knows more football than anyone else—and that if he doesn't, he can make people *think* he does.

John Sauer wasn't the only one of Al's superiors who felt undermined by him. Al did it to Don Clark during that next stop at USC, and later to the great Sid Gillman with the Los Angeles/San Diego Chargers. If it didn't go down Al's way, there was just no reason to discuss it. And why not? By the dawning of the sixties, Al Davis could reasonably feel this way, as a whole football league was arising as one result of his gall.

The impish flame of the American Football League was lit by Al Davis; he signed some of its marquee talent—most notably Lance Alworth, the first AFL player to be inducted into the National Football League Hall of Fame—and his big-bomb theory (or rather, his applications of Sid Gillman's big-bomb theories) provided a large part of the AFL's identity and dash. Al, with Chuck Noll, Hank Stram, Chuck Knox, and a clutch of others, represented the young, dynamic blood of the new league, in growing contrast to the sclerotic game played in the NFL.

Davis, a hard-liner in foreign affairs and a supporter of militarism (he himself had spent the Korean War making the world safe for democracy coaching football on an army base in Virginia), at the same time appreciates social upheaval, even if he doesn't quite understand it. He was made for the new era of football—and society—in which instant satisfaction, amorality, and antiheroism replaced Christian humility, and getting the "edge" and rubbing noses in the dirt supplanted good sportsmanship. Strategically, Davis had nothing on other top football minds—he just liked wasting people, physically and mentally, breaking their backs with big plays from anywhere on the field. Gall.

At thirty-two, Al Davis could hardly be contained any longer. He was named head coach and general manager of a then-moribund team, the Oakland Raiders, which within four years was re-vamped—Davisized—and an AFL contender. Sensing more, needing more, Al took on the job of AFL commissioner, with the charge of forcing the NFL to merge with a going-broke, six-year-old AFL. Having a public relations staffer write up his bio during his first day on the job, Al told him to start with two words: "Dynamic" and "Genius."

Davis's people then signed two of the older league's prime quarterbacks and were going for total annihilation when the AFL's owners—who may have appointed him as a way to be rid of him as a competitor—pulled back the reins and said, Whoa, boy, we got what we want. That was a sudden NFL offer to merge, on terms Al thought could be better. Some believe Al's own terms would have included Al Davis as commissioner of the new NFL, though in the Davis battlefield mosaic that may have been the last thing he wanted.

Early in the following year, 1967, the first Super Bowl was played. The next year, with Al back in Oakland as the team's co-owner—specifically, managing general partner, a term he was to make famous in football—the Raiders played in Super Bowl II, though as grist for the mighty Green Bay Packers of Vince Lombardi. Almost two and a half decades later, after gobbling up power and getting lodged in people's craws all over pro football, Al Davis is now president of the Raiders—the Los Angeles Raiders, through his graces and gall—though his title should be Generalissimo Al Davis.

In the interim, Al Davis's Raiders have notched the highest winning percentage of any team in pro sports. They have won sixteen division titles and have played in at least one Super Bowl in each of the last three decades, winning three after their initiation against Green Bay (in 1977, 1981, and 1984). For fifteen straight years, from 1965 to 1981, they had winning seasons. Twelve times they have won ten games or more.

How they achieved all this can only be traced to Al Davis, who went about building his teams in a manner that was anathema to the rest of the league. Always, they have been a mélange of odds and ends, oddities and irregulars, factory seconds and seeming chain-gang escapees. There were Ben Davidson's handlebar mustache; Fred Biletnikoff's stickum-stained fingers; George Blanda's ageless leg; Ted Hendricks wearing a pumpkin as a helmet; and the Jack Daniels poster boys, Ken Stabler and John Matuszak.

Given football life by Al Davis, they were in effect analogues *of* Al Davis. Outlaws. Outcasts. Hell Raiders. They played football his way, the way Al Davis would have loved to if only his tortured, feral soul could have been somehow transferred to his motor responses when he thought *he* might have been a storied athlete. But Willie Brown, Art Shell, Ike Lassiter, Phil Villapiano, Rod Martin, and, now, Marcus Allen and Bo Jackson, are also analogues of Al Davis, men with quiet dignity but frightful resolve; clean, efficient killers in response to a clear and present danger.

Yet, in many ways, to see Al Davis today is a great joy and a great pity. Joy because we can see him through a historical lens as the first great American antihero who could actually *get his way*, not merely seek to and fall back in defeat, a moral object lesson to the rest. Knowing what he *could* wreak, Davis minced no words or actions—he *acted* the part. He had his team wear black as its primary color and silver as its complement. Arriving in the sixties, he knew that bad could be marketable—men in white hats weren't necessarily the good guys anymore, not when you couldn't trust 'em for a minute.

Even the Raiders' motivational apothegms—"Pride and Poise," "Commitment to Excellence"—were devices of mockery, football vaudeville designed to parody the uptight sensibilities of the pro football world that despised Davis. Now, the bad guys could be as "excellent" as the prudes, use their kind of mottoes, scream in their faces. Their sepulchral colors and the eyepatched pirate they wore on their helmets became an icon of the times, playing well to baby boomers just starting to appreciate football as an updated art. Almost from the start, Al Davis was assured a wide audience even though he was in one of football's smallest and least wealthy markets.

There is more joy remembering how Al Davis beat the monolith of reactionary power in the old NFL. This corporate bureaucracy, gifted with an early antitrust exemption from Congress, is not quite the monopoly monster it once was, and this is Al Davis's doing. Gall. Davis, the old desperado, rode that steed right out of Oakland in 1982, even though the people of that decaying city supported him with maniacal fervor. Al liked them, too, but it wasn't as if they came out to see a bunch of feebs, either; Al never gave them a chance to prove their loyalty. But the point to Al was that other owners had much more lucrative perks and more money to help them keep competitive teams on the field. Al Davis did not. Also, the stadium in Oakland sucked.

So Al Davis became the first sports team owner since Walter O'Malley—the scourge of the Brooklyn streets on which Al grew up—to abscond from a city purely for greed. It was on this issue, of course, that the burghers of the NFL decided to make a grand stand against Al Davis. They had to. Pete Rozelle, the patrician commissioner, told them they had to. Pete Rozelle was so freaked out by the menace of Al Davis that he staked the league's money and its future on defeating Davis's move to Los Angeles. Rozelle was as confident as Napoleon on the march through the Russian winter, and just as foolhardy.

To Rozelle, Al was an urchin outside the NFL palace, an outcast who could not possibly alter the wishes of twenty-seven other lords. But Al had one thing Rozelle did not—he had the law. He sued his own league, claiming that it had abridged his rights as an owner and a citizen to make more money, and he proved it in court by hoisting the NFL with its own antitrust petard. For the league and for Rozelle, who never lost a bigger battle than this one, it stung more than the $18 million the other owners wound up paying Al Davis in damages. Risking everything, they lost their birthright because of arrogance and intolerance.

Winning, of course, has its privileges. When Al Davis was ostensibly considering moving his team *back* to Oakland last year—and only Al Davis *could* have considered it—the upshot was that, if he did, the league could have done nothing but watch him uproot again; after his example, after all, two other teams had done just that. More astonishingly, given the league's realignment in the 1980s and the retirement of Pete Rozelle in 1989, the shakeout was kindly disposed to Davis. Indeed, the new commissioner, Paul Tagliabue, was elected after Jim Finks was spurned by new-guard owners reverential to Al Davis. Though Al himself was partial to Finks, Davis, a Machiavelli from way back, broke the deadlock by turning his back on Finks and aligning with Tagliabue. Only a decade ago, it was even money that Al Davis would not survive such men, much less be able to veto them.

At the same time, it is also ironic that some of Al's allies in an NFL deregulated in part by his antitrust win have arguably left the league with a corporate face that excludes football men of simple means from ownership. But that is part of the downside of Al Davis's ascent into elitism. He is not the rebel of old. As Davis has admitted, he is quite frankly puzzled by the football and the players of the nineties.

Therein lies the pity, that with no more overt enemies to rouse his passions, Al Davis is too comfortable. Worse, he is today a victim of "modernization," his brand of football alien in an era of the sideline huddle, the one-back offense, and the "Run and Shoot." In the NFL of the nineties, *everyone* seems to be mean-spirited, not intimidating in the old Raider fashion, but out to dismember. It is as if the NFL has gotten back at Davis by forcing him to try to apply past rituals to future-schlock football. And, given Davis's stubborn and unrewarded faith in mediocre quarterbacks since the mid-eighties—Marc Wilson's futility is all but linked to Al Davis's name now—the question must arise: Has time passed Davis by?

We will not know the answer until the Raiders of the nineties emerge in earnest, but the Davis gall and the Davis ego are inviting targets for critics. Thus, it was inevitable that with the Raiders in a five-year playoff drought, Davis would be subject to a requiem sooner or later. *Sports Illustrated* got down on it first, painting Al

Davis in its December 1989 issue as a man "haunted by mortality and defeat," "not as defiant," and "practically Establishment."

People like Al Davis walk along the perilous edge of a great gorge; as long as they keep their balance they endure on their skills and instincts; a slip and the world tenses, anticipating a bloody end. But other than the fact that the Davis legend has been pronounced dead before—as far back as the late seventies, after John Madden quit as head coach, and yet the team went 70–35 over the next seven seasons and won two Super Bowls—there is a small problem with this "establishment" business. A man who cuts off his enemies' balls before they can cut off his is never on safe ground.

Though seven of Al's former players are in the Hall of Fame, Davis is not; and who knows how long it will take for the league and the sportswriters to admit he belongs. But, for now, the outlaw scent is still pungent around Davis, which he must love. Davis always said he wanted to be feared, not loved, and if it's not exactly fear today, neither is it anywhere near love.

We cannot write off Al Davis yet. He may at times sound like a bad actor who can't break away from an old role. When he speaks of his team playing with "controlled aggression," he says it as if no one else plays that way. But that's just the point about Al Davis— he's *always* said it as if no one else played that way, because Davis sincerely believes this is so. His rituals have a *context*, if an irrational one: only the Raiders are entitled to rely on such pap. This is a delusion, of course, but it solders team to owner like no other. Hell, even prototypical football men like George Halas and Paul Brown, who owned their teams because of passion for the game, made an eventual accommodation with the NFL power structure and lost the focus of their cause.

Although this book was written independently of Al Davis and without any expectation of Raider success as a propellant, the lessons—the entire *premise*—of these pages made it something less than shocking that as they were being written, the Raiders entered another renascence. Even less surprisingly, it was during this time that those who had been ready to bury Davis hastily backtracked —by early in the 1990 season, *Sports Illustrated* had this as a cover line: "Rebirth of the Raiders." By the end of the season, they were playing in the AFC championship game.

The lesson is that you don't count out the Raiders. Not while they are a function of Davis's force. And they are still. The Raiders do not belong to any scouting combine; why share information that Al Davis takes to be his and his alone? They have no public relations department; why be helpful to prying eyes? Al Davis is himself a classic loner, quilled for combat. He loves his family and his players, but he is essentially alone, a prisoner of football and his mystique.

That Al Davis has ignored moral imperatives does not mean he hasn't thought about them. A tip-off on this is his well-documented fear of death. To Al, this is the great equalizer, the door that could slam on him at any moment, even a victorious one. That many of his old friends—and several of his recent players—have died since the mid-eighties has reinforced what he first realized when his father died of a heart attack at age fifty-five: Al Davis was fallible.

Then, and now, all he could do was flee this burden, and try to bury concepts like fear, karma, and guilt—for example, whose fault is it that Raider players have died young, or that one of his most cherished analogues, Jack Tatum, now lives in Purgatory because of one literally paralyzing hit on a wide receiver? Is it *his* fault? Davis tries not to think about the answer, hiding within the amorality of Social Darwinism.

Davis has said he was heavily influenced as a young man by Theodore Dreiser's 1900 novel *Sister Carrie*, a grim parable of weakness and distraction. The story concerns a wealthy businessman, Hurstwood, who leaves his wife and comforts for the beautiful, innocent aspiring actress Carrie—and then loses everything he has as she eclipses and rejects him. In the end, he dies of starvation in a flophouse, and his body is carted off for burial in a potter's field, unclaimed. Al Davis has replayed that ending in his mind for years, a warning light flashing the dangers of flagging commitment and too much trust in others. When his football dream was still nascent, he vowed never to be a Hurstwood.

As a result, he became the most riveting figure in football since the great Lombardi. Certainly he is the most outrageous individual to cross this or any sport. In light of his holy war with the Pharisees of the old NFL order, he wears his sepulchral black and silver raiment with apostolic grace. A Disraeli he is not—nor was Lombardi. He has often ruled by deceit, and his obsessive purge of Wayne Valley, the man who brought him to the Raiders and to ownership, was in many ways beneath contempt.

He is also the most important and influential club owner of our time.

Al Davis has left his path littered with bodies he has stepped over, and he has made enough enemies to fill a large section of the Los Angeles Coliseum; this book includes their voices. Yet few begrudge Davis his brilliance, and neither do I. Indeed, if I have betrayed my own sociopolitical leanings in charting Al Davis's considerable legacy, it is because I could not help but see as heroic his crusades against the hoary, even bigoted ways of men in high places in sports. However, while this book has in many respects come to praise Al Davis, and not to bury him, readers would do well to keep in mind one simple truism: We will never know how good Al Davis is until we know how bad he is.

1

Carrie looked at him, while pedestrians stared at her. She felt the strain of publicity. So did Hurstwood.

"Why don't you tell me what's the matter with you?" she asked, hardly knowing what to do. "Where are you living?"

"Oh, I've got a room down in the Bowery," he answered. "There's no use trying to tell you here. I'm all right now."

He seemed in a way to resent her kindly inquiries—so much better had fate dealt with her.

—Theodore Dreiser, *Sister Carrie*

I've always been aggressive. Not to hurt anyone, but to get things done. To speed it up. To have the feeling that I can dominate.

—Al Davis

In May of 1950, one day after he graduated from Syracuse University, twenty-one-year-old Al Davis strode briskly into the office of Bill Altenberg, the athletic director at Adelphi University. A small school in Garden City, New York, near the western border of Long Island, Adelphi had only a few years before been an all-girl school. Turning coed as thousands of soldiers returned home after World War II, it had established a small but thriving football program. That is what brought Al Davis—unannounced and with no prior solicitation—into Bill Altenberg's office.

"He came in and asked for a job as assistant coach," Altenberg remembered. "He told me he had written an article on rule blocking, which is a system where your tackles call different blocking assignments at the line, depending on the defensive setup, so you get good angles.

"Well, I'd known about rule blocking for years. I did it when I was coaching at Adelphi. We did it at Columbia. I don't think there was any school that didn't have it, including Syracuse, and I think that's where he got it from—although his system worked it around to where he also had the center calling, too. I hadn't seen that before.

"Still, it wasn't anything new—and I didn't even think it was his article. I didn't know who Al Davis was. I already had two people as freshman coaches, guys who'd played football, both at Rutgers, and I told him I didn't have any vacancies—which was true, because we were allowed only two freshman coaches.

"He was polite about it. This is a very charming guy, Al Davis. He just left my office and I thought that was it for him."

Davis didn't. His next drop-in visit was to the office of the Adelphi president, Dr. Paul Dawson Eddy. What went on in there has been a matter of bemused speculation, and Eddy's death years ago guaranteed it would forever be so. It is certain that Al Davis used his charm. But the Davis charm is a compound of several ingredients: bluff and con are two of them.

Leon Cohen knew Davis from the old neighborhood in Brooklyn and then at Syracuse, where Cohen was cocaptain of the football team, while Davis never made the squad. "I heard that he walked in and said, 'I'm Davis from Syracuse,' and I think they might've thought he was George Davis, our great All-East halfback," Cohen said. "That's how I heard the story. It made the rounds for a long time—that was how he got in the door, because they assumed he was George Davis.

"Al may not have had to say anything false, just go with the mistaken identity. And the way he'd been studying those playbooks of Ben Schwartzwalder's at Syracuse, he could certainly talk football."

Bill Haskins, who shared the backfield with George Davis on Schwartzwalder's first Orange team in 1949, heard the story and had no trouble believing it. "George Davis was the star of the team, and Al used to impersonate him from time to time. The way I got it [at Adelphi], it was, 'I'm Davis from Syracuse'—and he had George Davis's clippings."

"Here's the thing about Al Davis. He never backed down from anything that could give him that extra edge, if it gave him something to trade on," explained Pascal Perri, captain of the Syracuse wrestling team, who Schwartzwalder brought onto the football squad. "I'm not saying he lied about it; in his mind, *he* was Davis. If people sometimes got the Davises mixed up, Al never backed away from the fact that he was *the* Davis. If people were introduced to him and they'd say, 'Oh, Davis. You're the football player,' it would be, 'Yeah. Yeah, I play football.'

"Listen, Al Davis's mind doesn't work like your mind and my mind. It's entirely different. Al will *beat* you, one way or another. So our buddies from Syracuse said, 'Did you hear what Al did?' The rumor was that they did confuse him for *the* Davis, and Al never backed down. And you know what? Looking back, he *is* the Davis from Syracuse."

Bill Altenberg only knew that, half an hour after Al Davis left his office, Dr. Paul Dawson Eddy called him and said, "Bill, you've got a new freshman coach." Davis hadn't only charmed the normally stern Eddy; he made Eddy rewrite the rules on freshman coaches. "Why? Because he sold Eddy a bill of goods," Altenberg said, "which he's been doing from time immemorial. How do you think he got all of his other football jobs?"

The next year, Altenberg gave up the AD job to teach phys ed at the school. Though Altenberg had not been close with Davis, he saw Davis strike up an almost familial personal relationship with Altenberg's successor, Ed Stanczyk. Altenberg suspected that Davis was playing favorites, for two reasons: to spite Altenberg and to suck up to Stanczyk. That second season at Adelphi, Davis was promoted to full-time varsity line coach.

"They were very, very close," according to Altenberg, "and there are reasons why they were that close. All I can say is, if an individual like Al Davis can't find his way, he could buy his way.

"I've got my ideas about what he did with Stanczyk. Stanczyk moved into a house, I understand, with the help of Al Davis's father. Al Davis came from money, his father was in the ladies' clothing business, and Stanczyk had two or three daughters. And Eddie Stanczyk set him up as the line coach. Need I say more?"

Altenberg's suspicions may have been heightened by his feeling that Davis spited him. "You know what? Al Davis says he doesn't even remember me. He's told people we both know that he doesn't know my name. This guy has a mind like you wouldn't believe. He can walk in a room and meet people he hasn't seen for years and he can call 'em by their first names. But he doesn't remember

me. Maybe he just doesn't like me because I didn't give him the
job."

At twenty-one, Al Davis began his football career with all the elements he needed. He had an aptitude for the game that many men
much older could not approach, an eye for detail, and, like all great
coaches, he had *presence*. Though he had been a washout as an
athlete, he had surrounded himself with players of distinction at
Syracuse, inhaling their sweaty air of conceit. The real point of the
Al/George Davis story wasn't whether it was apocryphal but rather
that Al Davis—big and wide enough at nearly six feet and 170 hard
pounds—could pass for an elite jock.

He had the look, the manner, the cool. He looked, well, *distinct*.
A giant, reddish-blond pompadour swirled in different directions
like a clump of rubber bands above a continent of forehead. His
pale blue eyes, small and darting, could give you the feeling you
were being watched as closely as a pea in a shell game—realizing
that his eyes could betray some hidden thought, he would a decade
later shield them behind tinted glasses. Conversely, the rest of his
face was caramel-smooth, his features soft and eternally adolescent,
engaging, unmarked except for a few squint lines at the eyes and
a small mole near the right corner of his top lip. His enormous two
front teeth gnawed into his bottom lip, and when he smiled he had
to bend his mouth into a crooked oval to accommodate them. Unhappy with the large and meandering nose of his youth, he had
already gotten it fixed, hammered into a sleek cruller, accentuating
his high, commanding cheekbones.

Al was so unique in look, it was hard to identify his ethnic origin,
which was Eastern European Jewish. Defying geographical place-
ment, his Brooklynese was blended with the pinched, hard-voweled
diction ingrained by living the first five years of his life in Brockton,
Massachusetts. With his weird twang and high-pitched voice, he
sounded like a cross between Jimmy Cagney in *The Public Enemy*
and those briny coaches in the South like Bear Bryant.

The latter, in fact, was a conscious affectation, a little trick he
picked up in the old neighborhood from Allie Sherman, the future
New York Giants coach who in Davis's youth quarterbacked at
Brooklyn College and then with the Philadelphia Eagles. Turning
his attention to coaching, Allie told Al that a Brooklyn guy could
recruit and relate to those ol' Southern baw-ahs better if he spoke

through his nose with a Mason-Dixon accent. And Al could talk; better than he did most things, in fact. That was, centrally, why he came off as such a confident cuss.

But Al had all kinds of tricks to make him seem larger, stronger, than he was—right down to his fingers. They were small and thin like gherkins, but Al could nonetheless forge a manly handshake by spreading them wide upon the grasp. Otherwise, as much as possible, his hands found their way into the security of his pockets. There was also the Al Davis walk: steps broad, toes pointing in, head erect. And the Paul Brown, hand-on-hip pose didn't hurt, either.

And yet Al couldn't have made any of his mannerisms work without his most persuasive trait—his boundless nerve. Al had no track record, had no recommendation from Ben Schwartzwalder, no sideline game experience at all. Davis made himself a football maven at Syracuse, but his blocking schemes were simply curiosities without his salesmanship.

"It wasn't just that he knew football," said Pascal Perri. "Al knew about all sports. But he had to make you think he knew *everything* about sports. He'd ask you who played first base for the New York Giants in 1901—and to refute him, you'd have to go look up the record, which you wouldn't do. So very often, Al got away with a lot of that 'expert' stuff on a bluff. He could talk you into believing anything."

This went for anybody. The men of the Syracuse football team were nothing that a sane person would fool with—especially if the person never wore a uniform himself. But Bill Haskins and quarterback Bernie Custis both were taken to the cleaners—quite literally—by a mere jock-sniffer named Al Davis.

"He sold me a suit," Haskins recalled, still wincing four decades later. "Goddamn brown suit that didn't fit. He did the old tailor routine on me. He was tellin' me to look in the mirror in the front and he was pullin' the back to make it look like it fit. And I'd turn around and look in the back and he'd pull it in the front. So I bought the damn suit. He took me for fifteen bucks and that was a lot to pay for a suit then. I pawned it like a year later for seven dollars. That was Al. He could sell anything, most of all himself."

"A green corduroy sport jacket," Custis remembered. "I was quite impressed with it and he said he was short of money for a date. He asked me if I was interested—you know, in that Al Davis way that says: 'Buy it or you're a fool.' And that's what I did."

Al was a visionary in at least one respect: he was an equal-opportunity con man. Bill Haskins and Bernie Custis were black, two of a very few who got to play for Syracuse on those teams in the late forties. That Al Davis snookered two racially isolated players for good-natured sport, the way homogeneous teammates snooker each other, was a small but meaningful blow for inclusion. "He was an open and, to use a term, a liberal kind of guy," said Horace Morris, a black lineman for Syracuse. "He never had all the hangups that some of the other guys had about race. As a black person, I felt very comfortable with him."

"Al made a point of associating with what we might call 'the best,' " Custis related. "That's the way he went, to be the best at what he did, and quite often that's through association, because you learn through association. With him being Jewish, I never thought that his interest would be where it turned out to be, but once he did he approached it only with the idea of what would get him where he wanted to go, whereas others more or less went according to what they *should* do. That's why Al recognized that he could learn about competitiveness from black guys."

Horace Morris thought about that often through the years. "I always thought," he said, "that the NFL owner who would name the first black head coach would be Al Davis."

The stout, stately brick buildings of Crown Heights were the gemstones of a vital, thriving community. In the Brooklyn of the thirties and forties, the marvelous structures of rust-red and tan were tranquil islands, their delicate gates and asphalt courtyards unlocked yet offering secure refuge from the crowded streets. They were built in neat rows after World War One, some of them squat, one- and two-family homes with clean white shutters and small patches of green grass, while others were taller and wider apartment houses with names like "Lincoln Terrace Court" and "President Court" carved into their doorways.

The broad strip of Utica Avenue was a corridor of traditional Jewish culture and fragrance. On either side of the avenue, *tchotchke* shops spilled dry goods onto the sidewalks, in between delicatessens in which turkeys and pastramis dangled from hooks in the front window. Looking south on Utica, one could look past Holy Cross Cemetery to the rolling valley of the Flatlands and the Atlantic Ocean; north to the teeming traffic and elegant brick row houses of Eastern Parkway. In thirty years, the neighborhood would begin to decline as the great middle-class core of the borough started to move out and an urban underclass of blacks and latinos replaced them.

When the revered Dodgers followed the trend, Brooklyn began to die. In another two decades, these same streets would change again, to include West Indian and Jamaican shops. Graffiti would smirch the terrain. But those wonderful homes would still stand, regal and unyielding, in testament to the pride of the men who worked too long and too hard for just a little fragment of prosperity.

These men were of the American generation that had braved the Depression, and nothing would stop them from worrying that it could happen to them again. So they worked, up to fifteen hours a day, sometimes seven days a week. Their wives and children would see them in fleeting glances and a generation of their children grew up knowing little more about their fathers than that they "worked for a living." If the fathers died before their time, and too many did, no autopsy would be necessary; it sufficed to say with a shrug that they "worked too hard."

For their children, the fruits of work meant they would have choice—they would finish high school and go to college and make something of themselves. Maybe they wouldn't have to work as hard. Maybe someday the fathers wouldn't have to, either, if they lived long enough. But for now, their two- and three-room slices of heaven meant more to them than they could ever express.

Louis and Rose Davis lived with their two sons, Jerry and Allen, in just such a bastion inside 1745 President Street, on a wide, tree-lined block lying east of Utica Avenue. The Davises entered the outside door of the six-story, brown-yellow brick building under an intricately constructed archway, then climbed five flights of stairs to their front-side, three-bedroom apartment.

Though these were hardly palatial surroundings, Louis Davis was content here, within walls symbolic of his success. Years before, in Brockton, Louis, who married late in life, had become a first-time father when Jerry was born in 1925. Four years later came Allen, born on the Fourth of July, 1929. To feed and house his family, Louis tried his hand at many professions, including working in a butcher shop, before eventually choosing garment manufacturing. Risking everything he had, in 1934 he moved the family to New York, the hub of the industry. He settled the family in Crown

Heights and opened a company called Little Dutchess Ladies Undergarments.

A superb, tireless businessman, Louis earned a substantial amount of money, yet he never thought to move to showier lodgings. He was comfortable on President Street; it was where he and tenacious men like him deposited their weary bodies for a few minutes of satisfied calm. The other men in the building were just as stubborn. Next door to the Davises lived Allen's best friend, Stanley Rabinowitz, whose father was a well-to-do doctor. Because of *his* father, Stanley would be able to go to law school and then go on to practice law as Stanley Roberts. Louis Davis would put his sons through school as well. Only then would he and Rose move, to a house in South Brooklyn's Atlantic Beach.

"You have to understand about Al's father and all our fathers," said Ernie Pugatch, who went to elementary school, junior high, and high school with Al Davis. "His father was a tough man who grew up in a tough age. The term 'well-off' didn't mean anything to them. In my building on Carroll Street, we had Florsheim of Florsheim Shoes living on the sixth floor. Teitelbaum, who owned Eagle Pencils, lived on the fifth floor.

"In those years, they weren't as 'home conscious' as we are today. They were in a beautiful community, they knew their neighbors, that was enough. It was strange, any sense of a social scene was almost confined to the *building*. These people worked such long hours that once you stepped outside, you were at work."

Hard and intractable as a slab of sheet metal, with a full head of hair and a truncheon of a nose, Louis Davis provided the iron in Al Davis's core.

"His father was a strong-minded but fair man, and I supposed Allen was an offshoot," Pugatch recalled. "Allen was very strong-minded. He was not a boisterous person, but when Al had to say something, he said it. He wasn't one of those kids that ran around shooting off his mouth. But if he wanted to do something, then you heard him and you heard him loudly. Believe me, he was the type of kid who could easily talk to you and influence you in your thinking."

Many years later, stories would be told about Al Davis and his childhood, tough-guy stories. Davis was said to be a fighter, a kid who could use his hands, a wiseguy prince of the street old beyond his years. One story had it that Davis found a screwdriver in the street, and when the guy who dropped it asked the kid if he'd found it, Davis asked him, "Did you lose one with a red handle?" "That's right," the guy said. "Well, I'm sorry," replied Davis. "This one has a green handle."

Louis Davis, in the street scenarios, was tolerant of almost any kind of nuisance behavior his son got into—provided he never got caught. The moral of these stories was that Al Davis was not *ever* supposed to knuckle under to any kind of confrontation. As it turns out, the source for all of the stories was Al Davis. "When your gang met our gang, and I got out in front to fight the other guy, I *had* to win," Al would confide to the nation in a *Look* magazine profile of him in 1969.

Neighborhood friends and schoolmates would read the blather and grin. "That was all media," said Louis Pinsky, a buddy of Al's back then. "I think Al had a good publicity agent, even as a teen-ager. He always wanted to come off as tough, more than he really was."

"He *was* tough, but he was more of a talker than a fighter," clarified Larry Krevins, another friend. "He was sometimes obnoxious, because his mouth was moving all the time and he'd always get people mad at him. He was absolutely egotistical and he had a terrible temper that was tough for him to control. But he had a way of ingratiating himself. He was very articulate and a real *schmoozer*.

"You couldn't stay mad at him, and that part of his personality came to define him. People who knew him loved him, and he was a guy who'd absolutely go out of his way for friends."

"Al's mouth was big but his mind was great," said Ernie Pugatch. "He knew how to express himself in an intelligent way. Why would he have to resort to fighting?"

If there *was* a forum, and an outlet, for Al's roughneck side, it was the hard, ungiving cement of the playground. In this, he was a mere speck in an entire generation of teenagers seeking ways to burn off their energy. These children of work-obsessed, New Deal parents, living in secure homes and relieved of having to work for their keep, turned like no previous generation to leisure time activities. In Brooklyn, where the pavement never ended, the playgrounds were where these children had *their* social scene. There, on baking or glacial asphalt, the "City Game" was born, with basketballs in the hands of thousands of mostly Jewish teenagers perfecting the deceptions of the give-and-go and pick-and-roll.

Al Davis, who played in parks far and wide, was fortunate to live right next to one playground of note, Lincoln Terrace Park, right across Rochester Avenue. Bounding out of his house, he would curse the interminable line of traffic, pick his spot, dart between cars into the park and in minutes be in a game. Playing so regularly here, adapting from the start to the exigencies of the competition, Al had little time to think about the special kind of toughness he was earning just surviving the games of Lincoln Terrace Park.

"I played at every park, I used to go from park to park all over Brooklyn. But no way would I go near Lincoln Terrace Park," said Bert Alpert, who was one of the best teenage basketball players in the city. "Never. The people who played there . . . it was because Al Davis played there that he got the nose he had then, because they probably wrapped it around the pole and it ballooned—that's why he was known as Al 'Hooker' Davis, because of his hook nose.

"Lincoln Terrace Park was the toughest park to play in. There were older ballplayers that came down there. Like Don Foreman. He was my idol, I followed him at Boys High and later when he went to NYU. He was able to play at Lincoln Terrace Park because he was a dirty ballplayer. I would never get on the same court with Don Foreman. He and those other guys wouldn't let you go up for a layup. If you'd go up, they'd grab both of your arms and hold you. Someone would push you against the fence and you wouldn't be able to move, and then the other guy would turn around and belt him.

"Al Davis was part of that scene. I wasn't. I was better with a referee around. He was the type of player who was better without one."

Larry Krevins was another schoolboy star who played at Lincoln Terrace Park. "Those were bloody games," he agreed. "And Al did well because he was a Philadelphia lawyer. You know, he used to bang and bang, and in that type of setup, there was no such thing as crying or complaining. But he had an indomitable will to always wanna win at whatever cost, and if it meant he had to split an infinitive to say, 'You stepped over the line'—when you were three feet away from the line—that's what he did. You'd get a pick and he'd say it was a foul, which was nonsense. But he'd do anything so that you didn't get the winning basket. Up until that point, you could play legit. But the winning basket, you were never allowed to make."

So Al Davis would play in an endless seam, season to season, year to year. When the war broke out—Stanley Roberts was being bar-mitzvahed when someone in the temple screamed that the Japanese had bombed Pearl Harbor—he played ball. When V-E and V-J days came, he played ball. He was never the best, but you knew The Hooker was there, sticking his battered nose into the middle of things, proving his toughness over and over again, getting off on the fact that he could go elbow-for-elbow with the Donnie Foremans and be smarter than they were—smarter than just about anyone he knew.

Later he would play baseball and football, too, which was rare for the Crown Heights crowd but, again, he was proving a point. By induction, Al took on the characteristics of a top jock. Though he played no sport overly well, he played the *part* flawlessly.

"I always thought he looked like an SMU halfback," remembered Al "Fat" Roth, a neighborhood guy who later played on the scandal-scarred CCNY team that won the national title in 1950. He was kinda skinny but the way he walked, the pigeon-toed thing, he just looked the part. And he was the most glib person I knew. He was usually the center of attraction, very good on his feet."

Sharp. That's how they thought of him around the Heights. Sharp as a tack. "Allen was one of the few people I ever met that could go to school and his mind was like a sponge, it absorbed everything," Ernie Pugatch said. "He hardly had to do any work at home compared to what others did, because he could retain.

"Allen was very different from us. He was an individual at an early age. He was his own person. He was aggressive; what he went after he would normally achieve—and he didn't eat off his parents to get it. Not at all. He went his own way, and give him credit for it because the rest of us would've been lost trying to do that. Al could've had a piece of his father's business but he didn't want it. Even then, he said: 'I'm gonna do it on my own.' "

Al's mindset was both a hand-me-down from Louis Davis and a polar reaction to him. Louis's own streak of independence had a fablelike quality. Anomalous as it was for a working man in the heart of Jewish Brooklyn, Louis was a rock-ribbed Republican who never wavered from the god of laissez faire capitalism during the FDR years. During the Reagan era, Al would recall that his parents "were into material things. My father liked a big house, a big car. He did it without being ostentatious, he did it with style. He was a Taft Republican and he fought the unions all his life. He was daring. He wasn't part of a crowd."

Around the dinner table, Al ingested daring and dogma along with corned beef. In fifth grade, he said, "We had these liberal teachers from places like [Univ. of] Penn. They were for Red China. I stood up and argued for Chiang Kai-Shek."*

Al had no idea that he was an iconoclast. Louis and Rose—a quietly cheery woman who willingly receded into her husband's stringent shadow—had themselves well-mannered, likable, thoughtful boys who knew they would have to excel on their own before there would be any offer of help from home. By then, they were too independent to want it. Jerry Davis went to Boys High School, served in the army, and then became wealthy in real estate while he owned a shoe store in Manhattan.

And then came Allen Davis. Sharp. A little vain—if he hadn't already been nicknamed "The Hooker," he surely would have been "The Comb," for he always had one at the ready, swirling up fresh waves in his pompadour. A little shy with the girls though he did all right. Al's big compulsion was sports, and even when he wasn't playing his mind was processing sports minutiae as though it was a Univac.

Neither boy felt a great deal of warmth from Louis, but they figured his kind of love was subliminal, that it came in forcing them to think for themselves. Jerry Davis once spoke of the "terrific arguments around the table," and how Louis would accuse his *sons* of being communists. But while Louis was "the most reactionary Jewish person you ever met," according to Jerry, such reaction was obviously a prod.

"My father would turn on us and make us come up with answers," Jerry said. "He'd say, 'Show me where you read it. I think you may have misunderstood it. Go get it and read it to us aloud.' It became a point of pride to prove it. We had to shield ourselves. If he thought you were going to cry he'd ride you to the finish. . . . You had to get an A. The B's didn't even count with them. If you came home from a game and lost or played badly, there was just no room for it. Second place was nowhere. When we ran on the beach, he ran us to our knees."†

---

*"Al Davis Isn't as Bad as He Thinks He Is," *Inside Sports*, May 1981, p. 49
†Ibid., pp. 38, 49.

Al put it this way: "They didn't give us a lot of love. They didn't know how. I don't regret it. They paved the way. I'd rather have what I have than the love."*

And, in fact, Louis's hard-fisted methods did produce impressive results, in the classroom, on the sports field, and beyond—but also a darkly foreboding ambivalence about him. Their battery cells charged by him, the boys still drifted away from him early on. The fact is, he made it easy for Al to read out the implicit privilege of being Louis Davis's son. Since it was of no hard relevance to him, Al wanted no one to *know* his father was wealthy. To do that, which required that he create his own reality, Al kept all references to Louis to a bare minimum.

"He was very close-mouthed about his family for some reason," Larry Krevins remembered. "He really didn't get involved with 'mamalution,' as we called it. We knew, faintly, that the father had money but he *never* talked about it. He presented himself as a guy fending for himself."

Al seemingly constructed this image as early as his years at PS 91 and Winthrop Junior High. He joined such boys' clubs as "The Panthers" and "Club 7," and was a fixture at Union Temple, a magnet for active kids, with its swimming pool and gym. But while popular with almost everybody, he was close with few. Stanley Roberts was a constant, a door away. And there was Danny Glassman, who lived on Schenectady Avenue near Empire Boulevard; big and easy-going, Danny didn't have to *work* as hard as Al to be liked, which let Al study and draw from Danny's popularity.

But he was probably happiest away from Brooklyn, at summer camps with their transient friendships far from the pressures of President Street. Filled with New York kids, these camps in the "borscht belt" of the Catskill mountains were basketball paradise. Leagues were formed that shuttled kids from one resort hotel to another, where they earned money as busboys between games. Allie Sherman was athletic director at the Tamarack Lodge, but more important was that Al Badain, the storied basketball coach at Brooklyn's Erasmus Hall High School, was head counselor and coach at Camp Withawind.

That was where *everyone* wanted to go, to play for Badain, and for Badain this grunion run was a ready-made recruiting pool; the

---

*Ibid.

best kids he would get to come to Erasmus Hall, maintaining Badain's unbroken chain of great teams. Al Davis at first went to other camps, better camps, because Louis and Rose never scrimped on their sons' summer vacations. But when he met Al Badain, for Davis it was like an oracle. Although other high schools were closer to President Street, he gladly walked or took the bus or subway each day to Flatbush, the location of Erasmus Hall, so he could call Al Badain coach.

Erasmus Hall High School, named after Desiderius Erasmus, the sixteenth-century Dutch theologian and humanist, was an imposing sight. Its Gothic architecture set off by huge archways and courtyards, it looked like a splendid college campus. Years later, after the likes of Barbra Streisand and basketball great Billy Cunningham graduated, Erasmus Hall—its students from neighborhoods of bitter, hard-core poverty—would be named the second-worst high school in New York state, based on reading and math scores.

But back then, its dignified beauty embodied upper-middle-class virtue. Rather than the arches and bronze statue of Erasmus, though, all Al Davis had eyes for was the basketball floor. He, Larry Krevins, Al Roth, and Bert Alpert all went to Erasmus Hall because of Al Badain. But while the others were varsity starters for the Dutchmen—Krevins as captain during the 1945–46 season, when he and Davis were juniors—Al left the bench only sporadically. Not inured to the politic "system" game of set plays used in scholastic basketball at that time, he also never struck a positive chord with Badain personally.

A stubby, black-haired, shrill-voiced man in his mid-thirties, Badain had intractable concepts and fancied himself as a kind of angel of mercy—but only to those whom he thought he could develop on his own terms. "Al Badain was a great coach, but it was hard to get on his good side," Al Roth said. "He had his favorites. He liked to pick *his* people, guys he would convert into a player *he* would want the kid to be rather than somebody coming from the schoolyard that had ability but was set in his ways.

"As a matter of fact, I don't think Al Badain really liked Al Davis. Al was sharp, and he would say things, like little innuendos. He would answer Al Badain, be 'equal' to him. He wouldn't shrivel from him. Al wasn't the kind of guy who lost his cool with anybody. He was very mature in how he handled himself, much more than any of us."

Bert Alpert elaborated: "Al really loved Al Badain, but it was very hard to *become* a favorite of Badain's. Badain never liked anyone. Maybe he loved everybody down deep, but he just wasn't your best friend. He was a system coach, everybody was part of a system. If there was something he liked about you, he fit you in his system, to play a role, and it would never vary.

"Also, once you weren't in the first seven, you would never get in a game. I was a guard, but you called it the 'middle man' then. I was in the center, I brought the ball up and guided the team. Al Davis did the same thing, but he could never get in."

Al was indeed a thorn in Badain's butt. He constantly pricked Badain to let the scrubs play the starters. When Badain gave in, the starters always blew away Davis's motley band, and his frothing mouth—"Come on, you can't get by me," he would growl—clashed with Badain's protocol of sportsmanship. As time went on, Davis became strictly a splinter-catcher. He could only watch as the Dutchmen in March of 1947 beat the team from Andrew Jackson High—whose star was Bob Cousy—in the PSAL semifinal playoff game in Madison Square Garden, before losing the title game to Benjamin Franklin High.

But even while stewing silently about not getting in, Al was also watching *Al Badain*. How he coached. How he ran his selfless, role-playing system. How he was a stickler for detail and practice —on Saturdays, with school closed, the team would have to climb over a fence to get on the court. How he took "incorrigibles" and low-IQ types from the streets and public school jungle and turned them around (the only black kid in the school, Sparky Smith, whom he got to come to Erasmus Hall, would become a school teacher and principal). Four decades later, when Badain was in his eighties and seriously ill, Davis paid his bills and brought him out to the Coast for a Super Bowl, ferried him and his wife around in a limousine, and put them up in a plush hotel. For Al, it was merely paying back a debt he felt he owed Badain, in whom he saw an apparition—how to get the most out of a team, and the importance of finding the right person for the right role.

All that was in Davis's data bank, subconsciously filed for possible future use somewhere and sometime. His immediate concern as a senior—with graduation coming up in January 1947—was to go to college and kick butt on the court the way he couldn't at Erasmus. Davis had also tried to play football and baseball—the latter with future big league pitcher Don McMahon—with the same meager results. But it was enough for Al to consider himself BMOC jock fodder, and on that premise he set up a one-man Office of Al Davis Information, dashing off a blizzard of letters to schools all over the nation. Larry Krevins, who was also going to graduate in January, was amazed when Davis reported on his campaign.

"All kids write to colleges, but he did it on a whole different level—he'd also write to the coaches themselves," Krevins said. "Al was a super letter-writer, and if you could get your hands on those letters they'd be classics.

"I mean, Al was so involved with this that he was trying to get *me* into a school at the same time. He'd use whatever feedback he got from these people and say, hey, I got somebody that might be interested in you. He was trying to pull strings for me—he was always an unbelievable manipulator. But his motivation was that I was a friend, it wasn't anything other than that. And he did it for other people as well."

Al's problem was that this was a time when great swarms of war veterans were returning home, and colleges were making special dispensations to allow them in under the GI Bill. For all the pen-pal relationships he struck up with coaches, none of the big sports factories could take him in. As usual, though, Al was a step or two ahead in the process. Academic regulations made it easier to get into a number of schools via the transfer route. Accordingly, he looked around for a good, middle-level college with a reasonably good sports program to use as a springboard.

As it happened, one of the schools he had queried, Wittenberg College, a Lutheran school in Springfield, Ohio, was making a sports push and had sent recruiters to Brooklyn. Obscure as it was—and as strange as it was for a Jewish kid to be in its *goyishe* environs— no one ever said Allen Davis did things the obvious way. His was an arcane mind, collating mounds of details, angles, and probabilities. Wittenberg offered a direct route somewhere. He would go there, without a scholarship, though Louis and Rose would take care of tuition and lodging—education being another exception to largesse—and, as he made sure to tell the Crown Heights boys, he would help put Wittenberg on the sports map.

His sendoff was the Erasmus Hall senior class yearbook. Although he lost out to Terence Fogarty as "Boy Most Likely to Succeed," and as "Class Politician" to Irwin Kaufman, Al did get "Most Popular Boy." In the centerfold, his picture sat on top of a stick-figure caricature in short pants and a bow tie, holding the receiver of a telephone. No one knew how prophetic this parody was, but no more so than the allusion to him on the "Class Prophecy" page, which read:

The crowd of autograph hounds are taking buttons as souvenirs from the suit of Allen Davis, whose life story, "The Great Profile," is now being filmed.

2

Al was not the guy who sat in the back of the pack. He had leadership qualities.

—Pascal Perri

He seemed to have a great understanding of people, and I think that's why he's gone as far as he has.

—Bernie Custis

Al Davis enrolled at Wittenberg College on January 6, 1947, entering a milieu that collided head-on with his hip, urban, cosmopolitan sensibilities. Big-time Al was at a school where football, baseball, and basketball were coached by *one* man, Howard "Red" Maurer, who also taught anatomy and hygiene classes.

The Wittenberg teams, named the Tigers, had until recently been the "Fighting Lutherans." They played a schedule that included the likes of the Kenyon Lords, the Ohio Wesleyan Battling Bishops, and the Heidelberg Student Princes. Davis played a little baseball, but mostly he brooded about being stuck in a rural outpost later apotheosized as *the* American goytown: the heartland home of Jim Anderson's TV family in *Father Knows Best*.

Doubling his efforts to effect a transfer consumed Davis's days until he got the go-ahead from Syracuse to slip in through a crack as a transfer athlete. This was an ideal repository for Al's more primeval street tendencies. Syracuse *was* big-time, and it had become a funnel for many New York kids, a number of them from

Erasmus Hall. Al was heady about the shift over the summer, when he vacationed with Larry Krevins at a camp in the Catskills called Oxford-Guilford.

"The first thing he did was save my job there," Krevins said. "We were counselors—Al got me the job—and they were gonna fire me because I let a toilet overflow in a bunkhouse. He charmed them into letting me stay." Then Davis got back to trying to get Larry into a school—using his Syracuse connection, which hadn't even begun yet.

"First Al said he was going to get me into Syracuse, but my marks weren't the greatest, and he decided for whatever reason that he wanted me to go to this new school, Champlain College, which was part of the new state university system. Evidently he had struck up a relationship with the coach, Slim Elliott or something like that, who had come out of Syracuse, and they were lookin' for guys to play ball. So that's where I went. Al did it all; he got the admission form and said to fill it out and that was it. He was helping me, but he already knew the ins and outs of recruiting."

It was also over that summer that an emboldened Al made a play for a pretty and bounteous blonde girl from Brooklyn named Winnie Joachem. Up until now, he had not been much of a blade, though he had an "understanding" with another Brooklyn girl, Carol Sagal, who went to Lincoln High and whom he had met at a New Year's Eve party a year before. Now, though, he had the hots for Winnie, and they burned up Oxford-Guilford. When camp broke up, they went back to Brooklyn and Al came to Winnie's home one night to pick her up. Her older brother Eddie let him in—but only until he could size Al up.

"I didn't like him so I threw him out," Eddie Joachem said of this moment, forty years removed. "He was smoking and he wore a gold chain in his pants. I believe he had on a zoot suit. There was no way I was gonna let my sister go out with this guy."

A smiling Winnie Joachem confirmed the story, up to a point. "I remember my brother said that Al was too much of a sharpie for me. I thought he was quite nice but I didn't continue seeing him."

(Larry Krevins was incredulous at the depiction of Davis as a clotheshorse with a Bogartlike cigarette on his lower lip: "Eddie Joachem is full of shit. Al Davis never wore a zoot suit in his life. Al was a modest, clean-living kid. I don't remember him as a smoker or a drinker. A beer, maybe, once in a while, but no hard liquor. Al's the same to this day.")

Syracuse University in the autumn of 1947 was a comber of sudden and immense transition. While its rustic, umber brick halls and wooded gardens stood in provincial calm, cheap bourgeois housing—in line after line of tin huts with pyramid roofs—snaked about around the edges of the grounds like tinsel on a Christmas tree. These abodes, as fragile as candy wrappers, were familiar domicile to thousands of returning servicemen who had lived in similar deprivation during and immediately following the war. Known as "prefabs" around the campus, they held six cramped rooms and twelve impatient young men, eleven or so normally standing on one leg while waiting to get into the one john. In four years, enrollment at Syracuse had zoomed from six thousand to twenty thousand as the pacific rural school inflated to the nation's ninth-largest. A huge concentration of the arriving crowd lived along winding, hilly Irving Avenue, which bordered on cavernous Archbold Stadium, home to the Orangemen football team, and the prefabs in the long shadow of the stadium were where the school's athletes were housed.

When Al Davis arrived, he was assigned to a prefab into which New York kids were funneled—The "Pastrami Prefab"—meaning that nearly the entire Jewish population of Syracuse was right here on Irving Avenue. In the room next to Al's were basketball players Bobby Wallach—who had played at Erasmus Hall in the early forties and then was in the Coast Guard for three years before coming to Syracuse—and Eddie Rosen. Down the hall were Pascal Perri, Horace Morris, and Leon Cohen. Al's original roommate was a football player from Queens, Ray Adams, but that lasted only one semester, because the leathery Adams had a hard time dealing with Davis's vanity.

"He was particularly concerned about his hair," Adams recalled. "If you made a move toward his head, his hair, he had a problem. He said he was an athlete but he was worried about getting kicked in the face—remember, there were no facemasks in those days, and if Al Davis never played football, that was possibly the reason why."

From the spring of 1948 on, Al would room with Wallach, who stood six feet five inches but was easily gregarious the way Danny

Glassman—who had gone off to college in Connecticut—had been; once again, Al's step was broadened by proximity to a real jock, but his ego could intimidate Bob, allowing Al to feel that he was on equal terms with him though he was not. As a freshman, Wallach had made the 1945–46 Orange basketball team that went 19–6 and lost by two points to CCNY in the NCAA Eastern finals.

Al craved this level of competition, but he never had a chance to scratch even the outer derma of the varsity football or basketball squads; he had to make do as a bench guy on the jayvee baseball team. Although he was a realist about most things, able to cut through layers of guano and get right to the core of truth, such was his competitive flame that his grip would not ease from the fiction that he was a real jock. Pissed about not seeing athletic daylight, he acted in spite and transferred in the fall of 1948 to Hartwick College, a pint-sized school in nearby Oneonta, New York.

One month later, his gut burbling again for the big time, he came back to Syracuse, to try out for and be rejected by the varsities all over again. And yet, the funny thing was that, among the varsity athletes Davis lived and mingled with, his stride was so broad that no one seemed aware that he *wasn't* playing: they just knew he wasn't playing with *them*. Football guys thought Davis was a basketball player; basketball guys thought he played football. Years later, Pascal Perri still wasn't sure just what Davis played.

"He wasn't a first-stringer, but he always gave the impression that he was one of the guys," Perri said. "You went to varsity clubs or one of the coffee shops the athletes went to and Al would always be with one of the starters, like they were best friends. When he first came to school, it was like he had been there all the time. He never seemed to need directions to get anywhere.

"The rumor always was that he was a very brilliant guy, like a genius, a whiz kid. He was younger than the rest of us, a lot of us had been in the service. Because Al had that authoritative way about him, he took the spotlight. He was recognizable."

The jocks dubbed him Al "Bummy" Davis, after the middleweight prizefighter of the same name. Al Davis the boxer came from Brooklyn and was brash. He also, like many fighters of the day, happened to fall in with the Mob—but only until they rubbed him out in front of a Brooklyn saloon. For the young men of Syracuse, especially homeboys fresh off the farms and apple orchards of upstate New York, the notion persisted that all the Al Davises from

Brooklyn might just be born with the same traits. To some, these traits were admirable, all spit and fire; to others, less so.

"Everybody liked Al, but he was not one of the guys," Horace Morris said. Much of it, he thought, had to do with Bummy's mouth. Al used to swear with amazing ease, and since he had a hair-trigger temper, the mouth would work overtime. Horace, who'd get on him all the time about his vocabulary, would ask him if he knew any nice words. "*Hell*, no," Davis would reply, clamping down hard on the first word.

As with Ernie Pugatch, Horace never saw Al—who was majoring in English—studying or even consulting a schoolbook. He once said to him, "Al, how the hell do you pass your courses?"—which Al did with ease.

"'Cause I'm smart enough to do it," Al rasped, emoting in character. And whenever he would deliver these bon mots, the other guys would grin at each other and roll their eyes in a gesture of forbearance. What else could they expect to hear from Bummy Davis?

"Oh, yeah, he was a big talker all right," acknowledged Bill Haskins, the football player. "Nobody ever saw Al play, but he would walk around saying you gotta do this, do that. But Al wasn't the kind of guy you liked or disliked, because nobody ever took him seriously. He was a character, a Dead End Kid, trying to look tough. We knew he wasn't but he'd be hangin' out with tough guys, like Ray Adams or Dick Bagley, who was a big tackle, like 285 pounds. Al was always there seconding their motion. Anytime they said something, he'd second it."

Bill Label, who was the manager of the basketball team, remembered Davis as "a gym rat" and "a very egotistical guy who was easy to dislike" on a surface level. But while Label got to know him as "a nice guy," he still shakes his head having seen what Davis made of himself. "If anyone would've told me that Al Davis would be where he is today, the people who knew him then would've said: 'Are you nuts?' You never would've expected him to be a coach, where you need a lot of finesse and brains, because he came across as a scatterbrain."

Still, there were things that made people wonder, little clues of studied grounding underneath the live-wire facade. Al was no more decipherable than he had been in Brooklyn, no more prone to reveal heartfelt thoughts. He still had a propensity to erupt in a hiccup-reflex of commie-bashing. "He hated the Russians. Molotov, the first Russian emissary; he'd go on about Molotov," Bob Wallach said. Dewey was his man in the '48 election—one of the few times in his life Davis picked a loser. However, little about him other than the safe harbor of sports filtered all the way through; if he had an aversion to humanity, sports was meant to obscure it. But it couldn't, not completely.

"He was a loner, a *real* loner," Morris concluded. "Al was his own person, and while he wanted people to like him, he really couldn't give a damn what they thought about him.

"Al always wore a sweatshirt reading 'SUAD,' for Syracuse University Athletic Department. He would never buy a new one either. The one he he wore got dirty and raggedy and he'd keep on wearing it. I would say to him, 'Al, you could make more friends if you'd stop wearin' that shirt and dress up.' He'd say, 'The hell with 'em!' He said they were gonna have to take him the way he was."

"Al just wanted to excel so much it was like it was at the expense of everything else," Pascal Perri believed. "Most guys hung out with the same guy. We ate together, roomed together, went on dates together. But I don't remember Al being that close to anyone. I didn't even know he had an older brother. He just didn't talk about his family the way we always talked about our brothers, our mothers and fathers. I never remember Al sitting down and saying, 'My brother did this and my father did that.' There was a rumor that he had money, but it was hard to believe because he *acted* very often like one of these underprivileged New York kids who have to fight their way through everything.

"Tooth and claw. It was always that with Al. He was always there with his chin out, and I just believed that in his childhood somewhere there was some demand to succeed and be better than the next guy. Either that or Al felt they tried to *deny* him that and he was gonna go out and do it on his own."

"He was definitely trying to prove something all the time," Bill Haskins said. "Maybe most of all to himself."

Bummy Davis saw the first hard reward for his obsession during the Thanksgiving break in 1948. Hearing that the team basketball picture was going to be taken earlier than usual, while the squad worked out before the cut-down for the season, Al decided to forgo his vacation and practiced with them. Given a uniform on picture day, he can be seen to this day in black and white glossy eternity, standing in the back row and grinning coyly—the beast in clover.

However, this was the closest he got to the Valhalla of wearing that uniform for real. Though Al still thought he could make the Orangemen in some form, the coach, Lew Andreas, had already picked his team, the core of which would win eighteen of twenty-five games that season and go to the quarter-finals of the NIT the next. Cemented as the team was, Al was embittered. Unlike his attitude toward Al Badain, here he cut no slack of overall redemption for the flinty, white-haired Andreas. Bill Label, the team's manager, was privy to Davis's unguarded rendering of a harsh judgment on the coach.

"He always complained that he never got a chance with Andreas because he was Jewish," Label recalled. "Al thought that Andreas was anti-Semitic. He was very outspoken about it."

Out of a squad of a dozen players, only two Jews made those Orange basketball teams—Bob Wallach and Eddie Rosen. Wallach, who had once started on an army team with Syracuse Nats' star Fuzzy Levane, had played his first two years, then rotted on the bench. Rosen, a superb two-hand set shooter, was used sparingly in Andreas's platoon system. In the Pastrami Prefab, Jewish kids wondered openly about the coach's motives. Andreas used to get tickets to the Syracuse Nats' home games and ask his team, "Who wants one?" When Wallach raised his hand, Andreas told him, snidely, "Why don't you ask your pal Fuzzy *Levine*?"—intentionally twisting Levane's Italian name into a Jewish one.

To Wallach, it was clear that Andreas wasn't much of a coach. "He wasn't in Al Badain's league; it was all run and gun with no rhyme or reason. He really didn't have a clue." Yet today he draws back from the issue of anti-Semitism. "Lew Andreas is dead, let him rest in peace," he said. Rosen begged off as well, preferring not to cloud the issue central to Al Davis's case—Davis's limited game. "Al wasn't a great shooter outside and he tried to use inside moves but he wasn't that big or strong. Al knew the game but he wasn't that good a ballplayer."

Eventually, even Al had to admit this—or at least give in to it. "He saw the handwriting on the wall," said Mike Stark, one of the starters, "and I think that's when he started gravitating to football." Al had already begun to hang out more with the cleated crowd, joining them in the far corner of the gym groaning in agony while lifting barbells; now, grown to just under six feet tall, the once-knobby body was pocketed with muscle tissue. But Davis's narcissism was adjusting to a new reality. Rather than sweat-covered glory, those old dalliances—processing data and steering the operating systems that made a team go—leaped into the breach. This did not occur, though, until Syracuse made an important move in April of 1949.

The two previous football seasons had been played almost apologetically, blunted in 1946 when coach Biggie Munn defected to Michigan State, taking with him his assistant coach, Duffy Daugherty. The Orange had gone 4–14 the next two years under the benign Ribs Baysinger, who had previously coached the jayvees for twenty years. With the program in disrepair, Lew Andreas, who was also athletic director, hired the thirty-nine-year-old coach at Muhlenberg College, Floyd "Ben" Schwartzwalder, who was coming off twenty-five wins in his last three seasons. Schwartzwalder was a small scarp of bedrock, an ex-Marine paratrooper with cauliflower ears, no visible neck, and a deliriously mangled nose. His diet seemed to be raw mutton and horseradish. At his practices he would instruct his players to be properly aboriginal—"I wanna take you guys to games in cages," he would tell them. Though the team didn't burn up Archbold Stadium right away, they stir-fried it; the creaky old oval swayed with student enthusiasm, and soon had to be enlarged by six thousand seats as Schwartzwalder established an East Coast factory that spawned three of the greatest runners football would see, Jimmy Brown, Ernie Davis, and Larry Csonka.

Al Davis, who could always perceive the big picture even as it developed, was drawn to the gathering flame. Back in the prefabs, his big interest became Schwartzwalder's playbooks. "When guys were either studying or just bullshitting, he would go through our playbook; he knew it better than the players did," Leon Cohen said. "He'd go through 'em for hours. He must've raked those things to death."

To be sure, Schwartzwalder's progressive theories caught Davis's fancy. Baysinger's archaic single-wing offense, with its static, cluttered backfield and wearisome pileups at the line, held little cerebral or aesthetic interest for Al. Schwartzwalder installed football's new wrinkle, the split-T, with the quarterback under the center as in the game's seminal days but with a modern skew. Haltbacks went in motion, and traps and misdirection plays ran in smooth conjunction with the offensive line. More and more coaches were warming up to the new-age wonders of the split-T, including Red Blaik at West Point, Bud Wilkinson at Oklahoma, and Frank Leahy at Notre Dame, who junked the old Irish "box" for it. In the pros, the split-T had been standard procedure since the beginning of the decade, when the Chicago Bears and the Cleveland Browns pioneered it, and the really new wrinkle was the way the Los Angeles Rams were flanking receivers and passing out of the formation.

Within this framework of renovation and innovation, in which new schemes were liable to cut a new and enduring swath, Al Davis saw the future—and himself squarely in the football vanguard. Davis tried explaining to the football players that basketball staples like setting picks could have useful applications on the gridiron. The response would be blank stares, but Davis was smitten. He became a regular at assistant coach Bud Barker's football strategy classes. This was a Mickey Mouse course for easy credit, but while Syracuse athletes sat and yawned, Al would take chalk in hand and go x for o with Barker on the blackboard.

Even Schwartzwalder was a mite perplexed by the curious young man in the SUAD shirt who would mount the concrete bleachers during team practices and make notes and diagrams in a spiral notebook. Forty years later, an elderly Schwartzwalder could still remember his presence up there in the stands, and his response to it.

"I wondered about him," he said. "I didn't know him. I knew he wasn't much of a player, that he'd withdrawn from the team because he couldn't make it. But I didn't know if he was a spy or whatever, if he was giving our plays away to other teams. You don't welcome people hanging around practice—and I still don't know if that's all he was doing. I got to the point where I didn't welcome him and I told him so. Some student shouldn't be sitting up there takin' notes on you."

With Al closing in on his English degree, he still had not stepped on a field in anger. But there seemed no doubt about what he wanted to do with himself upon graduation. "I thought he had designs about going into high school football coaching," Mike Stark recalled. But others sensed that Davis had bigger prey in mind.

Luke LaPorta, a football player, chatted with Davis after one of Barker's classes. Al's eyes had a particularly avid gaze as he displayed for Luke some kind of play he'd drawn up with x's and o's running into the margins. Luke, who would coach high school football, had an altogether logical question. "Will it work in high school?" he asked. Al, who judged himself far beyond the high school stage, seemed offended. "Of course it'll work!" he growled through gritted teeth—his visions of enterprise having blurred simple objectivity. An Al Davis play would *have* to work, anywhere. But, clearly, the Davis gaze was well beyond the high school stage.

To Eddie Rosen he was direct. "He said he was going to *own* a team, that was gonna be how he'd stay in sports," Rosen recalled. "I hadn't seen Al for a long time since the basketball team picture, there were a lot of gaps when Al was off in his own world. But when I saw him that time, he was different. *He* was the focus of his life, not Syracuse."

Accordingly, Al wasted no time leaving Syracuse in order to hasten the course of his life. Weeks before, knowing that his student draft deferment would be up at the end of the spring semester of 1950, Al, his Bachelor of Arts degree in English earned, had turned his attention on ways to go on fighting the Korean War on the home front instead of possibly at Pork Chop Hill. This would require postgraduate study leading to a Master's Degree—and, ideally, the defeat of the bloody communists by the time the sheepskin was in his hands. As he thought out his options, it did not take long before football found a place in the equation, which formed like this: he would work for tuition and sanctuary by taking a job as a football coach. He could land such a quid pro quo, he reasoned, if he could get face-to-face with *someone* in authority at a college, a college small enough to take him on despite his lack of coaching experience—small enough, say, not to know Al Davis from George Davis.

On the pretext of boredom, he talked Bobby Wallach, who'd completed his phys ed degree requirements, into leaving with him—"He said, 'Let's not hang around here, let's go home and start doin' somethin' '"—and in mid-May, a month before graduation ceremonies, they got into Al's black Plymouth convertible and headed down the highway toward Brooklyn. On the way, he told Bob about his plan, getting Bob to believe he could do the same thing, as a student basketball coach. The next morning, he picked up Bob and, with no appointment, they went to a school several miles east of Crown Heights just across the Long Island border, Hofstra University. There they were spurned by the athletic director, Houdy Meyers, a man whose acumen seemed immutable to Al.

Next they drove to Adelphi and to the naive graces of Dr. Paul

Dawson Eddy. Quickly forgotten in the shuffle, Bob Wallach, rejected as a basketball assistant—and unmentioned by Al in his colloquy with Dr. Eddy—wished Al well and went on his way toward a career as an FBI agent and later a Wall Street stockbroker.

Adelphi, more so than Syracuse, resembled a temporary holding bin. Its male students were mostly former servicemen, over a thousand in a campus enrollment of twenty-five hundred, and their lodging wasn't only military-like; they actually lived on a military airbase, in the barracks of Mitchell Field in nearby Hempstead. The coaches lived there, as well, and Al Davis's first coaching residence was a windowless room in a hutch called the Santini Barracks. Yet so low was he on the Adelphi briar that, as an adjunct freshman coach, neither his name nor his picture appeared in the school yearbook. For Al, though, the walls of his shelter were secure—and now they could be turned into the beams of a launchpad. As he put the freshmen through their paces with crisp precision, the eyes of the varsity were already on him.

"He made a fast impression on people," recalled Tony Piazza, an Adelphi senior that year. "When he had his guys on another field, I used to watch what he was doing as much as what we were doing, because he was so organized and he cut this large figure with his big flashing teeth and his booming voice. It just struck me that he had that burning desire and could communicate it to players."

He also had a burning ambition. Unconfined by the tag of freshman coach, he was soon spending more time with the varsity, wheedling, cajoling, teaching. Not everybody responded. One player, Andrew Tatom, remembered him as "a baloney artist," and for some players, cynicism about Al hung in the air all season. The "I'm Davis from Syracuse" story had made the rounds, and, according to Piazza, "A lot of people felt he was an impostor." Al would try to get tough when he had to. At one practice, he was disturbed by the play of a tackle named Howard Vogts.

"I forgot more football than you know!" he screamed at Vogts.

Vogts, who was older than Davis, hardly flinched, and when Al turned his back, he and some of his teammates could be heard laughing in derision. "That was the only way you could take the guy," Tatom said. "Here was a guy on the fringe, really, and you either laughed or ignored him." At this stage of his development, however, dealing with players personally was a secondary concern to Al. More crucial was making contacts, getting his name known in the coaching profession, turning the heads of people who could sanction a career. When Davis's freshman team played a scrimmage with the Columbia frosh, Bill Altenberg got a call in his AD's office from Lou Little, the famed Columbia coach whom Altenberg once played for.

"He wanted to know who this Al Davis was," Altenberg said. "Lou was quite impressed with the things Davis was doing. He said Davis had a good football mind."

In time, Al would visit with Little and other area coaches and talk football, which in combination with his personality made his name and face unforgettable. Making friends with Herman Masin, the editor of *Scholastic Coach* magazine, who carried much weight in the profession, Al got Masin to run the article he had presented to Bill Altenberg in that first meeting. Entitled "Line Quarterbacking at Its Best," it appeared in the May 1952 issue. Through Masin, Davis also became a regular at coaching clinics, exchanging ideas with men who had been in the business for eons.

Indeed, Lou Little had reason to be enamored with Davis's mind, and to pick it. For years, the Columbia Lions were the crown of New York football; Little's "A" formation, a variation of the single-wing from which All-American Lou Rossides ran wild, was aped by almost every college and high school team in the New York area. Now, in the split-T era, Lou Little had to listen to new voices. Al Davis came from upstate bearing the oracle of football's future. Even from watching Davis's freshmen, Little could see that Davis knew from motion football.

The Adelphi head coach, John Cerny, a Columbia graduate, had played the single-wing before Davis arrived. Now, overpowered by Davis's knowledge and sureness, Cerny, a big and mannerly man, installed the split-T, per Davis's specifications. By midseason, the team was effectively in the hands of the unacknowledged freshman coach. "Cerny just went along with whatever Al wanted to do," Altenberg said. "If Al could sell Lou Little, he could sell a John Cerny. But Cerny had a self-interest, too—whatever Al did, it worked."

Playing against the chaff of Eastern football—the opposition included Upsala, Ursinus, Long Island Agricultural College, and Massachusetts Maritime Academy—the Adelphi Panthers won three of their last four games and finished the 1950 season at 5–3 as their 155-pound fullback, Norm Davis, slashed through the line for huge gains. The next season—after Al padded his credentials and thirst for sports by coaching the varsity baseball team for the

first of two seasons (his record for those seasons was 19–13)—Ed
Stanczyk, Bill Altenberg's successor, recognized that the Al Davis
imprimatur was everywhere; in addition to his system, the team
had several players who were Davis recruits. Though Stanczyk
named Davis line coach, Adelphi players recall him as omnipresent.

"Basically, he was the offense coach," said David Finkle, a running back, "but he got his feet into everything. He was running
the defense, too. I remember he switched me to free safety one
game and I made a great play where I dove and knocked a pass
away. One of the other coaches started berating me, because I didn't
intercept the ball, and Al came at this guy and almost got into a
fistfight over it. It wasn't only because the other guy was wrong—
Al knew more than those guys, everybody knew that—but Al believed it was important to build up a guy. Besides, putting me back
there was his idea, so he was defending himself, too."

By that time, many of Al's old doubters were gone and the mood
was harmonious and hungry as the team went 5–2. "I thought Al
was a helluva guy, highly intelligent, and very keen. But if a guy
didn't take to him—and still not everybody did, because he was a
very forceful guy—Al's attitude was 'Go screw yourself,' " Finkle
said. "He would turn off to those guys rather than be patient with
them. He had no time to waste on guys that he thought didn't have
his kind of commitment. With Al, you had to know football, and
that was a radical change for a lot of guys, it scared 'em. Other
guys, like the older guys right out of the army, they just wouldn't
want to put up with him.

"That's why you knew Al was not gonna be long for Adelphi.
He was a dominant guy, you had to do it his way, and he wanted
that kind of authority on a higher level, compared to John Cerny,
who was a laid-back guy who later went into selling insurance. You
expected that from John. I think Al would've rather died first than
do something like that."

"As a coach later myself, I knew Al would be successful," Tony
Piazza insisted. "He taught guys the most important ingredient in
football. The desire to win. Al has used the word 'excellence' all
over the place and that goes back to the beginning. That was his
key. The x's and o's don't mean a goddamn—I mean, Al's big
thing, rule blocking, was something I had played in high school.
Football people use x's and o's to communicate; the guy who has
the chalk last wins the point, but can he motivate? Al Davis could
motivate. His kids had the same burning desire he did."

The spring of 1952 wrote an end to the brief but beneficial Adelphi chapter, the period on the last sentence provided by Al's draft board. His two-year Master's program successfully finished, the draft notice was inevitable. But even though the Korean War was stalemated, Al did not blanch at the prospect of seeing combat. Again, he had anticipated the situation, thinking hard about how he could turn discomfort to advantage. This time, he concluded, the United States Army would work for Al Davis.

3

When you spoke to him, when he started to talk, you'd say,
"Ah, there he goes again." But, now, we know he was
brilliant. He had it all planned, like an Army general, like a
war.

—Bill Label

Fort Belvoir's Engineer football squad for 1953 has the
unusual distinction of being coached by the youngest active
member of the National Football Coaches Association. Al
Davis . . . has been hailed as one of the most promising and
talented new faces in the coaching profession. . . . Three
years in the coaching end of the game is a long time for a
man Al's age, but is indicative of his ability. . . . Davis
played varsity ball for Syracuse in '48 and '49. Upon his
graduation in '50 he received coaching offers from major
schools. He accepted Adelphi's offer because it offered the
top assistant's job.

—from the *Belvoir Castle* (Fort Belvoir, Virginia),
October 30, 1953

Providentially, for Al Davis, football was practically a branch
of the armed services in the early fifties; no gunnery skill or
officer training could turn a base commander's head as fast as a GI,
tar, flyboy, or Marine who could effectually carry or throw a pig-
skin. Football (all sports, really, but chiefly football) was the most
virile and warlike vehicle of competition between rival branches of
the military outside of actual combat.

Bragging rights won hand-to-hand on the field were profitable and satisfying. Thus constructing hardy teams was something akin to an open meat market, with commanders—answerable to the top brass at the Pentagon—trying to beat each other to acquire the best players from a nationwide pool of officers, enlisted men, and draftees.

Pros, All-Americans, and lettermen became instant VIPs, granted immunity from the rigors of military subsistence and assigned to bases for "special services"—which might entail little other than arising at the crack of noon and playing ball against a schedule of service and small-college teams. As it turned out, the best sports bases were almost like elite big league franchises, the model being Paul Brown's great teams at the Great Lakes Naval Training Center during World War Two. A virtual farm team for the Cleveland Browns, Great Lakes was where Brown found Marion Motley.

Now, as men poured into camps during another interminable war, Al Davis found himself stationed at Fort Drum, an army base in Watertown, New York, not far from Syracuse. This was a preliminary training and orientation base where soldiers awaited permanent assignment, yet Al was on top of things even here. Leon Cohen happened to be at Fort Drum after he was drafted, but while he had to wear dingy work khakis, he saw Al Davis only in a sharply creased full-dress uniform, with waist-jacket and cap. "I was in a gym jumping up and down on a trampoline," Cohen said, "and a guy came in and he had a photographer trailing him. I turned to look and, sure enough, it's Al. Evidently he was in the public relations unit, getting pictures of athletes."

Still, the PR gig, and Fort Drum, was just a pit stop. When Davis was drafted, he had immediately used his affiliation in the National Football Coaches Association as a wedge to pry open the army football door. The problem was that service teams were normally coached by officers; since many players were themselves noncoms, it didn't seem possible that nonofficers could wield authority. But Al Davis, as pitched to the army by Al Davis, was a rare bird—and a base commander's dream. This was a guy who would know who the football players were just by looking at draft lists, and he could talk players and other base COs into propitious transfers.

Providentially as well for Al, the top kicks in charge of assignments were easy marks, Paul Dawson Eddys with shoulder braid. The Al Davis soft shoe—effected now in army boots—could have been done to the strains of "Anything Goes." Breezing into verbal overdrive, he was able to, ahem, *embellish* his credentials. At the same time, he was adequately versed in military enumeration as a product of Louis Davis's anticommunist instruction and his own fascination with man's conquest of man; Al could recite battlefield lore and lessons for long hours. Accordingly, he could talk about football as a lineal descendant of the infantry.

Annexing vast territory with his mouth, Al was summoned by General Stanley Scott, the head man at the Army Engineer Corps camp at Fort Belvoir, Virginia, ten miles south of Alexandria. Al understood Scott to be a "sports general," and a man dying to get a winning football team on his base. The impassioned Davis oratory would leave General Scott breathless and dewy-eyed, the private's vibrato possibly sounding something like what Davis emoted years later while summoning up tender images of a childhood passed by examining war maps and troop movement charts in the newspapers. In a Pattonlike fizz, he declared:

> I knew where all the armies were, who the generals were, where the Mediterranean and Singapore fleets were. I can still name the battleships in the Italian navy. I got a map and plotted where they all were.
>
> I've always had the *gestalt*, that ability to perceive things before they happened. I always used to be afraid to say that, but now I've proved it. Back then I could see the Germans knew what they were doing. I could see who was going to be good and bad. I'd look at maps and say, "We ought to try this." I did it with sports, too.
>
> I grew up hearing about how impregnable the Maginot Line was, and then I watched the Germans go through the lowlands, penetrate it and defeat it. It made a deep, indelible impression on me to look for other answers. I'd never accept convention as the final answer.
>
> Blitzkrieg. Expediency. Panzers. Wehrmacht. Quick strike. Bang. Boom. I admired them. I felt they had something. If the Russians took a city at 6 P.M., they'd have a wall built around it by the next morning. If the Germans took a city at 6 P.M., they'd be gone by 2 A.M. The German doesn't give a shit about the city. He's chasing. Bang. The next city. I didn't hate Hitler. He captivated me. I knew

he had to be stopped. Jesus Christ, he tried to take on the whole world, the cocksucker.*

When the chill of autumn bit into the air in 1953, Private First Class Al Davis was a head coach. Now he had to channel big talk into deed, and he did not tread lightly. Despite his enchantment with Herr Hitler's audacity, he also knew that the Third Reich was crushed by sheer force of numbers. Al had to have numbers if *he* were to take on the whole world.

Spiraling higher and higher to meet the challenge of his bravura—lest anyone call him a failure—he had sat with the Belvoir special services officer in charge, Major Dick Lewis, planning his onslaught, and it was with a certain aptness that on the day of the first game, *The Great Jesse James Raid*, with Tom Neal and Barbara Payton, was playing at the camp's movie theater. For months before, Al had been raiding army indexes, tabbing football-playing soldiers and running them into Fort Belvoir on an endless supply line. Some top-shelf players were already there, mainly Engineer Corps commissioned officers from the South who had combined ROTC with All-American football careers—one, "Shoo, Shoo" Shemonski, had played on the national champion Maryland team that beat favored Tennessee in the 1952 Sugar Bowl. From that Tennessee team came Hank Lauricella, Jim Haslam, and Pug Pearman. Georgia Tech center George Morris and Clemson receiver Glenn Smith were other All-American officer-players.

By the time the season arrived, a thirty-seven-man squad had been assembled, which counted Pittsburgh Steeler quarterback Ed Kissel, Washington Redskin running back Bobby Haner, and Don Engels, the quarterback of Illinois' Rose Bowl team. Other bases were doing similar routing and rerouting—the Quantico, Virginia, Marines combed the Notre Dame roster, and had the Detroit Lions' Buddy Parker that season—but Davis's was the most extensive and systematic. What was available, especially in the East, Davis went after—playing football off against the precarious terrain of Korea. He did that with two Adelphi players who were about to flunk out and lose their deferments. And he saw a particular ring of opportunity at Temple, where four starters had graduated and were awaiting draft notices, including cocaptain Pat Sarnese.

---

*"Al Davis Isn't as Bad as He Thinks He Is," *Inside Sports*, May 1981, p. 41.

"He came up to Philadelphia and told me he could get me to Belvoir to play football," recalled Sarnese, a six-foot-three-inch, 240-pound tackle. Drafted by the Steelers, he was convinced to enlist and go Al's way rather than risk the other draft. "Believe me, it was a helluva lot better than the alternative, and Al played on that. In recruiting, he was so far ahead of everybody. There was no way he should've known who was gonna be drafted, and the way he got all the Temple guys—Joe Tyrell, Lou Paludi, Gary Cooper, and me—was it legal or illegal, I don't know. But it was bein' done, because Gary Hennessy, an All-American from Villanova, was supposed to come to Belvoir and they fouled up on his papers and he wound up at Fort Eustis. And when the general there found out who he was, he said, 'Even Eisenhower can't get Hennessy out of this camp.' Cause that's the way it was, they'd do anything to get the best players."

In *this* kind of war, Al Davis was on the front lines and in the backroom councils. He needed an assistant coach, and *bang*, Temple's line coach, John Tutko, came with the Owl quartet. After nearly a year of this Army Shuffle, the squad that Al fielded was an odd, incongruous brew: buck privates from the ethnic, blue-collar East and Midwest, WASP second lieutenants from the Old Confederacy—and a Jewish private from Brooklyn at the helm. While all this was egalitarian in concept, human and army nature threatened to wreck Davis's meticulous handiwork from the start. "You had so many clashes going there," said Dick Bergeron, a holdover from a more homogeneous but mediocre Belvoir team the year before, which was coached by a captain.

"To begin with, you had guys like Pearman and Morris, who had tremendous coaching—Bobby Dodd, Frank Broyles, some of the greatest coaches in the game. Then you put 'em in with Al, a guy they never heard of, who's from New York and a *private*. All that put a helluva strain on Al."

If the officers, who lived off the base far from latrines and common barracks, were expecting army football to be a manor of blissful uniformity similar to the academic plantations they came from, Davis had news for them. Al, who loathed the idea of privilege—his original distaste for his father Louis's money had grown to include class and religious dissonance—was absolutely blind to color, rank, and status in choosing who played. His big gun turned out to be PFC Jim Leftwich, a five-eight, 160-pound black man who had played no college ball. At scatback, Leftwich would score six touchdowns—one off Bobby Haner's club lead—and make All-Army that season. An ideal agent of a diverse lot, Al was "a discipline guy, but the attitude was not unlike the Raiders," said Jim Haslam. "He was not the kind of guy that would make you line up and salute at everything." For all Davis's gung-ho yammering to the brass hats, Pug Pearman remembered Al as "the most un-Army guy I've ever known."

Yet Al at times did have moments of omnipotence. Tooling around the base in General Scott's staff car, a driver at the wheel —the spoils of being a base head coach could be considerable—he loved it that soldiers would assume that the natty soldier inside was the general, snap to attention, and salute him. In his vicarious reverie, Al Davis was old Blood and Guts himself. However, given the way some eyes saw him, getting some of his players to burnish the fantasy was a tall order on the field. There, the Jimmy Cagney/Bear Bryant mimickry did not play particularly well.

"The first time I saw Al Davis, he told me and George Morris, 'Let me see you get in position,' " said Pug Pearman. "We just laughed at him—I mean, at that point in our career, what's he gonna tell us about how to get down in position on the line? So we just laughed. We teased Al a lot 'cause he was a private and all, so we would hang him good if he didn't behave."

"Oh, shit," said a chortling Morris, "some of us were not impressed with that 'tough guy' crap. He's a disciplinarian, I guess, where he has control over people. But he didn't have any control over us. Hell, if he started tryin' to get too hard on us, we just wouldn't do it.

"I remember he had some weird deal about how to run a halfback trap, and we said, 'Al, you just get back out of the way, we're gonna show you how we're gonna run it.' He had to accept it— what the hell else was he gonna do? Because we knew more football than he did, from a *playing* standpoint. We had not learned it out of a book like he did. We played in some pretty fast leagues, pretty fast company. And he was learning to cope with those kind of athletes, not theoretical guys."

Morris, a first-round draft pick of the 49ers before his tour of duty, recalled Davis's pet theory. "Rule blocking at its best," he said, mocking the way Davis tried to indoctrinate them. "He had learned that by reading it. He had a whole folder of pamphlets on rule blocking and he mimeographed a bunch of that stuff for us. But we lined up and played football and he did all the reading.

Everybody knew what the hell they were gonna do, everybody knew the rule: if your guy's not over you or not inside, then you look outside; if he's not outside, there's a linebacker there somewhere, you can count on it. You didn't *say* it, call it on the line, you just done the rule.

"Even with his system, we called 'S' every time, that's all we ran. It just meant block as you would. Every once in a while we'd call 'CX' or however Al lettered it, just to confuse a guy—our *own* guys. What the hell, we were havin' a good time. It was just service football, not the Rose Bowl."

The Fort Belvoir Engineers could play with fire. Playing national-champion Maryland in a preseason scrimmage, with no spectators but an abundance of hitting, Hank Lauricella ran back two punts all the way to assure victory and Al was interviewed on local television as the coach who bested Jim Tatum and his mighty Terrapins. But after routing West Chester State Teachers College 21–0 in the season opener, they barely got by Kent State, 7–6—and during this game George Morris was kicked out for reacting to a clip by decking the other guy, "full in the face," as Morris put it. On the sideline, Al asked George what happened.

"Al," the big center said, straight-faced, "I didn't do a goddamn thing."

Recalled Morris: "'Course, Al saw it all in the film later—but what's he gonna say? I said, 'Al, I was raggin' your ass, don't worry 'bout it.' Al was a good guy, but you just didn't take it as seriously as he did. When we played hard, we were great. But we could've been better had we been more dedicated."

"We played good games when we had to, but we took the small schools too lightly," Pat Sarnese assented. "We were in Ohio for a week, to play Kent State and then Toledo, and we had a good time, partying and all. We beat Toledo 62–13 'cause we were goin' home, the party was over and so we got serious."

Al wouldn't stand for that kind of selective intensity. "He really worked us," Sarnese said. "They used to say the service teams were never in shape. But even when we didn't play well, we squeaked out a couple games in the last quarter because we were in shape."

Al turned up the heat when, after winning seven of eight games—the loss was to D.C.'s Bolling Air Force Base, quarterbacked by Michigan State's All-American Al Dorow—Belvoir had scrambled to a 13–13 tie with undefeated Fort Lee when Ed Kissel hit a long pass and then took it over in the last few seconds. Livid,

Al "broke our asses in practice the next week," Sarnese recalled. "We used a have a 'pit drill': the linemen would have to go one-on-one with the ball-carrier for a good half-hour and it killed you. So this intensified that week, and it started the ball rolling, where a lot of problems came up."

Like an open wound, the griping about Al Davis oozed and then gushed, over every issue and petty antipathy imaginable. Sides were being taken, and—incredibly—despite a very soft army life that other men dreamed of, even the PFCs were aligning against Davis.

"I felt a lot of enlisted guys were bein' egged on by the officers, the Southern crackers," Sarnese said. "Like Joe Tyrell. 'Cause Joe used to hang with the officers so he could go to the officers' club to drink. And Bobby Haner. Al loved him because he was tough-nosed, but Bobby's from Louisville so he went with the crackers.

"But I was an Al Davis man. I came out and openly defended Al. I felt that those Southern crackers didn't like guys from the North, and, you know, here was Al, who was Jewish and real New York. As a matter of fact, Pug Pearman and George Morris did not like me, and I never liked them from the word go. They were All-Americans from great teams and Temple always had mediocre teams; but, shit, I held my own if not better than George. Shit, George Morris got by on his name. George didn't put out that much and it made me mad. And once we started hittin', I felt he and those guys were no better than me."

The hot-blooded Sarnese, tired of the backbiting, called a team meeting. It was held on the second floor of the athletes' barracks —the one that, tellingly, was called "The Rest Home" around the camp. "It was a down and dirty meeting," Sarnese recalled with a slight shudder, "where everything came out. Guys were like embarrassed at all the shit that was comin' out."

Not shrinking an inch, Al attended the meeting, sitting silently as a procession of his players flayed him for inexperience and his grinding practices. At one point, he tried to talk tough by way of self-defense. As George Morris remembered it, "Al got up and he was all emotional and he said, 'You guys don't think I can play, y'all don't respect me. Well, I'm gonna put on my pads.' And Ed Kissel's sitting back there with his ankle big as your head, swollen from gettin' hurt. And he says, 'Whoa, wait. Wait 'til I get well, Al. If you're gonna put on pads, I want some of that action.'

"It's not like we hated Al. But, you know, service ball is different than any level of football. Service ball's crazy. Here you're worried you're gonna get your orders, you're gonna go to Korea, so what the hell did we care what Al Davis says?"

But Al did get points for courage on that day. "Al took all the crap everybody gave him," Sarnese said. "Al had brass balls."

Listening to all the bitching, Sarnese, by now boiling over, got up to say his piece.

"Al said to me, 'Well, how do you feel, Pat?' And I assume he knew I was gonna be positive, but I could've been negative, too."

In the hushed room, with nerves shorn and the mood mutinous, Sarnese delivered a brief but effective speech. "The only thing I gotta say," he began, his jaw locked in anger, "is that you have me here at this camp doin' something I like. The war's goin on, they're shooting at each other over there and I'm here playin' football. There's only one person I gotta thank for that, and that's the coach."

On reflection, Sarnese said, "I don't think he ever forgot that."

Moreover, Sarnese noticed a distinct change in attitude after the bloodletting—"I might not have been the best player, but I could always get a lot of people on my side"—and whether in cathartic relief or not, the Engineers went out and slaughtered the Norfolk Navy Tars 54–0 the following Saturday. Still, almost four decades later, some of the officers reserved a snide comment or two about Al Davis; and some of these asides, if scratched a notch below the surface, do not seem like the nicest things one can say about a Jew.

In surmising how Davis got the top job at Belvoir, for example, George Morris said with a crooked grin, "Somebody said he had some connections, or maybe his family had some money and some political clout in New York. That kinda stuff was goin' on, and you understood that. The world happens, but that doesn't mean Al Davis is the greatest football coach in America; it means that he had some clout someplace."

To that, Sarnese snorted: "Bullshit! Al Davis got by because that's what Al Davis could do. He could tell you who the third-string tight end was at TCU. He just outsmarts everybody, 'cause he's way ahead of everybody. I'd done rule blocking before, too, but Al's system was much, much better. And at halftime, he would make adjustments that were unbelievable.

"I remember one game when Al switched me from tackle to middle guard, where I'd never played before. And I said, 'Wait a second, this guy really respects me.' Well, I broke my ass that game because I wanted to repay his trust in me.

"I believe there's a jealousy factor with those other damn guys.

They may have had great college careers but Al Davis went way beyond them, and they're eatin' their hearts out. Al can be obnoxious, but if you get past the surface bullshit that gets bugs up people's asses, if you're a regular, down-to-earth guy and do what you're supposed to do, he'll be the greatest guy in the world to you. 'Cause Al's big thing is 'loyalty.' We had a guy, Dick Romanski, a little All-America from St. Norbert College in Milwaukee. Dick just couldn't break into our club but he was a beautiful person and a tough-assed guy. Al loved him, and he's still with Al today" (as the Raiders' equipment manager).

Hank Lauricella, one of the Johnny Reb officers, offered a fair-minded assessment of the novice head coach: "He was young but he was as strong-minded then as he is now; he knew what he wanted. But I had just left playing for Bob Neyland, and had a year in pro ball. I had played for some tough guys that had a real air of authority around them. Al had not been able to develop that yet.

"But, at the time, I was moving out of football and he was moving deeper into it. And his survival indicates his ability to know what it was about, and to know talent. I had been a single-wing tailback all through college. I wasn't a great T-formation strategist. I'd only known the basic T. If you were a quarterback, you were all pass; a running back and you were all run. You never got a chance to do both, like the quarterbacks do today. The whole spread-T was just evolving. But Al had me play some split-T quarterback. He saw something in me, and it worked for us.

"With his 'Line Quarterbacking' thing, he was trying to develop line strategy. They do a lot of that kind of thing today, and obviously he was on the cutting edge of a lot of this stuff. It was nothing compared to today with all the formations and sets, but it was very technical—but I appreciated that he didn't try to muscle his way through it. He was trying to teach it, he was organized, and he did a credible job. He couldn't demand of you what a Red Blaik could. But he demanded pretty much for the level he was on. And he got reasonable acceptance."

Even George Morris allowed: "Al matured a lot and I'm sure some of us had some maturing to do, too. But Al was a dedicated guy, the way he is today: hard-working, ruthless, dedicated."

And so the stoning of Al Davis eased—just in time for fresh wounds to be inflicted on the battle-weary Belvoir squad near the end of the season. In Washington, the foul odor of runamuck Red-baiting was wafting out of the Cold War councils on Capitol Hill—with the U.S. Army suddenly the prime target of the pernicious Senator Joe McCarthy. This escalated during the fall of 1953, after McCarthy subcommittee consultant David Schine was drafted and the army defied the demands of the bullying senator and his counsel Roy Cohn to let Schine out of basic training so he could continue his work.

In turn, they charged that the army was holding Schine "hostage" to suppress McCarthy's alleged "evidence" of Red spies infesting the armed services. Trying desperately to keep its house in order in the face of this inane bluster, the Pentagon clambered to show it was not doing what McCarthy had asked for Schine: conferring preferential treatment. In April of 1954, the army would face down its bogus accusers at the Army-McCarthy hearings. But, now, tension and rumors pervaded America's military bases—especially those with big-name "special services" jocks. As scuttlebutt had it, athletes were going to be scattered to other camps to finish basic training, or to the high mountains of Korea. "They were supposedly gonna ship us all out," Sarnese said. "We were scared to death. In the midst of all this, I had to testify to a colonel at Belvoir. They called me in and wanted to know if I'd ever had KP or guard duty, and, of course, I hadn't."

In this air of jittery uncertainty, the Belvoir team prepared to play Quantico in the last game of the season. For weeks, the players had been excited about this game—a televised, Thanksgiving Day charity event played before forty thousand people in Washington's Griffith Stadium. It was widely assumed that the winner in this game between these two of the country's best service teams would earn a trip to sunny San Diego to play in the service-football championship game, called the Poinsettia Bowl, against the powerful Fort Ord Army team of Ollie Matson and Don Heinrich. Now, more buzz circulated, which put even that in doubt.

"The officers were already goin' crazy," recalled Sarnese, " 'cause before the previous game, Major Lewis came into the locker room and said, 'Look, the general flew in to see the game and he wants you to look really good. If not, the twenty-one officers on this team will be in Korea.' It was like a pep talk, but now this is in everybody's head that something is in the air.

"So now, before Quantico, there were some bad rumors goin' around that it didn't matter whether we won, that we weren't gonna go to San Diego because Fort Ord was an army team and they wanted Quantico 'cause they were the Marines. So that was disheartening. We were all talkin' about San Diego, Tijuana, girls, the whole bit. And now we weren't gonna go no matter what."

Al Davis's army *commencement de la fin* was a 28–7 loss to Quantico. Behind 28–0 in the second half, the demoralized Engineers packed up for the expected passage to all points including Panmunjom. The campaign—which yielded an 8–2–1 record—ended, in the words of the camp newspaper, the *Belvoir Castle*, as "an anticlimax [to] one of the best football seasons in the history of Fort Belvoir."

Weeks later, Al was called to Washington to testify before a House Armed Services subcommittee chaired by Representative William Hess (R-Ohio), which was empaneled to examine the world-threatening issue of pampered soldier-athletes. Though it was the army's avarice for winning that led to the "coddling of athletes," as the politicians called it, Al—who was so good at the win-today–worry-tomorrow game—was set up to be the fall guy. Only he wasn't having any of it. He testified, but would not accept any blame. But, good and loyal soldier that he was, neither did he finger the brass who made human chattels move across the map at his whim. Basically, he did a former-days Ollie North—patriotic stonewalling, with a lot of hazy recollections—and walked out, unscathed.

Many years later, he was freer in directing blame, telling *Look* magazine, "You know how generals are. They want to win. This general gave me carte blanche. I also had very good contacts in the Pentagon that could move people. You follow me?"

Davis had reason to be cool and unworried. His gestalt as salient as ever, he could see that for all the static, the crisis was a tempest in a jockstrap. Instead of being shipped out, many top Belvoir players remained in camp and played during the 1954 season—though not under Al Davis, who finished his tour in the spring not in an East Asian foxhole but in the warm Virginia sun as both the McCarthy furor and the war died out.

In the interim, Al could only try to sate his sports habit by hanging around with the Fort Belvoir basketball team. During those last months, Pat Sarnese became close with him, maybe closer than anyone else at that time—or at least as close as Al would permit. "There was a place in Alexandria called the Italian Villa and he would like the pork chops there," Sarnese said. "We'd go out two or three times a week, but Al would never eat in camp. And some guys would put him down for *that*, because they were envious because we were all broke and he'd be gettin' the same private's pay, seventy-eight dollars a month, and be able to eat out 'cause he came from a few bucks.'' That Sarnese knew even that vague generality put him miles ahead of most others, but specifics were rare during dinner and barracks conversation.

"Al was a private guy, unbelievably private," Sarnese said. "We'd shoot the bull and Al would be open, but when Al didn't want to answer you, he just . . . he used to show his teeth. He'll go, '*Shee-ut*'—that was his favorite word—and he smiles that shit-eatin' smile. That's his trademark. It's the sign not to say anything more, not to go any further."

If there was one subject Al didn't mind going on about—next to football—it was Carol Sagal, about whom his desires were much more urgent now. Military isolation created obvious deprivation, but for Al the separation created a human void even he couldn't endure. Given the rumpus with his own players, Al felt lucky indeed to have someone who cared about and was willing to wait for him. For months, he kept his head together only by getting away on weekends and going back to Brooklyn to spend increasingly serious time with Carol—whom he had taken to calling by the pet name of "Carolee," after a local lingerie store—with the accent on the middle syllable. "He loved her, he was crazy about her," recalled Sarnese. "He said she was his first love, and to a guy so hung up on loyalty, that meant a lot to Al." Davis proclaimed a deep and abiding love for Carolee, and they became engaged and resolved to marry as soon as he was out of his army drabs.

Even so, neither military discharge nor impending marriage intruded on his football agenda. Soldiers would no longer salute him, but even as he was changing back into his civvies Al Davis was planning his next great offensive.

4

The [Southern] accent was an affectation. . . . If I was
recruiting three guys in one day, I'd change clothes three
times. Make them think you were fresh, that they were
special. I'd know their girlfriends' names. I can charm
anyone if I want.

—Al Davis

I'll tell you one thing. If there were no rules, he would have
the greatest football team in the history of the game.

—John Sauer

Al attacked the challenge of finding a suitably weighty coaching job through college football's flank—the increasingly
influential sphere of pro football. The vagabond, strictly mercenary
NFL of the thirties and forties—avoided by many college stars as
beneath their dignity and the poverty line—was barely recognizable
in 1954. Huge changes in pro ball were spurring the growth of the
league as a popular and profitable football showcase. At first following the colleges out of the anal-retentive, single-wing era, the
pros were now the daring and exciting game—the prudent quarterbacking of Sammy Baugh and Sid Luckman replaced by the
aerial madness of Otto Graham, Norm Van Brocklin, and Bobby
Layne.

Sprung from the scholarly minds of men like Paul Brown, Clark
Shaughnessy, Hamp Pool, and Greasy Neale, the pros' varied offenses and correspondingly flexible defenses reversed the old flow
of wisdom; now the colleges were taking coaches and concepts from

the pros, whose structure had itself become a legitimizing factor since the NFL-AAFC merger of 1949—taking the Cleveland, San Francisco, and Baltimore franchises into the league—charted the modern, bureaucratic NFL. When the league won a federal district court judgment in 1953 affirming the home-game television blackout rule, this invaluable marketing gambit sent ticket sales into orbit. The NFL was now inviolate.

Al Davis, whose urban jungle tastes drew him to the big-city, big-business aspects of commercialized football, had a clear slant on the new reality of pro ball eating into the imperial isolation of the colleges. During his two years in the army, he had all but bypassed the colleges altogether. Sitting atop a roster of former collegians, he found himself the curator of talented players coveted by the pros. Not only had the government become aware of Al Davis and his Belvoir stable of beefcake, but so had NFL people. Coaches and scouts would call Davis to get a line on potential pro fodder, and the Colts' head coach, Wilbur C. "Weeb" Ewbank, made a number of visits to the camp to see it for himself.

The round little rookie coach of the reconstituted Baltimore franchise (abandoned in 1951, it returned two years later with the inventory of the failed New York Yanks/Dallas Texans team) would sit and talk with the unripe but schnauzerlike young man and smile vacantly through Davis's big talk. If that was the only price for a pipeline to proven talent, he would gladly pay it. Besides, he knew that Davis's own talent did not end at his mouth. "I knew he was an ambitious guy," said Ewbank, pinpointing the quality that immediately spilled off Davis. "But he was also energetic, he liked to win, and he was willing to pay the price to do it; he'd spend the time and the energy."

Well aware of the "in" that Ewbank, a Paul Brown protégé, could provide for him, Al stroked the relationship. When he was discharged from the army, Al fully intended to use his cabinet-sized knowledge about recent graduates, where they were, and how well they could play as barter for pro contacts and conceivable jobs that could arise through them. But it was Ewbank that Al made his biggest chits with. While awaiting release from Fort Belvoir, Al had called around the league to pitch several of his players who had gone undrafted by the pros, among them linemen Bob Langas and Doug Eggers. Langas signed first with the Browns, then the following year wound up with the Colts. Eggers got tryouts with the Eagles and Colts, stuck with the latter and played on their 1958

championship team. Don Engels, the Illinois and Belvoir quarterback, also came to Ewbank's Colts in 1955.

"Al made all the calls for me, I had no idea of it," recalled Eggers,
who came from an obscure school, South Dakota State, and said
that if not for Davis's work on his behalf, "I would've ended up
right back in South Dakota," never tasting the pros.

"You don't know how Al manipulated," Pat Sarnese said of Al's
round of player Parcheesi. "You don't know what Al told Weeb.
Al might've said he was the agent for Eggers and Langas. Al would
do shit like that. He would call up and say he was somebody that
he wasn't. He was great at that, he could change his voice in a
minute. He loved those games. If something had to get done, he'd
find a way."

In short order, Al made a handshake deal with Ewbank as a very
loose Colts scout, and the keen-witted Ewbank knew the score—
Davis was using him as much as Weeb wanted to use him, only
more so.

"I hired a lot of college coaches as scouts," Ewbank said, "and
if I paid guys two hundred dollars for a report on a kid, that meant
a lot to them when they were gettin' paid four hundred dollars to
coach. But for Al, that was peanuts. Any money I paid him was
peanuts to him. It was more important just to get the association
with the Colts and the NFL. You'd never see a lot of scouts; they're
just out there somewhere. But Al would come to the Colt camp and
hang around with the players and coaches, like he belonged there."

In truth, Al provided Ewbank with little solid information,
though he handled the job with his usual intensity. Bill Label, the
onetime Syracuse basketball team manager, happened to be on a
plane about to fly from Washington to New York when the seat
next to him was taken by his old "scatterbrained" classmate. "He
had in his lap a card box," Label said, "and he must have had five
hundred three-by-five cards in there, which he guarded with his
life. He said he was scouting for the Colts and that he knew every
high school and college player in the country."

On another migration, Al ran across a young public relations man
for the Rams named Pete Rozelle. When Rozelle inquired about
players in the military, Al hinted that such details might be available
at a price. Davis was not acting out of mercenary interest: this was
a way of standing off Rozelle, whom he knew would spurn the
entreaty and be properly offended by it. Cordial as Rozelle was, Al
thought of him as distant and vaguely contemptuous, a skilled

apparatchik but no mensch. He sensed nothing in Rozelle that would repay any partiality. He wouldn't suck up to people like that—he would beat them.

Al did have reason to safeguard his card box. Most of the information on those index cards was earmarked for purposes other than use by the Colts or any pro club. Al knew all along that scouting, per se, was of little value as a career. Within weeks, with his emphasis now on high school players, he geared his vision to the most propitious career incubator: the benediction of academia. Schmoozing daily with college coaches and other scouts, Al knew where the job openings were, and when his travels took him to a college campus, he'd make a point of saying a few deferential words to the ADs. The nation's mail would usually contain an Al Davis resume—which could be preposterously far-fetched—en route to a school somewhere or other. The first reference would be the name of Weeb Ewbank.

Al worked the pro-college connection purposefully. Continuing on the coaching clinic circuit, he got into intensive symposiums with pro players and would-be coaches whom he believed to be on the same wavelength. "There was one clinic in Chicago," Pat Sarnese said, "where Al was in a room, up at the blackboard, and he had guys like Chuck Noll and Don Shula listening to him. I was told by a guy who was playing with the Bears at the time that Al Davis would take all these guys into the room and he would always wind up with the chalk."

At another clinic, in Atlantic City, he met a dwarfish young man with a lisp named Al LoCasale, who at age eighteen was helping to coach the Philadelphia high school team he couldn't ever make as a player. As much as Al was wary of the young Pete Rozelle, there was something ingenuous and reliable about LoCasale, in his obedience and his dogged, ordered approach to the game. Al spent hours with the pugged coach, doing x's and o's with him on napkins at a boardwalk deli called the Nosherai—but also seemingly doing a kind of security check for future reference. Someday, he had reason to believe, he might need a handyman, and those who offered paeans early would not be forgotten.

The Davis scouting caravan encompassed all of these considerations as time began to impel it with more urgency. His foraging was interrupted only briefly, in the fall of 1954. That was when Al and Carol Sagal married in a Brooklyn synagogue. They moved into a small rented house in comfortable Atlantic Beach, on the same oceanside strip of West Park Avenue that Louis and Rose Davis had chosen to move to several years before when Louis finally agreed to a life of leisurely recompense.

Al, though, was home so infrequently that he may have needed to write the address on his wrist in order to remember it. That Carol understood his football wanderlust amazed her friends, whom she often saw more than her new husband. But this was a marriage of immense rewards for Al; not only did he get the only girl he ever loved, but Carol's own ample family fortune—her parents owned a thriving department store in downtown Brooklyn—eased Al's festering guilt about taking Louis's money to stoke his gypsy moth existence. Their joint bank account bulging, he could turn away Louis's charity and pose more accurately now as the lean and hungry young turk. Able to afford much more glitzy wheels, he still rode around in his rusting black drop-top. There would be time aplenty for opulence, that he knew.

It took bare months for the pro connection to pay off—in an ironic twist that would have Al Davis back among army barracks. In January of 1955, The Citadel appointed John Sauer to rebuild a moribund football program as well as to serve as athletic director. Although Sauer had never heard of Al Davis, he became eternally yoked to Davis by a fate that seemed crafted by Al. For one thing, the thirty-year-old Sauer, a former player and assistant coach under Red Blaik at West Point, came to The Citadel from the pros, having been the backfield coach of the Rams. For another, his father had played in the early days of the NFL and was friendly with Weeb Ewbank, as was his son. Now, putting together a staff, Sauer called on Ewbank for some ideas.

"Weeb brought him to my attention," Sauer remembered, his voice curdled by a rueful harshness that gets acrid the longer he speaks of Davis. "Weeb didn't know anything about his coaching ability, but Davis was interested in getting started coaching and was willing to take very little money. He had been doing some scouting for Weeb and [the Colts' general manager] Don Kellett." Sauer paused. "Maybe I would've been better off if I'd talked to Kellett. As a matter of fact, I used to think maybe Weeb recommended him to get rid of him."

At the beginning, things were fine between them. Sauer, a compact, pleasant man with crisp army diction and a trusting nature, would have no clue that Davis would not fall firmly in line as an underling on his staff. When Sauer interviewed Davis, he found Al's knowledge of the game to be above reproach and his enthusiasm for erecting a winning program utterly maniacal. He promised Sauer he could get rock-ribbed kids from steelbed towns in the Northeast and Midwest—the kind Al was convinced made the hungriest football players—to come to a South Carolina military school, while keeping a steady number of Southern boys coming in to preserve the tradition of the school and please the alumni, dozens of whom lived in Charleston.

For all the swaggering, though, Al knew The Citadel would be a hellish sell to the kids he wanted to funnel to the school. Between his safarilike recruiting trips, he sidled up to the alumni, filling their heads with the same visions of Citadel glory that he used with impressionable high school quarry. Citadel alumni were vital to the lives of the young cadets. Away from home, chained at the neck by a code of military honor, their weary eyeballs pried open at dawn by reveille, and their bodies assaulted by drills before their first class, matriculation could be another word for masochism. For those kids with no bent for military life, the alumni would be the only lifeline to the necessary plebeian comforts: cars, girls, home-cooked meals in place of basic army swill. Permitted to leave the gate-encircled compound only on weekends, the two thousand cadets would shed their suffocating, brass-buttoned uniforms and stream lemminglike to the placid wood-framed homes of Charleston, the big flagpoles in their manicured front yards marking forty-eight hours of unwinding with the family assigned them.

As obliging as the alumni were in any case, they considered it to be virtually in their personal interest that football at The Citadel be redeemed after a season in which their Bulldogs had not won a single game. These men, who had stuck it out and sucked it up at the Academy, grieved that the military preparedness of The Citadel had drained on the football field. Now, this avid young Northerner was pledging victory and veneration, if they would be free with their largesse. As with his player pipelining at Fort Belvoir, Al did not appear to pay much attention to the letter of the law, in this case NCAA recruiting ordinances. If there would be a toll to pay for picayune statute violations, he would again worry about it later.

Established in 1842, The Citadel was, and is, an imposing shrine to a chivalric military ethos fighting the tides of social change. Lying serenely on one hundred acres just off the Ashley River, its ornamented gates and array of Civil War cannons balefully occluding the passage of time and traditional culture, The Citadel's fantasia was undisturbed. Wide thoroughfares crisscrossed the campus with names like Robert E. Lee Avenue. Colonial and rococo halls and chapels christened in the names of such Confederate war heroes as General Micah Jenkins stood in clean, dutiful rows surmounting the green expanse of Summerall Field. On that tract of virginal grass each Friday afternoon, the corps of cadets marched ramrod-straight in the ritualistic dress parade, which could make battle-hardened soldiers weep.

For Al Davis, who revered Red Blaik's army teams but who might have turned to mush as a cadet, this was the best of both worlds. It was as if he were back in General Scott's staff car, receiving salutes from imagined subordinates. Indeed, the scant pay of an assistant coach—five hundred dollars a month—was again irrelevant to status, and now to a deliciously ironic fancy. As a Citadel employee, he was given an honorary rank in the corps of cadets. This time Al Davis wasn't a PFC—he was a *lieutenant*!

This was what awaited when Al and a now-pregnant Carol (evidently, there was *enough* time spent at home) moved down to Charleston and rented a snug house in suburban West Oak Forest. John Sauer lived close by, and they would often come to work together, though Al would usually be hunkered down in his office long after Sauer and the others had left. In this challenge, as with all others—but now with so much on the line—he would not be caught short. No way. Although Al wouldn't admit openly that he required more football expertise, the realist in him quietly sought out Weeb Ewbank once again.

"He was the line coach, but I didn't think he knew too much about line play," Ewbank related. "So our line coach, John Sandusky, helped him along. John said he had to take him from scratch, pretty much."

Davis needed no assistance in recruiting. Hitting the road for weeks at a time, stalking the wild bullocks of his index cards, Lieutenant Davis retraced the paths of the early French-American fur traders—up and down the East Coast, through the Hudson, Mohawk, and Lehigh valleys, across the Three Rivers of Ohio and Pennsylvania, and finally to the shores of the Great Lakes. Less frequently, he would prowl the grottos and swamplands of the Carolinas and Florida.

But he did not sojourn in blind faith. Al had long before drawn his battle quilt. Since few of his prospective recruits had ever heard of The Citadel, and their idea of formality was lacing every eyelet of their work boots, he measured each kid not only by height and weight but by general awareness. The old Brainiac culling as he spoke with each, he quickly pegged them, his pitch to them running according to these variables:

1. See if they know what The Citadel is and feel out whether they have any affinity for the military lifestyle; if not, don't elaborate on it and go right down the line with football glory.
2. See if it is easy to convince them to come; if not, promise them perks according to how intelligent they are.
3. Obfuscate. *Never* be too specific.

In gauging the physical requirements of an Al Davis boy, he was no less painstaking—and, in this, he surely took recruiting to where it had never gone before. Showing up one day at the Allentown, Pennsylvania, high school of an end named Barry Thomas, he made a curious request.

"The first thing he wanted to do was see my legs. And then the next thing he wanted to do was go home and see my *mother's* legs," recalled Thomas, still a bit bemused. He had this theory about how big you would get. I was fairly big in high school, like six-two and 222 pounds, and he said if I had the potential to get any bigger, it depended on my mother's genes, and how developed her calves were. As it happened, my mother had been an athlete, so Al liked me right away. And my mother like him, which was another part of recruiting: getting the parents on your side. Al would come to our house, get a free meal, stay overnight while he looked at other guys in the area, and all the while he'd be charming my mom and dad. He played all the angles.

"What he would do was, he'd get you all caught up in a fever. That's how he got you down there, where he could really sell you. The majority of the guys he brought in there could've gone to the big schools, we were all heavily recruited. I'd never even heard of The Citadel, but Al made it sound larger than life. And when he got down there, he'd give it to you full blast. He'd take you to the stadium and say, 'By next year there'll be another deck on this stadium,' and 'I'm gonna recruit another thirty ballplayers and we're gonna be number one in the country'—and he's tellin' all this to a seventeen-year-old kid whose head would be so turned that he couldn't possibly say no.

"For just about everyone who played there those years, we ended up at The Citadel for only one reason: Al Davis."

Thomas was rare among them in that he didn't flinch when Al demurely mentioned what The Citadel was and was intrigued by the military thing. As a result, "He was up front with me. He brought out a yearbook for me to see. But with some people he wasn't up front. There were a handful of people that I'm sure Al didn't show a yearbook to and explain that it was a military school. A lot of guys didn't quite know the whole story. Some guys, like a couple from Youngstown, Ohio, didn't, people who weren't intelligent enough to understand whether it was a military school or not."

"He made sure you heard what you wanted to hear," explained Carl Wunderler, and All-State tackle from Northampton, Pennsylvania. "It could've been a little clearer text of the English language. You could take what he said in any number of ways."

And so, as Al went here and there and back again plucking big and fast football players off the vine, it was enough that Davis would beguile them, look at their thick calves and say in admiration, "Yep, yep. You're the kinda guy we want." Several of them weren't even football players—or even apparent athletes. On one expedition to New Jersey, he wooed Bob Schwarze, a quarterback who had flunked out at West Point. Then they stopped in at a track meet so Al could check out one of the sprinters. But instead of the sprinter, he became intrigued by a kid in the stands. "He spotted him and said, 'That kid looks like a football player,'" Schwarze remembered. "So he borrowed a stop watch and had the guy doing the forty-yard dash right during the meet."

That kid, Joe Chefalo, would become the starting halfback taking handoffs from Schwarze. The following year, Davis got a tip from Pat Sarnese about a blazing-fast Philadelphia track man whom he knew, Angelo Coia. Sarnese took Coia to a basketball game, where, as planned, Al was lying in wait. Before the night was over, Coia pledged to go to The Citadel as a kick returner.

"Angelo's father wasn't sure, he asked me if it was the right thing," Sarnese recalled. "I said one thing: 'Al will be loyal to Angelo, he won't let you down.'"

The recruiting of another important cog, a halfback from Chicago named Bob Daugherty, was an example of how Al Davis could control a kid's head. Though Daugherty was reluctant, Al got him to visit The Citadel. There, upon seeing the dress parade, Daugherty said, "The hair on the back of my neck went up." However, when it came time for him to go back home, Al was nowhere to be found and a Citadel aide had to drive him to the airport. "And I'm thinkin', 'Oh, God, I blew it, they don't want me.' So now I get back home and I'm walkin' into my house and as I'm goin' up the stairs the phone's ringin'—and it was Al Davis, sayin', 'What happened? You left before we could get together.' So I told him that I thought it was over for me and he goes, 'No, no, I got this contract here that I want you to sign.'

"Well, I'd be willing to bet that Al Davis knew exactly how long it took from the plane to land and for me to get to the door, and that I wouldn't have any time to think about this thing, that I'd have to say yes. And, sure enough, the letter of intent was in the mail."

John Sauer's first training camp was held at the Marine boot camp on Parris Island, off the South Carolina coast. The very locale hinted at a training regimen that many of the players—all but a handful of them Davis recruits—couldn't have imagined. Sequestered in barracks when not on the field, they were sent out in the torturous sun and choking humidity to perform two-a-day workouts run at double-time. "God, it was more like Devil's Island," said Carl Wunderler. "We had to run on sand dunes in Myrtle Beach, and those gnats chewed your calves up like you wouldn't believe. I was so damned homesick, first of all, and to go through that, I don't know how I survived it."

"We were just dying out there," Daugherty looked back with a shiver. "I'd see grown men start crying because somebody bumped their elbow and knocked the water out of their hands."

Four days into practice, Daugherty had had enough. "I went to Al after supper and said, Coach Davis, you told me when you got me into this thing that if I ever wanted to get out, all I had to do was come and tell you. Well, I wanna go home. I'm convinced I'm gonna die of a heart attack here.'

"And Al said, 'Bobby, what you're doin' out here is like climbin' up a hill and it's terrible'—and he gets into this dramatic storytelling and his voice rises—'but soon you're gonna get to the top, you're gonna start coasting, and, Bobby, it's gonna be the *greatest thing in your life*!' I said, 'No, I wanna go home,' and he said, 'I'll tell you what. Give me one more day. If you feel the same way tomorrow night, I got your plane ticket in my pocket.

"So we go out to this morning practice and I die. I was throwin' up, heavin' my guts out, and I could barely make it to the bus after practice. And I'm thinkin', 'This is it, the last day,' and you're going through this thing where you don't think you can muster another ounce of strength and all of a sudden something turns the light on. You break through this barrier and you do get your body in condition and the pain does go away and it *is* going downhill. And to this day, I'm very thankful to Al Davis because he didn't let me go home that day."

Not all of the battered players appreciated—or could even hear —the lesson. As if brutal practices weren't enough, there was more anguish when the players got a taste of military reality. Unaware of military dress codes and rules of conduct, the freshmen—even the largest behemoths—were constantly ragged by strutting upperclassmen who, by army tradition, were free to "brace" the plebes.

One Davis recruit, a huge lineman named Al Bansavage, never cared enough to button his shirt all the way to the neck or tuck it in. "He looked like a slob all the time," said Daugherty, "and these little upperclass wimps would pull rank and yell, 'Step to it, freshman.' And Al would sit there and just look at 'em. This one guy came in and held a pencil about an inch from Al's chest, sayin', 'Pump your chest up and touch this pencil.' Well, with that, Al swatted the pencil away with his hand and said, 'Is that good enough, sir?' The guy nearly exploded with anger and Al just looked at him, like, 'I don't need this,' and went on to his room."

Other players, faced with the same humiliation, went past their rooms. "After those early practices, when we got back to school," said Barry Thomas, "I think like twenty players just went home, and the rest of us weren't ecstatic to stay." One very homesick freshman, a farm boy named Bob Letcher, was recruited hotly. A fabulous athlete, he could run, catch, and punt with either foot. But Letcher gave it a go at The Citadel only until a letter came from home in which was a picture of a new John Deere tractor. He packed and left that same day.

The hardy ones who stayed learned a football system designed to reap the benefits of all this flagellation. Sauer felt he had little choice but to turn military rigor to his advantage, that since his team was going to be in fighting-ready shape, that quality would write the game plan. This, in a nutshell, was "Racehorse Football," which for Sauer was really a variation of a Red Blaik ploy used during Sauer's years at West Point. "If you recall Blaik's 'Lonesome End,' you saw an offense where a man didn't even come back to the huddle," Sauer said. Now, speed-up offenses—racing to the line of scrimmage before the defense could set—was being used by Bud Wilkinson at Oklahoma.

Faced with the daunting prospect of a team as green as Summerall Field, Sauer camouflaged reality with artifice. "We played nine freshmen on offense alone that year and we couldn't block out a grandmother, but if we were gonna do nothing else, we were gonna get eleven guys off the ball and hit the other guy before he could believe we got to him. We took a sprinter's stance and, man, off we went. And then I said, 'Now we're not gonna do it with a huddle.' I mean, for two weeks all we worked on was the cadence, the snap, so we didn't screw *that* up."

Yet, while Racehorse Football was an old idea wrenched by Sauer off other chalkboards, as the 1955 season wound on and Davis— as at Adelphi—gained more and more authority, the perception fattened that Al was somehow the power behind the throne. This happened not only because Al could mesmerize players with the chalk, but because he was able to transfer his crackling fervor to them in a way the low-key Sauer could not. Accordingly, Davis seemed to all eyes the progenitor of the racehorse game. With the short, nimble steps of a meadow mouse, Al would goose players by continually clapping his hands and yammering, "Go! Go! Go!" like a mantra.

So visible was he that the players—*his* players, *his* boys—assumed early that Al's jurisdiction went far beyond the line position. Whether that was his intention or not, Carl Wunderler could not help but feel Davis was a Socratic presence. "I thought Racehorse Football was Al's, but then again, we were seventeen-, eighteen-year-old kids. So whatever a grown-up would say to us—especially someone as exciting as Al Davis—we'd listen with awe."

But it wasn't only Al's boys who quickly swore by him. Jim McDaniel and Budgie Broome were holdovers from the comatose previous regime; vitalized by Davis's style and brains, they now excelled, acknowledging Al's influence. "I was the starting tackle but Al benched me and made me earn it back," McDaniel said. "He did the right thing. I took it for granted that I was a senior starter and I got lazy. Al set me straight."

Broome, a halfback who became team captain in 1956, recalled the impact Davis made when he swooped in on the program: "He was more vociferous than the other assistant coaches; he really was the personality of the coaching staff. I remember he said: 'This is a team everybody's gonna be talkin' about for years to come'—and it's true. I held four season records for almost twenty years at The Citadel—yards per carry, touchdowns, punt and kickoff returns—and it was because of the blockin', and that was Al's area."

What is more, John Sauer himself seemed to gild Davis's role. The novice who needed remedial instruction in line play was, by the start of the '55 season, calling the plays from up in the press box as the revved-up Bulldogs—often not even bothering with a cadence before the snap—careened through a lightweight schedule of teams like Elon, Wofford, Furman, and Newberry. Though they came back to earth after a 5–1 start, finishing 5–4—and lost their last two games 14–0 and 39–0—this was a season of splendor for one of college football's doormats of a year before. And with each win, Al's play calling took on a storied nature.

Against Richmond, down 12–7 late in the game, he sent down a long pass call that clicked and won the game for the Bulldogs, 14–12. When it happened, two former Fort Belvoir players Al had gotten to come to The Citadel, Dick Bergeron and Bill Righter, were sitting on the bench. "I remember that you could see the telephone line running from Al to John Sauer," Bergeron said, "and just before the play, Billy looked at me and said, 'You know what? I can see that play come right down the wire from Al.' It was just something you could *feel*, that Al was on top of it. That phone popped and—bingo—it was a touchdown." Just as crucial to that win, as Bergeron recalled it, was a slightly less intellectual Davis suggestion. "They had a fullback who had run wild every game. And Al decided we would hit this guy *every* play, even if he didn't have the ball. By the third quarter, this guy hadn't had any big gainers and he was tiptoeing up to the line each play, showing us he didn't have the ball. He was spooked, and Al knew he'd be."

The Citadel turnaround was an intriguing, if minor, college football headline of 1955, and Al had every intention of taking bows. In May of 1956, his third *Scholastic Coach* article ran, bombastically entitled "Racehorse Football!: A Revolutionary Go! Go! Go! Offense That Relentlessly Pressures the Defense." In it, Al cited the cover of the Citadel playbook, on which was written:

Within [these] covers are the essential factors of the greatest offense in football—The Citadel T . . . the fastest way of playing the game yet devised. It places a high premium on faith, discipline, and *speed! speed! speed!* . . . It's a continuous process of *go!-go!-go!*

Although the piece was rife with pronouns like "we" and "our," the name of John Sauer—to say nothing of Bud Wilkinson—did not appear once. When football people began to refer to the article, passing remarks that Davis must be one smart SOB to implement the system, Sauer's neck burned red. He said nothing, but the personal bond between him and Al was broken. During the '56 season, and for all the years after, Al Davis's games of ego and usurpation ate at Sauer like battery acid. Three decades later, the scald was permanent—explaining why Sauer's ruminations about the fallout with Davis often crossed into territory as ungracious as any Sauer thought Davis had entered.

"Here is a man that wanted credit for a lot of things," Sauer said, "because . . . maybe in his life he felt he was a minority, I don't know. But he was very ambitious and very cunning. He is one guy, the only guy I have ever known, that can change black to white in front of your face. That's not saying much for the people who listen to him. But I must say, he didn't change black to white in front of *my* face."

As it was, Sauer had no idea at the time that Davis's self-penned bio in the Citadel press materials and in the weekly football program—which listed him as a three-sport letterman at Syracuse and the former "head coach" at Adelphi and "assistant coach" with the Colts—was preposterously inaccurate. But the *Scholastic Coach* article, and its fallout, brought him dangerously close to imploding.

"I can remember the first time my hair got up on my back was when somebody said Bud Wilkinson got Racehorse Football *from Al Davis* for the Orange Bowl in 1956!" said Sauer. "And you could fill up books with the things that have been written that Al Davis was supposed to have done and it would be the most one hundred percent fiction you'd see in your life.

"I have known and worked for the greatest minds in football. Hamp Pool knew more football than any man who walked the earth, and so did Earl Blaik. And I know that I had to give a coaching clinic to every one of the [Citadel] assistant coaches, because they hadn't coached. Al Davis hadn't coached. Oh, Al learned football, and I claim that's where he learned it—*if* he learned any.

"I think Al Davis is probably a good teacher. But I don't think he could *demonstrate*. I used to watch him play pickup basketball with the kids and, hell, he could talk 'em out of makin' two points. It was easier than defending against 'em. He looked like he had the moves. He was a typical New Yorker—he fools people. He never lacked confidence, but sometimes that confidence is false but you make it *sound* like it's true. I cannot take offense to success, yet I will not promote the man because he is not my idea of the kind of man that I like. I do respect his ability, but I don't know many people that would want to pattern themselves after Al Davis."

And yet there is no question that the rousing terminology of the Citadel playbook *was* patently Al's; it is as distinctly his as are his fingerprints. And while Sauer insisted, "I was in charge of drawing playbooks every place I was," he probably rued the day he allowed Al so much latitude—and had every reason to fear that Al would stop at nothing less than taking his job. The '55 season was Al's study lab—'56 was going to be his petition for the head post.

But, as the football squad gathered for the 1956 season, things were happening—ominous things for both Davis and Sauer. Budgie Broome, whose role as team captain included calling the players together for gripe sessions, knew trouble was fermenting. "I listened to the stuff that Al promised 'em and, while I don't think Al told outright lies, I read between the lines. He walked a very fine line. Like if he said, 'We'll have a car available to you,' he did—but it was a big old gray van that could be made available to you for a few hours. Guys would say, 'Yeah, we got a car—a sixteen-seater.' "

"A lot of the fellas were bitter at Al because he did such a super selling job on 'em, and then they ended up at The Citadel and wished they were someplace else," Barry Thomas acknowledged. "He might have said, 'You'll be provided with a car every weekend,' and maybe they thought they were gonna be *given* a car. And, really, what Al was thinking was that the alumni would supply 'em with cars. But Al never spelled it out. So they would go to John Sauer and say, hey, the guy promised me a car and I'm not gettin' a car. And it was probably because Al couldn't find somebody in town to give him a car for the weekend."

The bitterness toward Al, however, was almost always ameliorated by the assumption that he was at least *trying* to come through for them. "Al *did* try to do what he said he would," Thomas believed. "He was sellin' all the time, goin' around town promising he'd get that upper deck on the stadium—which never happened

—and the alumni would work with him." That was made clear by certain regular practices. If Thomas played well, he could expect surreptitious rewards. "On Monday morning," he said, "there would be some money in the mail from 'anonymous benefactors' —although I never heard of Al having anything to do with it." But Thomas did conclude this about Davis: "He just would do and give anything to win; it wasn't the same with John Sauer. Al made a lot of enemies in Charleston because he promised everything and he couldn't *possibly* fulfill those promises. Nobody could have."

To his credit, Al *did* effect a modicum of change in a place where change was shunned. In line with his soft-pedaling of the military life, he talked Sauer into getting Mark Clark's assent to allow the team to spend the night before games in an off-campus motel, away from the constricting vibes of the compound. And for the first— and last—time, Citadel jocks ate at a training table, separated from the other cadets and served tastier, meatier grub.

"Al also wanted to organize a football company—the whole company would be nothin' but football players—but the general and the board of visitors didn't go for it," said Broome. " 'Cause as it stood, the other cadets resented the fact—and still do to this day —that the football players didn't have it as hard as them.

"But for a lot of guys on the team, they thought that it was gonna be nothin' but peaches and cream, pie in the sky, and Al may have thought he could do that, but it just doesn't happen at The Citadel. He and Sauer did a good job of it the first year, but it fell through the second. That's when all hell broke loose."

Even months before, right after the 1955 season, players were falling out like eczema-strangled hair—a good dozen of "Al's boys" went home, barely stopping to peel off their uniforms. Al could plaster over the cracks they left with a new crop of hungry and naive recruits, but he couldn't stop a mounting unease as the Bulldogs went 3–5–1 in '56, losing five of the last six games.

Not only had the opposition gotten wise to Racehorse Football —which Sauer stubbornly, and unwisely, clung to—but those wild grizzlies from the Northern tundra had, to Al's horror, gotten too used to the Virginia sun. At 3–3–1, with the season still salvageable, they went to Philadelphia to play Villanova—the only major college team they played those two seasons. "Before the game," said Carl Wunderler, "Al told us, 'Now we're in our own backyard,' but it was incredibly cold and the fellas from the South were freezing their behinds off. I was, too, because we were accustomed to warm weather. And nothing went right for us." The score was 46–0, Villanova. The next week, the season finale, they lost to George Washington, 20–0.

Now, the storm that had been gathering all season burst—directly over the heads of Al Davis and John Sauer.

It was Sauer who took the initial hits. For the better part of two seasons, players had come to Sauer with their complaints—directed there by Al, who unblushingly laid the blame on the coach. One of those players, end Paul Maguire—one of those prosaic Youngstown boys—years later described the carousel ride this way: "Al had offered everybody something. He said, 'There's going to be enough money, don't worry.' It turned out to be fifteen dollars a month for laundry. Guys went to Sauer and he'd say, 'Al promised that.' They'd go to Al and he'd say, 'Sauer reneged on his promise.' "

Perhaps because Al had stocked the team with capable players, Sauer had not kept a close watch on Al's recruiting ways, nor had he been vigilant when dissension arose—Sauer, in fact, privately suspected that Davis was secretly gleaning used cars for players from the nearby Darlington Auto Auction, but never confronted Al about it. Now, livid that players believed Al and not him, he finally reacted, with his usual military courtliness.

Addressing the team to deny that he ever had a hand in any promises, Sauer neither upbraided Al nor admitted to a passive duplicity in failing to keep Al in line from the get-go—though his next move made that moot. On December 7, Sauer dropped an incendiary bomb. Saying only that it was due to "personal reasons," he cashiered himself. Resigning as coach and AD, he took his leave, an old soldier fading away to the sad peal of carillon. Never again would he coach, except for the small change of the College All-Stars.

Sauer, still tight-lipped over three decades later, offered a third-person cryptogram by way of explaining his exile. "Earl Blaik once said when somebody asked him why did John Sauer get out of football when he was offered the army job and this job and that job. And Blaik said, 'He had a very ambitious coach with him.' Enough said."

Sauer's abrupt resignation was shrouded in mystery around the campus, and few on the outside knew of the subterranean stirring that threatened to blow the lid off the football program. Although Mark Clark publicly buffed the "personal reasons" varnish—bewailing, with crocodile tears, that Sauer's leaving was a "mistake"—he was well aware of the volatile situation with Al Davis and his flock of recruits. Budgie Broome had communicated to him the players' laments, as did a bulging knapsack of mail from the parents of many of those players.

The alumni, getting wind of the problem and fearing *they* might be implicated in improprieties, turned violently against Davis in letters of their own to Clark. Though the players kept the family feuding under their brass buttons, they knew the deal. "The hearsay was that some of the problems had gotten too outlandish with the recruiting," said Dick Bergeron, "and that John Sauer thought it may come back to haunt him and that's why he quit." So outlandish had things gotten, in fact, that Clark had asked the school's faculty chairman and NCAA representative, Colonel David McAlister, to look closely into the program. Included in McAlister's reading material, said John Sauer, was a "dossier" compiled on Al Davis by the athletic department.

All over Charleston, people concerned with the Citadel football program agonized. Al Davis, though, saw only a job opening.

5

Someone was writing an article one time and asked me, "How was Al Davis as an assistant coach?" I said, "I wouldn't know. He never coached for me."

—Weeb Ewbank

The words "cunning, shrewd, devious" don't have a bad connotation to me. Look at the history of people in positions of leadership. They've said of every one of my time that he's devious—from Roosevelt and Churchill to Eisenhower, Kissinger, and Mao.

—Al Davis

For his part, Al was very willing to risk scandal. The possibility of winning football games was, he trusted, a far stronger counterweight, and he was sure he had convinced The Citadel that winning rested in his hands. Even in the event of scandal, he had his defensive strategy, one that had not yet gone cold since the Hess Committee. If called on the carpet, he would stonewall. He was, after all, getting good at that. Besides, Al was sure he had done nothing grievously wrong—or else was sure he had been too smart (that is, hazy) to have erred. If he was careless, surely it was in small, selfless doses. "I didn't make any illegal offers," Davis said many years after, "but if a kid needed a couple bucks, I wouldn't be above giving it out of my pocket."

Still, he was not deceived—was he *ever*? Throughout the hemorrhage of the '56 season, he mobilized his best resource—the very players who were so unhappy. Knowing he had to keep them on his side was another reason he had tried to turn them against John Sauer; he could not manipulate them if he were a symbol of the establishment. Coach Davis, he etched into their subconscious, wasn't a "*them*"; he was an "*us*."

"Most of us weren't angry at Al," Barry Thomas said. "We all knew he was trying, that he wasn't just lying, because if it was up to him, he *would* have fulfilled all his promises. But it was either because of rules or because it was a military school that he couldn't do it."

"We all wanted Al to succeed Sauer—so that we would've gotten all the things he promised," added Bob Schwarze with a huge laugh. "It seemed like the logical choice anyway, because Al had made himself more than an assistant coach. As a quarterback, he was always helpful to me, telling me about different defenses and what to look for. There was no conversation you could have with him that he wasn't talking about how you could play a better game. It was absolutely his whole life.

"And we believed him. Maybe he didn't know as much about football as we thought, but you just felt he did."

Budgie Broome, as captain, earned special attention from Al. "I'd seen a pair of opal earrings in the canteen I wanted to buy for my fiancée. It may have been twenty-five dollars and Al said, 'Okay, I'll get 'em.' Well, a few days later, he says, 'Budgie, I got 'em,' and he gives 'em to me and all my money back. I don't know how he did it. He had all these connections."

Al also worked hard on the spit-and-polish image, so as to stand taller in Mark Clark's eyes—and the christening of newborn Mark Davis in 1955 would still make John Sauer smirk thirty-five years later. "He planted the seed early, didn't he?" Sauer mocked. "You don't think he had designs?" Beyond that, there was Al's carriage. Bridling the more coarse tendencies of his mouth—"I never heard Al swear, and I admired him for that," said Carl Wunderler—he emulated Sauer's gentleman-officer, wearing his clothes starched and his sideburns trimmed. There was only one exception: he refused to shear his beloved pompadour for the soldierly brush-cut. (Unfortunately, that could have an undermining effect—bathing in his shower cap after practices, he could look more like Mamie than Ike.)

Now, as a loyal leader of men, in solidarity with the players and the military, Al felt he deserved satisfaction, and said so to Clark when the general informed him of Sauer's resignation. The next day, he sent in reinforcements, first Budgie Broome and then Dick Bergeron, to express the players' support. "Al said, 'Budgie, I'd really like to have this job. I hope you'll put in a good word for me.' " But right after Budgie did that, he knew Al was a goner when Ernest Hollings, the lieutenant governor of South Carolina and a Citadel alumnus (who is now a United States senator) came by the barracks. "He was on the board of visitors and had a lot of influence," Broome said, "and he was very concerned about the recruiting abuses. I told him that if they wanted to win, Al was the man they oughta keep. But it went beyond that."

In fact, now even the school's professors were standing against Al. "He was a little too overbearing with the Citadel hierarchy," Wunderler said. "Al had pressured them to help guys' grades so they could stay eligible. He'd say, 'Could so-and-so write a paper, give a speech, be retested?' It was his attitude. These people had doctorate degrees, they didn't take kindly to that kind of arm twisting." Nor did they take kindly to the fact that Al had allegedly promised one farm boy that he could major in agrarian studies—a curriculum that did not exist at the school.

On Friday, December 17, five days after he had laid claim to the head coaching job, Al Davis's Citadel campaign was over, dashed by Mark Clark's blunt rejection of the moral and ethical price tag of an Al Davis regime. As Al had staked so much playing this hand, he knew the linear equation of failure—he had shot his wad at The Citadel. Clark didn't have to confirm it. The climactic headline in the *Charleston News and Courier*—DAVIS NO LONGER CANDIDATE FOR CITADEL COACHING POST—left him shucked like an ear of corn.

Realizing the high-stakes game he was playing, Al had covered his behind. Lately he had been courted by Don Clark, the former USC lineman who was about to move up from assistant coach to take over the Trojans in 1957. Al, who had met and become thick with Clark on the coaching/convention circuit, got a quick commitment as one of Clark's assistants. In January, when Clark was officially appointed, Al cashed in the chit.

But before he left Charleston, he had business to complete on two fronts—damage control and retribution. For Al, the cruelest blow of all was the pungent irony that this patriot son of America, born on the Fourth of July, was deemed not just unacceptable but near *seditious*.

"General Clark wanted a man he could look at and say, 'This is an upstanding man,' " noted Wunderler, needing to go no further.

John Sauer, who quit in order to be spared contamination by a scandal, was indeed spared—by the toxic cloud of Al's impeachment. Though they both were sacrificial Bulldogs, three decades later Sauer could pull moral rank and imply that *he* had really relieved the scourge of Al Davis from The Citadel.

"As long as he listened to me and took my orders, it was fine," Sauer said. "The minute he tried to run things himself, he was no longer there." And: "Let me say he didn't live within the rules. You have to abide by the rules."

Even the players that Al molded could not shed many tears for him. "I think the general probably used very good judgment," Bob Schwarze said.

But Al would never accept this as history's final judgment, and set out to revise history from the start. To the Charleston media, he erected humble but grotesquely self-serving obelisks around Clark's decision. In these remarkable figurations, Al was the martyred hero, killed by unexplained forces. "When I questioned General Clark as to the reason I could not be offered the . . . job, he gave me the reason," he told a newspaper with a tantalizing forthrightness—though he never identified the reason.

Yet, sparing no elaboration, he painted Clark as more pained by the decision than he was. "[Clark] said he was sorry it had to end this way [but] he commended me . . . and said he would be glad to give me the highest recommendation." Moreover, he declared that Clark had wanted him to *stay* on as an assistant coach, and even though the general rejected him, "He told me . . . he felt I could do the job and produce a winner here."

That was *if* he wanted the job. Unambitious a guy as he was, "I told the general that I didn't know whether I would be interested in the head coaching position." This he topped in a television interview, saying that while Clark kept the job from him, "He felt confident I was the man for the job." By *not* giving it to him, he swore, Clark acknowledged that the program would be "set back —but he had to do it."

Although Clark almost swallowed his epaulets upon hearing of this, he framed his response with military directness. "I told him I could not give him the job, period," he said. "If I had thought he was the best man for the job, I would have given it to him."

There was one Davis statement that no one could argue with: "I certainly would not want to remain here as line coach and hinder the work of the man who would be named head coach," he said.

(Long after The Citadel was a memory easily forgotten, Al offered a postscript he would have liked to stand as the final spin on the subject. "I really didn't want to stay," he told *Inside Sports*, "but a lot of the players wanted me to coach.")

His departure now definite, Al spent the last weeks at The Citadel doing his best to bite the hand that slapped him. Keeping the USC destination between him and his boys, he went about raiding the school of its football stock. He now tried to *un*sell the military to the best of the players—but was confronted with another slap that was actually an indirect compliment to him: the shambling kids who had survived the rigors of The Citadel were now hammered into prideful men, made better by it and unwilling to leave its security.

"He would've taken the whole team if he could," said Wunderler, who stayed put, as did all but three who abhorred the school and would have gone anywhere—Al Bansavage, lineman John Wilkins, and Angelo Coia.

"All those guys were makin' straight F's," said Budgie Broome, grinning, "and then they got awful smart all of a sudden at USC and made straight C's."

Still, Al had to be pleased with his take. Coia had become a blue-chip, all-around player who only needed a little more nose for contact to excel. And in Bansavage he had a big stud who was so valued by The Citadel that, in January, when Mark Clark named his new coach, Eddie Teague, a picture ran in the papers of team members greeting the new man, one of whom was Bansavage. A month later, Bansavage was on his way to USC.

His work done, Davis was gone, too, not even pausing to bid farewell to most of the young men who had gone to war for him— but also, by their unrest, betrayed him. He left as he had at Fort Belvoir, unsullied and polished in the art of the dare. With the carcasses of Sauer and Davis, the NCAA did not take action against The Citadel. It didn't have to. When Al Davis left, the school and its alumni were sentenced to losing football once again. Only no one complained about it quite as much as before.

In all ways, The Citadel was a warm-up for Al, an overture to the grand opera that was the University of Southern California—Davis had once told Bill Altenberg his big dream was to coach in the Rose Bowl. Yet the perils of the new job were at once made clear by what seemed an eerily timed object lesson. The year before, when scandal had broken at USC over alumni slipping money under the table to football players, NCAA retribution was swift and harsh: the team was barred from bowl games in 1956 and its offending seniors—including All-American halfback Jon Arnett—were ordered to sit out half the season. Sophomores and juniors on the take could accept the half-season edict or play the whole season and lose an entire year down the line.

The Trojans now faced a pothole-filled future in which several players would star and then vanish from sight, and this would mutilate any chance of Rose Bowl–quality teams the next two years. That instability, in fact, was what made Al Davis very appetizing to Don Clark. What Clark needed were players—fresh meat, ready to rumble—and Al had players, a large stash of them. To be certain, vengeance wasn't Al's only motive for raiding The Citadel's beefcake rack. Davis wanted the USC job, needed it, and that he could deposit Coia, Bansavage, and Wilkins, gift-wrapped, in Clark's lap may have been Clark's foremost reason for hiring him, which he did despite asking John Sauer if he could recommend Davis—"I told him I could not," Sauer said.

But not far behind were the coach's own limitations. A dark, lantern-jawed, and imposing man, Clark generated great and genuine affection among his players and assistants. Commanding by virtue of his mountainous presence and sympathetic manner, he could also end any disagreements with hard-staring eyes. But Clark had been no more than a line coach, in the strictest sense, at Navy and then for six years at USC, and his importance was somewhat confined to the choreography of the trenches.

"I loved Don Clark like a brother, and I hate to say it but he might have been in over his head," said Jim Sears, a former Trojan All-American defensive back who interrupted his pro career with the Chicago Cardinals to join Clark's staff. "Don was a very good player, but he was a tactician type of person. He was one-two-three turn, one-two-three cut."

Al, with his endless grasp of the game and snake-charmer guile, absolutely captivated the big man; Clark, who had fought in the Battle of the Bulge, would—like the generals at Fort Belvoir—get overheated by Al's military/football doggerel, and be almost ready to turn over the team to him. By the start of the 1959 season, two years down the line, Clark had in some ways done just that.

Although the fruits of Al's recruiting in the service of USC would not be seen for another year, they were gathering on the vine. Coia, Bansavage, and Wilkins were sent to junior colleges to obtain eligibility. Others, most from his Eastern futures cache, some of whom he had already worked on to go to The Citadel (Davis had no problem adapting their sights to high surf and blonde cheerleaders), were honed on the USC freshman team.

Nowhere was there a hint of deceit—nor was there a need for it, not with hordes all across the country eager to go to USC. But still Al recruited without end, and this could cause problems. Years later, Clark would recall Davis "calling recruits in the East at 11:00 P.M. even though it was 2:00 A.M. there. The administration used to come to me about the phone bill. He never wanted to go home." If this was not the normal modus operandi of an end coach—his supposed function—there was more proof that Al Davis was not bound by a mere job title. When the Trojans opened the season, they were playing none other than "Racehorse Football"—sold to Don Clark by the end coach who now provided the prevailing wind of the coaching staff.

One member of the administrative staff, Nick Pappas, who as field secretary did the paperwork in bringing recruits to the school, sometimes sat in on the new coaches' skull sessions. Of Davis he said, "He was brilliant. He set up a means of advance scouting films that we never had before. He could analyze film on a team and he'd see so many things. He'd tell the quarterback, 'If you see a five-man line, you can call these plays, a six-man these plays.' I'm telling you, it was brilliant."

Yet there were bigger problems inherent in the USC situation than paying hard for misdemeanors. Up to now, Al could do passable imitations of an insider, easing into the cameos of army and small-change football. Now, on this high-pressure public stage, he could not have gotten all the way inside with a bulldozer. USC was traditionally a stronghold of football chauvinism. Roiled by a perpetual inferiority complex about West Coast football—scorned by the Big Ten and Southwest conferences as little more than a caper in the sun—its disciples bonded in peevish pride.

And now here was Al Davis, his accomplishments unclear and his style unmistakably Eastern—you could not get any more Eastern—all but telling Don Clark how he should brush his teeth. Davis could seem arrogant, single-minded in his football ideology, and he could not help but read out lesser lights—lesser in *his* sightlines—from his world.

"He was very close with Don Clark," Nick Pappas remembered. "When Don died [on August 6, 1989], Al was tremendously broken up at the funeral. But the other guys, as far as he was concerned, they were nothin'."

Though this was not *intentional* discourtesy, Al had alighted on a Venus flytrap of fear and loathing from the start. Routinely going outside his job description to work with the linemen, the backs, or the linebackers, he drew glaring looks from the other coaches—two of whom, Don Doll and George Dickson, were the quintessence of parochial conventionalism and believed that Al Davis was staining their honor. Both backfield coaches, Doll and Dickson would nurse a private grudge with an unsuspecting Davis over the course of the '57 season, a season that triggered unpleasantness all around as the Trojans—devastated by the enforced absence of fullback C. R. Roberts and halfback Ernie Zampese—won one game and lost nine.

Week after losing week, Doll and Dickson fed their contempt for Al into corpulence. Though only in their mid-thirties, their lives had taken them through far more sanctified battlegrounds, in and out of football, than had been seen by the brash tenderfoot from Brooklyn. Doll, born in L.A., went from All-State schoolboy star to All-Coast Trojan star, separated only by a stretch in the Marines. He was then a Pro Bowl defensive back during a five-year career with the Lions, Redskins, and Rams and came to USC after a stint as a highly regarded backfield coach at Washington. Dickson was a high school star in Pasadena, then enlisted in the army. A paratrooper in the 101st Airborne Division, he saw combat on D-Day and won two Purple Hearts and two Bronze Stars. Then he played football and was a championship boxer at Notre Dame before his coaching career began on Terry Brennan's staff at South Bend—his prize pupil being Paul Hornung.

Encountering Al Davis, both men were mystified about why Don Clark gave him so much rein. The other assistants, though they took no sides in the matter, could smell trouble.

"I knew those guys really disliked Al," recalled Marv Goux, a former USC linebacker who coached the freshmen (and is now an assistant coach with the Rams), "and it made it tough for Don. Here you have coaches who really despise each other—or despise one guy—and Don could never make anybody happy, because those guys are always looking for this guy to do something wrong. If he does something right, they're gonna be jealous. If he does something wrong, they're gonna be happy and say, 'I told you so.'"

"Al was a very positive guy. I know I learned some things from Al. But he stepped on some toes. He wanted to make sure everything was done, and it's a very intricate thing when you're coaching that you coach your position and don't try to coach other guys'."

And yet Al knew no other way, even if just to coach his ends. If he got them back out on the field, he would need defensive backs to cover them, halfbacks to coordinate blocking with them, a quarterback to throw to them. And the others were sure to be better for his instruction. Simple, logical—and to Doll and Dickson, criminal. Late in that hellacious season, the one-sided feud fissured with the force of a split atom. Al had just finished one of those extra minisessions on the practice field and was sitting around with line coach Mel Hein, the old New York Giant great, in the locker room after the squad had gone to lunch. Into the near-empty room came Doll and Dickson, snorting like wild bulls.

"They let him have it, really cursed him out, and it was really kind of scary in there," recalled Hein all too well.

So stunned was he by the ambush that Al could hardly get out a word in his defense, and for a grim moment he wondered if he'd have to raise his fists for real, the way he always wanted people to think he did back in Crown Heights. But, just as suddenly as they had crashed through the door, the maniacal-eyed duo was gone, leaving Al white and stammering. Hein, who was shocked by the attack, commiserated with him.

"He said, 'What did I do wrong, Mel?' I told him, 'You didn't do anything wrong. I know what you're trying to do, but they didn't like you foolin' around with their boys.' He said he thought he was doin' them a favor, by helping everybody. And I stuck up for Al, because I know Al's style. I played with the Giants for fifteen years and I know how New Yorkers are, I understand 'em. I knew what Al was doing and I was on his side."

As soon as the blow-out happened, Hein thought there might be something else involved, a repugnant side issue that nobody wanted to mention but that had also occupied Al's mind. Part of understanding Al Davis, Hein knew, was understanding the long roots of hatred.

"Those two guys were Irish and Al is Jewish. Maybe that was one reason," Hein said, simply and saliently.

That Al thought about the worst implications of the incident was corroborated by his brother Jerry Davis in 1981. "He has had bloody fistfights on coaching staffs because he's Jewish," Jerry told

Inside Sports. For once the Davis hyperbole could be excused. For even though there had been no blood spilled and no fists in the air, in Al's mind the blows he took on that day hurt just as much.

For Doll and Dickson, the hurt they felt didn't go away either. Three decades later, they still recoiled at the mention of the name Al Davis; his success is like a personal affront to them, a blasphemy to football. "I'd rather lose with honor than win with dishonor," Dickson said in the eighties. "Davis was restricted by no moral principles. I'm not backstabbing him. I told him what I thought. I'm just a different breed of cat."

Doll, readily admitting an extreme bias about Davis, begged off explaining the specifics of his enmity for these pages, saying, "It would be slanted, but to me it would be truthful." Doll did allow some mostly bilious fragments. Of the gang-up incident, he said only, "My principles are much different than his."

Did Davis try to do Doll's job?

"No, he couldn't do my job."

Was there a rift between him and Davis?

"Where hasn't there been with him? Wherever he goes, there's been. On the Raiders, too. They just haven't talked."

How would Doll describe Al Davis as a coach?

"A disgrace to the coaching profession."

When the 1958 season began, George Dickson had quit and Don Doll was in his lame-duck year at USC before returning to the sanctuary of Notre Dame. Not coincidentally, Al's role was widening. His first USC recruiting crop yielded sure-fire players with a sense of urgency about them. Two of them would be pivotal as the Trojans went 4–5–1, with two of those losses by one point and another by two points. Dan Ficca, a 230-pound tackle from Atlas, Pennsylvania, ousted senior cocaptain Monte Clark (the future NFL All-Pro and coach) and made second-team All-Conference as a sophomore. And Angelo Coia finished third in rushing. Ficca and two other newcomers on the line, twin brothers Mike and Marlin McKeever, joined the rapidly maturing Ron Mix and Gary Finneran to form a monster row up front that made "Racehorse Football" unnecessary and unwise.

"We had a very restricted offense then—all teams did, that was the style," Mix said. "It was analogous to the Ohio State 'three yards in a cloud of dust.' We were big and not fast and we could only go-go once or we'd be go-goed into exhaustion." Rather, the big moose were a convoy in front of quarterback Tom Maudlin and scatback Don Buford (the future major league baseball player).

And yet, despite the betterment of the team, the transition and its alterations of playing time and philosophy pricked some of the players. Since Al was the boldest and most visible symbol of the change, he was subject to more—albeit quieter—locker room grumbling. One of the most irked was end Don Voyne, whose time was cut drastically. "Al and I sometimes would clash because I have a strong ego also," Voyne said, looking back. "It would be over how he wanted something done and how I wanted to. I felt we always had great teams. USC is a fine university and it's got a fine tradition and sometimes people that aren't from USC tend to go in there and change things around.

"Most of the guys who played in '57 and '58 would tell you there was a lot of turmoil. And we were from the old school, from Jess Hill, and here the attitude was: we're just gonna push you guys out. We want our kind of guys to play our kind of offense.

"Then, too, if you knew Al Davis, you knew Al Davis's career was not bent on being an assistant coach. Everyone knew that. This guy was going other places. I mean, I had no idea if he knew I had any disagreements, or even cared."

Concurrently, Al had strong voices of support among the holdovers. "Immediately, he was just a refreshing guy to have around, because most of the other coaches were so intense," said Mix, who began as a 200-pound end before beefing up to 250 during his Hall of Fame pro career.

"Al had an intensity about what he was doing, but his relationships with the players were far more cordial than anybody else on the staff. And Al liked Don Voyne, he really did. He gave Don a lot of playing time. I think Don was indicting the whole *system*. Don was way ahead of his time insofar as what college players' roles should be. In those days, college coaches were different than now; they felt they had to act like drill instructors and treat players in a demeaning way. Don was indicting a system that needed to be indicted. But I wouldn't single out Al Davis—my reaction was just the opposite. I thought Al was special, one of the few coaches you could simply talk to as a normal person.

"Remember this, too. He was a young man—he looked as young as we did, and he was still learning the best way to motivate a player. Some guys he would ride one way, other guys he would try to do it through praise. But he had a great work capacity, and I can remember working with him after every practice on exploding from the stance with a forearm shiver to the head. If it was borderline dirty, so what. Bottom line: Al Davis would improve your game."

Said Dan Ficca: "A lot of people didn't like him. Shit, there were people who didn't like Don Clark and Marv Goux and Mel Hein. Mel Hein, shit, his greatest contributions were the things he did before he got to USC. He used to talk about what he did when he was in pro ball. That was great. Didn't teach me a goddamn thing, but he was a well-liked guy. Whereas Al would get in there and fight like hell with you, show you things, preach and holler and kick and squirm and hope that you won on Saturday. Where Mel Hein would say, 'Well, I had days like that when I was playin','' and that would be it. Al was riding with you every play, and the good football players don't dislike that, the so-so players do.

"I keep taking his side here and it's not that there aren't other sides to the coin. You could see through him in certain ways, like how he lifted weights trying to make himself look big. We used to laugh about that. And if he wanted to coach everybody's position and teach everybody everything, that's ambition and it's gonna piss off a few people. But he also helped a few people because his way was the right way."

Even Don Voyne will give Davis that. As a movable part in the Age of Al Davis, now far removed, he can now see Davis from afar and admit to a simple source of his distaste. "A lot of it could be sour grapes, too," Voyne said. "Back then, you're young and you get pissed off. That's football, that's locker room stuff. When you don't have the controls, you want them in a different way.

"When I went to dental school and joined the real world, looking back, I knew Al Davis was an excellent coach; he knew the game and he brought in an offense. He's also a very forceful guy, a very intelligent man. He was more intelligent than the coaches around him. And when you're used to a level of intellect from coaches and you have somebody above and beyond that, who really was *too* bright to just coach, it's hard to deal with until it's over.

"Don Doll may have an axe to grind from a lot of years from a lot of different places and the magnet is Al Davis. When somebody carries that around, they haven't dealt with something and nothing positive has grown. It's probably that way with a lot of people in Al Davis's life."

There was, back then, a sense of either dread or titillation about Al Davis, something as yet unfocused that portended cataclysm or a wonderful new order in football.

Ben Charles, another of his recruits, a quarterback from Lancaster, Pennsylvania, rapidly fell under Al's spell—"He told me his IQ was 165 and I believed it," a smiling Charles recalled. "That was right after he told me he was assistant coach with the Colts and played defensive end for Syracuse." Yet Charles too carried an ambivalence about the man when he made varsity in '58 after a year in junior college.

"Some of the players questioned his ability to coach as opposed to his mind for the game. We all felt he was a genius as far as the game itself. But as far as getting right down on the line and showing how it should be done, I don't think he was respected in that area. I didn't know about the lies in his background, but he probably felt he had to say that stuff to get the respect of the players and the other coaches."

He would do that now by going to any length—including risking his unblemished anatomy. At one coach's meeting, he tried to sell Don Clark on a blocking scheme he called "Absorb with Oomph"—wherein, instead of firing out and hitting, the linemen absorb the blow first so as to keep equilibrium and neutralize their men longer. The old gut-tough lineman may have felt his expertise was questioned in the way Doll and Dickson had.

"You're full of shit, Al," he said with a dismissive wave of the hand.

But Al pressed on and—carrying out his threat levied at Fort Belvoir to lay his body on the line—he invited the 240-pound Clark to get down in a three-point stance, one-on-one against him. Even with his weight-lifting, Al was still no more than a ropy 190 pounds and when Clark came up and at Al, it was as if Clark was back in the Coliseum trenches after ten years.

No one had ever called Al on a dare quite like this—and this was something that must have occurred to Al when Clark displaced Al from the floor and nearly from his sneakers in the collision. Flying through the locker room air, Al bounced once on Clark's desk five feet behind him and landed half on and half off Clark's swivel chair. Unhurt except for his pride, Al was struggling to his feet, ringed by assistant coaches bent over in laughter, as Clark delivered his post-mortem.

"There's your Absorb with Oomph," intoned the coach.

Eventually, Al laughed, too. And why not? Despite the embarrassing scene, the kicker was that Al *still* got his way.

"There's nothing wrong with that style of blocking," Dan Ficca said. "We used it and Ron Mix, who was the greatest pupil of Don Clark and Al Davis, wound up being All-Pro ten out of eleven years."

It was 1959 now. The Trojans, free of shackled players and stocked with well-seasoned juniors and skilled seniors, were ready to drive for the Pacific Coast Conference title. The anticipation made Al's eyes dart faster, his step grow quicker. If this was to be USC's year, there would be huzzahs for Don Clark and the players—but, in the end, it would surely be *his* year, *Al Davis's* year. After two years in the frying pan, he figured he had earned at least that much.

6

I can't say that I didn't have a problem with Al Davis, but I don't think it's a problem that needs to be aired. It seems with everybody who has contact with Al Davis, they have a problem sooner or later. And the reason for that is because he's been very successful and as you go up the ladder you step on some people, and other people may not be as smart-witted. He hurt people along the way, no question about it. Because Al Davis said and did what was gonna get the job done for Al Davis.

—Dan Ficca

The people who govern the Brave New World may not be sane (in what may be called the absolute sense of the word), but they are not madmen, and their aim is not anarchy but social stability. It is in order to achieve stability that they carry out, by scientific means, the ultimate, personal, really revolutionary revolution.

—Aldous Huxley

Further identifying his name with the 1959 season, Al would own a title befitting his broadened power—backfield and end coach. Don Clark and Al may have believed this title was well-merited—and granting it had been made easy by the departure of Don Doll—but they didn't figure that two incoming assistants, both backfield coaches, would be as offended as Doll and George Dickson had been. One of the new tandem was Jim Sears, who at twenty-eight and with no coaching experience outside of the Air Force, had chosen to abort his pro career for the purpose of positioning himself for the head coaching job at USC someday. The other was an even more impatient man—thirty-six-year-old John McKay.

In John McKay there was potential for much territorial conflict for Al Davis, beyond just the topography of the backfield. Blunt and sarcastic, McKay seemed a compound clone of Doll and Dickson. A basketball and football star in West Virginia, he went into the Air Corps after high school and was a physical training instructor and B-29 tail gunner. Then, after playing halfback briefly at Purdue, he came to the West Coast. An honorable mention All-America and then assistant coach at Oregon, he had spent the last seven years at that school earning the same kind of power-behind-the-throne reputation Al had at USC. And while McKay did not begrudge Al his USC seniority and his plausibly good work in building this Trojan team, he watched Davis grab power seemingly while people's backs were turned, and it annoyed him.

The biggest point of irritation among the coaches, in fact, involved Al's new living quarters, or rather where they were—in Baldwin Hills, directly across La Brea Boulevard from Clark's house.

"Al would ride home with Don," Sears said, "and he was the instigator on the way home of a lot of things that were put in while the rest of the coaches weren't around. We would have our meetings and we'd be in there for hours—and then all of a sudden, the next morning, Don would say, 'Okay, we're gonna do it this way,' and it would be totally opposite of what we'd agreed on. And we knew it was because Al had talked to him on the way home. Which was all right because he had good ideas. But the way it always came about made us feel left out.

"John, in particular, didn't like it. John would say, 'Goddamn it, we worked all night on this thing and now it's all changed.' I don't think there were any real words exchanged but you felt there was a lot of uneasiness. He felt he had coached a long time, a lot longer than Al, and that Al should have more respect for him. And I don't know if Al *did* respect John at that point. So there was not the greatest feelings between those two. Because they were very alike. They both wanted to be the show."

Al's hauteur was suffered more civilly since the Doll-Dickson blowout—but, like a great Greenland whale, it bobbed in unfriendly waters, a tempting target for harpooning. In the spring of 1959, when the USC senior yearbook, *El Rodeo*, came out, the football page contained a tiny but venom-dipped inside joke that took dead aim at Davis's now-known mendacity. Planted by persons unknown in the athletic department—possibly including sundry coaches—a one-sentence bio of him solemnly stated that Davis had "played and coached at Notre Dame." This was a tiny jest stuck on the sharp head of a gargantuan lance.

"It was a put-up job," said a still-giggling Sears. "Because nobody really knew how much football Al ever played or whatever he did. So why not just have him go all the way to the top?"

However, if the aim of the prank was to humble Al, it actually worked in reverse. As audacious a liar as he was, it hardly mattered that for years Don Doll and other open Davis foes cited the "Notre Dame reference" as further proof that Davis was a reprobate— "Notre Dame wouldn't let him on campus," Doll could rabbit-punch after bringing it up. The pranksters, after all, had done his work for him, work even *he* would not have had the balls to do. If football people—*all* people—thought that Al Davis was a Notre Dame product, that was worth its weight in Brylcreem to him.

Only a year before, still on uncertain ground at USC, Al had felt alone even for a loner like him. He lived in a condominium in View Park, but it might as well have been on Alcatraz Island. "One Sunday my wife and I were out in his area and we stopped by," Mel Hein related, "and, by golly, we found out that I was the only coach who ever visited him, and he really appreciated that."

Needing a boost, Al had found use for the little football photo-copying machine from Philadelphia, Al LoCasale. While at the University of Pennsylvania, LoCasale had taken over the coaching at Olney High School. When he graduated, Davis secured a job for him in the USC sports information office, and his articles ran in the campus papers. Mostly, he stuck close by Al. "Al LoCasale was like chipped off of Al's hip," said Jim Sears. Al also paid for periodic trips by Herman Masin, the *Scholastic Coach* editor, to come and stay with him, Carol, and Mark. Now, though, his role cemented, Al had no time or inclination for a triviality like loneliness. This was foretold by the promise of 1959.

And then, just as Al Davis was reaching his goal, the fates that he had mastered suddenly rose up and knocked him down. By the time the season began, Davis had been stained once more by scandal.

* * *

Ironically for Al, it was a scrawny scandal almost unworthy of mention by comparison with what had worried Charleston half to death. The result not of overt or even latent venality but of a simple and dumb clerical error, it ran up and bit Al on the backside, laughing all the way. In actuality, it barely involved Al Davis at all. It had to do with Ben Charles, the quarterback from Pennsylania whom Al lured to the Coast. Charles had also been wooed by Miami University and had signed a letter of intent with that school when he came to visit USC, but he chose USC on the spot and stayed in L.A., not even going home first.

This would have been fine except that the NCAA—prodded not by Miami but by another school Charles had no intention of attending—looked into the particulars and found that USC had issued Charles a one-way ticket, not the required round-trip fare. At the same time the NCAA found that another Trojan, center Dave Morgan, had been brought out between semesters, another fine-print error. Together, and coming on the heels of the recent USC scandal, these were cause for punishment—although the terms were severe beyond reason. On April 29, 1959, the NCAA, citing "improper inducements," put the Trojans on a two-year probation, and this applied not only to football but *all* campus sports. The Rose Bowl, and all Bowl play, was again precluded, but so was all television coverage—the latter alone costing the school many thousands of dollars.

"It wasn't for illegal recruiting, it was for a ticket," Dan Ficca said. "That was kinda chickenshit."

Under the high magnification of big-deal football, though, small oversights were treated as crimes of the century—and in the eyes of many with a passing interest, traceable to Davis if for no other reason than his notoriety. While it seems strange that the only foul-up of this kind among thousands of USC football players over the years should happen to an Al Davis recruit, Nick Pappas—in whose office the problem occurred—removes the curse from Al's head.

"It wasn't his fault; it was my problem (as field secretary) and my hands that got slapped," Pappas said. "My secretary was on vacation and the replacement sent the ticket. And when the kid decided to stay out here, we forgot about it."

In the end, sadly, it was neither Davis nor Pappas who faced lingering obloquy. As always, it was the athlete. Years later, Ben

Charles lives in a muted kind of infamy, damned by ignorance for the sins of other men. "I still get comments from alumni that USC was on probation and couldn't get the national championship because of me, and I had nothing to do with it," he said, hurt showing in his voice.

Blameless as Al also was, Charles could not help but feel betrayed by those who could overlook small details that were big enough to alter his life. "I'm sure what happened was an oversight," he concluded, "but it's hard to prove that you're bringin' a young man out for a visit when you only send him a one-way ticket."

Al and Don Clark could still salvage much with a winning season, and the fact that Al could prove his worth stoking a team spirit that flew in the face of the NCAA had the Musketeer quality he adored—and he played on it from the get-go.

A strong scent of this was a season-opening 27–6 win against Oregon State in Portland. The next two weeks, the Trojans hosted two teams from the heartland of *real* football country, Pitt and Ohio State. Each went back home hurting, and without having scored a point, as USC won 23–0 and 17–0. The next five weeks went down roughly the same way—all USC wins, including those at Washington and Berkeley (against Cal). Standing 8–0, mashing out over 330 yards a game to their opponents' 180—and, in the Davis forearm-shiver fashion, taking nearly 200 more penalty yards—the Trojans were ranked number three in the nation. Predictably, they were getting notice across the country as the team that could be stopped *only* by the NCAA. But the two toughest games on its schedule remained, the mutual home game in the Coliseum against UCLA and then Notre Dame at South Bend.

Though UCLA came in at 3–3–1, they were wildly inconsistent, capable of a 0–0 tie with Purdue and a 55–13 win over Stanford. Against the Trojans, they yielded scads of yardage between the twenty yard lines, then clamped down. USC led 3–0 into the fourth quarter, then the Bruins—quarterbacked by Billy Kilmer—tied it, took a 10–3 lead, and then held fast on several crucial third-down plays to win. Notre Dame was next, and the surrealness of the sunshine boys challenging the Irish on their own turf—where USC had not won since 1939—was framed by their bright red and orange uniforms against the steel gray sky of a bitingly cold afternoon. With temperatures below zero, and their thunderous ground game useless on the frozen field, Clark turned Ben Charles loose to throw. But Charles went only eight for twenty-two, though he found Angelo Coia with a thirteen-yard touchdown pass, and the Irish rolled to a 16–6 win.

Although USC still won the conference and the distinction of deserving to be in the Rose Bowl, the deflation of the last two weeks left Al like a New Year's balloon on the morning after. Then, whatever air was left was pushed out when Don Clark stunned everyone at the school and resigned.

For Clark this was ostensibly a business move—his brother, the owner of an industrial laundry business, had had a heart attack and couldn't run the operation, so Clark stepped in. And yet, coming off three stomach-churning seasons—with as many problems between coaches as he had with the players—Clark may have jumped at the chance to run and hide.

"Honestly, Don relied too much on Al Davis and John McKay," said Jim Sears, "and because he did, it became an unbearable situation between Al and John. We had to spend hours together and you can't do that when there's that kind of tension. Maybe Don said, 'Hey, let me get out of here.' "

John Sauer refused to believe a word otherwise.

"I told Don Clark to beware of Al Davis," Sauer said, "and I guess maybe he learned that."

But where Sauer's retirement lit up Roman candles of opportunity before Al's eyes, Clark's left him off-balance. Al could never measure Clark's broad back for a stiletto, and now he felt as though he had *lost* leverage. It is even possible that, right then and there, he resolved nevermore to align himself too closely with *any* superior, for it was never again to happen.

At this point, if Al had considered what the success of '59 could do for him, it would have been clear to him that his position at USC was still peripheral, and he depended for that position on Don Clark. One, perhaps two more seasons would be needed to solidify his hold on the succession. Now, he suddenly had to shift the focus of his ambition—because he had no choice. It was apparent that, as at the Citadel, he could stay where he was only as the top man —but if he had thought that was a helpful squeeze play at the Citadel, here his hand was simply forced.

So, with not much enthusiasm or the Davis charm, as though events were simply pulling him along, he routinely put in for the head coach job by informing AD Jess Hill and USC president

Norman Topping. Davis's logic was ever firm—he was second in command and systems manager of a winning team—but his excess baggage consisted now not only of rumors and hard feelings but of violations. USC was on probation; what if *another* Davis recruit was nailed? And if Davis was anathema to other assistants, how could he run a harmonious ship?

Rather than with a miasmic gasp, Al Davis's second career death came with a wide-mouthed yawn. Few thought Davis would get the job, but the big stir came when Hill promoted one of Clark's assistants, John McKay, the safer of the two feuding rivals. When McKay named his staff, Al was—to the surprise of no one—not on it.

But by then, Davis was already gone. With his core of recruits only two years from winning the national title, Davis was again persona non grata in a program he had helped resurrect. Los Angeles was warm and sunny as a new decade dawned, but in the winter of 1960, Al was adrift in a cold football wilderness. Yet, while he did not figure on it, Al Davis was—in the fitting apothegm of another wunderkind of the fifties, John Fitzgerald Kennedy, who was about to announce his run for the White House—coming fast upon a new frontier.

Only months before, in August, the American Football League had begun in a hotel room in Chicago when half a dozen cockeyed optimists posted one hundred thousand dollars each for teams to challenge the NFL's hard-won universality. By the end of November, two more teams had been born, there had been a college draft, and a commissioner had been named. By the summer, the league had a five-year television contract with ABC worth $1.785 million drawn up, and had initiated a (losing) antitrust lawsuit against the NFL. It also had the 1959 Heisman Trophy winner, Billy Cannon, under contract to the aboriginal Houston Oilers. It missed out on almost everyone else it wanted.

And it very nearly did not have Al Davis.

As history stretched into folklore, it became football fact that Davis, born with the perfect timing and impulses for bringing pompous institutions to their knees, came upon the AFL with salivating glee. Here was Moses ascending Sinai to seek what was right and just—and he could hardly keep himself at USC one more day than was necessary before donning the AFL's coat of arms. This

assumption—lovingly encouraged by Al Davis—was of course salu-
brious in the making of a very profitable outlaw legend. As with
most legends, however, it is in large part myth.

In 1960, Al Davis—besides being a college football coach—was
an NFL traditionalist, in the sense that he was very fond of the
league's full-throttle professionalism, its leading edge of the football
culture. Having already been on good terms with the NFL, he had
little doubt that it would one day be his habitat. For now, the new
league, grounded in NFL envy (the germ was two Texans, Lamar
Hunt and Bud Adams, who couldn't get NFL franchises), and
stocked mainly with NFL chaff, had a petulant, hand-me-down
quality—not to mention that it was committing economic suicide
if it couldn't force entry into the NFL within a few years.

Al Davis hardly wanted to concede that a long-shot league was
his only recourse, nor was he turned off by the college game despite
the quick and opprobrious dim-out at USC. He believed himself
to be a victim of circumstances—and, on John McKay's part, of
outright jealousy. Indeed, when Sid Gillman, the coach and general
manager of the AFL's Los Angeles Chargers, at once offered Davis
a spot on the staff he was putting together, Al saw it—correctly—
as high flattery, if not exactly the shiniest bauble in the world.

The forty-nine-year-old Gillman was the longest tap into the
coaching sacrarium Al had met, and Gillman had thought favorably
of Al as far back as the early fifties when they intersected on the
clinic circuit. All Gillman recalls knowing of Davis then was that
he "was coaching some high school team or something," but the
eager young man would always be sitting in the front row when
Gillman, who was then building some leviathan teams at Cincinnati,
spoke—Socrates and pupil in the forum of Atlantic City. Different
as Minneapolis and Brooklyn (their geographical backgrounds) and
as an All-American and a benchwarmer (their athletic backgrounds), Gillman and Davis were nonetheless linked by a thirst
for erudite yet diabolical football.

Both had a vision of the game that took in the entire field, not
the tunnel vision from line of scrimmage to first-down marker. For
Al, this was due in part to God knows what environmental sources;
for Gillman, it was the product of personal achievement, as a true
pass receiver at Ohio State in the constipated era of the thirties.
For both, the pass offered delectable visions of yards eaten up in
one ferocious gulp—and the chance to finally use it after years of
microbic line-blocking absorption tickled Al; where before he could

locate a defensive flaw and attack it with a run, now a higher magnitude of destruction was at hand.

"There's a lot of Sid in Al; they're the same type of thinkers," said Jack Faulkner, a long-time Gillman assistant and the defensive backfield coach on that first Charger team. "They're not much on defense, I can tell you that. They say, 'Fuck the defense, just get the ball back for us and we'll score.' "

And still, when Gillman approached him, Al stalled. "He was lookin' for a job, but he didn't know whether he wanted to coach in the pros," Gillman recalled. "He was going to New York, to a college coaches' meeting a few days later, and I was going there too so I told him if he wanted it, he should tell me in New York. If somebody had offered him a job in college, he may not have ever gone to the pros."

But, with the well run dry, nobody made that offer and Al, who had heretofore used the pros only as a college lever, moved into the new world—a new world that was *really* new. He went on the condition that his footman, Al LoCasale, went with him as an administrative assistant. But if he had any trepidation, the needs of the Chargers—players, any players—made his first duties comfortingly familiar ones. With barely a pause, he was back recruiting, pulling strings and calling in vouchers.

Two of his old Citadel "boys," Paul Maguire—who led the nation in touchdown passes caught—and Barry Thomas were amazed when they got invitations to the Copper Bowl, a college All-Star game in Phoenix. "To this day, I know the only reason we went to that game was because Al somehow got us in," Thomas said. "And before the game, he came to our hotel room and offered us contracts with the Chargers." Thomas, about to marry back East, declined and instead signed with the Eagles. Maguire accepted, led the AFL in punting his rookie season, and played ten years as a linebacker/defensive end with the Chargers and Bills—building a gnarly reputation, to the shock of the original Chargers.

"I laugh when I see Paul on television today," said Jim Sears, who, disappointed that *he* hadn't gotten the USC head post, resumed his pro career with the AFL club. "Paul talks about how players should be tough—and he wasn't that tough. It's like with Al Davis: let's get to the credentials. Paul was a good punter, but not a very tough punter."

Out of Al's USC trough came Al Bansavage, who had made honorable mention All-America in 1959, and tackle Gary Finneran, another honorable mention All-America. Gillman used his Ohio State link to sign a massive tackle, Ernie Wright, after being tipped off that Wright was about to leave school before his senior year. The other assistants—including the thirty-year-old defensive line coach, just retired from playing, Chuck Noll—brought in players, as did LoCasale and the club's scouting director, Don Klosterman. When they and the other AFL people closed in on too much prime talent for the NFL's comfort, the NFL clubs began trying to "hide" potential draftees by having paid operatives blanket them with attention—an effective maneuver that Al would have loved to use but for time and money restrictions; still, he filed it prominently in his head.

Though the team's ownership and nickname were money-synonymous (so it wouldn't be a total loss, owner Barron Hilton, thirty-two-year-old heir of hotel magnate Conrad Hilton and head of the Carte Blanche credit card program, advertised the "charge" concept via his ballclub), the kiddie millionaire was not eager to lose any more than the bundle he knew he would on the team, which turned out to be nearly $1 million that first year. But Hilton, who admitted he didn't know the difference between a three-point field goal and a 3:00 P.M. checkout time, did make the expenditures to land some quality players—most notably Ron Mix, who was drafted by the Colts and wanted to play for them until Hilton paid big.

Gillman also moved to tie up hunch-bet castoffs from the NFL (halfback Paul Lowe, receiver Ralph Anderson), the Canadian Football League (tight end Dave Kocourek), or both (quarterback Jack Kemp). With the regularity of Greyhound, buses rolled into and out of tryout camps, and out of one of those came cornerback Dick Harris. In that maiden season, Lowe would average 6.3 yards a carry, Kemp would throw for 3,018 yards and twenty touchdowns, and seven receivers led by Anderson and Kocourek had over twenty receptions. Harris had six interceptions and was All-AFL (with Mix) for the first of two straight seasons.

Yet as much as for the players, there was great vindication that first year for coaches all around the league. Many of these men also had no place in the NFL. But the almost dementedly pass-happy new league had a clear brainwave advantage over the NFL, from Hank Stram's "moving pocket" to gargantuan fullbacks like Cookie Gilchrist going deep for passes. The early sixties class of assistant coaches would produce such head coaches as Joe Collier, Mike Holovak, Wally Lemm, and Chuck Knox. No staff would be more

sanctified, though, than Gillman's. All but one of them would become head men, and Jack Faulkner and Klosterman became successful executives. Al Davis, of course, became *both*.

In the very beginning, however, *he* would have to adapt to a
whole new deal—Gillman's, though as with Don Clark, Davis filled
in important crevices that made even Gillman a better coach. For
as accomplished a coach as Gillman had been with Miami (Ohio),
Cincinnati, and the Rams, he was not a popular man. He wore a
bow tie and he resembled a dowdy Jewish uncle—which he was—
but he could be an ogre. Short on patience, intolerant of imper-
fection, capable of purple rages in practice, the craggy-faced and
wide-nosed Gillman was most contented sitting in a darkened room
by himself watching football film—forward and reverse, until his
eyelids refused to stay up and he collapsed, projector controls still
in his hand.

But, by the same token, Gillman's obsession gave rise to a film
library bigger than Metro Goldwyn Mayer's. "He'd talk about running a comeback pass," Dave Kocourek said, "and he'd show you
five minutes of the all-time great receivers running a comeback pass.
You'd look at Raymond Berry and Billy Howton and Buddy Dial
and on and on." But Gillman could get lost in the abstruse, dealing
with his players as fleshy pieces on a chess board, their feelings
superfluous. When he won, which was frequently, few complained.
But when he went 2–11 with the Rams in 1959, he was bounced
with not a tear shed. In the AFL, he would quit or be dismissed
and then be brought back so often that he needn't have turned in
his key to the men's room.

Gillman had to be a genius because those who couldn't stand him
said he was, but what he needed were men who could teach his
system with an amiable kind of fanaticism. Maybe the best at doing
this was Al Davis.

"Al took the concept a step further, he took us through it step
by step," Kocourek explained. "He'd get down and trace the steps
you took right there in the dirt. Sid never would've done that. But
that was just the beginning. Al would take you through the phys-
iology of it, how body control would help your routes. In those
days, it was a lot of man-to-man so the moves were very important.
Al really emphasized that.

"And, God, he was such a hard worker. We'd be at practice and
when it would be ending, Al would bring up his relationship with
the Colts, whatever that was, and say, 'Right now Raymond Berry

and John Unitas are still workin', still practicin'.' And I'd say, 'If John Unitas was here, I'd still be workin', too,' and he'd laugh—but we'd always work a little more, on the most minute detail.''

Few souls were disposed to watch the AFL in its infancy—the crowd for the Chargers' first game was 17,724, looking like splotches of acne in the 100,000-seat Coliseum—and those who trickled in did so because of the fast impression made by wide-open, high-scoring games. That was how the AFL planned it, but the assumption among the fans and media was that these factory-second players were merely throwing the ball as deep as they could and seeing if anyone familiar could run under it. The truth was that Gillman's system—aped by the more astute coaches in the league—was an intricate, high-percentage one, constructed around a panoply of *short* passes in the pockets between the linebackers and deep backs, which with one or two critical blocks could allow the receiver to get into the open field.

As Kocourek synopsized it, "Our tight ends were called 'Y,' the flanker was 'Z,' the split end 'X.' And we had a block called 'Y Tag,' which meant the Y blocked the outside linebacker, and if he made a good block the play literally could go forever, 'cause it was a quick toss and the tackle kicked outside and the tight end could tie up the linebacker.

"And we walked through that step by step—I mean in inches, *half-inches*. Al would say, 'That step was too long,' or 'It's not long enough.' And, 'Which foot will you cross over?' Instead of striding with your outside foot, you had to cross over because it gives you better balance if the guy gets his hands on you quick. I mean, this was real, real detail, and that was Al's. Sid basically handled the passing game, but the nitty-gritty stuff was strictly Al."

Gillman's simple, precise plays were camouflaged by masses of formations that had men in motion (even the *tight end*), two receivers on one side of the field, and two tight ends in at the same time.

"Other than the 49ers of today, I've never seen anything like it," said Jack Faulkner, who is now administrator of football operations for the Rams. "And Bill Walsh [before becoming the 49ers' head coach] worked for both Sid and Al."

"We were so special and so far ahead of the time, it was shocking," addended Ron Mix. "Even today, it's a headline when a team has a total offense of six hundred yards in a game. We would always do that."

Out of necessity (all new players, most of limited talent) and convenience (easily exploited defenses), Gillman's offense wasn't nearly as complex as it had been with the Rams. But, because of that, it found its most effective level.

"I think we really gave it system," the old coach said. "We gave our quarterbacks good reads, simple reads, and we were able to cover the field. Our theory was that we were gonna throw based on what coverage was presented to us, but we were gonna stretch the field, horizontally, use every bit of the field. Our philosophy was, you throw so you're able to run, not the other way around."

This system, of course, was Al Davis's springboard, one he would learn inside out and be able to amplify on. And, later on, the suggestion would be made—again, with the encouragement of Al Davis—that it was really Davis who devised the Charger passing game, or at least should have shared cobilling for it. Each time Gillman heard this, every muscle in his body would tighten and he would do a slow burn, sometimes offering subtly cutting rejoinders. "I guess the longer you live, the greater you become," he once said. "We were throwing the ball when Al Davis was peeing in his pants."

Asked about the Davis-as-equal postulate for these pages, his frustration worked its way into a spume.

"That is a lot of bullshit," Gillman said, each syllable fairly dripping with carbolic acid. "He fit in *our* plans. I didn't fit in *his* plans. 'Cause he had no plans.

"I hired Al Davis for the same reason I hired Chuck Noll or anyone else. I hired guys because they were bright and could articulate. He coached our outside ends, but I didn't know what the hell he knew about it, because it didn't matter. The position didn't even matter because whatever they do, they were gonna have to fit into what we were doin'. I never had a coach where I gave him leeway to do things himself.

"In those days, the colleges didn't throw the ball. Al never threw a football, either, not even across the street. So I didn't expect that he knew much, except that I knew he was a bright guy and football was his life, and that's the kinda guys I look for. But since our ends were split all the time and we were throwin' the ball, my guess was that he didn't know too much.

"It was my system and my terminology. In fact, at that time, it was either the Bear terminology or the Ram/Charger terminology. We called our passes a 'hook' or an 'out' or a 'post-cover.' We developed that and it's the one they still use today. Sure, everyone on our staff made suggestions. That's what a staff is for. But what contribution he made to our football, I couldn't tell you."

In his singed pride, Gillman is likely disingenuous about Davis's importance. Certainly, Gillman knew what he had in Al, as well as Noll, whose almost effeminate, high-pitched voice and taste for fine wines masked an obduracy that made Al seem kittenish by comparison. Though Noll was, and is, what most people call "a tough SOB," he was also a man of depth and thought—all of it uncompromising. Even as a teenager, Noll was known as "Pius," after the famed pope, because he would never admit to fallibility. Gillman not only employed Davis and Noll, he played the strings of their obstinate brilliance, challenging them to top each other and thereby spring free football science. On matters from draft picks to personnel to the game plan, arguments—"loud and furious," Gillman describes them—would rage in coaches' meetings not only between Davis and Noll but among all the coaches.

"Sid encouraged that," Faulkner said. "He'd be a shit-disturber; he'd say something about a player or a team he didn't really mean, just to get us goin' and see who was on the ball." Unlike the irritated strife on the USC staff, in these contests egos had no part. Rather than vying for Gillman's favor, the coaches knew that to draw the coach's curt, unspoken approval they had to widen the gap between the Chargers and the other teams. By the midpoint of the season, they were all running on high octane. With the shrill sound of "hike" and pads hitting pads echoing through canyons of empty seats each week, the Chargers lost two of their first three games, then won nine of the last eleven to get into the AFL title game against the Oilers.

As a lesson in football and in early sixties sociology, the path was rubble-strewn. When the Chargers played in Houston, the club had to stay at the University of Houston dormitories because none of the hotels would book rooms to the black players. During a trip to Dallas, trouble erupted when the team went to see a movie at a local theater. "One of the blacks got up to get some candy," Dave Kocourek recalled, "and the guards in the lobby told him, 'Get back where you belong,' and in the next minute guns were pulled and things were getting really hairy. So Sid said, 'That's it, we're outta here,' and we all got up and got out."

Kocourek remembered that Al was particularly eager to decry bigotry—"He was really pissed off when that happened." Unable to right the wrongs of the world, Al would fight the war in microcosm, loudly bearing the streamer of the Good Guys on the Chargers. Jack Kemp, with a political career to come, was cutting his right-wing teeth on the churlish dogma of jackals—and he and anyone else who allied with him had to answer to Al for it.

"I used to run with Jack," Kocourek said, "and Jack was reading the John Birch Society stuff and I was reading a lot of it and some of it made sense to me. And we used to get into the most brutal arguments with Al and also Chuck Noll. Both of them were very liberal and they'd corner you and continue the argument wherever we were, on the bus, in the shower room, anywhere."

More of the hard, cruel realities of life—and death—intruded on the team. On November 26, 1960, Ralph Anderson, the greatly talented wide receiver, died after a diabetic seizure. For Al, it was the closest that death had come to his sphere. As immersed in his generation as he was, it hit him like a hammer blow. Immediately, he increased the pace of his weight-lifting, which now had a hard edge beyond vanity.

"He became really concerned about his health," Kocourek noticed. "Through the years you could always get to Al. You'd say, 'Hey, Al, aren't you feeling well?' And he'd say, really concerned, 'Why? Don't I look okay? What's the matter with me?' It was a joke, but even though it was funny, it wasn't to him. And I think his response reflected his fear of death."

Ralph Anderson's passing was a preamble. The soaring arc of life and the mocking doom-chord of death were, for Al, just now beginning to overlap.

7

He had good ideas, he really did. Otherwise, he couldn't
have gone as far as he did. You can con only so many
people. The rest was up to him.

—Jim Sears

Life, struck sharp on death,
  Makes awful lightning.

—Elizabeth Barrett Browning, "Aurora Leigh"

The first AFL championship game, played on New Year's Day
1961 in Houston's creaky Jeppesen Stadium, etched deeply
the character of the league's gilded age. Over the AFL's first eight
years, the Chargers or the Oilers would play in all but one title
game, and the goofy, amorphous nature of these games would parallel in reverse the NFL's re-descent into bullnose football, courtesy
of the Packers' Gothic-style domination.

Contrary to the age-old maxims about the benefits of the running
game, the Oilers had only four first downs rushing and had 65 yards
less on the ground than did Paul Lowe (who ran wild for 165
yards)—and won the game. This was due in the main to George
Blanda, who more than anyone else typified the new league's (by
exigency) land-of-opportunity bent. Hoary but unbowed after a
decade of keeping the Bears' bench warm, Blanda could take up
two vital roster spots with his arm and his leg; he threw twenty-
four touchdowns and kicked fifteen field goals in 1960, and his

passing was as effective in its unruly way as the Chargers' fine-print aeronautics.

And so, of course, as so often happens when a shootout is expected, defense ruled the game. Together, these two teams came in with over 6,500 yards passing—and when it was over, the only pass that broke long was a fluke. Leading 17–16 into the fourth quarter and on his own twelve yard line, Blanda hit Billy Cannon out of the backfield. Left uncovered from the start, Cannon looked like a jalopy on an open road as he ran, and ran, all the way for the touchdown, clinching a 24–16 win. "It was my fault, but it really wasn't," said Jim Sears. "I called the defenses and I called an all-out blitz, but the end cut down the linebacker who was supposed to take Cannon. And Blanda threw it, Cannon caught it, and I chased it."

Fresh from representing Los Angeles in the contest, the Chargers—each one richer by a dazzling $718.61 (the Oilers' split was $1,016.42)—came home just in time to take a last look around.

Coughing up red ink, Barron Hilton had been dickering with the city fathers of San Diego, an untapped sports province but close enough to Hilton's Santa Monica manse to qualify for the right to lose money for him at a slower rate than he did in L.A. San Diego was not unified on this idea. Its city council vote to lay an upper deck on Balboa Stadium—a stipulation to the deal, so as to increase seating to thirty-four thousand—was four to three, aye. Five days after the game, the deal was done, and the move went down on February 10—just one of several alterations leaguewide. Every team lost money, and with television money keeping the league afloat, ownership changed in Denver and Oakland. The New York Titans, their owner bankrupt, were about to be taken over by the league pending the team's sale. No one needed to speculate on why almost no high draft choices were coming into the league.

And yet, their internal organization a year firmer, the Chargers signed their top two picks—defensive end Earl Faison and fullback Keith Lincoln. Both became All-League players (Faison in his rookie year). But the biggest public relations splash of 1961 was the signing of six-nine, 312-pound defensive tackle Ernie "Big Cat" Ladd. If the hunky Lincoln was projected as the AFL's Paul Hornung, Ladd was to be its Big Daddy Lipscomb, and both came close to living up to the hype—to the benefit of Al Davis.

Knowing the power of this kind of hype, Al did not let it harden into history without his vivid signature. Thus, in future days, Ernie

Ladd became an epic in the storied life of Al Davis. Faithfully recounted by Gary Smith in *Inside Sports* in 1981, it supposedly happened like this:

> [Davis] asked . . . Ernie Ladd aboard the team plane after a game in Houston for a quick round of cards, then told the pilot to start the engines. "Oops, too late, Ernie, you have to go with us," Davis apologized. Ladd became a Charger.

Sid Gillman had to listen to *that* one, too, for years. He was not amused. "That is not a true story. Al Davis had no part in Ernie Ladd, no sir," he said, with wishful finality. "I sat with Ernie Ladd all night long with a couple of friends of Ernie Ladd's. He didn't sign Ernie Ladd and he didn't sign Earl Faison or Keith Lincoln."

Gillman allows that Davis was "a splendid recruiter," but with a rowel of sarcasm—"If you listen to Al, you'd think the rest of us just sat around and watched him do all the recruiting. And that he signed this guy, that guy, that guy. . . ."

Whomever signed whomever, the Chargers rolled on. They won their first eleven games, were watched by substantially more fans, and on November 19, 1961, they beat the Texans 24–14 before their largest home crowd yet, 34,788.

The following morning, very early, the phone rang in Al's Baja Drive home. On the other end was his brother Jerry, calling from his home in Far Rockaway, New York.

"Al, it's bad news," he said.

"How bad?" Al asked, and Jerry delayed a moment.

"The worst."

On that morning back in Long Beach, Louis Davis awoke with grinding chest pain that forbade him to even sit up in bed. Rose Davis phoned for an ambulance, but her husband was unconscious by the time the car got to 951 West Park Avenue. Taken to St. Joseph's Hospital in Far Rockaway, he was soon to be pronounced dead.

Suddenly, with no warning, but like many others like him, at age sixty-nine, Louis Davis had become another too-early casualty of the now-graying Depression generation, a staunch man who died because he had simply worked too hard.

Benumbed, Al flew back to New York for the funeral. Only

afterward was he overcome—by guilt as much as by grief. For the better part of three decades, the son had kept the father at arm's length, at first blotting his very existence, then resisting any kind of rapprochement. The dynamic of Al Davis's upward spiral was a continuous alienation; not even Carol could divert the anomie for very long. Looking for weakness in other people, he neglected his own. And now death had stepped in to mock him for his flaws, to lay bare the joke of wordly victory, and he was impotent to do anything about it.

"I never even had the chance to fight it," Davis said years later about his father's death. "He was gone. . . . I'd been out in the damn world fighting for what I wanted. Trying to climb all the mountains."

But, clearly, there was a residual defensiveness, and a self-pitying if tortured rationale to Al's guilt—ascribing a mutuality of alienation between him and Louis. Without missing a beat, he continued: "I never had a chance to talk to my father. He'd never given me that opening. I never had time to think about it. I could tell my friends I loved them when I was a boy. But I couldn't tell my dad. I think he knows. Christ, I hope he knows."*

Moreover, Al profoundly hoped such understanding would redeem what seemed to be a tepid relationship with *his* son. "[Carol] worries I don't spend enough time with our son," he once told *Sports Illustrated*. "I tell her I didn't spend a lot of time with my daddy, but we were close. I really loved my daddy. It's not how much time you spend, it's what you did [sic] with the time you've got."

If Louis did know, it would not have been as the result of their correspondence during Al's adult life. Indeed, their relationship may have soured, and it certainly cooled, after Al made his priorities evident. At times, as during the Citadel period, Louis had often beseeched his son to come home and help run the family business.

"I know that Al's dad called him probably every day," John Sauer remembered of those days. "He wanted him to come back and be executive vice-president and Al wouldn't go unless he could be president. Al had to be the boss." Providing that this cruel-sounding ultimatum was not some private joke between father and son (or one on Al's part to get out of the proposition without saying

---

*"Al Davis Isn't as Bad as He Thinks He Is," *Inside Sports*, May 1981, p. 49.

no), it could not have done much for Louis that he was being rejected—or even being subjected to extortion—in such a coldly mercenary way by his own boy.

When Louis died, he left no will, no final testament of love for the wandering son. But still he spoke from the grave. When his estate was probated on December 7, 1961, Louis's assets were appraised at just under $400,000—including $184,645.19 in mortgages, notes, and bank accounts, and $55,367.50 in stocks and bonds (safe, sturdy blue-chippers all, like General Electric, Long Island Lighting Company, and Standard Oil of New Jersey).

In 1951, Louis had incorporated Little Dutchess Underwear under the name of the 1013 Broadway Company, after the Brooklyn address where the firm was located. Holding 34 percent of the stock, he divided the rest among other family members, Herman, Martin, and Ben Davis, and left an 8 percent interest for Jerry, the son who *did* take time for the family business. Louis also had a one-third interest (the other Davises held two-thirds) in a warehouse on Ocean Avenue, and a 20 percent interest in a three-acre plot of land in a vacant industrial park in Islip, New York. All told, Louis's cut from these properties—and Rose, after a dispute with the other Davises, had to go to an arbitrator to confirm Louis's share of the 1013 Broadway Company—was worth nearly $56,000. The Long Beach home was worth over $78,000. And when Jerry broke into a safe deposit box under Louis's name at the East New York Savings Bank in the old neighborhood, he found 41 United States Savings Bonds at an original face value of $1,000 each, many purchased in Jerry's or Rose's name. Not a single one was taken out for Al.

In dividing the remains of Louis's world, according to probate law, Rose, Jerry, and Al were each entitled to one-third, excluding certain bank accounts, property interests, and bonds held in trust. Because Louis had provided for Rose and Jerry in these holdings, Rose was left $274,690.37 and Jerry $93,875.25. Al received a bare minimum $65,256.30—and while money had never mattered to him as a measure of wordly value, the ratios cannot help but hit the eye, as if expressing a sliding scale of approbation. If so, only Louis knew it would be this way, and he did not think to adjust the scales.

Later, when it was helpful to Al to have the hint of money as a chip on the ownership gaming tables—and even before that—speculation would run steady about how large *his* estate was. The first time Davis's name made the pages of *Sports Illustrated*, in November of 1963, the title of the piece, taken from a statement by Davis within, was "I Don't Need Money, I Need Points," and this fascination with his assets was apparent throughout three full pages. Of the "young, vigrorous and rich" Davis, Walter Bingham wrote, "He is a wealthy man. How wealthy he will not divulge. It has been reported that when his father died . . . Al inherited three-quarters of a million dollars. Davis scoffs at the figure, saying it is way too high, yet he drops little hints that indicate money is no problem with him. . . .

"Discussing how he met his wife, a tall, beautiful New York girl named Carol, Al says, 'A friend introduced us. . . . He thought she could handle me. You know, I wasn't a bad-looking kid and not a poor boy.' "

Such glibness about money probably made Al red with guilt. As adamant as he always was about the hunger-blunting aspect of money—for football executives and players alike, it was the root of all establishment evil—he never mentioned actual figures; most of the time, if he spoke of money at all, he would coyly imply that his wife was the moneybags, which, given the unadorned amount left him by Louis, was actually more truth than not. This, of course, only heightened the gossip, which Al hardly minded, since the enigma surrounding him, and arranged by him, was a myth-making propellant all its own. In 1966, for example, a *Sporting News* profile of him was headlined "AFL's Davis: Rich Boy Made Good."

Thus, he was trapped among maddening contradictions about money, and no one can know if he's sorted it all out to this very day. But he's had to live with them since as far back as 1961, when the rumors were already starting among the Chargers, some magnificently inane.

"The story was that Al inherited a lot of money," Jim Sears recalled, "and that his father owned the Fruit of the Loom company and he was in the 'Jewish Mafia.' Those were the kind of things that were told in beer halls and became fact."

If there was one thing Al could not hope to sort out, it was that most maddening contradiction of all, death. Its finality and immutability he could not stick his tongue out at. If Al had to have a humanist sensibility, death would inspire it. "I lost my father that same year," Dave Kocourek said, "and Al was very, very crushed by it. He's a hard guy but a very sensitive one."

Now, Al began to see clues about gaining karmic Brownie

points—or maybe erasing guilt points—even in *Sister Carrie*, his old Magna Carta of war against his environment.

"When Mae West died," he said in 1981, his sentimentality near the point of weirdness, "most people just passed over it. It bothered me. It all goes back to Hurstwood. I really don't have many insecurities. I'm kinda happy. But when someone dies I have to sit back and wonder where I'm going. Why is it? Sure, I'll cry. I'll go off for two minutes and do it by myself."

Upon Louis's death, Al discovered the lost implements of his religion. Herman Masin, the *Scholastic Coach* editor, recalled that Al began going to synagogue for the first time in his adult life. In his God, Al was able to find a kind of solace in reciting the Mourner's Kaddish. He would hang plaques in Louis's memory in whatever temple he prayed in. "I go to synagogue and pray for the sick and dead," he once said. "I believe in God. He lets me control. I don't believe in an afterlife . . . but when I'm at church or temple when someone has died, I'll close my eyes at the right time and say something to the person and see him. . . .

"It sounds crazy, but I feel they're listening to me. Maybe that *is* an afterlife. Maybe I've built a religion of my own."*

These catharses were indeed solitary—of Al's sacrosanct moments Jerry Davis once said, "He doesn't like people to know [about them] because he considers it a vulnerability"—and for Al they were a convenience: relieved of guilt, acquitted of burdens, he could go right on beating the crap out of his enemies. With all these otherworldly forces so much bigger than even he, if death were sealed at birth, if morality and amorality were ultimately without meaning—while he was here his worldly, bloodthirsty impulses would be his refuge.

Even as early as 1961, when death's sting pierced Al Davis as deeply as it could without claiming him, there was little time left and many battles still to be fought.

The Chargers and Oilers again met for the AFL championship on December 24, 1961, this time in Balboa Stadium. In a game that was a near-identical reprise of the year before, the maligned defenses dominated. There were six interceptions and seven fumbles, and neither team gained one hundred yards on the ground.

---

*Ibid., p. 48.

And the winning score came on a broken play, when Blanda was flushed out of the pocket, scrambled right, and hit Cannon for a thirty-five-yard touchdown to make it 10–0 Oilers late in the third quarter. The Chargers cut it to 10–3 and were driving late in the game when Jack Kemp, throwing long for Dave Kocourek, was intercepted by strong safety Julian Spence.

Less than two months later, death again struck at Al Davis and the Chargers. On February 16, 1962, backup halfback/linebacker Bob Laraba was killed in a car crash. It was a portent of impending disaster for the team, even though they reeled in the biggest AFL catch yet. Al would take credit for this one, too, and this time he deserved it. For many months he had been on the trail of Lance Alworth, a lithe but undersized halfback at Arkansas. In Frank Broyles's rumbling game plan, the forward pass was purely hearsay and Alworth mainly was a blocking back. But Gillman and Davis —as did most everyone in the pros—agreed that Alworth had the body structure and speed to be a nifty receiver. Al worked on him all during his senior year—doing his sidewalk act for the guileless young man and his down-home parents, as well as sending garlands of flowers to Alworth's girlfriend.

Alworth was called "Bambi" because he had ears like lettuce leaves and a withering innocence that turned his face into a Botticelli painting. He was quick kill for Al. "My parents loved him," Alworth recalled. "In fact, Al still will call my parents. He'll say, 'Mrs. Alworth, this is your favorite coach.' " If Al had a particular fondness for this assignment, it was because its timing offered a vicariously soothing form of absolution. "My father had died a week before I [first] went to see Lance," he told *Look* in 1969, "and he's very close with *his* father, and somehow there was a lot of warmth."

That may have been, but if Al felt warm inside as he courted Alworth, much of the heat rose from incinerating the NFL's plans for Alworth. The 49ers were on the kid's tail as well, and they dispatched their head coach, Red Hickey, an Arkansas alumnus, to sign him right after his last college game. Already committed to Davis, Alworth went through an uncomfortable charade with Hickey, assuring him the 49ers were in the picture—and, in fact, Hickey almost got a long and last laugh on Al, the result of some typically bizarre AFL hijinx.

Trying to scoop the NFL on college talent, AFL owners had held a "secret" draft in November—keeping in the dark AFL commissioner Joe Foss, who had set the AFL draft for December.

Among the undercover picks—through "gentleman's agreements"—were Alworth by the Chargers and Syracuse fullback Ernie Davis by the moribund Jets. When Foss found out about this, he voided the whole business. Since the official draft would go along the usual lines, in inverse order of the standings, the Chargers were in real danger of losing rights to Alworth. They avoided that the only way they could have, by bilking the *yutzes* in the front office of football's very worst team, the Oakland Raiders. Gillman and Davis tantalized the Raiders with four roster players—and though the only useful one was halfback Bo Roberson, a former Olympic broad jumper, the Raiders agreed to draft Alworth number one and then trade him to San Diego for the four "proven" talents, all of whom, except Roberson, refused to report to the club. With dibs on Alworth restored, Al moved in fast.

"I'm naive now, and I was really naive then," Alworth said. "Both the Chargers and 49ers asked me what I wanted and all that was to be able to go to law school and get a no-cut contract. Both of 'em said okay, but the difference was Al Davis. It was really a personality thing."

The clincher came when Al went to Little Rock as the Razorbacks were getting ready to play number-one-ranked Alabama in the Sugar Bowl. Taking the kid to a coffee shop, Al grandly flourished a pen and began scribbling on the white tablecloth.

"He was drawing all these circles, standing for all the players, and then he puts this big X out there on the left side, where the flanker lines up. And he says, 'See that X? Lance, the minute you sign with us, you're my X, that's your position and nobody can take it away from you.' And I'm sittin' there, with my mouth open."

The contract agreed to, Al had only to wait until after the Sugar Bowl for Alworth to sign. Licking his lips, he decided a mere signing was not enough. He wanted a public relations hit on the NFL, hard to the body. So he schemed with Alworth to sign right after the game's last play, when Alworth, walking in the national spotlight, would step right into the AFL.

"He said, 'I'd like to do it under the goalpost,' and set it up like a battle plan," Alworth recalled, with an apt metaphor.

As it turned out, Alworth was not in the best mood to accommodate Al's big PR coup in New Orleans. With time running out and Arkansas down 10–3, a desperation pass for Alworth nestled in his long fingers but was then knocked loose. For Al, this only heightened the scenario, with even more attention on Alworth. And the dejected Alworth, the feel of the potential game-winning ball still on his hands, dutifully strode under the crossbar and inked the contract held in a beaming Davis's hands.

Though just six feet tall and weighing 185 pounds, Alworth's body control and tubular vertical leap was such that he could shield the ball from harm by *jumping*, without losing a millimeter of balance. This made him a natural in the Chargers' exacting system— even though he quickly discovered something common to all Charger pass-catchers. During training camp, Alworth overheard Davis sidle up to the other receivers and give them the "You're my X" routine, just as he had with Alworth in the coffee shop. "That was Al's pitch to *all* of us," Alworth chortled. Later, when chicken-armed Tobin Rote replaced Kemp, Alworth would have to truncate his routes and curl back to get the ball, and that would become a designed and devastating play; coming back, he could gain more room to break into the clear.

Now, though, as the 1962 season progressed with Alworth assimilated into the offense, the Chargers stood no better than 3–2 by early October. Then, during practice, Alworth was fooling around kicking field goals when he tore a muscle in his leg, finishing him for the season. As killing a blow as it was, that was just one in a terrible string of injuries that wiped out the season. Paul Lowe broke his arm and Kemp broke his hand in preseason games and were gone; and All-League middle linebacker Chuck Allen and defensive back Charley McNeil went down during the season, which ended with a 4–10 record. It was a temporary fall. The following season, the Chargers won their only AFL title.

But, just as with the USC team he helped turn into champs, Al wouldn't be there for it. As the miserable season of 1962 wound to a close, the conditions were set for Al Davis to parlay what he was, and what he wasn't, into the bluff of a lifetime.

The Oakland Raiders, looking for a new head coach, called on Al Davis in early January of 1963. As it happened, they were brought together in large measure by happenstance—the AFL All-Star game was going to be played in San Diego, and thus it was an opportune moment for the Raiders' two general partners, Wayne Valley and Ed McGah, to check him out as a potential head coach for their afflicted team (Packers assistant coach Bill Austin had already turned the job down). After an initial feeling-out, Valley and McGah met with Davis in a hotel room. But instead of being properly obsequious, Al was characteristically coltish and fringe-line obnoxious as he began a new game of dare. In the room were two newspapermen from the *Oakland Tribune*, sports editor George Ross and football writer Scotty Stirling—they, and the paper, had been heavily influential in making football a reality, such as it was, in the city—and Al seemed to pay more attention to them than to the clubowners.

"He was very outgoing and asked Scotty and me about the team," Ross said, looking back. "Were they gonna make it, did they have the finances, and so on. Al had a very low opinion of the Raiders. He said the Chargers looked upon the Raiders as two exhibition games and two W's in the win column. And so he had no respect for the owners.

"At one point there was a break because Wayne and Ed had to go to the bathroom and when they left the room Al began laughing about them. He said, 'Christ, these guys don't even know the right questions to ask.' Al thought all owners were dilettantes playing with a new toy. He said to me many times through the years that owners are often the problem with their franchises, that too many of them think they can run things when they cannot, and the teams that succeed are the ones where the owner hires the best people he can and turns the game over to them."

Because Valley and McGah didn't immediately cede the breadth of power that Davis was seeking, and that he would need with this pitiful franchise, Al turned down their one-year deal. Risky as it seemed for a man with no head coaching experience, he told them he would need a contract for two years or more. Biting at the bait, Valley and McGah deliberated, then came back with a three-year deal. Without blinking, Al again turned them down; now he wanted to be the general manager as well. Although few football people would have considered Davis qualified for such a job, the audacity of the demand worked to convince Valley and McGah that this was a man they *had* to have.

Within ten days of the initial meeting, the deal was made, and on January 15, 1963, a press conference was called to introduce the new Raider coach and GM. In rarefied air now, as a coach and executive, Al sanguinely defined his caliphlike powers to the press.

"I have," he said, "sole and complete control of the operations of this football team."

It was a famous victory for brass balls, and just as it wasn't the first, neither would it be the last. With the synapse of power—real power—crossed, Davis would from now on see every little strand in the world in terms of *potential* power. Able to read a game by its underlying components—and there were games when Al, his mind threading matchups and tendencies, could call the opposing coach's plays right along with him—Al came to Oakland with a similar, if reverse, syllogism, one of effect and cause. Already taking the long view, he had to know the conditions would be right for opportunity.

"I remember he called me just before he took the job," George Ross recalled, "and he said he wouldn't take the job unless he knew he could be sure of some things. He wanted to know that these owners—principally Wayne Valley, because Ed McGah was not a factor at that time, he was really a cipher in the ownership—were not gonna cut and run and move the franchise to Seattle or someplace. And I told him that I thought Wayne was a heavyweight guy, that he had a lot more money than he had put into football and he was not gonna see it go down the tubes. Then he asked me if there really was gonna be a new stadium built, which was on the drawing board, and I told him the guys in charge of putting the Coliseum over had an excellent plan to finance and build the thing away from politics. And his last question was, 'Where will the *Tribune* be?' "

That, in fact, was an ethical question Ross had debated with himself since he took over the *Tribune* sports desk in 1961. As the largest newspaper in Oakland, with a circulation of two hundred thousand—which was still only about a quarter of the readership of the big San Francisco papers—the *Tribune* had a large vested interest in the doings of the Raiders. If home-town pride—which had heretofore been expunged by the corona of the *real* city lying west of the Bay—could be unearthed by a popular sports franchise, the *Trib*'s circulation and prestige would be enhanced proportionately. And the *Trib* was in a position to prick the Raiders' growth process. The rub was whether the paper could do it in good journalistic conscience. Ross would try to hold the line on outright puffery, but he did not deny that the *Trib* was also in the business of Raider boosterism, if not overtly in its pages then covertly in its sponsorship of booster clubs and press luncheons.

"My view was this," Ross said. "If we're ever gonna be a major league paper and not just a satellite, it was gonna be by nursing a sick baby."

Ross was also soothed by the fact that Al came in not expecting a free ride but offering a quid pro quo: news breaks about the Raiders would be funneled right to George Ross and his boys. "If you're close enough to a source like that—and this guy was the number-one sports source in Oakland and he had a fantastic knowledge of the game and what was going on around the league—as a journalist you accept it, you appreciate it, and you use it. Listen, if Al was using me, I was using him, too." While Davis was after manipulation, so as not to be hounded if upcoming years were lean ones, Ross had an answer to Al's phone query that—for now—satisfied both men. "I told him that we were both going in the same direction, that we might get on opposite sides of the street here and there, but that we were headed in the same direction."

Al Davis's big-time manipulations were just beginning. In the poor Oakland Raiders, Al now saw in football a king's ransom of personal power. While everyone else in football saw in the Raiders only raw sewage, Al saw raw material that could be transformed by time, space, and hard labor. Al had often let his mind play on the fantasies of coaching in the old-money power base of New York, or in newly cosmopolitan Los Angeles; but would he *be* Al Davis in those places, or only a siphoned-off product of already entrenched power?

When the Raiders came to him, it was as if the AFL was *really* summoning the future. Because by Al's going there, he would surely make the team and the league an experiment in the Davis Method, which was so new that even Al didn't entirely know what it would wreak. But he did know this: he would not *think* of going there without a salary that would guarantee his security—for all his years on earth, if need be, and Al was preoccupied with such conditions at the moment—and that certainly would extend far beyond the almost-immaterial thirty-five thousand dollars with which he would begin.

Cognitively, organically, chemically—whatever the prod—getting all he wanted from the Raiders would pit Al against Wayne Valley in a foot race alongside a forbidding third rail. A multimillionaire, Valley was one of the West Coast's most dominant home-building contractors and a man accustomed to getting his way. Unable to buy into the 49ers for many years, he saw the Raiders as his payback, which was why, despite regarding Al Davis as a particularly unpleasant fellow, he had to have him; the club didn't need just a coach but a man so committed to winning that he was obsessed. Valley did not have much problem with what he recognized as Al's little gambits of control and ego. Davis was smart, he was young, he was hip—the guy knew how to effect the *combustion* of winning, through tightly controlled organization.

As a man who had risen to the good life on just those precepts, Valley was impressed by Al's near-visionary attention to the chalkboard and the ledger book. "Wayne told me after the first meeting with Al how well-prepared Al was," Ross related. "If they didn't know the right questions, Al definitely had the right answers." And, at least some of the time, the right cons: asked to fill out a dummy budget, Al rummaged around back in the Chargers' front office, found the team's budget, and gave it to Valley and McGah, with the name "Chargers" whited out.

What Valley could not know then, of course, was that he hadn't seen nothin' yet of how Al's business reflexes worked with his viper instincts. While he gave Davis a large margin, he thought he would be able to keep him in line. For Valley was hardly a rube when it came to identifying and dealing with problems within the company store. Sometimes, he could do that by scaring them out. In his mid-fifties, Valley was as granite-cut as in the days when he was an offensive lineman at Oregon State. An Irish Catholic, he had carbon-dark eyes, a product of his part-Portuguese blood, and his horn-rimmed glasses and long nose were an austere contrast to his smooth, unlined brow and large-crowned, hairless head. Valley's eyes were warning lights; suddenly restricting like a tomcat's in some uncontrolled rage, they ignited a conflagration of malice.

He was once described by a fellow owner as "a tough guy who would come across the table at you." George Ross called him "abrasive . . . more like the hod-carriers than the big builder." But Ross was close enough to Valley to know better. "Underneath," he said, "all that tough stuff was a facade. Wayne wanted to be horny-handed, but he was really a shrewd guy, and a sensitive one." Ross would never forget the night when, after negotiating some nugget of Raider business with the Oakland City Council, Valley stood on a dark downtown street corner and dreamed his big dream. "He said, 'I don't have to make a nickel out of this team. I'm an Oakland man, this is where I've made my life. I just want this thing to work.' That was the rarely seen side of Wayne Valley, who was generally a hard-nosed guy with a nickel."

Strong as Valley was, to Al he was nothing but a challenge. From the start, he would not be intimidated by Valley, and in his mind he would devalue Valley's physical and mental strength, always looking for signs of weakness and inflating them. To confidants there would be continual insults of Valley, delivered with so much glee and bile that it seemed as though Al was constantly trying to convince himself that he could outwit and outmaneuver Valley if he had to. The battle lines were already clear. Though Al had his on-field and front-office oligarchy, Valley was going to collect on the Al Davis genius. Wayne Valley seemed to be a bigger, stronger, wealthier man. Al had all the reasons he needed already to detest him.

To Valley—who felt a mild but mutual personal contempt for Al—it was enough to dream on, of glories that he prayed would someday unlock the 49ers' hold on the Bay Area. Valley had, during the previous season, served as president of the AFL; now, he stepped down to train his undivided attention to his own team, whose brash new coach and general manager he would refer to over and over in the same words: "You don't have to love Al Davis," Wayne Valley would say. "You just have to turn him loose."

8

When young, dynamic Al Davis accepted the [Raiders] job, an organization was created dedicated to the development of the Raiders into a professional football power. Davis, only 33 years old, has 13 brilliant coaching seasons behind him; yet, nobody close to the new Raider scene expects the new Raider administration to work miracles. This is a team that won one game in 1962 and only three out of the last 28.

—from the 1963 Raiders media guide

In order to run an efficient organization, there has to be a dictator.

—Al Davis

The Oakland Raiders grew out of a hole sand-blasted into the AFL profile by a vengeant NFL. Originally, the AFL's eight start-up franchises had included an ownership group out of Minneapolis, headed by Max Winter. But the NFL, knowing it could expose the underlying motives of those willing to war with it, dug a cavity in the new league's credibility by awarding an NFL franchise to Winter, who almost hurt himself scrambling out of the AFL picture late in 1959.

Left with a gorge where a team was supposed to be, the league sires desperately looked for new takers, and when there were none, they decided to simply make one up—in Oakland, it turned out, only because Barron Hilton knew that if a team could be put there, his Chargers would have a geographical rival and he would be able to cut transportation costs on road trips. But the announcement that a new franchise had been awarded to Oakland was news to everyone *in* Oakland. Sitting in the news room of the *Tribune* when the item came over the wire, Scotty Stirling called around to anyone in town he knew who had ever expressed an interest in owning a football team. He found no one who actually *had* one, but—as the league hoped—people *became* interested, primarily because George Ross and Stirling kept trumpeting the idea of football in Oakland in the *Trib*.

Quickly, an eight-man syndicate of builder-millionaires emerged, fronted by Y. C. Chet Soda and including Wayne Valley, Ed McGah, and Charles Harney, who was responsible for building San Francisco's Candlestick Park. Magnifying Oakland's lack of identity, the group was split, with Harney heading the San Francisco faction and Soda the Oakland one (the latter was humiliated that the Raiders played their games across the Bay their first two seasons, first in Kezar Stadium and then in Candlestick Park, though almost nobody came to see those games).

In time, heavy financial losses and fratricidal bickering altered the syndicate. All but three of the original owners cashed out, their shares bought up by those who remained: Valley, McGah, and Robert Osborne, who changed the ownership structure in 1961 from a closed stock company to a trilateral limited partnership. Each man, with a $50,000 investment, held the title of general partner, and they were empowered to bring in limited partners—with no power, only as investors—in equal thirds. (In future years, many would fail to understand the meaning of the general partners' ownership "shares"; *not* a stock company, the Raiders are divided among *all* the partners but only the general partners can sell as well as buy shares, and their authority is technically equal regardless of how many shares they own. In 1961—with the franchise worth about $180,000—Valley, McGah, and Osborne each owned only about 10 percent of the shares but had 100 percent of the authority.)

Valley, who had originally brought in McGah, and who seemed to rule by force of personality, populated the limiteds with longtime cronies, many going as far back with him as Oregon State. But Osborne, unable to find investors and with his building business in trouble, could not go on, even applying his losses as a tax writeoff as the others did, and sold out to Valley and McGah at the end of the 1961 season. That season had borne a $70,000 loss for the club, leaving it $120,000 in debt.

Although Valley could have bought and sold the entire AFL, he maintained his policy of curbing his Raider endowment, unwilling to risk his fortune on this risky investment. Instead, needing immediate capital just to keep the club afloat, he struck a quiet and remarkable deal that was probably unprecedented in sports history. The deal had the Buffalo Bills' owner, Ralph Wilson, become a (very) silent partner in the *Oakland Raiders*. Wilson kicked a whopping $250,000 into the Raiders through his father's Devoir Management Company in Detroit. Through Devoir, which officially owned limited partner shares, Wilson would thus share in Raider profits and receive dividends, an incestuous arrangement that had to violate the AFL's conflict-of-interest bylaws. Yet Valley succeeded in keeping the arrangement sealed from the outside world, and those who did know of it apparently went along with Valley's suggestion that the Wilson investment was really a "loan," without which the Raiders would die.

As the Raiders were indeed close to cadavers on the field, the least Valley wanted for the 1962 season was to have the team do its dance of death in Oakland. He had already begun to work out a deal with the city to build an Oakland–Alameda County Coliseum, so *any* feasible land mass would do for now. Unfortunately, after the people at UC-Berkeley nixed the use of their stadium, not a one was available, and Valley and George Ross began to pressure Oakland's mayor, John Houlihan, to provide some land. Finally, a wartime housing project on Recreation Department land was cleared and, in the manner of a large Erector set, a skeletal stadium was built with city funds. The last stage was to forklift an existing press box and porta-potty—christened the "George Ross Memorial Men's Room"—and plop them onto its outer rim. Receiving hot running water infrequently and seating barely 18,000, this aluminum crate, named Frank Youell Field (after a civic-minded sports booster who, appropriately, happened to be an undertaker) housed the Raiders for four years.

In 1963, few could imagine that they would ever deserve any better than this cow-pie treatment. Through three seasons, the Raiders—originally named the "Señors" by Chet Soda before he came to his senses and went with the sobriquet chosen in a contest run by the *Tribune*—were not only *not* very professional but were more an annex of the University of the Pacific football team. Beginning as late as it did, the club had had to equip itself by buying surplus uniforms from the school, taking the field in the same black and gold colors. The uniforms were accompanied by a coterie of

Through these portals: 1745 President Street, Brooklyn. The Davis family lived on the fifth floor. *Author's collection*

At seventeen: gym rat Al Davis (*back row, third from left*) sidles up to letterman Larry Krevins. *Courtesy of Leon Cohen*

From the Erasmus Hall yearbook, January 1947. Being popular could open doors. *Courtesy of Leon Cohen*

The Syracuse Orangemen, 1949. Al *(back row, fourth from right)* was a member of the team very briefly. *Courtesy of Bob Wallach*

On the USC coaching staff, rubbing elbows with head coach Don Clark. So what if he never won a letter and never went to Notre Dame? *Courtesy of the University of Southern California*

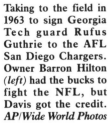

The next year, smiling through scandal. But John McKay *(second from right)* got the job Al wanted. *Courtesy of the University of Southern California*

Taking to the field in 1963 to sign Georgia Tech guard Rufus Guthrie to the AFL San Diego Chargers. Owner Barron Hilton *(left)* had the bucks to fight the NFL, but Davis got the credit. *AP/Wide World Photos*

Davis shows good posture and casts a mean eye as a rookie head coach in 1963— the year the Raiders, quarterbacked by Tom Flores (15), became a real football team. *Courtesy of Russ Reed/NFL Photos*

For his ten-victory season in 1963, Coach of the Year honors. *AP/Wide World Photos*

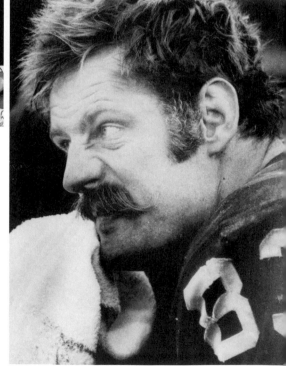

Signing a new contract in 1965, under the gaze of Raider general partners Wayne Valley (*center*) and Ed McGah. Valley seemed to know he'd have the least to smile about. *AP/Wide World Photos*

Ben Davidson, the first Raider antihero, and the mustache that made him famous. *AP/Wide World Photos*

A family portrait in 1966: Al with his wife, Carol, and son, Mark. *UPI/Bettmann Newsphotos*

Newly named AFL commissioner Al Davis huddles with Buffalo Bills owner Ralph Wilson. They shared a secret—Wilson's quiet financial interest in the Raiders—but kept tight-lipped about it. *AP/Wide World Photos*

The AFL commissioner with Buffalo quarterback and AFL union president Jack Kemp: both had bigger things on their minds for the future. *AP/Wide World Photos*

Raiders head coach John Rauch exhorts the team during the 1967 AFL title game against Houston. But the team's future belonged to hulking John Madden (then an assistant coach), who tolerated Al's front office meddling far more easily. *AP/Wide World Photos*

A defensive back's nightmare: Fred Biletnikoff extends his sticky fingers to grab a pass. *AP/Wide World Photos*

Arm cocked and impervious to the rush, Daryle Lamonica follows the Davis game plan to the letter—throwing long. *AP/Wide World Photos*

Old goat George Blanda found an elixir in Oakland and became a miracle man . . . *AP/Wide World Photos*

. . while carousing Ken Stabler found mentor in Blanda and became the aider's messiah. *AP/Wide World hotos*

Raider reprobate Warren Wells *(left)*—released from prison after serving time for rape and parole violations—greets his probation officer, Sam Lacey, in January 1972. *AP/Wide World Photos*

The ever-excitable John Madden nearly busts a gut urging Clarence Davis down the sideline during the Raiders' thrashing of the Vikings, 32–14, in Super Bowl XI. *AP/Wide World Photos*

Wedged between Gene Upshaw (63), Willie Brown, and Mark van Eeghen, Madden revels in his post-Super Bowl dousing. Then came the ulcers. *AP/Wide World Photos*

A common sight: the ref calls a penalty on George Atkinson (43) for assault on a wide receiver. With Atkinson and Jack Tatum (32), the penalty and body counts were always high. (*AP/Wide World Photos*)

former Pacific players and its public relations director, Bill Tunnell. And when Chet Soda, who had been the Raiders' general manager their first year, sold out and left, his place was taken by a former Pacific man, Bud Hastings.

Incompetent as most of the front-office people and the team were—ironically, one of the Raiders' early assistant coaches, in 1961, was Al's old USC nemesis George Dickson—when Al Davis made his entrance he fired one after another, even bringing in as ticket manager the guy who had served that role with the Chargers, George Glace. He also bought spiffy new uniforms, changing the color scheme to black and *silver*, which jibed more forcefully with that wonderful eye-patched-pirate-and-sword logo. In a subtle way, the more sinister look of the Raiders linked Al's boyhood romance with the Black Knights of West Point to the self-possessed clawing of his adult life.

"Al told me he had been impressed as a boy watching the Cadets come out on the field—the way the black made them look so much bigger than the other teams," George Ross recalled. "At first, I disagreed with the black and silver thing. We were just starting to run some color action photos in the sports section and I got a vision of guys standing there looking like a black and white photo. But once I saw the uniforms, I came around.

"These kinds of macho symbols were important to Al. He thought it influenced guys' psyches. In San Diego, the Chargers used to come out of their locker room, these great big guys they had, and they'd just bowl their way through the Raiders—who'd be moseying to the field—with no regret at all. When Al got here, he wasn't going to stand for that, he wanted that sort of respect for the Raiders. He didn't want them to look shabby, and they didn't."

However, everything else about the Raiders *was* shabby, the product of a loser's mentality. Inspecting the business premises of the club, Al was horrified by its smallness. The team office was located on an open mezzanine overhanging the lobby of the Hotel Leamington in downtown Oakland. Raiders business was conducted amid the din of guests milling, luggage thudding, and bells clanging at the check-in counter.

Given this sandal-string operation, the Raiders had become resigned to staying ineffectual. One survivor of the Davis purge was Ollie Spencer, a thirty-one-year-old one-time guard with the Lions who had been offensive line coach in the previous regime. Kept on for continuity's sake by Al, who made him a player-coach, Spencer recalled the Raiders in an unwitting but suitable paraphrase of the Gertrude Stein refrain about the city of Oakland. "There wasn't anything there," Spencer said. "They'd drafted guys but then they wouldn't even try to sign 'em. It wasn't only money. The guy before Al was good buddies with somebody on the 49ers and I think he probably had a little deal about not going after certain people."

With the Raiders so immersed in debt, Al had no hope of doing any better in the draft, at least in 1963, and his first strategy was to draft key "futures" who still had time left in college. His immediate focus was on recruiting, only this time the fodder wasn't raw schoolboys but a vast, shifting surfeit of pros cut loose by NFL and AFL teams. Men matured by the pro experience were a paramount need for Al in restocking this bereft club, and when hiring his staff he chose two types of men: those with a first-hand knowledge of who could play and of why some players hadn't played up to their level, and those who could talk players into coming to play in what they regarded as the penal colony of football.

In hiring his first assistant, Al's emphasis, significantly, was on the latter. Even before he took the job, he had made overtures to Tulane assistant coach John Rauch—the stimulus being an obscure event (to all but Al) of years before, when Al was at the Citadel and Rauch was an assistant coach at Georgia, where he'd been an All-America quarterback. Both had hotly recruited the same high school player, a running back named Bill Strumpke. When Rauch won in the end, Al gritted his buck teeth in high admiration. Anyone who could beat Al Davis to a recruit was good, very good, and he did not forget Rauch's name.

In 1961, Rauch had moved to West Point, and he still had never met Davis when Al came through on a scouting mission for the Chargers. The first thing Al did was bring up the Strumpke thing. Then he hired Rauch as an ad-hoc scout, filing reports on college players for the Chargers. A year later, Rauch was an assistant at Tulane. That team went 0–10 but still Al remembered. When Rauch came out to a coaches' convention in Los Angeles, "Al came runnin' up to me and told me he was going to Oakland that night to discuss the job there and would I join him as an assistant," Rauch said. "Well, I didn't know Al that well to give him an answer, but the next morning, before I even got out of bed, the phone rings and it's him. He'd accepted the job and he wanted to know again if I'd join him. Again I didn't give him a commitment and I went home. I no sooner walked in the door when the phone rings and it's him wanting me to visit Oakland. The next morning I was on the plane and in twenty-four hours I bought a house there."

Named offensive back coach, Rauch could still say years later, "I really didn't know why he wanted me, other than I beat him out of Bill Strumpke."

Settling in, Al—taking no chances—*rented* his house, a small house on Fairlane Drive, high in the hills of Oakland, and then chose two other assistant coaches from among pro types. On a recommendation from Dallas Cowboys coach Tom Landry came Tom Dahms, a journeyman NFL lineman who had been the Cowboys' defensive line coach for three years. Al hired him and Charlie Sumner, fresh off his career as a defensive back with the Bears and Vikings. The two of them, with Ollie Spencer, began a catechism, learning the Al Davis/Sid Gillman offense.

"I sat in in some of those sessions," said George Ross, "and Al was showing John Rauch the concept of 'lateral' football, getting the ball down the field with as many as five receivers going out. And Rauch—who was a four-year All-American at Georgia—was just open-mouthed."

Rauch—whose union with Al would flourish, then turn laceratingly sour—remembered it a bit differently. "What he did was pick everybody's brain. You might not get a point across and he would ask you to get up and expound on the blackboard. And then he wouldn't make a decision on whether this was worth puttin' in our playbook or not. But a week later you came in and he said, 'And I think we oughta put this thing in'—and it was what you talked about a week ago. But it was now *his* idea. That was the way he operated: it's mine because I'm the head coach. But that's one of his great faculties, too, being able to pick people's brains and put it to use."

The new Raider assistants had no choice *but* to talk football. Working late, then later, Al would say that they'd have to go on "because I know that old bastard in San Diego is still watching films," meaning Gillman. By Al's edict, no clocks were allowed on the office walls. "And Al never had a watch himself," said Rauch. "He'd ask somebody, 'What time is it?' and you'd say, 'It's one-thirty in the morning,' and he'd go, 'God, we gotta get the hell out of here,' and boom, we were gone. At one time, Al borrowed three watches from me. When he had to be somewhere at a certain time, he'd borrow somebody's watch. He came in two years later holding three of 'em and said, 'Here, these are yours.' He just didn't want one himself. He didn't want to go by a clock."

Always, the late-night brainstorming would address the acute problem of acquiring players. Al had resolved at the start to excise the dead wood from a team that was last in offense, defense, and right feet in 1962. By any measure, the Raiders had two NFL-grade players, three-time All-AFL center Jim Otto and halfback Clem Daniels, with guard Wayne Hawkins close. Craving anything human that could stand and think at the same time, Al would bring in people who might fit the bill, even if all other coaches wanted to avoid them.

Latter-day historians would draw a correlation between Al Davis and chronic malcontents—and even insurrectionists—and this was with much good reason. However, in 1963, the truth was that he couldn't *afford* to be scared off by any player's dark reputation. Not if he was able enough to fit a *role*, since, at face value, these recidivist players were likely going to remind no one of Lance Alworth, nor anything in a civics club.

And yet, strikingly, Al's first player catch hit the jackpot—the next-best thing to Alworth, as it turned out—Art Powell, a royally gifted receiver hung by coaches with the tag of "attitude problem." Sullen and sometimes surly, Powell was big—six-two, 212—agile, and blazing fast. But the price for his services—and they were considerable, as Powell had been one of the AFL's top receivers the last three seasons—included cold silence and alienation from teammates and coaches.

By 1962, when he played out his option with the Jets (the Titans, saved from extinction by Sonny Werblin, had gotten a new name and a new coach, Weeb Ewbank, that season), the book on Powell was that he couldn't get along with people, mainly white people, and thus had a racial chip on his shoulder pad. As a free agent, Powell was thought to be headed to the Bills, but Al had inside information that he intended to use as a sledgehammer to get Powell—to wit, that the Bills had signed Powell before the season had ended, which constituted tampering.

Knowing he had Buffalo by the gonads, Davis investigated Powell's character with numerous sources, including Bernie Custis, his old classmate at Syracuse who had played with Powell in the Canadian League. Assured that Powell was no devil (rather than being a white-hater, he had married a white Canadian woman), Al flew into Chicago in the middle of a terrible storm to meet with Powell.

"Art, he said, "we're gonna build a franchise around you.""

Powell ate up the adulation, but he told Al he'd signed with the Bills.

"I know," Al said. "But those sons of bitches signed you illegally. They can't pull that contract out of the drawer."

Powell signed with the Raiders that night, and as Al already knew, the Bills were helpless to challenge *his* Art Powell contract—though he couldn't help but think that if he were on the other side, he'd fight to the death in court to keep Powell. But there was no Al Davis in Buffalo.

If Al would not be getting many other Art Powells, his face-down of the Bills showed that, at the least, the better teams would not be able to slip something by the Raiders anymore. And he would victimize teams as weakly managed as the Raiders once had been. One of his first player transactions was to trade four players he had no use for to the very same Bills for All-League middle linebacker Archie Matsos, who at a puny six feet and 212 pounds was downgraded as that team sought bigger people; not incidentally, Matsos was also known as a "clubhouse lawyer" who urged players to stand up to management. If Buffalo figured the trade as a way of getting back at Al, it became a fleeting thought. While only one of the ex-Raiders stuck with the Bills, Matsos—an untamed free-lancer, guided by instinct rather than plan—made hits from sideline to sideline and was a folk hero in Oakland for three seasons.

Another Davis heist involved Dan Ficca, his one-time USC recruit, who was on the Raiders roster when Al arrived but had gone into military service and would not be out until after the 1963 season began. So Al beguiled his old mentor, Weeb Ewbank, into a trade of guards, straight up—Ficca for thirty-year-old Bob Mischak, who'd made All-AFL at guard but whom Al remembered as a wide receiver at West Point and moved back to that position in Oakland. Ewbank was delighted to get a much younger player, except that Al never mentioned that Ficca was out of commission for a while.

"I remember when Weeb finally found out and called me on my army base, he said, 'That bastard Al Davis tricked me,' " Ficca related. "So, if that was wrong for Al Davis to do or not, Weeb Ewbank gets egg on his face 'cause Al outsmarted him. That's Al Davis. That's his whole goddamn life."

It was also the kind of duplicity that, repeated over and over, would soon earn Davis an unsavory reputation around the football beltway.

"Al pulled several of those," George Ross noted, "to the extent that many people were awfully leery about making trades with him." Al, though, was undisturbed if anyone cried foul. "I would say," Ross concluded, "that he ignored being popular."

Trying to upgrade the Raiders' operation, Al demanded that the office be moved to more suitable quarters—which became a three-room suite in a building connected to the Hotel Leamington, which was metaphoric of the still-patchwork quality of the team.

"Everything was kind of skimpy at the time," John Rauch recalled, "but Al handled the budget so nobody really knew what we could afford. I remember Al said, 'See if you can get any furniture for the place,' so Ollie and I rummaged through the hotel and stole tables and chairs from a ballroom and took it up in the service elevator. There was this big oak conference table we found, which we used to haul every year up to our training camp in Santa Rosa."

Most of the budget went toward recruiting players, and Al sent the assistant coaches out across the country that winter and spring. Often, though, they found themselves high and dry in the hinterlands.

"Al gave us this big pep talk about the job we gotta do on the road," said Rauch, "and then he'd give us air travel cards through United Airlines. He said we'd be able to use the cards to pay for cars and hotel bills. Well, after I got out on the road, I found out the hotels and the car people won't take the card, and I'm $2,500 in the hole. When I got home I told him and he said, 'Well, let's wait for the bills to come in,' and, Jesus, I got a dozen or more letters from collection agencies threatening lawsuits. Eventually, it got taken care of but, shit, for a time I didn't know if I'd be able to keep up my house payments. For Al, payin' people off was way down the list of priorities."

Those "people" also included the players, even Art Powell, who with roommate Clem Daniels would stage a series of training camp holdouts in the ensuing years before Al—extremely comfortable in the dictator's robes—relented and paid his two most valuable players slightly more than table scraps. In giving players the newfound Raider spiel, Al used other inducements than money, well-polished ones dating back in theme to the Citadel era. The highest draft choice the Raiders signed that year was their number seven, Dave Costa, a wild-eyed defensive tackle from Utah who was a first-round pick of the Rams as well.

"Al told me that they were gonna name a bridge after me," Costa rasped in recollection. "He said, 'Leo Nomellini is nothin',' " referring to the 49ers' huge defensive tackle, a future Hall of Famer. "He said, 'You're gonna be better than Leo Nomellini and one day they'll name a bridge after you in San Francisco.' "

Unlike most of Al's prey, Costa was unfazed by the Davis manure dray. "Nah. Hey, I'm from New York, too, from Yonkers. Brooklyn's just a couple miles down the street. I said, 'I know what I'm dealin' with,' and I think that's why we got along. He wasn't gonna put no boogie-woogie on the king of rock 'n' roll."

Costa did play for Oakland, he said, after the foursquare, no-bull pitch of Wayne Valley. But he would learn this of Al Davis: "He was the best coach I ever had. I tell you, he really knew football."

At the outset, this was something Al had to prove to his motley crew. Discredited by losing and rejection, censured as incorrigibles, many of these men were wary of authority—now personified for them much the way he had as a fast-talking PFC/coach with a staff car at Fort Belvoir. Assembling under a hot July sun at the Raiders' training camp in Santa Rosa, Raiders new and old were fed heavy rations of motivational pablum. With all the dynamics of group therapy, they spent nine weeks in the secluded suburb having their negative dispositions reordered, inoculated by a rasher of drumbeatlike maxims that few could know would one day become uppercase Raider synonyms.

" 'Pride and Poise,' that came in from day one," recalled Clem Daniels, whose bank account was down to fourteen dollars after he failed in Canadian football before finding redemption of a sort with the Raiders. "You know, 'We are the Oakland Raiders and we have pride and poise. We have a commitment to excellence.' And on every itinerary, next to the time of the game, was 'We Go to War!'

"See, Al was an enthusiast of military tactics and I was a military man, I held a second lieutenant's commission in the army. And we'd sit around and talk about the great generals and strategies in war. Al knew *all* the battles, and he applied a lot of those lessons in terms of football, breaking a team's will, striking hard and fast."

Others were less convinced that the slogans and doggerel had any hard significance for football. Dalva Allen, one of the holdover Raiders—and a raw-necked Texas guy in the mold of the Fort Belvoir crackers—said, "The first dealings I had with Al Davis, I thought he was full of shit. I thought he was the most arrogant . . . I thought, that guy won't last through the exhibition season. It wasn't just what he was sayin', it was just the whole take-charge attitude didn't ring true. It just seemed like he was one of the boys. He tried to come off tough, but he just kinda laughed and joked and was generally full of shit. All he'd ever been was something like a third-team wide receiver in junior high or somethin', and Al just didn't look like a football player or a football coach."

And still there was method in every bit of Davis's words and moves. Again, without option—but also by inclination—Al was not averse to the chain-gang nature of his roster, and he had to relate to and use it somehow in the pursuit of winning football. While Al had his disciplinary strictures, he let the players—among whom were several whose sleep was sometimes cushioned by the sawdust on taproom floors—determine their own incentives to comply.

"He *was* a dictator," said Ollie Spencer, "but he did a great job of coverin' up that he was to the players. He's a pretty good salesman and he was willing to give up some of the easy things, the dress codes and so on. While everybody else was wearin' suits and ties on the road, Al—who hated that himself—let guys skate on that and they would think they were gettin' away with something. The real important things he was always strict on, the football stuff."

John Rauch saw a real benefit in true crazies being allowed to blow off steam after hours. "[Fullback] Alan Miller and [defensive back Claude] 'Hoot' Gibson would have their little beer parties and sometimes one thing led to another, but they never got into any real serious trouble. And Al was smart enough to know when to let guys have off. The rest of the time they worked their asses off and when he gave 'em a little time off, he knew they were gonna run to the closest bar—but he knew what bars they were at. If he wanted to find 'em, he could."

"Some of the guys broke curfew, but they got fined and they didn't care," explained Jim Otto, the wondrous center whose rapacious presence was enhanced by the semi-eponymous "OO" he wore as his uniform number. "Al had his set of rules and we were supposed to live by 'em: be in by eleven o'clock; if you're not, you're fined. Then you're fined for every minute after eleven, three dollars per minute. We worked hard and we played hard, but we were controllable. I was never bound to my room, but I never got fined either."

Dave Costa, on the other hand, paid enough fines to finance a small country. On one particular foray, he emerged from a bar that was around the corner from the Raiders office. "I came out drunker than shit about midnight and I bumped right into Al Davis—I mean, literally, bumped into him—and he pushed me back inside. He says, 'Get back in that bar,' and he just kept on walking down the street.

"I think, y'know, that's that New York street-tough stuff, you know what I mean? As long as you played and did your job, man. It was like, I got a bunch of rebels out there, so what. As long as you could play, that's all he cared about."

"That's the same old military mentality," Daniels reiterated. "You go out and you have a beer before you go to war. That's the way Al ran it, like a military base"—although, unlike his courtly officer-gentleman pose at the Citadel, now he was an unabashed foot soldier, Drill Sergeant Davis.

"He'd get into it with you, with his mouth," Daniels said. "You know, Al's mouth wasn't the cleanest in the world. He'd say, 'Hey, you cocksucker, you don't know what you're talkin' about,' and I'd tell him the same thing, give it right back to him.

"This was all geared to getting you involved. He would talk to you about *anything*. He'd solicit your opinion. Before a game or at halftime, he would always come up to you and say, 'What do you see? What do you think you can do?' And I could respect that, and if I recommended something and he put it in, that was more incentive for me to make the damn thing work.

"Al Davis felt that he had athletes who could think, and it was like a shock to many of us. Back in the fifties and early sixties, most coaches felt that the players couldn't think, that they had to make all the calls because the players couldn't do that. But with Al, if you have something on your mind, he'll talk to you about it. You don't have to pull punches with him. You may end up cussin' each other out, but at least he'll listen."

An example of how far Al could bend while listening—and of his tunnel-vision quest for winning—was Bob Mischak, the player traded for Dan Ficca. Another military man, out of West Point, Mischak was, like Costa, familiar with the Davis archetype, having grown up in Union, New Jersey. Mischak had also been around the football block, a veteran of Paul Brown's system in Cleveland

and Vince Lombardi's line instructions while with the Giants. Now in his thirties, Mischak was in no mood for an Al Davis.

Midway through that first camp, Mischak, under torrid Davis criticism, sought out Al in his office and told him, "I respect you as a coach, Al, but I don't like you worth a shit as a man."

The two of them—Mischak the irritable soldier, Davis the prickly play-actor—often clashed. Yet Mischak played three seasons for the Raiders, having switched back to guard after one year. And in future years, Al would hire Mischak as an assistant coach—two separate times. "Al always said, in fact, he told me this," Clem Daniels said, "that Mischak was one of the smartest ballplayers ever to come into the game. So I wasn't surprised when he brought him back as a coach."

Indeed, while some of Al's assistant coaches were strong personalities—Charlie Sumner, for one—and others were mere sycophants, *all* would be savants of "Raider Football." To be useful to Al, a player or a coach could be just about anything but an imbecile. "He loved to test you, to see if you knew what you were doing," Ollie Spencer said. "If you had an idea, he'd say, 'Well I wouldn't do it that way,' and you'd have to justify it. And he might not mean what he said but he wanted to be sure you thought the thing all the way through."

In Santa Rosa, the Raiders learned the game from the inside out. Players practically lived with their position coaches, while Al flitted from one meeting room to another, dotting i's and crossing t's. The practice field was the great synod, with Al in his black sweatsuit overseeing workouts.

Sometimes an hour could be spent rerunning a single play, on the geometry of every step; a simple change of angle in relation to the parallel white lines, he stressed, could add yards to that play. "I mean, it was even down to what foot you moved first," said Dalva Allen. Fully installed, the denominator of Raider Football was the deep, killing strikes of the "lateral" game—though in the emerging Raider methodology, Al distanced himself from Sid Gillman by renaming it the "vertical" game. The knockout punch, of course, was to be the whippetlike Art Powell, the unrenamed X end. Shooting downfield, he would, like Lance Alworth, run letter-perfect routes, but to deeper destinations.

"Al was more committed to the deep throw," Spencer said. "Al's brand of ball is, the deeper the better, and the running backs always had to catch and be able to go deep. Nowadays, there's a whole bunch of 'em who do but he was way ahead of his time with that."

"I can't recall that we actually patterned a bomb-type offense right from the beginning," John Rauch clarified. "When we made out our game plan, it involved what we would do when we got to the other team's twenty-yard line, because we knew when we got closer to the twenty, they would start playing more man-to-man coverage and we could get the ball into the end zone quick.

"But Art was such a classic receiver. He didn't appear to be fast but he had a lope that was deceiving to defensive backs, and you'd get him on a five-seven, 175-pound guy and he'd take the ball away from him. You could just lay it out there. So we had him come out on a quick post pattern. He'd go down eight, ten yards and make a break to the inside and if you'd get the ball in there close, he'd pick it out of the air.

"But, as far as a big-bomb attack, to be honest we really didn't know what the heck we had. We wanted to play good defense— which we didn't—and we did have in our minds that we had to be strong in the front lines, and that's where I think Al worked the hardest at picking up people to improve the ballclub."

Said Clem Daniels: "The average team runs their patterns from twelve to fourteen yards. The Raiders run theirs from eighteen to twenty. So that means the offensive line has to block longer. We always stressed that we gotta hold for four seconds before the ball is thrown. Most teams hold for two seconds and they expect the ball to be gone. That's why the 49ers are so successful now; they hold that damn ball for four or five seconds, and the offensive line is able to do that. Well, the Raiders were able to do that for years. If you can't block for four seconds, you can't play with the Raiders."

Luckily, fate had dealt Davis an ace in Jim Otto. In working with the linemen, Al knew he had the penultimate cogwheel for his old rule blocking scheme. One of the AFL's profound success stories, Otto was an undrafted, 200-pound center when he came out of The University of Miami (Florida) in 1959. Signed as a free agent, he had bulked up to 250 when—even with the handicap of his team—he made All-League in 1960 for the first of nine straight times. It was almost impossible to knock Otto off his feet, on which he was so light that, leading sweeps around the corner, he seemed to do a buck and wing aligning for the best hitting angle.

Seeing this, Al at once inculcated his "line quarterbacking" system—focused almost exclusively on Otto, who was to call nearly all the blocking patterns. "There were some things that the guards would call, like if there was a sudden shift of the defense and they could see it better," Otto recalled, "but, yeah, I used to call all the blocking for the line and a lot of the backs and the tight end. Almost everybody does that today, but back then nobody did. Obviously, I'd never done, or seen, anything like that before and here I was an All-Star and I was getting a whole new system.

"For a while, it was hell on me. I used to wake up in the middle of the night callin' out blocking signals. I'd scare my wife half to death. And then, even when I got it all, Al would keep adding different things."

"The rule blocking," Ollie Spencer mused. "That was something he stole from somebody. Al probably didn't have an original thought in his mind about football, and you can tell him I said so. But he talked to everybody and, hey, if you wanna find out something, go to the best. That was Sid Gillman, and Sid always said that if an idea was good enough, somebody should steal it."

Al's thirst for the clean, swift beheading of jackals in his midst—in pungent contrast to his extended neck-stroking of loyal allies—was a grim subtext in Santa Rosa. Weeks before camp began, Al, who understood that Al LoCasale chose to stay in a good job in San Diego, had hired a scout/personnel assistant out of the Canadian Football League named J. I. Albrecht. After just one week in Santa Rosa, thinking Albrecht was trying to take undue credit for the trades and signings, Al fired him on the spot. "But he didn't do it," Spencer emphasized, "until he'd pumped the guy for all the information he had." This information would later reap some important players from Canada.

He then replaced Albrecht with a twenty-four-year-old editor of a pro football magazine in Texas, Ron Wolf. Wolf was obsessed with football and could usually predict draft selections accurately round after round. But perhaps more important to Al was that Wolf had been an army intelligence officer in West Berlin in the late fifties and a history major at Oklahoma. Like LoCasale, his eyes were like Xerox machines, and his evaluations of potential player trades took into account the *motives*, as well as the front office IQ, of the other teams. He had no great attachment to winning with grace.

Most of all, he was uninfected by the football job rat-race and he was a good soldier. He would serve his master, gladly.

The real stir of training camp, though, came just one week before the first game of the season. Although the Raiders won three of five exhibition games, Al had been unhappy with his starting offensive tackles, Charlie Brown and Jack Stone. With no compunction, he cut both and picked up two vets with middling credentials, Dick Klein and Frank Youso. Coming so late, this caused a conniption among the players, who couldn't be sure of *their* security or Raider stability.

"I woke up and those two guys were gone," said quarterback Cotton Davidson, "and I thought, 'What the hell is he doin'? It's a week from the opening game. Where does that leave us?' It really shook us up, but when I talked to him that morning he said, 'I didn't feel like we could win with those guys.' " To John Rauch, that was all the explanation needed. "Those two guys," he agreed, "didn't have a big winning attitude."

The charged-up newcomers, joining seventeen other fresh Raider faces, stepped into the opener against the Oilers and played the whole game, effectively. And the Raiders as one, knowing now that Al would accept nothing but full raging effort, went into the game a two-touchdown underdog and practically set Jeppesen Stadium afire with the vertical game and won 24–13. Art Powell, soaring like a great cleated cormorant, migrated through the Oiler secondary with 181 yards worth of pass yardage, seven yards shy of the club record.

Eight days later, in the Frank Youell ricketyshack, they demolished the Bills 35–17, with Cotton Davidson passing for 315 yards—most of which went not to Powell but to Clem Daniels (172), whisking far out of the backfield past startled and overmatched linebackers and defensive backs.

Rare as it was, the good Raider fortune could hardly have mattered less in the grand scale of pro football, or even the AFL. On paper, this was still a team of blown tires held together by baling wire. Even so, the Raiders themselves were thinking some audacious thoughts. "Al Davis brought us a winning philosophy, which is the only way you win," said Davidson, a twenty-nine-year-old veteran at the time. "He gave us an offense that we had a chance to win, and I don't think I ever came into ballgames better prepared to handle whatever confronted me. When he walked on the field, you felt like things were gonna happen, that we were gonna win and win quick."

Even Dalva Allen came around rapidly. "I started respectin' him when we realized that he really had somethin' on the ball. Looking back, I know he was the most brilliant football mind that I ever played for, and I played for a lot of 'em."

A belly-jigglin' laugh. "Now I'm not sayin' he *ain't* full of shit, and I'm not blowin' smoke on him, tryin' to brave up to Al or nothin', but he was the most brilliant football mind of any coach I ever played for."

He convinced me that his ideas on what an end can do jibed with mine. Al Davis can talk an athlete's language.

—Art Powell

I'm going to dominate, but I have to be intelligent enough to adjust to cultures. I understood the sixties, the black renaissance. You didn't have to give anything [to athletes] in the fifties and early sixties. They accepted everything. But once you saw the Catholic Church starting to give—and there's no more paramilitary group than that—you knew it was time to change.

—Al Davis

After the win over the Bills—before 17,568 fans, a good 5,000 more than had ever seen a Raider home game—George Ross and Scotty Stirling clambered into the locker room flushed with glee. "It was very exciting to us," Ross said. "We hadn't seen many wins in Oakland." But they found Al in a less than festive mood. Far too sensible to get carried away, Al told them, "Hey, you guys, don't put the balloons up. We haven't done anything yet."

He was right. The next week, the Patriots came in and beat the Raiders 20–14. True, it was a close enough game to keep a roll going, except that for the following three weeks the team had games on the road, a long road—to save on transportation costs, they played successive games in New York, Buffalo, and Boston. The timing could not have been less helpful.

Over the first few weeks, "the league sort of went to sleep on

Davis," Ross said. "Really, what he had was a wired-together front four, an inverted linebacker playing tight end, and a decoy as one wide receiver. And he was changing things around week to week, because he had to. The game films that the other teams studied weren't gonna tell them much because Al had changed his defense around so much. He confused everybody away from the basic fact that they weren't a very good football team."

The road was the great equalizer, where a lack of skill could not be disguised. For seventeen days, the Raiders' shortcomings were magnified by conditions that could not have been any worse on the Lewis and Clark expedition.

"We lived like gypsies on those East Coast trips," recalled John Rauch. "We'd have to find places to practice because those teams wouldn't let us use their stadiums. So we'd go to some playground or something. One time in Boston we got off the bus and were out there in this public park warmin' up and here comes about ten buses loaded with kids, little kids in football uniforms, and they said, 'This is our field, you can't stay here.' And then a police car comes over and the cops tell us, 'You guys gotta get off this field, it belongs to the kids.' So that's the way we lived, third rate, and that's how we would play during that time."

Still, the losses were not unreasonable—10–7 to the Jets, 12–0 to the Bills, again 20–14 to the Patriots. But with a 2–4 record reminiscent of past years, it might have been crisis time if Al had not shown particular calm and strength. "He just kept on an even keel, that it was gonna turn around, and I guess that's what made me realize that he wasn't just a flash-in-the-pan type of coach," said David Allen. "He just kept on, matter-of-factly, like 'just keep workin' toward your game plan.' Al always had his sights right. He didn't ever care whether we won an exhibition game or not. It was when the season started, then it was 'win, baby, win.' "

The fulcrum of the season was the homecoming game at Frank Youell Field, against the Jets. Al's pep talks had become *too* matter-of-fact lately, as cool as his normal sideline pose—stoic, tense lips puckered, a Rodinesque hand cupped under his chin—but before this one he ladled Pride and Poise as though out of a soup kettle. "He broke a sweat on that one," Clem Daniels said.

Catching the fire, the Raiders won 49–26 as Daniels ran for 200 yards, which stood as a club record for twenty-four years. Now the Raiders had three wins and three different ways of doing it—first with the X end, then with the halfback out deep, then with the ground game. For Al this presented an encouraging prelude to the next game, the biggest one in his life to then—against the Chargers in San Diego. The Chargers, though, hardly noticed. They had beaten the Raiders all six times they'd played, some of the scores being 52–28, 44–0, and 41–10. The Chargers were 5–1 so far in 1963, and this game had the look of another walkover.

But the Raiders scored first, a twenty-yard pass to Art Powell, and when they fell behind 10–7 they came right back down the field and Alan Miller took a dump-off pass in to make it 14–10. With little workable defense—the biggest defensive play was a blocked point after touchdown by the Raiders—this was how Oakland would have to play it, coming from behind, and Al had thought of just such scenarios before the season.

To maximize offensive diversity, he had decided to go with two proficient quarterbacks, neither one more entrenched than the other. The usual starter was twenty-five-year-old Tom Flores, the son of immigrant Mexicans and an original Raider who had to sit out the previous season with a serious lung infection. But whenever he faltered, Davis sat him and sent in Cotton Davidson, a twenty-nine-year-old veteran who had played three years with the Colts and was an AFL All-Star in 1961 with the Dallas Texans. Asked about the efficacy of alternating quarterbacks, Al would say, "They won't keep us out of the end zone." And they did not.

"Flores was an excellent deep passer," said George Ross, "a very courageous player who played hurt a lot. And Davidson, sitting on the bench during the first half, would see where he could go with the ball and was able to come in and throw under the defenses a little more and begin changing the tempo around. They won a lot of games with that system." And Davidson—who threw hard enough to lacerate a receiver's chest—made the All-Star game even with limited playing time. He and Flores were also close, their resentments about not playing full-time suppressed for the benefit of the system.

Al again called on Davidson in San Diego when the Chargers regained the lead just before halftime. Backed up near his own goal line at the start of the third quarter, Davidson threw a pass that was intercepted and run into the end zone by Dick Harris. Dying with each down, Al's poise became unwrapped. "He came running down the sideline and was chewing me out all the way back to midfield," Davidson recalled. "He was yelling, 'You chunkhead, you,' but the thing was, he stuck with me and that gave me a lot of confidence."

And on the next series Davidson threw a thirty-nine-yard touchdown pass to speedy wide receiver Dobie Craig to cut the deficit to 23–21. Then, after a Charger field goal, Davidson hit Art Powell with a forty-six-yard heave to go up 28–26. Again the Chargers broke back, Keith Lincoln running fifty-one yards for a 33–28 lead with less than two minutes left. His nerve dripping like vinegar, Davidson cranked up for one last shot, but—looking pass—the Chargers allowed Clem Daniels a wide roadway up the middle and his forty-one-yard run put the ball on the nine-yard line. With time running out and drama running high, Davidson then found halfback Glenn Shaw with a dart over the middle. Touchdown. Game, 34–33.

With the victory and Sid Gillman's congratulatory handshake in the bank, *now* Al could plant the Raider banner in the belly of the AFL. Bathed in hard sweat, he screamed "We've arrived!" to George Ross in the dank and delirious locker room. And, in fact, at this stage of their awakening, little pebbles of significance were starting to collect in their path. There were *lines* now at the thimblesized Raider ticket office on Madison Avenue, Raider bumper stickers could be seen up and down the Nimitz Freeway, and newspaper ads even in the San Francisco papers were offering swaps of 49ers tickets for a place in the splintered bleachers at Youell Field.

By happy coincidence, as the Raiders were taking flight in 1963, the NFL cornerstone team across the water was en route to a lastplace finish. And this was just as the Davis name was becoming a neat little juggernaut in the media. As an emolument for winning in Oakland, the Davis *style* was getting national exposure. In late October, the name appeared for the first time in *Sports Illustrated*, in the Walter Bingham "I Don't Need Money, I Need Points" article. This piece was more puffery than a study of Davis, a true bamboozle job by Al that—as happened with many other journalists he stroked along the nation's football meridians—made Bingham go over the edge, as goofy in his truckling as a tumbling, rolling borzoi:

> [Davis] is a tall, good-looking man with powerful arms and shoulders which he keeps hard by lifting weights in his cellar. He has white,

shining teeth and blond, wavy hair which, despite constant attention, is receding on either side of the middle. Stand him on a pedestal and there he is, Mr. America.

With an examination as cooperative as this, Al was free to stack the bricks of his nascent legend. There was rare candor about his undistinguished athletic grounding—oddly, at a time when Raider promotional materials presented the requisite "three-sport letter-man" bunk, Al admitted otherwise to Bingham, but with a vitiating self-defense.

"I really wasn't much of an athlete," he said. "It would be in-accurate to say I started or anything like that. . . . I didn't get along with coaches—you follow me. I didn't feel that I was understood."

He went on: "I majored in English, but it was pointless. I re-member thinking, what am I studying English for when all I want to do is coach. . . . I don't want to give the feeling I'm above and beyond, but I've always had the perception to understand these games. Do you follow me? I was the organizer."

Then there was Bingham on the Davis mien:

Davis, the salesman, speaks in a soft, persuasive voice, looking his listener in the eye. "Come in, sit down and let me tell you some lies," is one of his opening gambits. He often closes a conversation with, "Hey, give me your right hand." It is slick, but friendly and apparently genuine. . . . [T]he word "sell" itself is active in Davis' vocabulary. "The owners sold me on the idea that they would spend more money for players," Davis said recently. And to his team: "This is what I'm trying to sell you on. Let them have the short gains."*

People on the Raiders would read this persiflage, see the evolving caricaturization of Al Davis as a bold New Frontier icon, and giggle among themselves. In the gaze of many, Mr. America was a front, a put-on, a cover blown every day they saw him struggling with insecurities swollen by billowing success.

"There was always two levels to Al," John Rauch surmised. "A lot of times you heard things from other people and then you'd see

---

*Sports Illustrated, November 4, 1963, pp. 27–29.

things. You always thought, you know, that he worked out with weights but he didn't like to have anybody *see* him work out because he's really not that strong; he's got skinny legs and he doesn't have an athlete's body. If he did lift weights, I don't think it helped him too much."

"Oh yeah," said Dave Costa, still in hysterics, "in training camp he'd put a bunch of weights on the bar and sit in his room with like three hundred pounds on his little bedspread, sit there with a towel around his neck and make believe he was liftin'. Somebody would walk by the room and he'd go *aaargh* like he just got through workin' out, the fuckin' guy. I mean, he had a *big* complex about lookin' strong for everybody."

It was around this time that Al took to living behind his dark glasses much of the day. If he was hiding his betraying eyes, he may also have been shading another insecurity. "Al needed to wear glasses," Costa said, "but he thought that would make him look less like an athlete, so he wore prescription sunglasses and it was like he was Joe Cool."

So, while one caricature was embedding itself in the football loam, another was rising in the Raider subsoil—an Al Davis fleeing his real self. It was the prepared image of him that he wished to stick and instruct. "He *was* like Mr. America when he got to Oakland," George Ross said. "He looked like a boy, a good-looking boy. And, Christ, you didn't know whether to believe this guy was capable of walking on water.

"But there's a misconception about Al, like his body. Very early he got on weights and he's got a great upper body. People say that he wears padded jackets. I don't think so. He's built like a horse from the waist up. But from the waist on down, Al is very sparse. He's got skinny legs and a flat butt. And he had an order that none of the coaches on the field, even up at hot Santa Rosa in August, could wear shorts. They all wore long pants and he wore the same."

Living daily with Al's quirks, it was possible that these people would come to define him with a weird freeze-frame totally irrelevant to football. "It's crazy but the one thing I remember most about him was the goose grease he puts in his hair," John Rauch confessed. "He always had that little can of grease and he'd put it in the back of his hair, make it like a ducktail, and it would stand straight up."

So piquant were these deviations that it was as though Al was fitting himself into an aberrant contour of the world in which he could live contentedly. If he was "weird," it was only because no one else could occupy this space. And once inside there, his insecurities could be made to seem like pieces of inscrutable genius. That was why Al Davis believed he *was* a genius. He had to.

"When you're with him for a long time, you see that Al is really a shy person," Rauch ventured. "He always picked his spots for appearances very carefully."

"I don't know about shy but certainly he's a sensitive man," Ross decided. "A guy who would not want to seem to be a bully, even though he is."

Given his ego and need to be noticed, Al could sustain a heroic pose under layers of protective camouflage and not have to stand naked in the revealing spotlight. That way, beneficially, one could never think he *had* any inner clackings of weakness. "He likes the mystique," Ross said. "He likes to be able to walk away from a scene and know that behind him all the heads are gonna follow."

While Al could be equally abstruse in player moves and information-gathering, the rampaging Raider passing attack of 1963 and beyond was not concerned with deception or hidden motives. Like a raw nerve, it throbbed in and through the open air. With Davis's verticals keeping pace with Sid Gillman's laterals in San Diego, Art Powell would lead the AFL in receiving (1,304 yards) and touchdowns (16); five other Raiders would have over 200 receiving yards. Tom Flores passed for 20 touchdowns and Cotton Davidson 11. In the end, the Chargers finished the season with 24 more yards passing than the Raiders—but Oakland had three more aerial touchdowns, 31 to 28; and though attempting 85 more passes, and longer passes, had precisely the same number of interceptions (24).

If there was one key to this long-ball efficiency, it was Clem Daniels. A remarkable anomaly, Daniels became a running back after starting his career as a linebacker, and when the Raiders put him in the backfield in 1961 their wisdom was as inspired as it was rare. At 6-1 and 220 gristly pounds, Daniels ran the hundred-yard dash in 9.8 seconds, and anyone who got in his way on the field felt as if he'd met the front end of a cement mixer. If Powell's speed deceived defensive backs, when Daniels began rumbling past them it must have seemed as if they were mired in mud. "Clem fit in just perfect for Al's type of offense," said Rauch, "because we liked to throw the ball to the back out of the backfield whenever we knew that there was man-to-man coverage by the linebacker, and with Clem it was a mismatch. And if they doubled up on Art you could throw to Clem thirty, forty yards down the field."

Thus, Al often sent him out on a wing, in endless permutations of a formation called "East," which could embrace as many as five receivers. Five times in 1963 Daniels took a pass all the way, and his average per catch was an astounding *twenty-three* yards. And this was by and large a sidelight; running the ball 214 times, second-most in the league, Daniels rushed for a league-high 1,099 yards.

For Daniels, as for all the Raiders, it was football so new that it was almost scary to be part of it. What was so scary was that it could not have been simpler in essence. "Al's philosophy was to go for the end zone, and when they stopped that, take whatever's left," he said. "Art and I were able to open up that offense. We were so good that we were isolating a back on a linebacker or a safety, because most safeties I could beat. We had enough flexibility where the backs could call plays at the line for themselves.

"There were other teams that tried to utilize similar concepts but these were limited editions of it—they didn't get the whole concept. It was a matter of subordinating the call to the players and what they saw. It's not just running a play; it's knowing *when*. And nowadays it's so sophisticated the players are almost forgotten in the call; all the communication is between the coaches.

"The stuff Al came up with . . . we would put three wide receivers on the same side, with Art in the slot between a wingback like me and a wide receiver; or you'd have two tight ends on the same side and you'd flare the running back and *another* tight end to the weak side and you'd have five wide receivers out. Art would kinda get lost in the crowd coming out and, bang, he'd go to the corner and be able to walk into the end zone."

The problem with the Raiders was in Al's least favorite distraction—defense, the temper of which was shaped, with Al's full assent, by Charlie Sumner. As defensive back coach, Sumner's prize piece of work was All-League cornerback Fred Williamson. At six-three and 215 pounds, Williamson was bigger and stronger than most defensive backs; in college he was a shot-putter and he also ran the hundred yards in 9.7 seconds. He also had a vicious streak that Sumner exploited to the max—Williamson would use his forearms as truncheons to smash ball-carriers across the face-mask. Dazed and with his teeth loosened, the victim would then

have to hear Williamson trash him verbally about getting too close
to his "hammer," which became his nickname.

Amazingly, the more the Hammer was associated with this subtle
technique, the fewer penalties were called on him and the less often
other teams would try to take him out—the way they tried to do
with the more peaceable Art Powell, by cutting him at the knees
when he sprang into his routes. It was as though molestation was
made acceptable by its sincerity, and this played right into Sumner's
hands.

"That was Charlie's tactic, usin' that hammer," John Rauch said.
"They used that with the old Chicago Bears and Charlie used to
teach it. Of course, Freddy kind of exaggerated it a great deal. It
was, when you're gonna make a tackle, make the guy know it, and
one way to ensure you're gettin' your arm around him is that you
come with the hammer. Later they made that illegal, you couldn't
strike the guy above the shoulder, but then it was like a wrestling
match and talkin' a lot of shit: 'Hey, I'm out here, baby, come my
way and I'll hammer you.' If you did that back in the old days,
somebody would break your leg under the pile."

In the coagulating sixties, however, this passed for defensive
philosophy all around the AFL—mainly because the alternative
was letting receivers waltz across the open field in peace. In 1963,
with similar numbers for years to follow, all but one AFL team
scored an average of *at least* three touchdowns a game. The *only*
defense, it seemed, was to try to scare people about what would
ensue *after* they caught the ball—yet roughing penalties would often
set the defense back more. "We wanted to be known as an aggressive
team," Rauch said, "but we weren't what you'd call intimidating;
that came later, when the defense was good enough for penalties
like that not to hurt us. But we kept playin' the same style."

Still, no amount of yard-letting stopped Al from devising, almost
as a hobby, Rube Goldberg–style defensive schemes with the over-
think of his offensive quilts but little of their workability.

"Al played a lot of crazy coverages," Rauch recalled. "It was his
big toy to come up with crazy things, which used to drive me up
a wall because a lot of times we'd end up with a guy not covered.
But we had 'em fooled enough that they wouldn't pick us apart all
the time." In fact, true to form, some of Al's notions were light
years ahead of the game, if only in concept.

"People talk about the nickel defense being new," said Rauch, referring to five-defensive-back alignments, mostly used on sure passing downs. "Well, Al had a defense called 'The Five Brothers.' That was five defensive backs—although it wasn't in a passing situation. And he had the 'Backers Four,' which was a four-man front and four linebackers, which predated the 3-4 defenses by several years."

Even so, these figurations rarely worked then. "I remember we were playing the Patriots and we had 'em down something like 27–3 at halftime and we were usin' all these crazy coverages and we had 'em all confused but something was wrong. I was up in the press box seeing these breakdowns and I told Al at halftime, 'Al, in a couple of these coverages, nobody's covering the tight end.' And he said, 'Nah, they'll never figure it out.' Well we had to kick a field goal with about thirty seconds left to win something like 42–39. They had figured it out and they started bombin' us out there, pickin' us apart. But he was always . . . it was like writing those articles. He thought he knew it all."

Offensively, it seemed he did. The formulae he created to hide gaps in talent were sound—and bestial—in practice as they were in theory. One such procedure he devised the week before the Charger game, aimed at the mammoth Ernie Ladd. Although Wayne Hawkins was a marvelous guard, he stood barely six feet tall, a pygmy next to the six-nine, 312-pound monster he'd have to contain. Accordingly, Al concocted a blocking mode appropriately called "Turmoil," wherein Hawkins took the first shot at Ladd—at the knees, it was stipulated.

"Big Ernie hated anybody to go at his legs," John Rauch explained, "and Wayne would try to cut Ernie's legs out from under him. And when Ernie got untangled from Wayne, Jim Otto would back off and take on Ernie straight up, and then Wayne would get up and wheel around again and chop Ernie from the side—of course now it's illegal to do that stuff. And in the meantime the quarterback took five steps back in the pocket, planted like he was gonna throw, and then he'd start rolling out to the side where Wayne was gonna chop Ernie Ladd down. They did a great job. They had Ernie lookin' all over the place and sayin', 'Where are they gonna come from next?' "

In its effectiveness, the passing game proved Al's and Art Powell's assumptions about attitude versus football. Powell flourished without altering his character. Smiling no more frequently, as separated as ever from team bonding rituals, Powell also "had a big black-white thing," said Ollie Spencer. The Raiders coped with it by ignoring it.

According to Spencer, "Al took that approach with everybody: I'm not gonna dictate what you do and feel but we're gonna depend on you as a football player."

And the truth was, Powell posed far fewer problems to Al than other Raiders did. As versed in his system as they were, a good many Raiders away from the field had the minds and habits of small children. To certain loyal friends Davis would lament about it.

"He told me he could talk to maybe three of those guys adult-to-adult," remarked Bob Wallach, Al's old Syracuse roommate, in whom he still confided. "The quarterback, the backup quarterback, and one wide receiver. Otherwise, he said, 'I can't talk to anybody because they're so dense.' He said that when the guys would stay in motels they would break through the transoms and overturn the rooms. On the plane rides he'd hear the stewardesses screaming; they'd put the stewardesses up in the clothing racks. Al would be embarrassed about them and worry that they'd get themselves thrown in jail."

More worrisome was a frightening and grotesque incident during training camp one of those early years—an eruption of racial hatred that Al simply could not believe would have ever happened on his team. Indeed, there was no slow, curdling buildup of tensions but rather a match struck to an open gas jet. It began when a white player got into an argument with a black player in the locker room as the team was dressing for a workout in Santa Rosa. John Rauch was in the coaches' office when the phone rang. In the locker room, Dick Romanski, the equipment manager, screamed into the receiver, 'Somebody get over here! There's a guy in here with a gun and he's threatening to shoot."

"So I went over there," Rauch recalled, "and sure enough, you had the white guys on one side of the locker room and the black guys on the other side and one guy had a gun and it looked like there was gonna be a messy situation. I had never experienced anything like that before so I just walked into the middle of the thing and said, 'What are you guys doing? Are you all crazy?' Like a fool, I reached out and said, 'Give me that gun,' and the guy handed it to me. Then I said, 'Look, you guys got half an hour to be on the field. Anybody that's not is fined a hundred dollars, so get your asses goin'.' And that was it.

"This had stemmed from what happened in the dining hall involving a black guy and a waitress, some bitch of a waitress, and one thing led to another and we had a couple white guys on the team that were notable rednecks. But here's the thing, it happened and twenty-four hours after that there was a little talk about it here and there, but we never saw anything more of it. And I think Al had a lot to do with that. Things like that didn't fester too long. I mean, at almost every practice we would have one or two fights out there on the field, but nobody took it as a serious thing."

Said Clem Daniels: "It was pretty hot at the time, but Al handled it very well. He called a team meeting and he made it very emphatic, in terms of what he was gonna stand for. He said that prejudice and racial issues would not become a part of the Raiders organization. He really stuck his neck out and took a stand that wasn't all that popular with the white guys."

And not for the only time. During another early training camp, an exhibition game was scheduled between the Raiders and Oilers in Mobile, Alabama. But the week before the game, a San José reporter, Sam Skinner, called the game's promoters and found out that the stadium in Mobile was segregated, with blacks routed into a "special" section way up in the stands. When the story ran, the black Raiders resolved en masse to boycott the game if it were played as scheduled. "I remember that I was the one who went to Al and told him, 'We're not goin' to Mobile,' " Clem Daniels said. "And then Al called the league office and demanded that Joe Foss do something about it. And within three days they decided they would move the game and it was played in Houston."

Davis had no patience for a football establishment turning its back on racism with all deliberate speed. Another time, the AFL All-Star game was slated to be played in New Orleans' Sugar Bowl. But when the same seating restrictions arose and black players on the All-Star team voted to boycott the game, Al again was on the phone to Joe Foss, pushing for the game to be taken away from that city—no matter that powerful interests there were lobbying the league for a franchise. Finally, the game was moved to Houston. New Orleans didn't get an AFL team and instead wound up in the NFL; though some regarded this as a blow to the AFL, the fact that the city was still years away from racial equity made Al Davis believe that New Orleans and the NFL plainly deserved each other.

Not consciously perhaps, but not incidentally, Al also stood to gain from his courage. "He scored a lot of points with the black players around the league," Dalva Allen pointed out, "and there were a lot of black players who just wanted to come play for him after all that. It was one of the most brilliant things he ever did."

For the Raiders, a team that had been a slender thread away from a mortifying racial incident, life went along with a healthy, unifying abandoning of convention—even that of racial etiquette. "I remember during that Mobile thing," Allen said, "I was kiddin' Freddy Williamson. He told me, 'I'm gonna be down there and I'm gonna be up in the stands with a white woman drinkin' beer.' And I said, 'Yeah, and after the game I'm gonna be drinkin' me some beer watchin' 'em hang your black ass.'"

And all the while, these glorious, half-a-bubble social misfits prospered. The Raiders finished the 1963 season at 10–4, one game behind the Western Division and impending AFL champion Chargers—whom they beat twice, the second time a 41–27 thumping in Youell Field. His game plans picked from his pocket by Al, Sid Gillman gave his protégé all due credit, then and now. "Listen, if he beat us, he did a better job than we did," Gillman said. "That's all there is to it."

This shocking consequence earned Al the Coach of the Year award from AP, UPI, and publications on down to the *7-Up Digest*; he was also named Oakland's Young Man of the Year by the Junior Chamber of Commerce. For that, the city did all it could to honor him with a show of gratitude—which, even then, was the crux of something faintly disturbing to Al about the city he had revived: that all the resources of Oakland could not muster more. As Al tried to smile while accepting the city's praise, he silently railed at its limitations.

"Here he was winning all this adulation around the country and they had this little damn parade up Broadway," George Ross remembered, "about ten antique cars and a high school band. Oakland simply did not know how to put a guy on a pedestal, and never would. And while that wasn't all of the problem Al had with the city, of course, I think it stuck a little bit in Al's craw."

As far back as 1963, then, there was a small clue to a very large puzzle to come.

10

A prince being thus obliged to know well how to act as a
beast must imitate the fox and the lion, for the lion cannot
protect himself from traps, and the fox cannot defend
himself from wolves. One must therefore be a fox to
recognize traps, and a lion to frighten wolves.

—Niccolo Machiavelli

Remember John Foster Dulles? . . . He was a one-man
foreign affairs deal. . . . [T]hey tried to pin him down one
time on a certain philosophy about the nuclear bomb. He
didn't use the word *pragmatic*, but he said that every day is a
different situation and you have to say 'I'd rather be right
than be consistent.' I've always used that.

—Al Davis

It was late in the 1963 season when the Camelot dreams of a new
generation of Americans were ended by the cold, dull corpo-
reality of a Mannlicher-Carkano rifle in Dallas. When those gun-
shots tore through history on that day and a young president died,
Al Davis was so shaken that he called off practice and sat ashen in
front of his television for the next three mournful days—the AFL
postponed its games that weekend, the NFL did not—watching
the eclipse of idealism.

A scion of Camelot, Al had considered his and John Kennedy's
fates to be so interwoven that he seemed to fit himself into the First
Family. "I think they were friends," Cotton Davidson said. "Al
used to talk about Kennedy like they knew each other." In what

was already a chilling bell-toll of death all around him, maybe only Louis's hit him harder. And yet, Davis's ensuing fatalism was in a sense a professional aid. Given his function in Oakland—and the seemingly concentric development of the AFL within this irascible decade—their raw idealism needed to crust over now.

Having taken first breath in a New Frontier, the league was in early 1964 turning toward the entrenchment and long-term gains adumbrated by the Great Society. In survival terms, the smashing economic success of the New York Jets and the Kansas City Chiefs (Lamar Hunt's old Dallas Texans) in 1963 was far more important than the Raiders' unlikely season, and prefaced the Richter-scale consequence of the Jets' signing of Joe Namath in January of 1965. The real seeds of survival came exactly a year before that when the league closed a five-year, $36 million deal with NBC—dwarfing the NFL's new two-year, $14 million pact with CBS and stoking each franchise with heavy coin to go after talent.

And in Oakland—fathoms from the power centers where such news was made—Al Davis too was concerned with permanence. Seeking parts for his mechanism, he renovated with careful abandon. Effecting nine trades, again losing little, and signing three of those key "futures" drafted the year before—linebackers Dan Conners and J. R. Williamson and offensive tackle Rex Mirich—the Raiders went 5–7–2 in 1964. Though done in early by another damaging East Coast trip, they played with essentially a *better* team than in 1963. Having traded for Billy Cannon, the first AFL superstar who had become an injury-prone castaway in Houston, Al—perhaps remembering Cannon's long, long pass catch in the 1960 title game—converted him from halfback to tight end.

"Very few tight ends had the burst of speed off the line that Billy did," John Rauch said, "and he was an excellent blocker when he wanted to be; he could move 280-pound defensive ends by himself if he put his mind to it." Cannon caught thirty-four passes, five for touchdowns, and gave the passing game even *more* length—the Raiders led the league by over one hundred passing yards—but it wasn't until the following season that the patchwork, transient look of the team began to solidify in earnest.

Before that season, Wayne Valley had torn up Al's contract and given him a new five-year deal at a substantial raise. And now, with the NBC money kicking in, Al made his first big push on prime college seniors—with the light-footed Al Davis touch of larceny.

As with most teams, he resolved to draft only those whom he

had already signed before draft day. But he took this a step further—he'd try to get them signed before they were eligible to sign, before their college seasons expired. Not willing to gamble with his own and his league's future, Al Davis didn't intend to lose high-visibility players to the NFL, and if that meant he'd have to play fast and loose with the rules yet again . . . well, nobody would know it, not if he had to swear to silence every object in his kingdom.

By the time the Raiders chose their top three draft picks in November of 1964—Memphis State offensive tackle Harry Schuh, Florida State receiver Fred Biletnikoff, and USC offensive tackle Bob Svihus—at *least* the first two had signed before their eligibility ran out, though no one in the league office or in the press would know about it. Twenty-five years later, many if not all of those people still didn't. However, a member then of the tight inner Raider circle—Scotty Stirling—provided some intriguing details in recounting the days when he quit covering the team for the *Oakland Tribune* and began working for Al as the club's public relations man and Al Davis factotum in 1964.

"I signed Harry Schuh in a hotel room in Memphis," Stirling said. "He was ready to sign but I laid out all these greenbacks on the goddamn bed, five thousand of 'em, and he signed."

Schuh, when interviewed for this book, had maintained that the signing took place elsewhere. Told this, Stirling, his voice dipping slightly, said, "Well . . . the reason he told you that was, his season wasn't quite over . . . and we didn't want it known."

Thus, what resulted was an elaborate cover-up lurching over thousands of land and nautical miles and about as many alibis—though at the time and for years afterward the saga vitrified as merely another wacked-out fresco of Al Davis excess, this time in pusuit of an offensive tackle. It *was* that, of course, but only because the quest was over *so* early, and for Schuh with a simple explanation. "I signed with them because of John Rauch," he related. "I'd known John Rauch since I was in the ninth grade in New Jersey and he was at West Point. He asked me if I wanted to play for the Raiders and I said okay."

Needing to keep the signing quiet, Al called back to mind the NFL's effective tool of the early sixties, its "baby-sitting" of seniors, keeping them sequestered from AFL hands so that they could be romanced and signed in peace. In Al's hands, this method now expanded to include police warrants and all-points bulletins. His enemy was the Rams, who would also draft Schuh and were on his tail even as Stirling was on his Memphis mission. If the Rams could sign Schuh they could likely get the Raider signing voided in court, so when Schuh's season ended Al sent Stirling back to Memphis —with lots of money and instructions to get Schuh out of town.

First, Schuh, his wife Joyce, and their baby daughter stopped in New Orleans; then they and Stirling flew to Las Vegas. "That was to be the hideout until draft day," chuckled Schuh—who played ten years of pro ball and never was as famous as he was during this mad excursion—and the location was thought out carefully by Al. As Stirling recounted, "It was West but away from L.A., and it was attractive to twenty-two-year-old kids." Once there, Stirling and Schuh rendezvoused with Ron Wolf—whose cloak and dagger background, merged with Al's obsessiveness, made these kinds of escapades so maniacal—as well as with Maury Schleicher, an ex-Charger linebacker whom Al hired as a Raiders operative because Schleicher had played for the same high school coach as had Schuh.

Clearly, Al was sparing nothing to keep Schuh pacified, yet after only a day in Vegas the Rams caught up to him. Schuh remembered, "My wife had gone to bed and I was sittin' in the casino of the Sands Hotel playin' blackjack and these two fellas walk over. One of 'em says, 'Hi Harry,' and put a card down in front of me with the logo of the Rams. I said, 'I'll be with you in a minute,' and I got up and ran and showed the card to Ron Wolf. And like in a second, he told Maury Schleicher to get a car and call Al Davis. And before I could take a breath, I was in the car with Maury— leaving my wife and daughter behind without a word—going to L.A., then at the airport, and then in two hours I was in Hawaii, on the beach with all these whales lookin' at me."

"The dumb shits," Stirling said of the Rams twosome, as contemptuous now as he was then. "They had him but they hand him a card instead of scurrying him out of there."

And so Schuh and Schleicher would stay in Kalakaua, on the sun-bleached island of Oahu, for a bucolic week while most of America lay frozen in the late November winter. "Oh man, with the ocean out there and all the citrus food around the pool," Schuh looked back, still basking, "I really was in heaven. I mean, when would you ever do something like that again?"

But, meanwhile, back stateside, Schuh was the subject of frenzied activity. When the Rams reported him missing in Las Vegas, the local police found that Schuh's wife had been registered under a false name in a different room and they wanted answers—not that

Joyce Schuh could give them any. Whisked out of Vegas so fast, her husband had not spoken to her since—Al feared her phone would be tapped—though she had been assured by Raider people that he was okay. The very next day, in fact, she had been brought to Oakland, to secretly stay in John Rauch's home while the entire world, it seemed, looked for Harry Schuh.

For that week, no one found him, and—in the role of NFL guardian—Vince Lombardi wondered aloud whether Schuh might have even been kidnapped. That gave Al his biggest laugh of the year, but it prompted New Jersey state police to go to Schuh's parents' home to pump *them* for information. But Al had that covered, too. "He'd already contacted my high school coach and told him to tell my parents I was fine," Schuh said.

During that week, the ruse played out: Schuh was drafted, then "signed"—according to Schuh—in Hawaii, and then he was brought back to meet his new team as they played in snowy Denver. There, months before he first put on a pro uniform, Schuh learned a couple of things about his new coach and the nature of pro ball. "I stood there," he said, "and they were throwin' frozen oranges and beer bottles out of the stands. I knew that when you played in Denver, you'd better keep your helmet on at all times."

And of Al Davis? "Al would always say . . . he'd take his hands, run 'em through his hair, suck air through his teeth and he'd say, " 'Let me just say this, young man. Anything good in this life is worth cheating for.' "

The Fred Biletnikoff scenario was far less extensive, and again a bit different from the official, Davis-told story—which was that he signed Biletnikoff a la Lance Alworth, under the goalpost after the Gator Bowl that year.

"No, I signed him," Scotty Stirling said. "That other thing was all for TV. He was signed by Al under the goalpost but it had already been done three weeks before that. I signed Bob Svihus, too. I did most of the signings and we got everybody we ever wanted. We got [Utah State tackle] Richie Zecher that year too, even though he turned out to be a bust, and we got [Missouri linebacker] Gus Otto—we got everybody. We never lost anybody to the NFL. We lost one guy, Tony Loric, to the Colts. That's the only guy we ever lost. We beat the NFL at every turn."

Al was deadly serious about signing *all* of his picks and turning over every stone to get them. Pat Sarnese, the old Temple lineman and Al's old locker room defender at Fort Belvoir, hadn't heard from Davis in years when, just around Thanksgiving of that year, he picked up the phone in his Philadelphia home and was greeted by Al as though they'd never parted company.

"You gotta get on the plane and get right out here," Al beseeched him.

"But Al, I got my whole family comin' over for Thanksgiving tomorrow," Sarnese told him.

"Well, I got somethin' goin' on you might like. Get down to the airport. There's a ticket waitin' for you. I'll pick you up in San Francisco."

Said Sarnese: "Al Davis can talk you into anything. So I went out there and he was gettin' calls from all over the country where different guys were bein' baby-sat. He had 'em hidden all over. And he wanted me to baby-sit Gus Otto. I took him to San Francisco, took him in and out of a couple of motels in God knows where. I took other guys to Vegas.

"Then the night before the draft I said to him, 'Listen, Al, I'm goin' back home. I'm exhausted and I miss my family,' and he said, 'Okay, but, hey, stay up, let's talk old times,' and I stayed up all night with him and he got a call at about 4:00 A.M. that Harry Schuh was still safely tied up. And damn if I didn't wind up stayin' out there four more days, in case he needed me. He just has that power over you. And then he had me doin' some scouting for him.

"Al Davis is a funny guy. Al has more scouts than anybody. He doesn't need to belong to the scouting combines. He has his own scouting, he had guys like me all over the country workin' for nothin'. I remember that the next year he asked me about a kid named Tom Mitchell, a receiver out of Bucknell. Well, Tom Mitchell went to Plymouth Whitemarsh High School outside of Philadelphia, and his coach and I played at Temple together. And besides me, Al had somebody *else* in this area, so he had Mitchell covered. Mitchell was drafted by the Colts, who are close by, but he played for Al [as a number-three draft pick] and played well for him. That's how Al does it; he got these guys on his side however he could."

And even if it went right down to the last second. The top draft pick two slots ahead of Mitchell in 1966 was Kentucky defensive back Rodger Bird. Unable to sign him before draft day, Al worked on Bird up until and then right *through* the draft. "That's when we passed in the draft for eight or nine hours," Stirling recalled. "I was with Bird, baby-sitting him in Lexington, and Al kept passin' his turn 'cause we were havin' trouble signing him. Finally I did, and it took about nine hours."

What Al couldn't get in the draft he dealt for. Needing to shore up the Raiders' secondary, he had already made a bold move early in 1965—using as bait the darkly effective Fred "The Hammer" Williamson, whose ego had grown along with his press clippings. "Freddy was always presenting this or that little problem," John Rauch said, "and I think it got to where Fred had made the All-League team a couple of times and he was asking for a big jump in salary and his age was mounting up. Then he got an injury and Al just felt he couldn't justify givin' him all that money. And, really, the last few years with us, he went downhill."

Ridding himself of a problem case too much even for him, Al dumped Williamson on Hank Stram in Kansas City. The Hammer got loads of ink there when the Chiefs went to the first Super Bowl—and just desserts when the Packers knocked him cold in that, his last game before taking to acting in blaxploitation movies. Al, meanwhile, gained a real gem in exchange, twenty-five-year-old All-League free safety Dave Grayson, who in 1961 had a record ninety-nine-yard interception return.

Then, in a throwaway deal that would later set the tone of the entire Raider defense, he sent three has-been players to the Oilers for their number-eleven draft pick, Nebraska cornerback Kent McCloughan. He also sent the Bills the little-used and now aging Bo Roberson, whose athletic prowess never really developed on the football field; in return he was delivered twenty-five-year-old Tom Keating, a 250-pound defensive tackle with a latent talent for rushing the quarterback, and guard George Flint.

While Williamson and Roberson were out of football within three years, the younger Raider blue-chippers were moving comfortably into pivotal and enduring roles—at the expense of the stopgap Raiders who hadn't realized how disposable they were. One of them, veteran linebacker Clancy Osborne, became nearly homicidal when he read in the paper during training camp in 1965 that he had lost his starting job to Gus Otto—and took Al's give-and-take largesse a tad too far.

Waking up early one morning, Harry Schuh was walking outside the dormitory building when he heard a crash, spun around, and saw the booted feet of someone who had kicked in the window of

Al's room. "I saw just the two feet but I knew it was Clancy by those cowboy boots and because that old cowboy always got up at the crack of dawn," Schuh recalled. "I got closer and I hear this high-pitched, pleading voice saying, 'I promise you, Clancy, I didn't know nothin' about it. I didn't put it in the paper.' And I look in and there was Clancy Osborne sittin' on top of Al in Al's bed. Finally Clancy came to his senses—but he was gone right after that." And if Al was momentarily stunned by the assault, he had no trouble going right back to sleep. "That kind of thing was life to Al," Schuh said. "That's how it was living with the renegades."

Indeed, the new generation of Raiders, while more skilled, behaved the same way as the older generation under Al's relaxed manner of discipline away from the field. Schuh, entertained and instructed by the redoubtable Dave Costa, would sit in conference with kindred spirits like defensive tackle Dan Birdwell and defensive end Ben Davidson and debate the merits of mayhem.

"Dave was always doin' something weird," Schuh said, "but he was beautiful people. I mean, when he and [tackle] Rex Mirich got together, man, forget it. They got me out one time and one time only—'cause I didn't remember anything the next day. They told me, 'Let's go make a beer run,' and that was the last thing I remembered."

Fondly recalling Birdwell—who played with the Raiders eight years and later died of a sudden and premature heart attack—Schuh paid homage as only a Raider could. "Danny Birdwell was the only guy I knew who could take off his shirt and still have a Mohair sweater on. That guy was the hairiest man I ever saw. But he had the biggest heart in the world and it just busted on him."

In time, six-foot-eight-inch Ben Davidson would himself make hair a cause célèbre. In 1965, though, clean-shaven and thin as a spar, he was in his second year with the Raiders after signing as a free agent NFL reject and close to washing out.

"Ben wasn't very impressive to start with," John Rauch said. "He was only about 230 pounds at that time and he'd been let go by two NFL clubs. In fact, the first year he stayed on the taxi squad. We were probably payin' him like two hundred dollars a week just to stay around because Al liked him. Then in the last game of the [1964] season our right end, Jon Jelacic, got hurt and we moved Ben in there and he got blown out. So the next year I told him, hey, you gotta beef up and get on a weight program."

Ben complied. In 1965 he came in weighing 260, but the big defensive line find that year was 270-pound free agent Ike Lassiter, who was cut by the Broncos only to become a brute in Oakland.

Gradually, Davidson got more action and headlines, and nearly made the All-Star team. Yet while Ben could mount an impressive pass rush with his added bulk, his success was due largely to the less-noticed Lassiter charging hard from the other side. "Ike wouldn't say five words the whole season, he'd just play," Rauch said. "And he wasn't that recognizable because here's big Ben leapin' over blockers and makin' these sacks. But, actually, after lookin at the films . . . nowadays they give credit for a sack and a pressure. Well, Ike would have like ten pressures a game and Ben would have two or three sacks, and what happened was that Ike would be the first one to get to the quarterback and he'd turn away from Ike and run right into Ben."

With those two pincers, most of the Raiders' defensive people went on raw instinct, gambling in the Archie Matsos straying style. When Matsos was slowed by recurring injuries, Al hatched another of his forerunning defensive schemes, this a most practical one. He allowed the six-four, 250-pound Birdwell—a former offensive lineman with speed and a cold predator of a player—to line up either at tackle or end, or in a stand-up linebacker stance. With Birdwell upright, football saw its first three-lineman, four-blitzing-linebacker look—seven years before the Miami Dolphins won two straight Super Bowls using an identical-looking "53" Defense.

When Chuck Fairbanks then brought the strict 3-4 alignment from Oklahoma to the Patriots, with the linebackers going deep in coverage as well as blitzing and plugging up the run, it bred into the standard NFL defense—with one of the last holdouts, ironically, being the Raiders. Uniform speed in the defensive backfield would also be a latter-day NFL standard, and Al was hip to it back then with small but blur-fast Dave Grayson and Howie Williams —like Davidson, a 1964 free agent—now installed at free and strong safety. However, while Kent McCloughan moved in easily at left cornerback, neither he nor the other deep backs weighed as much as two hundred pounds; manhandled by big receivers, they yielded the second-most passing yardage in the league in 1965.

The other side of the line was the most effective side, and its future took half a season to arrive. That was when Harry Schuh and Bob Svihus became the starting tackles. These twin elephants were comfortable with the bog that was the turf at Frank Youell Field. Intricate trap-blocking was useless on grounds frequently sloshed by rain—and Al knew the same would be the case in the now-rising Coliseum—and the Raider blocking game was declared early: it would be straight ahead, a mule train.

"It was like a ball of jelly on the field," Schuh recalled. "You couldn't get traction. You'd be like a big old hog wallowin' in the mud." And still he, like everyone else, combined scholarship and slop.

"There were four different ways of blocking. Al had his odds, evens, treys, deuces; the terminology was fantastic, and if you made a mistake he would ask you why did you make that call, what did you see in your stance, son? Because, standing up, you see one thing, but down in your stance you see something else. He was totally involved in all aspects of the game." And, now, Schuh and Svihus made possible an expansion of communication. "Jim Otto made most of the calls but the tackles would talk to the backs, the tight end, and the guard depending on the play. There was a *lot* of conversation goin' on."

Still, this was primarily old-time power blocking, and the Raiders were masters of it. Later, this meat grinder style would become a mark of the team's manhood when everyone else was going to more finesse blocking. It also more than accommodated the blocking idea that had gotten Al knocked over Don Clark's desk at USC—Absorb with Oomph. Human fire hydrants like Schuh could take the first blow without quailing, then push away onrushing linemen with their bratwurst-thick arms.

Knowing his linemen were flirting with holding almost every down, Al played a game of diversion—with his mouth and wiles. After losing to the Chargers early in 1965, he went public in accusing Sid Gillman of "coaching holding." By this he hoped not only to deflect such suspicion from his own linemen but also to psych out the old man, so as to divert *him* from the verities of beating the Raiders.

In Davis fashion, he went full tilt with the charge. Gillman's linemen, he said, held no less than *75 percent* of the time, and Oilers coach Bones Taylor had agreed with him—thus putting Taylor on the spot the very week his team was going to play the Chargers, who then mauled the Oilers 31–14. Having made the complaint, Al would never back off it, boiling the bad blood already between him and Gillman. Asked about the long-ago accusation, Gillman still bristles as if it had been made yesterday. "I never listen to anything Al Davis says," he snapped.

Any kind of visceral reaction like that was a moral victory to Al Davis, and he would get a lot of them. In November of 1965, *Sports Illustrated* again gazed at Al, again favorably. Yet the piece, by Edwin Shrake, was more tempered and harder-edged than the fatuous Walter Bingham "Mr. America" take. Among its findings were these:

> Davis is a fast man with a waiver list and frequently claims players on other teams are trying to sneak through with injuries. At Buffalo he once held his team in the locker room during TV player introductions while the Bills obediently stood around on the field, and that did not endear him to [Bills coach] Lou Saban. "Davis always acts like he's got some kind of secret information nobody else knows about," an AFL coach says, "and much of the time that's true. He knows the members of every taxi squad in both leagues and what players are having trouble with their coaches, and he's always ready to make a deal, although you'd better look out when you deal with him. But Al has done a fine job."

With Al releasing information as grudgingly as Captain Queeg, the press and sometimes the league office wouldn't know which Raiders were injured or, for days, which ones had been moved. As constantly as queries came in from the press, his response would be smug and insulting, though Scotty Stirling—who said it for him much of the time, as Davis's press windshield—laughed about it years later. "He would say to the press, 'I'm not telling you who I'm cutting. You're here every day in training camp—count heads.' And the smart guys who could count figured it out. Besides, George Halas did the same thing." And yet, at the same time, Al was still using the press as a *collaborator*.

"Al would get together with George Ross the night before a game," John Rauch recalled, "and there'd be player matchups in the Sunday morning paper, and they would always put that the opponent was gonna kill our little guys. They did that just so the other guys, reading the paper at breakfast, would think they wouldn't have to play hard against us."

If Al got off on having it both ways with the press—or was intoxicated being a maestro of manipulation—it may have provided

Al his only moments of hilarity. One anonymous former Raider employee would later say, "Tell him a joke and you'll get a blank look. But if a general manager on another club calls him up and congratulates him on some fast deal he put through, he'll laugh like hell." Stirling, however, believed Al was always too preoccupied with winning to take much joy in exploiting lesser men.

"I think he enjoyed the wheeler-dealer image, but not from any ego rub," Stirling said. "It was because it helped him to do what he wanted to do. He let people focus on an image because it kept them from focusing on what he was really doin'. Everybody got into it. One of the all-time great spreaders of stories was Tom Keating. He used to have fun with it, which is how we thought of it. He used to tell the press all kinds of bullshit things and they'd believe it and write it."

"I got Tex Maule of *Sports Illustrated* one time," recalled Keating. "Tex wasn't very kind to the AFL, and he came in after a ballgame and he started tellin' me about our defense—instead of *asking* me questions, he was tellin' me what we were doin'. We played an 'over' defense, which everyone uses now, a three-man line, and there was a gap between myself and Ben Davidson. So Tex starts sayin' something about how we would 'go to the bubble.'

"And I didn't know what he was talkin' about, but I was goin' right along with him, like, 'Oh yeah, sure—that's what we play, the Bubble Defense.' It was all bullshit but, I mean, if a guy's comin' to ask me about my business and then proceeds to tell me about my business, and he's wrong, I'm not gonna tell him. Let him go make a fool of himself."

Every time a reference appeared thereafter to the club's "Bubble Defense," the Raiders gained a little credibility. And laughed themselves silly.

"I tell you, we used to do a lot of stories just to keep people off balance, because it kept them focusing on stuff that didn't mean anything," said Stirling. "Like that we had listening devices in the locker room and we watered down the field at home to slow down other people, all that kind of crap. We didn't *need* to water the field the way it rained, but why would Al do that? He'd hurt his own team. Why wouldn't people be smart enough to understand that?"

The San Diego "holding" issue was surely a dodge, Stirling said—the real holding grievance Al had was *not* with the Chargers but with the Jets, who beat him to the publicity punch with it. "Weeb Ewbank used to accuse us of holding all the time and no one coached holding as well as Weeb. The best in the world at holding were those Jets, they had to for Namath. But Weeb was smart, too. He had everybody lookin' at us."

Which was why, from the mid-sixties on, Al had written off the Chargers, Oilers, and Bills as his main threats. The menaces now were the Jets of Joe Namath and the Chiefs with their huge front lines, tricky plays, and *really* dirty tactics (when Fred Williamson arrived, *everyone* there began to play with a hammer).

But Al had a new lethal weapon of his own—Fred Biletnikoff, though his accession was delayed. The bright beacons that shone on him under the goalpost at the Gator Bowl had gone dark as the overwound, almost ethereally precise receiver spent the first half of the season fettered by injuries and self-doubt. Biletnikoff did not catch a ball until the seventh game, against the Patriots.

Harry Schuh remembered that moment as though a new binary star had burst into the heavens. "Up to then, they threw passes to him and he dropped 'em, and Freddy *never* dropped balls," Schuh said. "You know when people are really fightin' it and we were rookies together and I knew what he was goin' through. He was really down on himself and then he made this one hellacious catch up over the middle. He jumped up about four feet and made a circus catch and the guy hit him around the ankles and he did a flip in the air and landed on his head, but he held on to the ball. From then on, Freddy was on his go." Biletnikoff, stretching the field to its limit with Art Powell and Clem Daniels, caught seven passes that day for 118 yards, and 17 more over the last seven games.

Not incidentally, the Raiders—with nine rookies on the roster —won five of their last eight games and finished a strong 8–5–1 in 1965. In a year of shifting earth in the AFL, they lost to the last of Sid Gillman's division-winning Charger teams, who went 9–2–3 and twice beat the Raiders (that would not happen again for the next sixteen years). What was affecting about this team was not any strategy but its ethic. "Dan Conners, Gus Otto . . . those guys worked their fool asses off," John Rauch said, "and they were such loyal football players. They loved to practice, loved to just be around the field. And Dan Birdwell was the first guy on the field and the last guy to leave. He'd play anywhere you wanted; he played center, guard, nose tackle, defensive end, linebacker, and he snapped on punts."

And, of course, there was Al Davis.

"He'd be sitting there watchin' films on special teams," Schuh remembered, "and he'd say to no one in particular, 'Young man, be reckless with that body, be reckless!' Then, just before guys would be piling into each other on the screen, he'd jump up and scream, '*Sacrifice yourself!*'

"You just knew when Al's presence was there, 'cause all the watches got rolled back. If he showed up a little late, they all rolled back to the time practice was supposed to begin. Time officially began when Al arrived."

Just in time to showcase the Raiders' turned-up sense of professionalism, the Oakland–Alameda County Coliseum was nearing completion. This horseshoe-shaped stadium and its environs, set to open at the beginning of the 1966 season, was a paradigm of fiscal planning and foresight—and commendable independence from political meddlers. Credit for all this lay with Wayne Valley. In the beginning, in 1960, the city and county were going to put the stadium project to public vote as a bond issue. But that risky proposition was averted when Valley steered the matter clear of the voting booth and politicians' caprices and into a nonprofit corporation named Coliseum, Inc., which would build its complex by selling revenue bonds estimated at around $30 million and then lease it to the city and county for $250,000 per annum.

Oakland's taxpayers were not liable for a dime; spectators would, in effect, repay the bonds by buying their tickets and paying parking fees, with the cash that flowed from the place run straight into city and county coffers. Expedient as this concept was, Valley had to twist arms and pat backs until it hurt before the city council and the board of supervisors voted aye. Al Davis's whirlwind 1963 season clinched the deal. Then the members of the Coliseum board all but conducted a civics lesson in its management; their engineers weighted each bid without charge, and two big builder board members—Edgar Kaiser and George Loorz—did not enter the bidding so as to avoid conflicts of interest. Unlike future stadia elsewhere, which practically sank in cost overruns, the stadium came in at $22.5 million, with the surplus going to operating capital.

The 55,000-seat stadium was the hub of an "entertainment center," which also included an indoor arena and a 9,000-car parking lot. Centrally located to the whole of the Bay area, the grounds were tangential to the Nimitz Freeway, along the path of the rapid transit system, and within ten miles of the Oakland airport. For all the astute planning, though, the stadium itself turned out to be a lackluster, dull gray cement oval built to be convertible to football and baseball—a then-popular idea that actually made the contours of the park imperfect for either sport. Still, Coliseum, Inc., could now approach Charlie Finley, the owner of the Kansas City Athletics, about moving his failing baseball team to Oakland, with a twenty-year lease beginning in 1968. The Raiders' lease, however, had been a touchy business; while they were clearly the biggest draw here, they still could not be called major league, as Valley well knew. Before Al Davis, when Valley was still losing money in great gobs, the Coliseum, Inc. wanted him to sign a twenty-year lease, and Valley had to say no. Unbending, Valley spent two years negotiating with Coliseum, Inc., for a five-year lease that would give way to five three-year options.

The upshot of the deal—which, looking back now, groans with agony and irony—was that Coliseum, Inc., agreed to these provisions on condition that the Raiders would not leave Oakland for as long as the team was successful both on the field and at the ticket office. With the notion of real success for now mere drollery, Valley closed the deal with a nervous handshake.

Three years later, with his team whirring like a fine timepiece, there was more irony. Even as the Raiders were turning their first profit—the team's book value was up to $4 million—Valley had to sacrifice his coach and general manager to the cause of a greater good, lest his team perish nonetheless. As the last touches of paint were being splashed about the Coliseum, Al Davis went East, drafted again for the kind of war he adored—one in which the dank air hung heavy not with self-preservation but with self-promotion.

11

Davis said he would have complete command of league policy and of the owners. "I have dictatorial powers," he said. "We'll eliminate fighting one another." He is looking forward to taking on the competition, meaning the older National Football League. "We will fight for players. We'll do a-n-y-t-h-i-n-g we think necessary."

—from *The New York Times*, April 29, 1966

I won the war, but the politicians lost the peace.

—Al Davis

In the light of history, Al Davis's path to ownership in Oakland had its on-ramp three thousand miles away, in the Madison Avenue offices of the American Football League. In the light of the Davis version of history, such ownership was the least of all possible rewards for a job well done in New York. And yet all it really may have been was the bum result of a horrible miscalculation by Wayne Valley designed to *rid* football of the Al Davis plague.

The opening for Al's biggest ascent came when Joe Foss informed the league's owners that he was out as their titular stooge. Foss, a decorated war hero and a rugged outdoorsman, had lost his appetite for being circumvented by ham-handed yahoo millionaires in a league with no executive discipline. Sitting like a caged tern in an airless Manhattan office, given little authority to stop them from rewriting their draft and procedural rules almost daily to fit their needs, Foss had no stomach to spearhead a merger strategy with the NFL by standing in for a nine-headed beast. Foss was hamstrung to the end; instead of speaking his true feelings, the war hero faded away and went home to South Dakota, passively denying accusations floated by the owners that he was fired for allowing the NFL to co-opt the Atlanta franchise many thought was headed into the AFL.

With the league finding no one else who would consent to be the new figurehead of this legion of chaos, Wayne Valley did some quick and drastic thinking, combining the useful with the wistful. In early April, as the owners convened in Houston, Valley proferred the name of Al Davis as AFL commissioner. He did so "reluctantly," he said, as it would be a grievous loss to his team, but surely in the best interests of the AFL.

And in this he was correct. Without a strong-looking commissioner, the thinking was, the NFL would not take the AFL as a serious entity; and with all the league's gains, its owners stood no chance of survival without a merger. As suicidal as the draft-signing war was—it had cost both leagues $25 million to sign players drafted in 1965, $7 million for the top twenty picks alone—the NFL was surely going to die harder.

Al Davis, of course, was a boffo recruiter of talent, an unrivaled salesman, and in Valley's view, a gut-fighter who could turn scheming, misanthropic drives on the NFL and scare them to death. Yes, Davis would be the ideal ignition key in turning over the AFL's image. But this arrangement had inherent problems. As Edwin Share had said in his Davis piece in *Sports Illustrated*, "Outside the city of Oakland . . . it is not certain where Al Davis would finish in a popularity contest among sharks, the mumps, the income tax and himself. If the voters were the other American Football League coaches, Davis probably would be third, edging out income tax in a thriller." The same applied to the owners. "Sure," said Scotty Stirling, "because we were kickin' their asses. I mean, people don't like that."

More central was the problem of Al Davis *representing* their league. This was like Al Capone being named police chief, and few believed Davis was in line for any kind of reward for his conduct. It was Valley's enlisting of Ralph Wilson—the AFL president and the Raiders' still-silent ownership partner—to work the crowd in Houston on Al's behalf that changed many minds. Yet only by dint of pressing need—and the shared supposition and secret design to ignore Davis as they had Joe Foss—did Valley carry the motion, by one vote.

Valley's widow, Gladys, recalled the train of thought in Houston as Davis's appointment materialized. "Nobody wanted the job and Wayne said, 'Well, Al's a dirty fighter and he comes from New York and he'll only be a figurehead—we'll do the dickering with the NFL,' " she said, her voice tense with the frozen loathing the Valleys held for Davis as the result of the bitter days yet to come. "So finally everybody said all right and they gave him a limo and let him use the title of commissioner."

For many AFL barons, even this intended chimera was too great a concession. "Most of them hated him," Gladys Valley said. "Billy Sullivan (of the Patriots) grew up in the same gutters [in Massachusetts] as Al Davis did and likes to claim the honor of being the first one that Al Davis lied to, when they were both kids." (Actually, Sullivan is fifteen years older than Davis.) Others reasoned among themselves that vesting Davis with this prearranged nominal authority might have the effect of getting him out of their way by kicking him upstairs, then, they hoped, into pasture after their merger.

Wayne Valley, too, had private considerations regarding the move, according to his wife. These had to do with Valley's uneasy alliance with Al. For the most part, the relationship—which was a rivalry to Al—played itself out in little escalating doses of Davis nerve and tart Valley jabs to Al's inflated self-importance. Setting down his jurisdiction early, Al had in his first Raider season politely ejected Valley from the locker room when Valley walked in and sat down during a film-watching session. Stopping the meeting, Al told him, "I will sit down personally with you tomorrow, Mr. Valley, but you're not sitting here now."

"That taught Wayne something," said John Rauch. "Al didn't want to be stepped on. And Wayne and Al didn't see eye-to-eye on a lot of things. Talk about some heated disagreements. There was always something goin' on between those two, about money, about football tactics, everything."

Perhaps this was a function not of Al's stated opinions regarding owner dilettantes but of his unstated personal envy of Valley. Said Gladys Valley: "I tell you what Al didn't like was, Wayne played football and the guys just adored him. He'd come into the locker room and talk with them. Al didn't know how to do that. He's no athlete—he can't even dance. And they all sneered at Al. He'd come in with his little skinny legs and all humped up with pads under his jacket. And Wayne came in and they had a real rapport. But Al never had that because he always felt inferior. That was the monkey on his back."

For Al, picking fights with Valley was ordered from within his psyche, though the order could not have come easily, if Gladys Valley is correct—"Al was scared to death of Wayne," she said. And yet Valley did understand Al's discomfort and didn't get into any real macho turf wars with him. Obligingly, in deference to his coach's matrix of insecurities, Valley usually kept away from hard football convocations, and his building business afforded him the distance to see Al in an almost comical perspective for a time. Accordingly, he reacted to Davis in that manner, with thorned sarcasm that would dig at Al's hide.

After that first season, Al had suggested to George Ross that *Tribune* stories about him include the word "genius," which they did, and often. While for Al this was a serious matter, Valley couldn't help but skewer Al with this product of his pomposity.

"George Ross always kept Wayne and I apprised of everything Al was thinking," Gladys Valley said. "Al thought he was conning George but George was a pipeline to us, as were many of the players. He conned Al Davis. So when the 'genius' thing happened, the next time Wayne saw Al he said, 'Hi, Genius'—and Al's eyes about popped out of his head. Wayne called him 'Genius' from then on, in derision."

She added: "Wayne had nothing against Al, except that he was a liar and a cheat and a despicable cad."

That feeling, however, was kept far under the Raider surface at the time. But for the Valleys, existing with Al Davis had become a too constant strain.

"I remember we had a few dinners when we first hired him," she said, "and our friends tried to be nice to him and his wife, tried to include them in social events, but they never accepted, they ran and hid. He's a very insecure man. She's his only friend and she's as bad as he is. She upheld his lying. I used to question things Al said. I'd say to her, 'You know, Carol, that's not the truth.' And she said. 'Well, Al has to say those things, that's the only way you get by.' She's another Al Davis, in feminine clothing."

By 1966, these fissures, still known only deep inside the Raider family, drove the Valleys to excise a problem they didn't need. Many years later, Gladys Valley would scale back time and wonder aloud about how football anthropology would have been altered if her husband hadn't latched on to the Davis-as-commissioner solution—which was fraught with danger, as Al was adept at manipulating any form of power—and simply fired him before he could fortify a power base. But for the convenient out (or so it seemed), she insisted, "I think Wayne would've fired him, because he was taking the fun and the sport out of it. Al was showing his true colors and he wasn't very nice to be around, and Wayne said that by that time, John Rauch should've learned enough to be able to coach."

And yet that appraisal is highly questionable—even according to Rauch himself. "Wayne Valley was skeptical about me becoming head coach," Rauch said, "but then Wayne was not gonna be enthusiastic about many people; he was just that way. In fact, I always had the feeling that Valley didn't want to push that hard for Al to be the commissioner, but he saw that something had to be done because our league was losing ground."

Ironically, in the end, it was by Al's choosing that Rauch finally got his dreamed-of head coaching job—and with the kind of inane subterfuge that Al so loved. "When he was accepted as commissioner," Rauch related, "he called me and said to meet him in Las Vegas (where he was vacationing), and when I signed in at the Riviera Hotel to use an alias he gave me, and then to stand in the lobby until I heard that name paged. And when that happened and I saw him, he asked me if anybody had been following me. He really thought this whole thing was a big deal. For Al, everything's a big deal."

Indeed, like Valley and like the AFL owners, Al may have had a hidden game plan with this commissioner thing. Although he was immediately turned on by the newest scent of war, and clearly bought the sham of leadership the owners had contrived for him, he also saw only potential positives in closing the book on coaching. As he saw it, this job would drive up the stakes of his game of dare; what would await him was a leverage he could not have attained by the usual means.

But Al Davis was too bright, his antennae too sensitive *not* to know of the bear trap the AFL was setting for him by its one-vote mandate. Now he *really* had to entrench, quickly and effectively, and if need be, in diametric opposition to whatever the AFL's millionaires wanted to do. Thus was Al's entrée into New York football society every bit like the opening of a Broadway show—

played in acts of broad farce and narrow skulduggery. Having elicited tacit approval from the owners to cater to the city's sporting press, Al boxed the *owners* in by going public so loudly that they couldn't buck him without seeming to act against the league's interests.

Spoon feeding the influential New York columnists—Arthur Daley of the *Times*, Dick Young of the *Daily News*, Milton Richman of United Press—with information and flattery, within weeks Al could pose as a hard symbol of an AFL strength and unity that in reality did not exist. With everything he did accompanied by a press release from the fanciful mind of Ron Wolf (whom Al brought to New York with him), Davis now had an agenda beyond just merger bluster. Casting out Joe Foss's staff of inert bookkeepers, he assembled a retinue of young PR-wise aides—including Irv Kaze of CBS, Houston sportswriter Mickey Herskowitz, and Syracuse PR man Val Pinchbeck. He also found time to repay an old favor. Remembering how Mel Hein had befriended him during the Doll-Dickson gang-up at USC, he named Hein, who was still at USC, supervisor of AFL officials.

"That job paid me twice as much as I was makin' at USC, an expense account, and a new car every year," Hein recalled. "That was the only time I ever made any real money in football."

An activist commissioner—and, singularly among sports commissioners, one sympathetic to the players as much as to the owners—Al stabbed in many directions in an effort to carve out actual authority. He consulted Bob Wallach, who was then an insurance broker in New York, about drawing up a pension plan for the AFL rank and file. At the same time, he held all players subordinate to AFL concerns. When Ernie Ladd played out his contract with the Chargers and wanted to sign with another team, Al—fearing fratricide when a united front was needed—issued a fiat that no club could bid for him. Ladd remained in San Diego.

Al's first press conference, on April 28, was a virtuoso performance. A star-struck William Wallace of the *Times* wrote of Davis's "gritted pearly white teeth" and "blue eyes under moving eyebrows." Al, bathed in klieg-lit, Napoleonic grandeur, boasted that "I have dictatorial powers" and announced the AFL's desire to "fight for players. . . . Give us three months to get organized and we'll drop a bomb somewhere and get everybody excited."

At the time, the spoils of this crusade were ostensibly college players, not those with existing NFL contracts. Al, in fact, was working on the theory that the AFL didn't need the NFL for its own health. Of a merger Al—speaking for what he thought was common AFL sentiment—said, "I didn't take this job with any concern about the other league. I'm interested in winning the war, and believe me, it's going to be a good scrap."

Within days, Al took his league further into his war. Whether or not it wanted to go that far with him, the AFL was now in for the duration. As every war-maker needs an excuse, Al looked around for the battleship *Maine* and instead found a Hungarian placekicker. On May 17, Pete Gogolak, a kicker for the Bills, routinely played out his contract—and, unroutinely, signed with the New York Giants. This was the first time a signed player had ever jumped leagues, and while it was completely legal and binding, Davis jumped on it as an act of aggression punishable to the fullest extent of Al Davis jungle law.

"It was a flimsy excuse," said George Ross, "but it opened the door just an inch—enough for Al to shove his foot through it."

Now, suddenly, like lumberjacks attacking a gigantic oak, Al's PR minions went to work. On May 19, an "AFL source" threatened retaliation if the NFL approved the Gogolak deal. Wanting just the opposite, Al's office began to leak items to the press about the AFL raiding NFL rosters. According to these reports, guys who hadn't even played out their contracts were either signed, close to being signed, or close to close to being signed. Some of the leaks were actual news, some were grossly premature, some all hot air. Still, Al was on the trail of NFL blood, directing a small but wolfish gang to hustle players. Prime among these leg men were Scotty Stirling in Oakland and Don Klosterman in Houston, and Ron Wolf kept tabs on the operation the way he did during the baby-sitting forays. "He was always convincing his people that, hey, you sign these guys and we'll decide where they're gonna play," Ross related.

After Gogolak, he also began convincing the owners—who had given him a huge war chest as part of the bargain that elevated him to commissioner—that they had been reviled by the league they wanted so dearly to join; and though most of these men still loathed him, and still had him earmarked for eventual decapitation, they saw how Davis had made the AFL seem virulently nationalistic and turned loose their own charges to play by the Davis style. In response to the Gogolak signing, Sid Gillman was reported to have offered three New York Giants deals to play out their contracts and sign with the Chargers. Five days later, Weeb Ewbank, denying the AFL raids were going on, said NFL players were *seeking* AFL offers—which several were, but merely to extort better deals from their clubs.

Then, on May 26, punctuating this burgeoning discord, Scotty Stirling dropped the Davis bomb out in Oakland—the Raiders had signed Rams quarterback Roman Gabriel to a three-year contract plus an option year, effective when his Ram contract expired after the 1966 season. Not only was the legality of *this* contract seriously disputable, it was even less plausible when the Rams pointed out that they had just signed Gabriel to a new contract running through 1968. Then, in early June, Don Klosterman weighed in with *his* depth charge—the Oilers had signed 49ers quarterback John Brodie to a monstrous quarter-million-dollar deal, also commencing in 1967.

The rumor mill now crackled, and Scotty Stirling years later loves to relive the high of sanctioned hyperbole. "We had *all* their quarterbacks ready to fall," he burbled.

What Al Davis did not know was that the owners had bypassed him fully in dealing on the side with merger-minded NFL counterparts. Removed from the battle of newspaper headlines, such plenary sessions had been going on for over a year. In January of 1965, Ralph Wilson and the Colts' Carroll Rosenbloom met a number of times regarding terms of a merger agreement, stalling on the issue of AFL indemnity money to the NFL, postmerger. A new round of secret talks began in February of 1966, and even as Al Davis took over as AFL commissioner, Lamar Hunt and the Cowboys' Tex Schramm were meeting in a parked car at a Dallas airport.

Hunt and Schramm continued merger discussions during and independent of Davis's hostilities. In early June, a twenty-six-point armistice was drafted. Now, intermingled with the player raids, other news leaks began to surface about an impending merger— news that Al first dismissed as NFL counterpropaganda, but that slapped him hard when he learned the truth. Feeling betrayed and made to look foolish, Davis at first tried to squelch the merger rumors. Knowing events were rapidly moving further from his hands, he sounded unconvincing when he called merger talks "speculation" and "conjecture."

Inside, though, Al was smoldering in disgust—not only because he was personally affronted by the deception but because of the ignominious irony of it all. Through his work, things had begun falling the AFL's way. Only days before, none other than George Halas had dealt his league a credibility blow when he called the Pete Gogolak signing "a mistake." And now, finally privy to the merger terms he had no part in formulating, he read every clause as treason, defeat, and surrender. For overjoyed AFL owners, acceptance into the NFL—even at an indemnity price of $18 million over twenty years—was a victory, but it was a pyrrhic one that burned with shame to the survivors of the old Davis war brigade.

"We were sold down the river," Scotty Stirling said. "We whipped their ass and then we turned around and gave it right back to 'em. There was no fight left. We had won."

Al Davis found out that his war of the roses was over when Billy Sullivan, who loathed him the most, told him of the agreement over dinner on June 7. The very next day, the two leagues would hold a joint press conference at the Warwick Hotel to announce it to the public. Al, with no time or means to hold back the dawn, would shrink into the shadows of men celebrating capitulation.

The swiftness of it was startling. The moment Sullivan told him of the peace at hand, Davis's commissionership was adjourned, his network of scavengers shut down, his future too suddenly delivered. It could not have been an easily digested meal. Years later Al allowed that he would have loved to kill the messenger on that June night. "Mr. Sullivan was kind of emotionally happy because we were going ahead with this merger," he said. "I told him I thought he had abandoned me and personally had sold me out." He even considered that there had been a conspiracy headed by Sullivan to shut him out. "It is a possibility," Al said. "I would not deny it."

That was part of the spin Al intended to put on the merger and his place in the act that took pro football into the modern era. Once again, history would not be written without an Al Davis augmentation. As the spin took form, the merger was unspeakable— "Yalta," as Al would take to calling it—but that it happened was due to . . . Al Davis. Lamar Hunt and Tex Schramm were dismissed as amoebic, and these faceless businessmen stood no chance versus the Davis PR thresher.

"They weren't gettin' it done," declared Scotty Stirling, who wrote much of the Davis primer of self-adulation in the Raider press guides. "What brought the NFL to the table was the fact that we were goin' after their quarterbacks. What got it done was when Davis said, 'Look, we're gonna take their fuckin' best players.'

"Some [AFL] people were afraid of what Al was doing. Maybe

they were afraid he was too aggressive. That shows you how unthinking they were at the time, 'cause he brought 'em a merger, he brought 'em all success. It would not have gotten done otherwise, there was no way."

This, of course, is mostly hogwash. The NFL never subsided in anyone's mind as the *big* league. The AFL's player raids only tightened the NFL's hold as the league with the big names and big teams. Never did the old league lose its leverage to cut a deal on its terms, and a deal was what it wanted. The NFL didn't respond in kind to Davis's shoplifting—not because of weakness, but because its owners knew a merger was on the way. And in the end, the AFL's commitment to the player raids was ephemeral; most owners, convinced that these signings were illegal, laid off the entire business. No one outside Oakland and Houston actually signed a player—and those two signings, Gabriel and Brodie, were later rescinded.

"Oh, he didn't do anything," Gladys Valley huffed. "He was just a lot of talk. He'd get on the phone and say, 'Go for the quarterbacks' but it was never official, that never meant anything. The owners did it all."

Yet Al *did* have a profound effect on the temper and alacrity of the negotiations, by giving the AFL sharp teeth. And he had every right to feel snubbed when the peace accords were announced with scarcely a mention of his name. For that he blamed not Billy Sullivan nor any of the AFL cadre. For that, there was a more visceral enemy.

For that, there was Pete Rozelle.

It had been a good ten years since Davis and Rozelle had crossed paths along the scouting cordon. Now, with both having beaten a path upward, they were the top hands of the rival leagues—though the range and conditions of their authority could not have been more antithetical. This had everything to do with the differences in the two men themselves.

Rozelle, who turned forty in 1966, had used his soothing, honey-coated manner of diplomacy to amass a barrow of goodwill. But that was old news for the long-snouted Rozelle. Fashionably attired and sloe-eyed, as West Coast as Al Davis was East Coast, Rozelle reeked of the airy, dreamy, unfazable pace of Southern California. Born in South Gate, near Los Angeles, as Alvin Ray Rozelle and nicknamed by an uncle as "Pete," the young man adopted the moniker as a more facile, jaunty identity. Of the same generation as Louis Davis, Pete's father was a Depression survivor and symbol of earnest pluck, losing a grocery store he owned but then forging a comfortable life as a purchasing clerk in an Alcoa plant in Compton. The Rozelles led an unhurried, Methodist lifestyle in a tidy house with a garage.

Pete Rozelle, like Al Davis, played basketball in his youth. Unlike Al Davis, he also played tennis. During World War II, Rozelle enlisted in the navy, then went to Compton Junior College, earning side money by working as the school's athletic news director. Eventually he began covering high school sports for a Long Beach newspaper. When the Cleveland Rams moved to L.A. in 1946—the first big league sports team on the West Coast—and they trained at Compton Junior College, Rozelle's easy charm endeared him to the club's publicity director, who hired him to help edit game programs. He then went to the University of San Francisco and he graduated to become that school's SID—but came back to the Rams as PR director in 1952 at age twenty-six. Except for Rozelle's handling press relations during the 1956 Olympics in Australia—while also working for a San Francisco PR firm—the Rams and the NFL would have a chokehold on Rozelle's life.

In 1957, Rozelle rejoined the team, personally recruited by NFL Commissioner Bert Bell to ameliorate a growing power struggle between owner Dan Reeves and his two partners. Because of this deadlock, the club's management was stagnant and this had led the Rams' general manager, Tex Schramm, to quit. Rozelle took the job and disentangled the angry knot by massaging egos on all sides.

But Rozelle was quick to admit that he was not enough of a hard football man to run the team's operation—marketing and mediation being his meat—though he had already made a clutch of allies in high football places. And when Bert Bell abruptly died on October 11, 1959, and the league's owners could not agree on a successor for over three months, Reeves—acting much like Wayne Valley, though with complete sincerity—put forth *his* young GM as a compromise candidate. Where the AFL knew all too much about Al Davis, the NFL didn't know much at all about Rozelle, only that no one had an unkind word about him. In their stalemate, that was good enough to appoint him. "The Boy Czar," the press dubbed him—a designation Al Davis would have loved if Rozelle had not gotten there first.

Rozelle earned his bold title. Once in power he executed an enormous change in league policy and philosophy. Although the NFL was booming at the turn of the decade, it was clear to Rozelle that the weaker teams were being victimized by the stronger ones because the latter could sell their own television packages to local stations; TV revenues varied wildly, some teams weren't carried at all, and broadcast rights were completely out of the hands of the league.

Rozelle's solution was socialism—a centralized package yielding *equal* revenues to *all* the league's teams. Though the idea was not new (the AFL's first TV contracts were designed to work in the same way), Rozelle had a much tougher sell, having to convince long-time profiteer-owners in the top markets of New York, Los Angeles, and Chicago to share the wealth. Rozelle did it with his artful tact and persuasion—the same qualities he used to gain a limited antitrust exemption from Congress to facilitate the plan without fear that it would be ruled a monopoly practice by the federal courts. Rozelle lobbied adroitly, and in September of 1961, Congress passed the Sports Antitrust Broadcast Act, paving the way for all sports to pool TV rights. (Rozelle would just as effectively lobby to gain another antitrust exemption in 1966, which was critical for the merger to go through. He did that by dangling a New Orleans expansion franchise before two powerful Louisiana congressmen— who promptly got the measure attached as a rider to an anti-inflation bill.)

Al Davis did not begrudge Pete Rozelle his successes. But his original sense about Rozelle's glacial, sanctimonious underskin was now underlined when Rozelle—dealing on the side with the AFL owners—ignored him to the point of insult on Merger Day. It was Rozelle, smiling broadly at the Warwick Hotel between Tex Schramm and Lamar Hunt, who avidly drank in the credit for the union Al thought he made possible. He saw that smile taunting him. Vicious as he could be in team matters, Al could not imagine himself being so cruel if the roles were reversed; certainly there would be a sop, a place in a ceremonial rite of passage. In his value system, Al called every other coach "great"—that was his favorite word, *great*, and everyone in football shared it in his public pronouncements.

Above all, Al Davis considered himself a gentleman. Never before had he really *hated* anyone—he didn't care about anyone enough to do that. But for a million little reasons, Al Davis could not abide Pete Rozelle.

And so Davis did not go along with the charade of peaceful succession that Rozelle ordained, and he would not be a Rozelle retainer. Denied the battlefield by the Warwick Treaty, he drew breath for a conference table war as a mandatory member of the executive committee making the final merger agreements. Trying to turn these deliberations into a passionate defense of his league and himself, he raised point after point of dissent, delaying the ratification vote for days.

Not all of this was done in the spirit of petulance or nihilism. In its rush to merge, the AFL had left for later dispensation many points of agreement, several of them extremely disadvantageous to the league. Al made a grand show in contesting the $18 million indemnity-tribute, which worked out to about $100,000 a club per year. He was also outraged that the league was forced to turn over to the NFL $8.5 million of the entrance fee taken from the next AFL expansion team. Inasmuch as television revenues alone for the AFL teams would now jump from $600,000 to $2 *million* by joining the NFL's broadcast package, Al got nowhere with these quarrels.

More meaningful were his objections to smaller, near-nebulous details about taxes accrued from the indemnity. This issue particularly disturbed Wayne Valley, who may well have been the wisest businessman in either league, and in this Al was acting as an agent for Valley.

"A lot has been said about Al 'holding up' the merger," Scotty Stirling said. "It wasn't Davis, it was Valley. Al had no vote; only the owners voted and they had a big fight over the tax implications. And Valley came up with this little accountant in Oakland who figured the whole thing out for people. Valley knew the deal was gonna fuck the AFL teams. It was Wayne, in fact, who climbed across the table going after [the new Chargers owners] Gene Klein and Sam Schulman, trying to make the point to them.

"They just wanted to merge, no matter what, and when Valley explained it to Al, he wasn't gonna let it happen. He was helpin' everybody and they didn't even know it."

Sid Gillman, in the room with Klein and Schulman, had no idea what Al was driving at. "I mean, here I was runnin' out of money in San Diego and now we have a chance to play the Browns, Colts, and Steelers—they were gonna join our league in the merger—and

Al was holding everything up. I didn't know what the hell he wanted, he was talkin' about guarantees and this and that. God, it was frustrating."

Davis wasn't through there, either—and, as became apparent to Valley, Al's help was invaluable to the very continuance of the Oakland Raiders. Goaded by the 49ers, NFL draftsmen had included in the merger agreement sixteen unconscionable demands of the Raider franchise. Some of these were the right to oversee Raider schedules to avoid head-to-head competition, control over which NFL teams the Raiders would now play, and some 49ers games to be played at the Coliseum. Apparently, the 49ers—and the NFL—meant for these interdictions to force the Raiders out of the Bay Area.

"The NFL had come to me before that, through a liaison, about the possibility of convincing the Raiders to move to Seattle," George Ross recalled. "They were using the 49ers' share of the indemnity as a bribe—they'd give it up if the Raiders moved. I said go to hell. And then, right at the end of the merger, the 49ers went to the NFL with the same idea, to get the territory to themselves."

Valley, Davis, and Sonny Werblin, standing firm, scared the NFL out of holding to the demands. For Rozelle, it was worth it to end a week of negotiations reminiscent of those at Panmunjom. Sid Gillman remembered Rozelle "beggin' our owners and our GMs, 'Come on, let's get this thing together.' Pete was almost bawling." This was a very different Pete Rozelle from the ever-composed man with the fixed smile, and Al must have luxuriated in Rozelle's torture. Indeed, through the years, the interpretations of what went on in that room have rarely gotten further than the private dance of Al Davis and Pete Rozelle. In his 1988 autobiography, Gene Klein wrote:

> Davis was against the merger. As Wayne Valley later explained to me, Davis felt he was responsible for the merger taking place and he wanted to serve as commissioner of the combined leagues. . . .
> "I was on the phone with Davis when it was announced that Pete Rozelle would be the NFL commissioner," Valley recalled. "Al was really upset. 'I deserve to be commissioner,' he insisted. I reminded him that I'd had a difficult time getting him the job as AFL commissioner in the first place . . . and since then he'd succeeded in alienating three or four of the people who'd voted for him. . . . Davis

didn't listen, he just kept repeating that he deserved to be commissioner. I don't think he ever forgave Pete Rozelle for that."*

Gladys Valley said: "That's what Al held against Wayne. He said, 'You know, you have enough influence over the other owners. You could've influenced them to make me commissioner.' And Wayne said, '*I* wouldn't want you as commissioner—and nobody else would either!' "

But could Al Davis have seriously coveted a job wainscotted with social graces and convention? Could he have devoted himself to protecting owners' interests? Certainly the liturgical fragrance of the designation offered an immense rush, and a sense of closure to the arc of power Davis had followed all his adult life. But Al gave the notion the back of his hand in 1969—"I didn't want to be commissioner. No way. It's a desk job." Scotty Stirling believes it.

"You don't understand Al Davis if you think he wanted that job, or that jealousy of Pete Rozelle was what possessed him after that," Stirling said. "Because there were no real wins there. As commissioner, you don't have any wins. All right, you can do a TV contract and you can consider that as a win, but who are you competing against?

"I know this for certain. As hard as this is for people to believe, revenge and getting even is not in his nature. It doesn't make any fuckin' difference to him, 'cause he has other fish to fry. First of all, he had goals. And you can see today what those goals were. And unlike most people, he sees the barriers and the problems getting to his goals. Now, to be involved in some kind of a vendetta based on the fact that he didn't get this commissionership way back when, that's ridiculous; that's not him.

"But a lot of people *think* it's him—mostly people whose ass he kicked on the field—like Gene Klein on a regular basis."

Said George Ross: "I think he was interested in the job from this standpoint. He had just undressed the other guys and out of that great victory should've come more than just a handshake and a thank-you down the road. He ripped their nuts off and he felt that being commissioner was giving him something the league deserved."

First Down and a Billion: The Funny Business of Pro Football, by Gene Klein and David Fisher (New York: Morrow, 1987), p. 81.

"What Al had with Pete Rozelle wasn't a personal problem," Stirling concluded. "If you wanna create a situation between them, why don't you start from the point of view that Davis kicked the shit out of Rozelle to bring the merger? Now, given that as a basis, where is the motivation to be pissed off? Who then would look for revenge? It wouldn't be Davis. Just maybe, it was Pete Rozelle who held the grudge."

In July of 1966, the big fish in Davis's frying pan was quickly found. Once again it would be Wayne Valley, whose gratitude to Al for his aid and comfort in New York would cost him dearly.

12

The Al Davis Story has been variously described as remarkable, astounding, stunning and, even, unbelievable. And it is all of these.

—from the Raider press guide, 1966

Wayne thought that being good to him and giving him a piece of ownership and pride in ownership would maybe make him honest and that he'd get back some respect from the other owners. But all it did was make him worse.

—Gladys Valley

Beneath Al's anger there was a cold reality. The sly game of euchre by the AFL's owners had done more than exploit him; now, in the fallout of the merger, Al could see what the plan had been, and with all the trouble he could make on the executive committee, he did not kid himself. His were the last acts of a man trying to save face. Noble as his cause was, in working for Wayne Valley, he was working for himself.

As part of the settlement that foaled the NFL-AFL championship game—with the inaugural "Super Bowl," as Lamar Hunt informally dubbed it, to follow the 1966 season—and the realignment and interleague play that would begin in 1970, the post of AFL commissioner was at once expunged, thoroughly absorbed into the clerical duties of the league president. Al recognized this as a dictate to remove himself from the AFL's offices in the coming weeks. Facing his own extirpation, he must have felt the way he did when he looked at the USC head coaching seat and saw John McKay sitting in it. An in-demand bright light only four weeks before, Al Davis now needed a job.

Much has been made of the world of opportunity open to Davis following the merger. This, too, was part of the history rewriting that accompanied the re-empowering of Al Davis. George Ross, as was usual then, was the viaduct of Al's assertion that job offers awaited him throughout the NFL, and the *Tribune* went along with it. But Ross decided later to check this one out for himself.

"Al said he had other options than the Raiders, but Al is apt to say anything," Ross said. "He said that Carroll Rosenbloom made him an offer with the Colts. Well, years later I asked Rosenbloom's GM (after Rosenbloom took over ownership of the Rams), which was Don Klosterman at the time, and he said Rosenbloom always said of Davis, 'There wouldn't have been room for the two of us.' And Al was one of the few owners Rosenbloom had a good relationship with. He liked Al personally, and Al delivered the eulogy at Rosenbloom's funeral. But working together was another story.

"Through the years, Al has made similar claims, and I talked to a guy whose name Al dropped, Billy Sullivan, and he said he had phoned Al several times in the past when he was looking around for a coach or a GM and asked Al about guys, what he thought about so-and-so, and Sullivan would say, in a passing remark, 'Christ, Al, you're the guy I want.' It was a joke that both of them would laugh about.

"It was probably the same with all of the teams he said had 'talked to him.' It was, 'Goddamn, Al, where can we find another Al Davis?' And out of that, these claims would be born."

Of the alleged postmerger offers, Scotty Stirling adamantly said, "Of course he had 'em, and he could've gone anywhere he wanted. Carroll Rosenbloom wanted him real bad."

In the end, the best—if not the only—offer came from Valley, of which Gladys Valley remarked, "Al felt everybody would want him, that he could demand any job he wanted. But nobody wanted him. There wasn't an owner that would touch him, they wouldn't waste their spit on him. Because he was dangerous, and he lied to too many. That's why he kept calling Wayne, so that he could come back to the Raiders.

"I was against that. In fact, Wayne would tell the other owners, 'Gladys doesn't want to bring Al back,' and they said, 'She's right.' "

But Valley owed Davis. The ready-to-open Oakland–Alameda

County Coliseum was a nagging reminder that the viability of the Raiders—which Davis actualized—was to be preserved because Davis had taken his cues well in New York, even if he was looking out for his own tail. The Raiders, a jest of a team three years ago, were going to be an NFL franchise—a tax-reduced NFL franchise—in no small measure due to Al Davis, a man who had willingly stepped down when Valley pointed him toward New York. Then, Valley hadn't minded losing Al to a deserved oblivion. Now, seeing him twist in the New York wind, Valley's Irish guilt kicked in. Not incidentally, many of the Raiders' powerless but valued limited partners were aghast when Al left, and were now pushing Valley to repatriate him.

But having an Al Davis back was not as easy as it seemed. Even with his demise in New York, Al had been right about the stratifying ramifications of the commissioner's job. As Valley told *Look* in 1969, "Davis wanted to be an owner. [He's] very image-conscious. He felt being an owner was a step up from being commissioner. Anything else would have been a step down."

What Valley had in mind was for Al to resume his old duties as head coach, owner or not, but things were complicated now from a number of sides. Valley would not have minded if John Rauch and Scotty Stirling—the new coach and new GM in Davis's absence—had just evaporated, but Al knew the perils of a crassly done shakeup with the Raiders already in training camp. As it was, logistical problems abounded. Back in Oakland, Al was having lunch with George Ross as he and Valley were putting together a deal.

"What do I do about these two guys?" he asked George. "One's a head coach, one's a GM, and I'm upstairs. Where's the breakdown of responsibility?"

"Al," Ross told him, "there *is* no breakdown. There's only room for one dictator."

And though he was still uncertain about the structural quandary, that was Al's attitude in yet another round of dare. Sensing a give in Valley, he pounced hard. What Davis, Valley, and team attorney Bill Hayes worked out was completely unique to sports management; in effect, Davis would become a general manager in the corporate sense and a part-owner in the *business* of football. Power, money, influence—where once Al could claim an implicit right to these, they were now the covenants of a thirty-six-year-old football man who never gave or took a hit on a field, and, as it turned out, wouldn't have more than a few thousand dollars of his own riding on the fate of this franchise.

The deal was this: since the third Raider general partnership vacated by Robert Osborne was still open, Al could buy into this tier of absolute ownership. Valley, boosting Al's cut, freed up 10 percent of the partnership shares—roughly the same as Valley's, and double Ed McGah's—through a process in which the twenty-four limited partners gave up a prorated tenth share apiece. To facilitate the transaction, Valley listed the book value of the club at an emaciated $180,000. Thus, Al's one-tenth interest cost him just $18,000—which he acquired on a *letter of credit*. As the Raiders were worth many millions more, Al Davis, without going far into his pocket, suddenly was worth something like $1 million.

Davis's new title—the corporate-sounding "managing general partner"—which made him general manager of the Raiders' general partners, was the operational part of his function. Running on a contract from July 1, 1966, through December 31, 1975, it carried a nominal salary of $35,000 a year, a pittance that Al was willing to give on since he would also be collecting on his salary as AFL commissioner—$50,000 a year—until the end of the decade. The boundaries of Al's monarchy, as set forth in his "employment agreement," were swollen with his victory.

"Allen Davis," it read, "shall have the exclusive authority . . . to direct and manage the [Raiders], including but not limited to all of the details of the procurement . . . of football players and football coaches . . . and to do all other things which he may consider necessary . . . to the best interests of the football team and the partnership."

When he signed it, Al Davis was made. Now was opened a *new* circle of power. He would run every phase of the operation. He would be attending league meetings in place of Wayne Valley. Only by dint of a paper association did Valley and McGah retain any semblance of authority. As Al pronounced it, his partners' roles were those of "consultant" and "sounding board." In all important matters, Al Davis *was* the Raiders.

Gladys Valley read Al's contract and cringed.

"What Wayne had always done in our building company was take in a young partner when he was ready to give him a piece of ownership at a small price," she said. "So we did the same thing with Davis, and I was all against it. That was the only time I was opposed to what Wayne wanted to do.

"Wayne thought it might make Al stand up and tell the truth. And he thought he could handle Al, even though he knew Al was a conniver and a liar." Sadly, she finished, "But we learned a lot of other things about his psyche and his meanness later. . . . He's a very sick man."

Valley's only illusion of priority control was that, by terms, Davis had to serve at least ten years or he could sell out his partnership only for the incremental value of his shares over the elapsed time; after ten years, the resale value was a full third. In addition, Valley could—theoretically—fire Al from his managing general partner job.

"As a general partner, no; as the managing partner, he might've had some vulnerability," said George Ross. "It possibly could've been done by the other two partners."

Al made a strong mental note of that arithmetic. Though Ed McGah was nearly unseen as a Raider owner, he now was of critical importance to Al; verily, though McGah hardly recognized it as patronizing, Al was paying him the kind of attention that Valley never did.

And yet at this stage, as far as Valley was concerned, any potential threat from Davis was outweighed by the more tangible threat of growing power by the limited partners, specifically, Ralph Wilson's Devoir Management Company, which by now owned no less than 23.625 percent of Raider shares, many times more than any of Valley's building-business colleagues—the most involved of which, John Brooks, owned 5.25 percent. Thus, Valley snuck into Davis's contract—which had to be ratified, though not read, by all the limiteds—a clause that read:

> At the end of the term of this agreement the general partners shall be entitled to purchase the assets of this partnership from the partnership at fair market value.

This would mean that, at any time after 1975, any of the three general partners could buy out any of the limited partners at their whim. And while it appeared in small print as part of Davis's contract, Valley never imagined that Al would ever have any cause to use it to turn on Valley. He was wrong.

Al also had reason to be satisfied with the present. Having gotten all he wanted from Valley, he all but devalued Valley and McGah right out of existence.

"Even before, when he was coach and GM," Ross observed, "he privately referred to both Valley and McGah as 'my two dummies.' He'd tell me about what went on at a league meeting, at which he'd be a GM without a vote and the other two would be the team spokesmen. And he'd say, in disgust, 'My two dummies did this and did that.'

"Al's attitude was that Ed McGah was a big joke and he hated Wayne Valley. And he just stiff-armed those two out of his way until he began to stroke Ed McGah."

Davis had little time for concepts like gratitude and common cause, and the main threat to *Al*—Wayne Valley's presence—now shrank before his eyes, though not enough to suit him. In his contempt, Al had always wanted to hate Valley. Now he could, because in the eyes of Al Davis, Valley was the worst of all creatures—one who gave in to him.

"To Al, Wayne made himself weak because he gave him ten points of ownership for almost nothing," Gladys Valley related. "Al thought that if Wayne were really powerful he wouldn't give him anything. Because that's how Al Davis saw life—if you were powerful, you had to get more powerful."

As Al still was not omnipotent, it is likely that by this attitude he was steeling himself for future trench warfare with Valley. But, as the Valleys came to believe, the roots of Al's hatred were sunk in much deeper earth, the manifestations of which made them flinch.

Wayne Valley once observed that Davis "was a great admirer of Hitler and the Nazis. He and I would have these conversations and he'd call them a 'great organization' that 'drove their point home.' "

That a Jew could say things like that, even in the broadest figurative context (and even with the addendum that Hitler was a "cocksucker" who "had to be stopped"), was not just insensitive; it had disturbing undertones of self-loathing. But Al seemed to have no capacity for shame. And he drove *his* point home.

"He has a psyche that says power means everything," Gladys Valley recognized. "Al doesn't care too much about money, per se, except that it might mean power. That's why he worshiped Hitler. He'd say Hitler was one of the greatest men who ever lived by getting all this power, that he was the only man who really knew how to get power."

That kind of power has no room for morality. But for Al Davis, it is as though he has asked for a cross to bear.

★   ★   ★

If Wayne Valley was wary but sanguine about the reborn shadow of Al Davis, John Rauch was completely unnerved. Even before Al's return, taking over a team so identified with Davis had made Rauch come undone. "They were just reporting to Santa Rosa," said George Ross, "and in just a few days Scotty was calling Al back in New York, saying, 'Al, you gotta talk to Rauch. He's ready to climb out the window.' Rauch was just so nervous about this thing."

After Al made his re-entry early in training camp, Rauch was never convinced that Al would not at any time step back in as head coach. As bizarre a notion as that was given Al's new station, there was no law against an owner coaching his team, and as Rauch reflected, "He said he was giving up the coaching end but when he came back, in my mind, there was always that thing that, well, if things didn't work out, he would always be . . . available."

A round-faced, almost cherubic-looking Irishman, Rauch had a high-pitched voice that in its loudest upper ranges sounded more like an agitated whipporwill than an angry head coach. He had a nature that seemed to appeal for cooperation rather than command action or else. Rauch was an army man used to taking orders. Partly because of his nature—and mostly because of Al's—few around the Raiders could swear to Rauch's security. No one thought that, if necessary, he could stand up to Al and assert his own coaching authority—least of all Wayne Valley.

"Wayne was sure that Al's ego was such that once he returned, no matter what the titles were, Al was gonna be head coach," Ross said. "Al was not gonna let Rauch muck up his football team. And I sort of thought that Al might assert himself on the field."

Holding the same expectations, Rauch had an immediate solution. "When Al came back I went to Wayne Valley and I offered to step down and give the job back to Al because, after all, it was his job. Valley said . . . well, he didn't know what to say, really. He said, 'I'll talk it over with Al.' And then, my first meeting with Al, I expressed the same thing to him and he said, 'No, this is your opportunity, see how far you can take it.' But then things started to slide backwards between Al and I on a lot of things and we didn't get along too well."

The first sour note came when Al informed Rauch that once the club broke camp and went back to Oakland, the coaching staff—

which now included a Rauch hiree, thirty-four-year-old Stanford assistant Bill Walsh, who coached the offensive backfield—would have to find their own office space outside of the Raiders' Franklin Street quarters.

"He said there wasn't enough room there because he'd brought so many people back from New York with him," Rauch recalled. "And I really didn't think he had that many people, but now all of a sudden we couldn't use the office. And then he said we couldn't use our practice facilities at this little field in West Oakland called Bushrod Park. So I had to find my own practice grounds when we got back to Oakland."

Both the coaches' offices and the practice site turned out to be an old high school in Hayward that had been abandoned because it sat on an earthquake fault. For the next two years, this lonely, crack-riddled monument to man's helplessness in the face of higher powers was where Rauch contemplated games and Al Davis's next moves. Rauch, his office a converted cafeteria kitchen, already felt as though he were splattered by suet.

"To be honest with you," he said, "my thought right there was, well, he was doing all this to throw obstacles out in front of me. Like, let's see how you can get over this one."

Scotty Stirling—allowed to stay in his office—did not feel the same usurpation as general manager, and decades later still had no sympathy for Rauch's stewing. "That's nonsense," he scoffed. "First of all, practice facilities were always a problem, finding a place to practice. There just aren't that many fields in Oakland, and it didn't get good until Davis built his own [in 1967]. They used Hayward, Bushrod Park, the Alameda Naval Air Station. I mean, they bounced around. And it wasn't that Davis prevented them from using anything—they *couldn't*, because it rained so much that year that the grounds were inadequate.

"Same with the office thing. We were in a little downtown office building that wasn't adequate, and Al wanted room because he knew the operation was gonna grow. I found that place in Hayward, and it was for the coaches' convenience. They all lived out that way to start with. Why should they have to drive all the way into Oakland if you got 'em in a place out there where they could put a desk and a telephone?"

Stirling had his own problems during that volatile training camp of 1966. In his first days as GM, he had to face growing player alienation about money. The two most celebrated Raiders, Art Powell and Clem Daniels, did not show up when camp began, holding out in tandem after the fashion of Dodger pitchers Sandy Koufax and Don Drysdale, who had linked their salary demands during baseball spring training that year and came away with huge contracts for it. Holding the Raider salary line Al had set before he went to New York, Stirling was no pushover. "I probably negotiated harder than Al," he believed.

During a tense few days, not only were Powell and Daniels out, but Ben Davidson, Bob Svihus, and Ken Herock walked out of camp over money, and Dave Costa was demanding a trade if *he* wasn't paid more. Naturally, Costa had his own way of showing his displeasure. Said Harry Schuh: "Dave wanted to get traded so he walked from one building to the next totally in the nude. That was his form of protest. I couldn't believe what I saw, Dave Costa walkin' across the hotel roof with not a stitch of clothing on."

Stirling talked Powell, Daniels, Davidson, and Svihus back into the fold, but not the other two. Unsatisfied with Stirling's final offer, Herock opted to quit. And Costa's dare was met with a ticket to ride—all the way to lush and lovely Buffalo.

In Costa's case, at least, the sense of angst that grew around money had been already aggravated by the loss of Davis as head coach. "John Rauch took over and it wasn't the same," he said, "I was makin' fifteen thousand dollars and I was goin' for the big eighteen my fourth year and they wanted to give me seventeen. I went to Scotty Stirling and it was, 'Yes ma'am, no ma'am,' and I was just disgusted by the whole thing and I said, shit, I'm gettin' the hell out of here."

In years past, Costa had lamented about money, but at least he knew Al's quirkily autocratic methods. "My first year I made twelve thousand dollars and played in the All-Star game and they gave me a thousand-dollar raise. But the night before opening day against Kansas City that year, Al came in and says, 'I'm rippin' up your contract. You're gettin' thirteen-five. And Ben Davidson was my roommate and Al ripped up Ben's contract and gave him a five-hundred-dollar raise. And then he said, 'Now let's go get Lenny Dawson tomorrow, boys!' It was like a psych thing.

"That's how he did it. Y'know, like you'd say, 'Wow, the coach likes us, he gives us a five-hundred-dollar raise'—and then you go to sign the next year and he says, 'Hey, didn't I always take care of you?' and you'd get nothin'."

By the time Al returned, it was too late for Costa. "I was taping up for the first game and Ron Wolf told me, 'You got twenty minutes to get out of here.' I got traded to Buffalo so I went to the airport, got to L.A., slept in the airport there, went to San Diego, where the Bills were playing, and then went cross-country to Buffalo—nine thousand miles in about three days for a thousand bucks! Oh yeah, I'm a smart sonofabitch."

Although Al had no *overt* influence on salary negotiations, the trouble over money receded only after he was back in his Raider office. To Rauch—who had no part in the negotiations—this was hardly coincidental. And even "finished business" could be more evidence to Rauch of the contrary apparition of Al Davis.

"It wasn't a very good working arrangement," said Rauch. "Scotty was allowed to go anywhere from $250 to $2,500 in raises and of course those guys weren't gonna sit for that and so they were walkin' out of camp. And then Al came back and boom, boom, boom, they all fell in line. And I wasn't that stupid that I couldn't go into the file cabinet and see their contracts and that instead of bein' $2,500 it's $5,000 or $10,000.

"Naturally, I felt that Scotty and I were being undermined and that Al was exercising his control by using the players as pawns. Some players he would make happy and others he could care less about. And all the while he was acting like he didn't want to interfere with our jobs."

Stirling saw it in a different light. "Listen," he said, "if Davis is around he's in charge, it's his team. If he wants to give guys more money, he can—and I thought he was very fair with the players. That's been one of his great strengths. So, no, I never felt undermined."

For the moment, the "interference" issue faded, kept to no more than a low boil by a consciously hermitized Davis. Keeping to the office, he went about the business of running the team and mustering scouting data from his standing army of information hounds. During the 1966 season, Rauch longingly remembered that "we very seldom saw Al"—which was more than a little startling to most people around the Raiders, including Wayne Valley and George Ross.

"I'm sure Al felt uncomfortable with Rauch as head coach," Ross said. "He didn't feel that—even inheriting Al's system and all the players—he didn't feel that Rauch was a take-charge guy, and he may have been right. But, just the same, Al told Wayne straight out, 'You're wrong about me. I'm not going to coach again.' He had to keep saying that over and over, and he held to it."

Wayne Valley believed it to be only a matter of time—*hoped* it would be. Even at the beginning, Gladys Valley said, "Al was the managing general partner but he was really the coach. But he said, 'I can't be called coach because that's demeaning.' "

Valley had a solution for that. He told Al, "You can call yourself Mr. God."

While a death watch lingered for him, Rauch took a hammer and tongs to the Raider roster. As Rauch had helped to construct the team's big-play system, he was pledged to its perpetuation. Still, he was prepared to make some changes, especially in Al's old fire-drill schemes in the defensive secondary.

"I said, hey, we're not gonna play all these crazy coverages," Rauch claims, "because when I broke down all the coverages I saw that we played best when we played what we called 'Cover-One With a Free Safety.' We'd get our cornerbacks up real close on the receivers, force 'em into the middle of the field, and our free safety, Dave Grayson, who was a speed merchant, had the responsibility to read the play and go get the ball."

In that way did the Raiders' signature defense—"Bump and Run"—evolve. No longer did Rauch want to see Kent McCloughan, the fleet but none-too-agile cornerback, being turned inside out by nimble-footed receivers downfield. Instead, Rauch went full time with a gambol used in practice-field drills.

"Bump and Run," Rauch mused with a taut grin. "That was another thing that Al jumped on as his own. It was his, but only in that when we would go to training camp every year, Al would test our receivers by playin' up on 'em real tight. And this was also a test on a defensive back, to see how close he could cover. So the first week in camp was all Bump and Run. But we didn't really play that way at the time."

Now they did "95 percent of the time," as Rauch estimated it. McCloughan and the other cornerback, usually Rodger Bird, lined up almost inside the wideouts' shirts, and at the snap "bumped" them, and continued poking and shoving them while running shoulder-to-shoulder with them downfield. Ideally, this disrupted the receivers' rhythm and slowed their routes. The danger lay in a meek or missed hit, which would spring the receivers into a meadow of open field. That's where "Cover-One" kicked in, by turning the safeties into guided missiles. "If the receivers got more than two steps on our corners," explained Rauch, "our safetymen—particularly the strong safety—were supposed to cover from sideline to sideline. It was a totally man-to-man thing."

An extension of Charlie Sumner's primeval methods of defense, Bump and Run affixed the pins of a workable system of intimidation. Even so, in its grittiness, few completely grasped the subtle physics of this high-risk concept. "Bump and Run," Dave Grayson said, "is *not* physical football, not to the extent that you're hittin' guys hard. You're *impedin'* guys, makin' 'em think about bein' hit. When you try and knock the devil out of a guy, he's not there. Play it in that manner and you're gonna get beat. The reason we were so successful with it was because our cornerbacks *weren't* as physical as everybody thought."

It *was* basic football, though, and for Grayson it was a world removed from the "mod" cybernetic football he had played under Hank Stram in K.C. "That was like a maze, the way it is today in football. You did so many things. In Oakland you knew we were gonna be in a certain defense. We'd say: you can't beat us, we're gonna tell you what we're gonna be in—now beat us. We had a lot of pride in that because at that time, a lot of people still thought we were all individuals and negative-type people in Oakland."

Instead, the Raiders were now shaping up as a team of smooth, round pegs; holes were being filled not by journeymen but by talented players. The 1965 season was the end of the line for stopgap guys like Archie Matsos, Claude Gibson, Bob Mischak, and Frank Youso. While none of them would play another down in football, Al was still able to use Matsos, the old folk hero, as trade bait to obtain from the Broncos their 225-pound tight end, Hewritt Dixon, though Al had a different job in mind for him.

"Dixon is the best fullback in the league, and nobody knows it," he had told George Ross months before, knowing that the truck-sized Dixon ran the hundred in 9.9. And in 1966, like two gargantuan warthogs, Dixon and Clem Daniels gouged out enormous yardage, combining for nineteen touchdowns—twelve on the ground, seven more through the air. The problem was, they—and Art Powell, who caught eleven touchdown passes—could have opened up *more* space on defensive backs if they had had a surer-armed quarterback than the often-injured Cotton Davidson and the now-declining Tom Flores. And while Flores threw for twenty-four touchdowns in 1966, Al was concerned about how much longer his quarterbacks would hold up.

When the Raiders, with three straight early-season losses, failed to keep pace with Hank Stram's raging Chiefs and finished second to them—with the same 8–5–1 record as the year before—Al made his boldest move thus far. However, rather than with the usual Davis growl, he made it with all the courage of a timorous tabby cat, and was ready to pass blame if it backfired on him—onto the back of John Rauch, who came to Al with the idea and would have paid hard for its failure.

In talking with Joe Collier, the coach of the Bills, Rauch had inquired whether the Bills' backup quarterback, Daryle Lamonica, might be available in a trade. When Collier said yes, Rauch thought Al would jump, since Al had often remarked that Lamonica was a Raider kind of quarterback.

Burly—six-two, 218 pounds—and Notre Dame–bred, Lamonica threw a football with the delicate touch of an anvil. Finesse was not in his arsenal, an absurd joke in the presence of his shotgun arm. Built for power passing, Lamonica's stocky body and horn-beam-thick legs worked in leveraged unison with his arm and allowed him to stand up to a torrential charge of rushing linemen while releasing the ball. Though Lamonica had been used sparingly as Jack Kemp's backup, he had won several games coming off the bench. Al, in fact, remembered him for one single obscure play against the Raiders.

"He once told me he'd made up his mind about me," Lamonica said, "when Ben Davidson came in on me and I stood in even as Ben unloaded on me. He said, 'Hell, you didn't even care about gettin' hit, you just got to your knees lookin' to see if the pass was complete.' Al wanted that, a guy who could stand in and keep throwin' the long one."

Now, with Joe Collier looking to fill needs, he proposed a deal that cut to the Raiders'—and Al's—heart. Lamonica and middling receiver Glenn Bass would go to Oakland for Flores and none other than Art Powell. While this was an emotional torture for Al—Powell, his first Raider building block, had notched almost 4,500 yards and fifty touchdowns in four years, and Al liked him immensely—Powell was pushing thirty and coming off an Achilles injury; Fred Biletnikoff was clearly ready to emerge as the Raiders' primary receiver.

Conversely, on its face, the deal looked like a steal by the Bills —getting two Raider starters for two Bill backups—and Al was unwilling to consummate it. The Bills, who were kept dangling, finally issued an ultimatum: the deal had to go down before the Bills chose their first draft pick or Al could forget about Lamonica. On the day of the draft, Rauch was in New York, on a cross-country phone line to Al as the deadline closed in.

"Every time I got on the phone to him, Al got cold feet," said Rauch. "And so with about ten minutes left, he says, 'Look, if you wanna make the deal, go ahead.' But then he tried to muck up the thing by demanding a draft choice thrown in. Finally, with like a minute to go, we got the draft choice too and I made the deal. And then when I got back and told Al, he yelled, 'You idiot! Why'd you do it?' "

Lost in the importance of the deal in Raiders history was the sad termination of Art Powell's career. Having soldered his troubled soul to the team, he was "in shock" when the trade was made, according to Clem Daniels: "I think Al got some medical advice that Art wasn't gonna make it back from his injury. But that judgment came from the team trainer, the guy who took care of the Band-Aids, not a real doctor." And yet, the very next year, with the Bills, Powell, possibly favoring his Achilles, hurt his knee and missed half the season. The next year, he went to the Vikings and caught exactly one pass the whole season—the last of his brilliant career.

A similarly melancholy fate awaited Clem Daniels. The 1967 season would be his last. Like Powell, he was a victim of Raider modernization and attrition, out of which almost every position would be filled with a young and gifted player—the latest being the club's number-one draft pick, Gene Upshaw, a Gorgon-like guard from Texas A&I. The streamlining was moving so rapidly that Al worried about the team losing its sense of ragged-edged heroism.

Trying to soften the hard chrome of progress, Al dealt for two veterans merely for their weight in pockmarked wisdom. First he brought in Dave Kocourek, the old Charger tight end who had played in 1966 for the expansion Miami Dolphins. Next came George Blanda. The gnarly warhorse, now forty, was still chuckin' in Houston but for a team in dire need of youth. Still, the old boy had rousted the Raiders 31–0 in 1966, and when the Oilers cut Blanda after the season, Al claimed him.

"Al said he wanted a winning attitude on the team," Kocourek said, "but with Al nothing is that simple. I didn't contribute as much as I would have liked for the Raiders—I backed up Billy Cannon. But Al kept me around for three years."

John Rauch pondered Kocourek's role as well—and, along with many other things forced on him by Al, it made sense only in terms of interference from above.

"Rauch thought I was a locker room spy for Al Davis," Kocourek recalled, "that I was runnin' to Al with whatever John wanted to do, which was bullshit."

"I might have been skeptical along those lines," Rauch would admit. "I had to be skeptical of everything."

13

The old story was that Al used to pass the game plan underneath the door on Tuesday night, that everybody would sit around and pretend to go through the motions and all of a sudden the game plan mysteriously would slide under the door. I think that was a lot of bullshit.

—Dave Kocourek

Al shuns the spotlight but it's like Greta Garbo shunned the spotlight. Garbo did shun the spotlight, but by shunning the spotlight you become the act.

—Tom Keating

The 1967 season was the debut of the Raiders that most of the world first came to know about. With Al Davis as the managing general partner and great ghostly demigod of the team, the Oakland–Alameda County Coliseum—within which a fevered spirit unfolded in contrast to its cold gray minarets—bred a fanaticism drawn from all corners of the Bay Area. On opening day, over fifty thousand fans jammed their way in—twenty-one thousand more than had ever thought to attend a Raiders game. The Raiders, of course, won, a habit that would be disconcerting to visiting teams over the next two decades.

On the floor of the arena, players molded in the Al Davis style —Fred Biletnikoff, Jim Otto, Dan Conners—began to run with the gods. And, for now, the coach was all but forgotten.

Though there had been an infusion of new Raider blood, the basic, lethal simplicity of the team's operating systems—Al's old mad blackboard contortions having been cauterized to their ball-busting core—made it easy for newcomers to step onto a moving sidewalk now en route to serious winning. Now, in 1967, expectations ran fever-high.

"It was in training camp that year that we knew we had it," Harry Schuh remembered. "You had a lot of new, quality people and everyone was willing to learn all over again. We worked together, got together after games as a family, and it really helped bring the Raiders to a head."

One other of the new crowd took them over the mountaintop—Willie Brown. An unheralded cornerback for the Broncos, Brown had been a tight end at Grambling, but went undrafted. He was signed by the Oilers, who converted him into a cornerback but then cut him. He then signed with Denver and in three seasons he had a mere four interceptions. But Al, who closely scouted the small black colleges and mined them for men of great physical gifts, knew that Brown was good because, as terrible as the Broncos were, quarterbacks could throw *away* from him. This lesson was lost on Lou Saban, who took over as that team's coach in 1967. Al, cashing in on Saban's ignorance, grabbed Brown for a modest exaction—little-used defensive lineman Rex Mirich.

This trade, barely noticed in agate newspaper type, gave the Raiders perfection in the defensive secondary. At six-one and 190 pounds, Brown was like a large sock filled with hobnails; when he bumped receivers, marks were left. His ball-reading smarts were transmitted to his feet in an instant. As hard to get off his feet as was Lamonica, Brown took Bump and Run to its apogee—by not allowing receivers to breathe, he could practically determine the character of a game all by himself, actively or passively; if quarterbacks threw away from him now, the rest of the Raider wolfpack of linebackers and deep backs could load up on the other side.

Moreover, to their benefit, the defensive line was now peaking. In 1966, the Raiders led the league with thirty-six quarterback sacks, and this unit—Davidson and Lassiter on the outside, Birdwell and Keating on the inside—was perhaps Al's finest achievement, with their skill and an insouciant Raider hip. Davidson, in fact, had already become a marketing tool as a sixties-generation icon of antiheroism.

Mostly, that identity was nonsense, though Big Ben had no objection to it. The father of three daughters, he was a paragon of virtue and decency, but he did have feral habits. Even at six feet seven inches, Davidson raced motorcycles, a habit made for hype and a Hell's Angels metaphor. When he came to training camp in 1966, he had a full growth of beard, sprouted during a summer on the motorcross circuit. Ben put his football helmet on but with the shrubbery on his jowls, he couldn't fasten the chinstrap. Indifferent as Al was to physical crudity, he wanted Ben to find a razor. However, Davis had no intention of telling this to Ben himself.

"Al said during the coaches' meetings, 'Something's gotta be done with that asshole Davidson about that beard,' " John Rauch remembered. "And so it happened to be my night for bed-check and he says, 'When you go by there, tell Ben he's gotta shave that goddamn beard off his face.'

"So I went in there, apprehensive to do it. But Ben wasn't a mean guy, he was a very nice guy. He said, 'Coach, I've been cut by three clubs and nobody recognized me until I grew this beard.' And I said, 'Lookit, Ben, Al wants it off but you can keep the mustache part of it.' And he did, only he turned it into that big handlebar thing."

That bushy appendage, of course, soon became the single most identifiable symbol of Raider deviation. Davidson looked like a wayward Norseman out of *Die Götterdämmerung*, and his on-the-field theatrics now had a dramatic context. Though Ike Lassiter spun many quarterbacks Ben's way, Clem Daniels noted, "Ben would stand up and beat on his chest and hold his arms up and get all the credit."

As individual expression shook off the trammels of orthodoxy throughout the land, Davidson's exaltation of his destruction wasn't only an augury of a perverse new form of sportsmanship—it was *marketable*. He was an absurd and cuddly kind of reprobate whose style would play in Peoria, or at least in Palo Alto. Not long after, Harry Schuh, to his amazement, saw the future of American pop culture through the windshield of his car.

"I was driving across the Bay Bridge," he said, "and I look up and there on a billboard was Ben Davidson with his handlebar mustache holding a glass of milk. He was doin' a *milk* ad!"

Ben couldn't help but get attention, it seemed. During another off-season, he took his motor home to Mexico. Pulling into a gas station, he stepped right into the middle of a stick-up. The bandit was a kid with a knife; nonplussed, Ben strode over and, towering above the kid, said, "You don't really wanna do this, gimme the knife." Almost peeing in his pants, the kid surrendered. The story, naturally, fueled the legend of Big Ben.

Next to Joe Namath, Davidson was the AFL's most recognizable figure, and this microcosmic rivalry was at once delineated whenever Ben met Joe on the field. As Tom Keating recalls it, the sight of Namath would curdle the greased ends of Ben's mustache. "Ben would just . . . if Namath was comin' on the field, Ben would just go after him." As fast and elongated as Davidson was, he would routinely elude the Jet's tackle and be right in Namath's face.

"Ben used to come flyin' around the corner and he had a real good reach," Keating said, "and Namath would have to step back or step up. Well, this one time he steps up and Ben just *nails* him, and this was when the goalpost was on the goal line and Namath goes head-first into the post.

"I mean, I think he's dead. I go over and pick him up—Ben won't pick him up, he just walks away. And Joe's kinda wobblin' around. Well, damned if the sonofabitch doesn't get up and on the next play throws the ball for about sixty-five yards. I mean, it's just disgusting.

"But that didn't happen a lot; many times those guys just stayed down. And those were the days when you could just go right after the guy. There was no in-the-grasp or any of that shit. And offensive linemen couldn't use their hands—although I'm not sayin' they didn't anyway. But what they ended up doin', and it started in New York because of Namath, the league would station the referee right behind Namath. They were protectin' their big meal ticket because we always banged him around pretty good.

"The first time they did it, I was shocked. That was the first time I ever saw any referee do that. All he did the whole game was, he stood back there and when we'd get close to Namath when he got rid of the ball, he'd yell, 'Lay off! Lay off!' Damndest thing I ever saw—and they never did it for *our* quarterbacks. I bitched and moaned about that, boy.

"I guess they were right, though, because we were probably as guilty as anybody on late hits. Hell, we always figured if we kept on hittin' these guys enough, sooner or later they wouldn't wanna get up, or make some mistake. With Joe, with his quick release, you had to take the shot at him. And we still did. We still hit him. We just ended up gettin' two or three fifteen-yard penalties every game. Sometimes, Ben got called three times for it all by himself."

Like piranha, the Raiders' front four—with almost no blitzing from the linebackers, as Al had always deemed that an admission of weakness as well as a needless risk—went on a bacchanal of quarterback sacking in 1967. Revealingly, none of these men were highly regarded players when they came to the Raiders, before Al turned loose their primal urges. Keating had been injured during his first two seasons in Buffalo. "But Al's gonna find his kind of people, he knows who and where they are," he said. "I'd gotten hurt late in 1965 and Lou Saban, when he was coaching in Buffalo, called and told Al, 'I guess you don't want him, huh?' And Al goes, 'I still want him.' A guy does that and you say, 'I gotta do well for this guy.' "

As for Dave Grayson, his coming to Oakland meant liberation for Keating. "In Buffalo I had to check a lot of things at the line before rushing. With Al's system, I could just put my foot to the floorboard." With Birdwell playing the stand-up rover, Keating became the middle man in that overshifted line. As such, he was likely the world's first real nose tackle, though Al and defensive line coach Tom Dahms lifted the concept from Hank Stram's Chiefs.

"Hank would put Buck Buchanan in the middle, over the center, on a three-man line," Keating said, "The difference with us was, we played the four-man and slid with it. We'd sometimes line up even, two guys on each side, and then shift odd the next play. We had so many looks that offensive linemen always had to change their blocking techniques.

"And with the Raiders, you could break rules. Before I came to Oakland coaches would tell me that when a guard pulled, *never* run through the vacated gap, 'cause you might get sucker-blocked. Al's philosophy was that you might get caught one time a game on a trap, but you could make a helluva lot of tackles in the backfield all the other times.

"I mean, we had days. We were just *hammerin'* guys. One time in Denver, they had a guy named Max Choboian. Well, we hit Max Choboian *twenty-seven* times with the ball, even though he went down only eleven or twelve times. Ben hit him in the testicles so hard that we heard one of his testicles swelled up like a softball. God, it was just terrible. But it was that kind of thing when you'd get goin'."

By season's end, they had recorded a then-pro-record sixty-seven sacks —an average of almost *five* a game. Aided to no end by their relentless pressure on quarterbacks, the defensive backs grabbed a league-high thirty interceptions. All around, 1967 was not so much a season as it was a carnage. Daryle Lamonica arrived in Oakland throwing. Though he would often be criticized for not throwing short, surgical passes, he never wavered in his fealty to Al's incontinent brand of passing. That first year, Lamonica aired it out for 3,228 yards and a league-high thirty touchdowns.

In this windfall, many Raider receivers prospered. Fred Biletnikoff darted and dodged for forty catches and an average per catch of *twenty-two yards*. Warren Wells, a sylphlike receiver with ocelot speed but unproven abilities, was picked off the waiver list from the Chiefs and caught thirteen balls—*six* for touchdowns. Six others had at least ten receptions, with Hewritt Dixon coming out of the backfield for a team-high fifty-nine.

Wells was both startling and disturbing. As became clear to the Raiders, he was a man of drastic highs and lows. Out of uniform, demons seemed to run rampant within him, and far too often he took his refuge in a bottle of Jack Daniels. Yet on the field, he was a player of immeasurable talent—"probably the best athlete I ever played with," according to Tom Keating. "He could throw the ball as far as our quarterbacks, outkick our punters, and he got in great shape all the time." As the new "X" receiver in the Lance Alworth–Art Powell mold, Wells presented myriad options racing downfield with Biletnikoff—whose prissy moves led many to believe he was slow, much to their regret.

"People didn't realize that Freddy timed in the forty as fast as Warren did," Lamonica related. "Warren had a little better burst to the ball but you had to throw it equally hard to Freddy's side of the field. With any of those receivers—including the backs—if I saw man-to-man coverage, I would automatically go deep."

Then there was the effect of Gene Upshaw. At six-five and 255 pounds he was faster than most of the backs. Stationed in the left guard spot, he immediately became the nucleus of the running game. Often, Rauch would run two or three sweeps behind Upshaw on the first series of the game—right at the other team's best cornerback, so that the ungodly Upshaw would put a hurtin' on him early.

The next season, a third-round draft pick would bring another mastodon lineman: Art Shell, six-five, 255, and a two-way tackle at Maryland–Eastern Shore. When Shell matured and moved into the tackle spot next to Upshaw, the Raiders would slant their running plays almost exclusively toward the left side—and would do so until 1982, when both men had finally retired.

Among a cast of flagrant oddballs, Biletnikoff may have been the kookiest—although the man was clearly putting himself through hell. Nervous to the point of self-flagellation, his sallow face furrowed in anxiety, he looked as if he might snap at any minute. Watching Biletnikoff before a game was like watching a man about to be executed.

"As soon as he'd get done with the pregame meal," John Rauch said, "he'd make a mad dash to the locker room and throw it all up. God, he'd tear the locker room down with those roars he was makin' in there. Then he'd smoke two packs of cigarettes before the game started."

As much as Ben Davidson's mustache, Biletnikoff's signature was the gooky brown "stickum" he used as an aid in holding on to passes. Many players used stickum, but Biletnikoff accessorized it. He began by putting the stuff on the underside of a wristband, but he was allergic to it and when his arms broke out in a rash he reversed the band—which meant that anything that touched him was immediately branded by the gook. And because Freddy was a touchy-feely kind of nervous, everything on *him* was smeared: his arms, ankles, helmet, the whole inventory.

"He had so much of it caked on his hands," Harry Schuh remembered, "he'd ask me to pull some off as we were walkin' up to the line, because he usually lined up next to me. And I got so dirty with it that it was a liability—if I'm gonna get caught for holding, I didn't need to advertise it by havin' glue on my hands. So finally I told him to keep his distance."

His uniform crusted with muck and mucilage, Freddy became an alter ego of football fashionability—in other words, the archetypal Raider. But all his agonies created art on the field, where his jittery energy burned off in his intricate moves and his concentration. "We used to run a drill where the receiver was told not to look for the ball until he was fifty yards downfield and three to six yards from the sideline," Rauch said. "They'd look up at the last minute and find the blur of the ball. Well, Freddy would catch 'em one-handed while reachin' out of bounds. He was so good it was scary."

★   ★   ★

By the midpoint of the 1967 season, their reputation preceded them. "It was always Ben Davidson and the bad guys from Oakland were coming to town," Harry Schuh noted. The players themselves were not just dedicated to winning, but saw it as a kind of crusade for a lunchpail ethic. While Al hadn't planned it this way, Tom Keating—who played for two more teams but made his permanent home there—could smell the soot and silt of Oakland all over the Raiders.

"The town's a reflection of the team, and the team's a reflection of this town," Keating said. "Hey, it's just win, baby, 'cause if you don't win, what else is there?

"I mean, shit, Jack London can write best-sellers in Oakland, right? It's the kind of town that spawns that kind of people. Rickey Henderson might've made money in New York, but he sure didn't have any fun.

"I had some great coaches and owners in my career. I was blessed, from Hank Stram and Lou Saban and Chuck Noll, and Ralph Wilson and the Rooneys and Al—all just totally different guys but the cities are like that. Buffalo, Kansas City, Pittsburgh, Oakland. All overachievers. You gotta win, 'cause, hell, how are you gonna go into a restaurant that night? It isn't that people are gonna boo you, 'cause they never boo you in Oakland. It's just that, Jesus, you've gotta give 'em something to get 'em through the week."

In 1973, when Keating was traded to the Steelers, he thought it was because that team sought lessons on the Al Davis method—so *they* could meld team to town. "I tell you, I felt like a mercenary going there, to tell these guys how to win. And it's not like I had to do a whole lot. It was, y'know, hey, you guys are really good and you don't have to wear suits and ties on the road, all you gotta do is play and be a decent family guy—that was one thing Al liked, but he didn't go in for psychological testing and dress codes. You could have long hair or no hair, wear a jumpsuit or a three-piece suit, carry a lunchbox or a briefcase, he didn't give a damn and neither did we."

John Rauch had made more changes in 1967. Bill Walsh had left to become head coach and general manager of the San Jose Apaches in the short-lived Continental Football League, and Rauch hired two new coaches in his place. One, the new linebacker coach, was a thirty-one-year-old assistant under Don Coryell at San Diego State—John Madden.

Al, meanwhile, was consolidating as well. He had bought a spacious wood-frame home at 300 Mountain Boulevard in Piedmont, in the same upper-crust neighborhood Wayne and Gladys Valley lived in, staring down into the russet basins of Oakland. Fittingly, an old fallout shelter had been built into the basement, which may have comforted Al as he went about running the Raiders with a bunker mentality. There was, for example, the new Raiders office building and practice facilities he had ordered to be constructed in 1966, just across the Nimitz Freeway beside the Coliseum. It was now ready for occupation, and Rauch recalled bitingly, "We were allowed to come back in"—but to no less of a class system.

"Al's office was in the front and he was the only one that had a window that looked out over the freeway and into the stadium. The rest of us were back in the corner."

Yet, physically proximate as Al now was to the coaches, he still resisted the temptation to push himself into their affairs. "We saw more of him, naturally," said Rauch, "but we never had any meetings or anything like that, other than personnel meetings." But Al Davis still coursed through the Raider system like a kind of plasma. As Wayne Valley had foreseen, it hardly mattered that Al was not *nominally* the coach. While the coaches and players had little contact with him, nor did Davis ever stipple on the chalkboard anymore, Daryle Lamonica *did* assume the game plan came from the office of the managing general partner.

"I gotta believe," he looked back, "that very strongly in the background Al would look at those things and maybe not say anything, but at some point during the season they would be discussed. It would be crazy to think that Al didn't have a big influence over the Raiders."

Still, that was hardly evidenced, rarely glimpsed in the hard light of a locker room or coach's office—which, of course, led everyone to believe his presence was that much more cosmic. Thus, when Al *did* huddle up with a player, during meals, at airports, or on other meeting grounds, it could seem like a chat with Hermes.

"I always felt," Lamonica said, "that if I had an opportunity to sit and talk with Al Davis and try to get into his mind—and you really couldn't get near his level—that was a plus, because it only made us better as a team and me better as a player.

"Because you knew what he told you was right, and it would work. I would say, 'Al, I got an idea, what do you think?' and he'd say, 'Let me think about it.' And you could bank on it that the next day he'd meet up with you and say, 'I thought about it and it *looked* like it would work but it wouldn't. But if you use *this* formation, it would work in our system.' He wouldn't give you a flat no. He'd give you a football lesson."

Lamonica, then, could accurately say, "He was involved on a day-to-day basis. He was involved in the offense, defense, and special teams. He knew what we were doing at all times."

John Rauch, still addled by real or imagined obstacles, toddled on, feeling ever smaller. And then Al came too far from the eaves for Rauch to endure. To Rauch, it wasn't only that he did but *when* he did—after the Raiders began their rampage through the league in 1967.

"He had acted like he didn't want to get involved—up until we started winning," Rauch said. "We won four or five games in a row and then he came out to practice and he's got the same kind of trousers and shirt the coaches wore. And he just joins in, he starts tellin' guys this and that, and we had to pause every once in a while for him to get some coaching points in.

"And so my blood was boiling and I stepped out and said, 'Al, we don't have time for all this extra coaching. When I made the schedule for today, I didn't know you were gonna be out here.' And he backed off."

Clem Daniels, stunned like most of the players at Rauch's outburst, recalled it with a cold shiver. "I'll never forget it," he said. "Al said to somebody, 'You're doing that wrong,' and John stopped him in front of the players and said, 'Hey Al, *I'm* the coach.' And Al turned around and looked at him and walked off the field. I knew at that moment that John Rauch was not gonna get along with Al Davis."

Said Dave Grayson: "It took a lot of guts for John to do that. But Rauch also could've been there for another seven or eight years if he *didn't* do that."

Rauch surely figured there would be hell to pay. Seemingly with a dirge playing, he was called in to Al's office as soon as drills were done. Scolded by Al, Rauch then spoke his fermenting piece.

"My feeling was that him doing whatever he wanted to do with the club was like a cancer," Rauch said, "and anybody with cancer has to . . . the best thing to do is to get it cut out. And I said, 'If you want to fire me, go ahead and fire me.' He said, 'You know I can't do that.' And so it kept getting worse.

"I had the feeling that he tampered with a couple of the coaches. He had a couple of 'em . . . he was meeting secretly, with Madden and other guys, to find out what I was doin', pick up the game plan so he could act like, you know, he knew what was goin' on—which was his right, and I didn't feel badly against those guys because they told me everytime that they met with Al, or when Al called 'em. But it just made it an impossible situation."

Among the players and other coaches, Rauch's chafing became the source of amusement and derision—a marionette, for that's what he was, but one with *pride*, for God's sake.

"John was a really fine coach, maybe the best that Al ever hired," Ollie Spencer said. "But he was not a *head* coach, 'cause he got paranoid. It was hard for him to make decisions in the first place, so he should have welcomed Al's advice."

"Davis had one goal, the success of that franchise," Scotty Stirling asserted. "To do what John suggests would've been counterproductive. I was there and I didn't see any of that. Al was helping, because he understood the game so well."

Now, Davis's tongue-tying title, as it applied to football, was Al's license to trespass on property he owned. "He was a strong managing general partner," Spencer put it, "and there were very few times when he made an executive decision that everybody but John didn't agree with. We were a small organization, and it stayed small because Al could make all the decisions."

Harry Schuh, who was a Raider because of Rauch, was torn and saddened by the whole silly business. "John Rauch was a personal friend as well as a coach," he said, "and I thought John had probable cause, because he was winning; he had an opportunity to lead and tried to be his own man. And he did a helluva job, the record proved that.

"But this wasn't your normal situation. Al knew the offense and he was the boss; and if you're Al, you don't just drop out of sight and not be heard."

Interestingly enough, for all the hearsay around the club about Al's hard ties to game strategy, direct meddling was one thing Rauch never pinned on Al; his irritations were more textural, involving power-tripping games only an Al Davis could find edifying.

"I had no problems with him insofar as my ability to coach," Rauch clarified. "I and the staff made the game plan up and we gave the game plan to the players—although I'm sure Al got a copy of it, since the secretaries all had extra copies."

Actually, among Rauch's problems were his own personality and priorities. As a star quarterback who had worked in and with backfields for so long, Rauch on the practice field hardly altered his routine; to all appearances, he was still a backfield coach. And while a Daryle Lamonica could love that, Tom Keating shook his head and said, "I never understood Rauch—because I didn't really *see* him that much. I never really had much to do with him."

By the end of the season, Rauch and Al weren't on speaking terms. "I was the go-between for them," Scotty Stirling said, "because they had stopped talking to each other." But Rauch did win a small victory. Al continued appearing at practices, but abridged his visits to Wednesdays and Fridays; he also said little that was technical. "He came only to watch and stand on the sidelines," Rauch recalled. Al refrained from second-guessing Rauch and did not enter the locker room at all.

"I can't ever remember Al bein' a big guy in the locker room," said Tom Keating. "I mean, he wasn't a guy that spent a lot of time criticizing your performance. For the most part he'd tell you if you did something good."

All the same, Rauch could not have failed to grasp the dynamics of Al's mesmerizing mythology. When he showed his abbreviated but kingly countenance, he could swell or atrophy the egos and pride of huge and fearless men with just a few words, or a mere look.

"You'd lose two games and . . . I had a span of four years where we lost like eight games," Keating said. "If we lost two games in a row, I mean, *Fred Biletnikoff* was worryin' about where he was gonna be traded. *Everybody* was worried.

"'Cause Al's upstairs but, see, he's on the sideline and he's bitin' his fingernails down to the quick. He's kinda loomin' over your shoulder and it would be such a concern at all times to win, an all-consuming passion. I mean, to the extent that he would be in the airport and he'd be talking to Warren Wells, and he'd say, 'Son, if you just run the pattern like this . . .' and you would *watch* him doin' this and, Jesus Christ, other guys are in the bar or gettin' on the plane—but not him. And you realize that this is *it*. This is the whole show.

"And, you know, as much as you laugh about it, you're so goddamn . . . you can't let him down. Like when you see him on the field goin', 'C'mon, baby, we gotta win, we gotta win,' and he's dressed in the silver and black and at first you say, 'He's goofy,' but then you go, 'Hey, the guy's right down there with you.'

"Shit, he'd be workin' on guys on *other* teams. He'd stand out on the field before the game and tell 'em, 'Jesus, if we could just have you. Y'know, I don't care about money, I just wanna win,' and we're all dressed in black and we got Ben Davidson with a mustache and other guys that looked like they just got out of jail. And these guys are figurin', Jeez, I'd really like to be over there—and they wouldn't pay attention to the game. It really worked.

"Our whole team was like that. I know I always thought that we never lost games, we just ran out of time. Most of the time, I never worried. We'd be losin' goin' into the fourth quarter, and that never bothered me at all. I figured we were gonna win, that sooner or later those other guys were gonna quit, they were gonna stop and we were gonna beat 'em."

Al certainly knew the Garbolike merits of a minimalist mystique. In writing the rules of his unprecedented incumbency as he went along, he also could be pleased that as a shadowy figure he could quarantine himself from the scrutiny he hated. Al always wanted, needed, the power to control men and images without being visibly on the line himself. Now he had it, and was learning how to use it.

At the same time, in keeping away from Rauch's toes, he was at times sensitive to Rauch's feelings. After the Raiders ran away with the division title—going 13–1—Al did not seek attention during the postseason swirl. In fact, the first time most people saw him was after the Raiders trampled the poor Oilers 40–7 in the AFL championship game. Making an understandable breech in his locker-room withdrawal, he was summarily lifted off his feet by several players and tossed into the running showers—together with Wayne Valley.

"Al wore the wet clothes all the way home," Keating giggled. "It was a sign of honor. You gotta love it, *love* it! *He* loved it. He'd been waitin' all his life to get thrown in that shower."

Then, during Super Bowl week in Miami, while the Raiders were quartered at a Holiday Inn in Boca Raton, working out nearby in seclusion, Al stayed at the Doral Hotel in Miami.

But still Rauch found fresh ways to be distracted and anguished by Al. Before leaving Oakland, Rauch had a run-in with Al after the coach told his players they could bring a relative, a wife or whomever, to the game. When Al found out, Rauch remembered, "He called me in and said, 'Uh, uh. I don't have enough places on the plane. I got so many commitments for seats that there's no room. You didn't have the right to do that.' "

Rauch told him. "Al, the players take a relative or we don't go." The coach won.

But then came another skirmish, involving Billy Cannon. The veteran tight end, who was studying to be an orthodontist in the off-season at the University of Tennessee, had to take an exam there during Super Bowl week. Instructed to come to Miami on his own, Cannon didn't show when the Raiders hit town, and told Rauch he wouldn't come unless he could bring his entire family. Livid, Rauch ordered Cannon to Miami. "I said, 'You be here by such-and-such time or you're not gonna play in the Super Bowl and you won't play with the Raiders again as long as I'm the coach here.'

"Well, he came in the next day, with kind of a chip on his shoulder, and I had the feeling that Al set him up for that, encouraged him, to be another obstacle for me."

With the Green Bay Packers waiting for the Raiders to show up in the pit of the Orange Bowl, John Rauch's mind was occupied by travel arrangements and Al Davis. It wasn't a good omen.

14

We're going to go our way and our way is to create an
environment where people can come in and express
themselves. Sure, we're paramilitary, sure. But in our
organization, it's okay to dissent. Dissent is not an evil, it's
a virtue. It's the nature of America to dissent.

—Al Davis

Al wouldn't let me be myself.

—John Rauch

Al Davis chose to believe that his gains—which paralleled his
league's—had come at the NFL's expense. And he was on
to something. Though the elder league had those enormous flagship
franchises, the AFL now had more formidable quarterbacks, more
speed from top to bottom, more game-breaking receivers, more
imaginative methodologies—the NFL's most quickly evolving
team, the Dallas Cowboys, had an AFL look. And the Raiders and
Chiefs had size in the trenches to stand with the NFL's big front
lines.

But the Cowboys' problem—and the Chiefs', and now the
Raiders'—was the personal force of Vince Lombardi.

Lombardi, of course, was the living prototype of football czarism,
and Al had studied him closely, with reverence. But Al thought he
had taken the model a step further, and that he had something on
the great Lombardi—as an overall administrator of genius (which
was somewhat proven by Lombardi's subsequent failure as general
manager of the Pack in 1968).

What's more, even Lombardi knew that time was not on his side in Green Bay. Aging figurines of a dying football era, the Packers were running their stampeding sweeps now with Donny Anderson and Ben Wilson instead of Paul Hornung and Jim Taylor, and winning was taking a bigger chunk out of Lombardi's gut. He was fifty-four, and this Super Bowl would be his last game as coach of the Pack, which would crumble and fall from grace thereafter. Sensing they all were on the precipice, they rose up each week for Lombardi, tears in their eyes, as though they were holding off the Etruscans at the Tiber Bridge to save the glory of Rome.

Two weeks before coming to Miami, they had beaten the Cowboys in the famous "Ice Bowl" game, when the frozen Green Bay turf allowed just enough access for Bart Starr's last-second quarterback sneak. The afterglow of that dramatic victory all but trivialized the Raiders.

The Lombardi specter was the only thing that could have unnerved the Raiders the afternoon of January 14, 1968. "Hey, I thought we could beat 'em," remembered Tom Keating, who had hurt his Achilles tendon against Houston but played on—and well—against Green Bay. "But it was the kind of thing where, y'know, nobody on our club had ever gone against anything like that before."

"Everyone was so damn uptight for that game," Ollie Spencer grumped. "The press down there was brutal. Every day for two weeks it was Packers, Packers, Packers, and we didn't do a very good job of handling it. When we finally realized we could play with those guys, we'd dug our own grave."

Actually, one large trowelful had already been dug when Clem Daniels broke his ankle late in the season, an injury that would end his Raider career. When Al refused to re-sign him the next year Daniels, like Art Powell, played out a morose, one-year final act, carrying the ball twelve times for thirty-seven yards with the 49ers. Daniels's replacement against Green Bay, Pete Banaszak, was the kind of rabid plowhorse Al loved to sprinkle among the lab-specimen jocks; a five-eleven, two-hundred-pound drudge, Banaszak had little speed but could find a hole and hit it with every ounce of his being—his average per carry, 5.5 yards, was not small change—and he would play thirteen seasons for the Raiders as an effective short-yardage and special-teams bulldozer.

Mettlesome as he was, though, Banaszak simply could not shake loose the skies; passing to him out of the backfield might get a first down or two but it was hardly in keeping with the vertical game. On a team that otherwise scared defenses to death, Banaszak scored twice on sixty-eight running and sixteen passing plays. In the Super Bowl, he carried six times for sixteen yards.

Still, what may have been the killer was a strange lineup move by John Rauch. Trumpeting his ability to make a bold decision, he benched Dave Grayson and started Howie Williams at free safety, the idea being to have Grayson—who could also play cornerback —ready to spell any injured defensive back. Years later, Grayson was still miffed. "I'd had three interceptions against Houston the game before, then I sat at the Super Bowl because I was *versatile*. You don't think that hurt?"

It hurt the Raiders big time. Two-touchdown underdogs—an effect of NFL pomp and Lombardi—they were down 6–0 in the second quarter when Starr hit Boyd Dowler long downfield. Normally, on such plays, Grayson would follow the ball, but neither Williams nor anyone else came near Dowler, who ran it sixty-two yards for a touchdown. Lamonica then threw a twenty-two-yard touchdown pass to end Bill Miller, but just before halftime Rodger Bird fumbled a punt, setting up a Packer field goal and a 16–7 lead.

Thus staked, the second half was marked by Packer ball control and Herb Adderley's lightning-bolt, sixty-yard interception return. Though Grayson did eventually play, at corner and safety, the Packers were by then safely running the ball—forty-one times in all—and they won 33–14.

"Physically, we were on the field with 'em," Rauch reflected, "but we had busted coverages that gave 'em two scores."

"We went in at halftime and it was still doable," Keating said, "but it was big plays. They made 'em, and they had a running game that just hit it."

After his first taste of the football penultimate—the live gate was 75,546, the take $3 million, the TV audience 60 million—Al went home in a sour mood. "You couldn't talk to him; oh yeah, he was pissed," Grayson recalled. Though he held his tongue, Davis simmered inside about Rauch's coaching against the Packers. Years later, Ollie Spencer recounted what must have occupied Al's mind on the plane ride back to Oakland.

"The Packers had played their 4-3 defense in a certain way all year," he said, "but the first time we ran Hewritt Dixon to the weak side, they played it differently and I tried to get Rauch to make an adjustment, to run inside more with it, but it didn't sink in. They weren't gonna give us that play, but we didn't do a thing about it for the whole first half and that was kinda frustrating."

And yet Al took the loss harder than did the players, who were satisfied they put some hurtin' on the Pack. "I ended up gettin' the quarterback twice and got nine tackles, so I wasn't exactly in awe of 'em," said Keating. To these men, their season was more significant. In 1967, Lamonica was the AFL's Most Valuable Player, *fifteen* Raiders went to the All-Star game, and George Blanda—a horned toad of a man, irritated by nearly everything under the sun, and specifically by not being allowed to play quarterback—took it out on the football, kicking twenty field goals and racking up a league-high 116 points. Surely, there would be other Super Bowls. "I always figured," Keating said, "that we'd be back there fast."

Al did not stand pat over the summer. Because there had been some pieces missing against the Packers, he flooded Santa Rosa with any number of new people who might be the magical amulet. He didn't know if he found it, but his talent-reading expertise again proved to be unmatched. The 1968 Raiders were speckled with thirteen new players.

The key man all along had been Charlie Smith, a speed-rich halfback from Utah who had once beaten Olympic gold medal sprinter Jim Hynes in the hundred-yard dash. Smith was penciled in right away to replace Clem Daniels, and in 1968 he ran for 504 yards and caught twenty-two passes, with seven touchdowns. But the real savers turned out to be two defensive backs—George "Butch" Atkinson, a seventh-round draft pick out of Morris Brown, one of those tiny black colleges, and Nemiah Wilson, a veteran acquired at almost no cost from Denver.

But for them, 1968 could have been calamitous. From the start, injuries turned Santa Rosa into a hospital ward. Tom Keating never even made it to camp; after the Super Bowl, he played in the All-Star game and was chasing Joe Namath when his wounded Achilles ripped, an injury that would force him to miss the entire 1968 season. A much bigger hurt for Keating, though, was that Al refused to pay him while he sat out—his rationale being that *he* wasn't getting paid, since injuries incurred in All-Star games weren't insured.

"That was a nice rationale," Keating said, "but it didn't help me any. Then he wanted to pay me on the previous year's contract, and I thought I'd had a pretty fair year so I said no and I was gonna play out my option. I said, hey, you're not gonna pay me, I don't have to play here. And so this went on all season. I didn't draw a paycheck all year and I wasn't exactly Mr. Personality about it, either. I was motherfuckin' about it the whole time."

Toward the end of the season, Keating, who was the Raiders' representative to the players union, prevailed on the union—headed by the politically carnivorous Jack Kemp—to act on his behalf. Finally, Keating was paid, but Al never did lose the war. "The check came from the league, not the Raiders," Keating recalled.

Keating's place in the middle of the defensive line was taken by 260-pound Carleton Oats. Hardly missing a beat, the Raiders again led the AFL in sacks, though with a more mortal forty-nine. And when Kent McCloughan was lost with an injured knee, Atkinson and Wilson vied for playing time in the secondary; they did so well that they *both* had to be accommodated, at cornerback and safety. Though both looked as if they could be blown over by a small wind—neither tipped 170 on the scale—they were as frigidly aloof to pain (their own and that of others) as brass knuckles. Quickly, Atkinson, who liked to scream at and taunt receivers from first down to last, had acquired the league's worst reputation. In his rookie year, he also took back three interceptions for touchdowns. Dave Grayson, collecting the spoils of a secondary manned by killers, had a league-high ten interceptions.

The Tom Keating back-pay squabble was symptomatic of a general fretfulness about money as the decade began to dim. Because Al's capricious reward system was applied to so many disparate players, no one really knew what anyone else in the new Raider "family" was making.

"Hell, we were a put-together team from all over," Harry Schuh said. "Some guys didn't sign contracts with the Raiders, they were workin' on their old contracts, like the Lamonicas and the Dixons. And now we were winnin' so they would go in the next year to sign a contract and come out smellin' like a rose, while a lot of other people didn't feel they were bein' bumped up like that."

Most players of the era worked on one-year contracts, negotiated by themselves, and were easy marks for Al's heavy syrup about Raider Pride and his strategically fickle bonuses. Soon enough, in an era of multiyear deals and checkbook loyalties, these men would look back and blame the old plantation system for their plight, not Al Davis. Indeed, it was a perverse irony that Al could be effusively sympathetic in *personal* matters. It was Al who found a doctor for Keating's treatment, including twice-weekly trips to Los Angeles for therapy. And when Pete Banaszak's infant daughter was diagnosed as possibly having leukemia, Al vowed to send the child to the best doctors in the country.

And yet it is balefully tragic that Jim Otto—the Raider original who never missed a game for Al until he could barely walk—never made over seventy thousand dollars in a season (perhaps out of guilt, Al would keep Otto on the payroll after his retirement, in a variety of paper jobs). Though irked, Otto never made it an issue. "I never made a lot of money," he said, with no rancor. "When I retired there were a lot of players of lesser caliber makin' a whole lot more. Some other guys on the team were gettin' more and they weren't even playin'. But when you start out makin' seven thousand dollars. . . ."

Even players with open grievances with the Raiders were pacified. Ken Herock, the tight end who'd quit the team in 1965, sat out that year and then returned, was given a two-year contract. In 1968, though, Herock wanted out of the second year so he could sign with the Colts. When Al refused, Herock took the case to the players' union—and lost. But despite the wrangle, Herock stayed in the organization, as a Raider scout (and he is now general manager of the Atlanta Falcons).

Al, who'd always been in favor of the *concept* of a viable players' union, clutched his power of the purse tightly in the interim. But he knew the old system was going down. In 1968, the evening-up process was just under way. For the first time in a Raider camp, players' agents came to negotiate for players—and while they were few, Al was too smart to dismiss the implications of their kind.

Knowing the importance of the salary game from here on in, he did not replace Scotty Stirling when Stirling left to become GM of the newborn American Basketball Association's Oakland Oaks. Now there was a *technical* finality to Al's role; nevermore would he indulge in the burlesque of having a general manager. And as player hegemony rose and then free agency options became real in the seventies—and salaries were made public in the newspapers—Al had no choice but to pay big to stay competitive; his reputation as a guy who paid his players without compunction then was made retroactive. This would be prime among the forces that led him to consider options for the economic security of his team that no one could have ever imagined.

In the meantime, Al marked time with the exercise of heavy-handed duplicity when he felt like it. There was, by example, his handling of the great old pro, Billy Cannon. As Harry Schuh tells it, Cannon had a clause in his contract in 1969 stipulating a bonus if he started half, or seven, of the team's games.

"We had one game to go," Schuh related, "and Billy had started the last four or five and needed that game to make it seven. But Roger Hagberg started the first series—and then Billy came in and finished the game. So he didn't start half the season and Al didn't have to pay him that bonus.

"Needless to say, I heard about *that* whole summer, because Billy was goin' to dental school in Memphis and I would see him and that's how I found out about it. He was hurt, too. He had a chunk of money comin' and didn't get it when he deserved it. That's why a lot of the fellas didn't want to deal straight up with Al after that, and that's when agents started comin' in."

There was no leverage available to the long-suffering John Rauch. He was still terrorized by Al, and he and Davis maintained their lethal separation. "We were starin' daggers at each other through most of the season," he said of 1968. Worse, he could count on no sympathy from Wayne Valley, who helped usher him toward the brink by openly referring to Rauch as "Charlie McCarthy." Al Davis, of course, was Edgar Bergen.

"John Rauch was a good assistant coach," said Gladys Valley. "He was an army man and used to taking orders, not giving them. Al knew that and played on it. He lied to John and tried to make a gofer out of him.

"John Rauch was a straight-up guy, army all the way, as honest as he could be. And Al was disgusting to him. Al can't find things too small to use to get his way."

The Raiders again plundered the league, going 12–2, losing only on successive weekends in October. They were on the edge of another defeat on November 17, trailing the Jets 32–29 with under two minutes left. Joe Namath had shredded their impregnable secondary on that day, and it seemed like sweet revenge for Namath —the year before, in a late-season Raider win, a pass rush had leveled him and left him with a fractured cheekbone.

That event was of such import to the Raiders that the usually tongueless Ike Lassiter for once complained when Ben Davidson got credit for the butchering, after a photo ran the next day of Big Ben astride a flying Namath, his helmet separated from his head. The game films later showed it *was* an earlier Lassiter elbow-shot that did in Namath's cheekbone, but that photo added another briquet to the smoldering Raiders-Jets rivalry. Giddily, Al made a blow-up of the picture and hung it in the Raider office.

Now, Namath had his way, hitting Don Maynard alone for 228 yards in taking the lead. And that was the storyline millions of viewers were left with. Because the game was running into prime time, NBC pulled off the game and showed its scheduled program—the soon-to-be invidious *Heidi*, the name by which history remembers this signal game in crackpot AFL lore: "The Heidi Game," when nobody at home saw the Raiders score and then score again after a Jets' fumble to win 43–32.

As usual, Rauch could only laugh a little at such moments. As the season went on, he said, "Things got worse with the assistant coaches and the players. I had some players come to me saying that Al told them to do this or that, and I'd say, 'Look, Al's the boss but on the field you work for me.' "

Dave Kocourek was one of those players. Out injured during one game, he sat with Davis in the pressbox. "Just before halftime," he recalled, "Al grabbed me and said, 'This is what you've gotta tell Rauch.'' And so I'm rememberin' these things and I get down and I say, 'This is what Al told me.' And Rauch just looked at me like, 'What the hell kind of deal is *this*?' "

Taking satisfaction in small doses, Rauch's means of getting back at Al was to annoy him. When the Raiders practiced away from the Coliseum, Al wanted to know where they'd be going. Rauch would have someone tell Al a certain locale and then take the team elsewhere. "Al didn't call me in about it, but it probably didn't sit too well," he said, happily.

Still, Al was not eager for a confrontation, and he went to amazing lengths to spare Rauch from *public* embarrassment. When the Raiders played in Miami early in the season, a newspaper column appeared about the team that praised Al grandly. Going over it with Bob Bestor, the Raiders' business manager, he asked, "Does it flatter me too much, Bob?"

"He lays it on you, but it's a good column," Bestor said.

"Well, listen. Don't you think it makes the coach look bad?"

"He doesn't even *mention* him."

"I know. Listen, that's what I'm worried about. I tell you what. Why don't you go down to the lobby and buy all the papers so the coach can't get one."

Bestor and the club's public relations man, Lee Grosscup, did just that. Rauch never did see that column. Later, when Tom Keating heard the story, he was duly impressed—"Jesus Christ," he said, "the man spends $250 on newspapers at a time when you were payin' players $1,000 a week. Hey, that's a big-time guy."

Even had Al wanted to fire Rauch, he probably could not have. For all his nerve, he needed *distant* targets, dehumanized by over-riding crusades and nebulous causes. This was the same Al Davis who as a boy lost himself in troop movements all about Europe—and the same Al Davis who fought the Korean War in the PX at Fort Belvoir. In confrontations where actual wounds and actual lives were concerned, his nerve was drawn off by loyalties, sensi-tivites, and guilt. In these confrontations, often he turned tail and ran.

"Al won't fight face to face with anyone," said Gladys Valley. "He's a worm."

In part, Tom Keating agreed. "He can't fire *anybody*. Al will plant insecurity in coaches, but he just . . . it hurts him to fire anybody." Keating's huge body rumbled in laughter. "Hunter Thompson once wrote that Al Davis made Darth Vader look like a punk. But if he was as cold as Hunter Thompson says he is. . . . Hey, even Darth Vader couldn't kill Luke Skywalker."

Scotty Stirling said it this way: "People don't get fired on the Raiders, they just leave."

George Ross wasn't sure Al had so little to do with it. He saw too many faces move in and—unhappily—out of the front office. Al's relationship with Stirling, Ross believed, was hardly sanguine. "It deteriorated," he said. "I think it came short of bitterness but certainly it wasn't a happy evolution."

There was also the case of Bob Bestor, who as a young naval officer had been brought in by Stirling as a PR assistant and then became business manager—and a favorite Davis whipping boy. Tom Keating recalled Bestor as an "on and off" presence. "He was on the team, then off. I never knew which it was. Al was always on him about something. Like if the plane was late. Everyone would be bitchin' at the airport—especially in Kansas City, 'cause the bars were closed there on Sundays, with the blue laws—and so Al would hear the bitchin' and blame Bestor for the plane bein' late."

When Bestor wound up "leaving" in 1969, Ross had a theory. "Bestor had perfected an Al Davis accent and he was entertaining the coaches one afternoon and Al walked in behind him. I'm not sure if it was A-B-C you're out but it was shortly after that stunt that he was told to find other employment," which turned out to be back with Stirling, in pro basketball.

By then, Lee Grosscup was also gone—fired by Al after the 1968 season, but sadly and with justification given Grosscup's vehement self-destruction. A former NFL and AFL quarterback, author, and television sportscaster, Grosscup had worked for Al as a scout and talked his way into the PR job when Stirling left. But the job was an invitation for disaster. An alcoholic and addicted to painkillers, he was given an unlimited expense account, and used it to dine and knock back drinks with sportswriters. He also shared a house with Tom Keating—who could outdrink a small elephant—and moved about in the grottos of Raider excess. However, unlike them, he shared no self-imposed restrictions or sense of ultimate morality. Soon, he was out of control.

"Booze, pills, and funny cigarettes," is the lineup Grosscup recalled of the era, not any that ever played on the field. He went on: "I had a tendency to mix tequila and amphetamines. Then I'd take a hangover pill, Desbutol, with methamphetamine and phenobarbitol. A terrible, vicious cycle." Grosscup staged some truly sick scenes, none worse than when he insulted Wayne Valley in front of a large group of media people. "I had too much firewater in me, and Wayne just happened to get in the way," he said. Valley got Al to fire Grosscup. At the time, he raged about it. When he could again focus his eyes, he was grateful.

He says today: "A lot of people think I don't like Al because he fired me. But in some ways I owe my life to Al Davis. He was the first person who did not enable me to continue my ways. He looked me in the eye and said, 'You've got a major problem.' I think a lot of people misinterpret Al. He's very much of a humanitarian.

"In many ways I really was one of Al's first reclamation projects. By the grace of God, I haven't had a drink now in nearly twenty years and I have a very manageable life today so I'm grateful to Al Davis for telling me the truth about myself."

And yet for years after he was fired, Grosscup was on the outs with Al because he had told the truth about *Al*. Interviewed over a dozen-Martini lunch by the acerbic sportswriter Leonard Schecter for *Look* magazine, he hit Al where it most hurt—in his false bravado. "He wants to be thought of as an athlete," Schecter quoted Grosscup, "but he isn't even particularly well-coordinated. And he may have the skinniest pair of wheels in America, which is why he never takes off his pants where anyone can see."

In a sense, the *Look* profile—playfully jabbing at but affirming the Davis genius—might have been a source of pride, as Schecter had done similar tickle-penned studies of Vince Lombardi and Paul Brown. Now the trilogy of football majesty was completed with Al Davis. But Al, his vanity inflamed, saw it as heresy.

"He never spoke to me after that for a long time," said Grosscup, who was immediately contrite when the piece ran and still is. "I came off as the villain, and I was horrified. Schecter got me drunk and it was like someone who wakes up and finds he's murdered his wife. I had character-assassinated Al Davis."

Perhaps not coincidentally, Bob Bestor had some choice words about Al in *Look* as well. Among the choicest were these: "Davis's theory is that people are motivated by fear. He thinks people perform better if they're afraid." Today, Bestor will flinch when asked about the relationship.

"I'm not interested in talking about it," he says, curtly.

The Raiders steamrolled the Chiefs 41–6 in the semifinal playoff and on December 29 went to New York to play the Jets for the AFL championship. New York was an iceberg that day. The swirling, vicious wind that normally swept off Flushing Bay and pounded Shea Stadium was whipping human flesh like razor strokes on a barber's strop; glazing over an already-frozen field, it made game plans immediately inert, since both passing *and* running were problematic. Seeking any small comfort, the Raiders' equipment people built a clear plastic bus-stop–like shelter on the Oakland sideline to shield the players—an idea always assumed, incorrectly, to be Davis's. Actually, it was the work of an old high school buddy of Harry Schuh's named Stan Canter, whose sports equipment company in New Jersey made the pirate decals on the Raiders' helmets.

Canter, who sometimes traveled with the team, came to New York with his tools, spent Saturday foraging for materials, and helped assemble the shelter on Sunday morning. Al knew nothing of it until he saw it—by which time Weeb Ewbank and the Jets were getting AFL president Milt Woodard to order the thing torn down, saying it obstructed fans' view.

Weeb played hard on the shelter in his pregame pep talk—with no doubt in his mind Al had set up the farce to unnerve the Jets, off past form. "He'd do anything to get an edge," Ewbank said. "My wife used to get mad at me because he'd call me the week before a game at about 12:30 or one in the morning, just to talk. I'd say, 'Al, I'm in bed,' and he'd say, 'Oh, I forgot about the time difference.' Hell, he knew the time. He'd just wait until he knew I was in bed, to bug me."

Regardless of who got the edge this time, the result was less a game than a cockfight. Even in the tundra of Shea, there was 860 yards of total offense, with Namath and Lamonica heaving rockets that cut right through the wind. Namath had the Jets out to a 10–0 lead, but then Lamonica began finding Fred Biletnikoff on what had become Freddy's most dependable play—"91 Comeback," on which he streaked long downfield and curled *back* to the ball; he then did a little toe dance to shake defenders, who had to follow him backward.

Against the Jets, he caught a twenty-nine-yard touchdown and six other passes, 190 yards in all, and Warren Wells caught three for 83 yards. The Raiders tied it 13–13 in the third quarter, gave back the lead, then went ahead in the fourth quarter after George Atkinson ran an interception thirty-two yards and Pete Banaszak jammed it over from the four. Namath then made the pass of his life. He hung one out that Don Maynard caught over his shoulder, then tumbling out of bounds—fifty-two yards downfield, to the Raider six—and next whistled a dart to Maynard slanting into the end zone. Jets, 27–23.

But a dogged Lamonica dragged the Raiders right back, deep into Jet territory. And then he made the mistake of *his* life, one grounded in irony. Lamonica, the man who hated to throw short, chose now to throw short. But, meaning to lead Charlie Smith with a screen pass out of the backfield, he threw *behind* Smith. When Smith reached back for the ball, it glanced off his shoulder pad and fell to the ground. Thinking it was an incomplete pass, Smith and almost everyone else just stopped; but when no whistle blew, Jets linebacker Ralph Baker picked up the ball and ran it all the way into the end zone. While people stood around confused, the officials met and ruled it *lateral*, not a forward pass; the Jets got the ball where Baker recovered it and ran out the clock.

Lamonica still grieves, his eyes haunted by the pass. "I worked on that play the whole week," he said. "It was the right play, had we executed it. But Charlie got bumped around and I threw a bad ball. Gosh, we had no doubt we'd win that game. If I'd just thrown a good ball. Gosh."

Tom Keating, standing feet-frozen on the sideline in street clothes, spoke of it with pain. "I'm standin' there goin', 'Oooh, *noooo*.' You talk about depressing. It was dark out, it was cold. And it was a *long* ride home."

For Al it was another ride filled with anger. It was the Jets who went on to the football apocalypse, goring the wheezing beast of the NFL by beating the Colts in the Super Bowl. Quickly, the recriminations began in Oakland. While Al had not second-guessed Rauch before, now he did. In clipped but cutting verbiage, he used the *Tribune* to question Rauch's wisdom against the Jets. That finally tore it for Rauch.

"He had some comments about 'We never should've lost,' " Rauch said. "And so this was running through my mind and I just knew I had to get out. I had three different opportunities to go someplace, and even though I was still under contract to the Raiders I got things squared away with Buffalo to be their head coach."

That's when he went to Al—an indentured servant risen against the lord of the manor.

"Al, I'm leaving," Rauch said.

"You can't do that," Al told him. "You're under contract."

Rauch stiffened, then—with a line he had dreamed of someday using—calmly pronounced, "Al, if you stand in my way, I'll tell everybody what I know about you."

Rauch recalled that sublime moment as deliverance. "He looked at me a minute and then he said, 'Say no more. Do what you wanna do.' "

And what *did* Rauch have on Davis? Even while backing off, Rauch tantalized the senses.

"I don't even want to reveal it," he decided. Then, with an elusive grin: "But so many things he did back in those days, like business stuff, make Watergate seem like child's play."

★   ★   ★

The top candidates to replace Rauch became John Madden and Ollie Spencer. They were the most malleable of those who knew the Raiders' system. A defensive guy and a line guy, they would not only be amenable to Al's advice but they would *need* it; unlike Charlie Sumner they weren't too tart, and unlike Tom Dahms they weren't too trollish.

Al, of course, would make this choice a demonstration of his Raider loyalty, but the man he really wanted was Chuck Noll, his old mulish compeer with the Chargers. But Noll, by then an assistant under Don Shula in Baltimore and a hot property in the football orchard, took the top job with the Steelers. Of the others, Madden clinched it on intangibles, an innate sort of symmetry with the Raider typology.

Still just thirty-two, Madden was uncorrupted by football convention, so much so as to seem not just ingenuous but *nutty*. To Tom Keating he was "an absolutely absurd figure, with his little nameplate flapping on his belt and screamin' at referees, the bare arms in the cold and runnin' all around. God, he was great."

The Raiders knew Madden as "Pinky," for his big-top elephant size, his red hair, and the way his pulpy, pale-salmon face and neck lit up neon-red when he got agitated. Once *off* the field, that part of him drained away along with his melanin. Madden had no pretension of a kaisership, and would have laughed out loud if anyone ever suggested he should. Because he had a sense about him that he knew himself, Al thought it probably followed that he would know his players. And in fact nobody on the Raiders disliked him, and very many learned a lot from him—yet, as natural a "man's man" as Madden was, he had also put a good deal of work into his craft, and his easy ways were more ordered than most knew.

Always a huge man, with a California kind of balm beneath the surface—he grew up in Daly City, near Oakland—Madden was a guard at Cal Poly at San Luis Obispo and was drafted by the Eagles in 1959. But in his first pro camp he tore up his knee. Out the whole season, he would take whirlpool treatment in the morning at Franklin Field and then wander into the room where the Eagles' great quarterback Norm Van Brocklin would be studying game films. The Dutchman would point things out to him, things he would remember, but with his career finished, Madden went back to Cal Poly, earned a Master's Degree in education, and began teaching at San Luis Obispo High School. When the football coach there was fired, Madden took over. Then, as line coach at Hancock

Junior College in Santa Maria, he met Don Coryell at a coaches' clinic. Coryell hired him as defensive coordinator at San Diego State in 1964.

All the while Madden continued teaching at whatever school he was at, and an important root of his coaching style was his knowledge of the group dynamics of infants. "As a coach," he once said, "the class that helped me the most was child psychology. I learned that, as a group, football players react like children." Translating these lessons to adults, Madden let them *act* like children while learning to take ultimate control of their own subjection—which was, in a more structured essence, right out of the Al Davis textbook.

Keating, to whom Rauch was a rumor, could sit with Madden over beers one minute, then be torn into by a beet-faced Madden on the field. In either case, he would love it. "It was a different approach," he said. "John Rauch wasn't a lot of laughs."

"Madden's biggest asset was his people skills," Pete Banaszak recognized. "He knew each player, what made 'em tick, what made 'em go. He knew if he had to pat a guy on the back or kiss him on the ear. We had quite a few guys that he had to grab by the shirt collar and kick 'em in the ass, be belligerent and obnoxious to get 'em to play. He'd say, 'I'm gonna trade you to Buffalo,' and you'd sit up and listen.

"He related that way to Al, too, because John knew what Al's quirks were, and when Al needed to be stroked. He knew *when* to have Al involved, and he also knew when to take the bull by the horns himself."

Madden used his "big lug" outer shell to maneuver into authority without sirens blaring. As George Ross put it, Madden "bargained" with Al to get on solid footing. To be sure, Madden's situation was severely different from Rauch's. The Raiders had already won a championship (AFL) and Al was definitely in power. Thrilled to be a head coach, Madden had no fantasies of "taking over" for Al, or crises of confidence. While Rauch looked for things to brood about, Madden simply did not care what Al was doing or whether anyone thought he was a puppet.

Disposition aside, he also knew how much he *did* need the kind of life support Al could provide. At first Madden sat in awe as Al instructed him. "Madden's expression was, 'What better counsel can I get than Al Davis?' " Ross said. Once entrenched as a Raider symbol himself, Madden was moved to prose that both flattered and distanced Al. "If I had an idea, I had to sell it," he said many years later. "But it's the same with Al. He didn't tell me, he sold me." There would be small tensions between them down the line, but by that time Al appreciated not only Madden's authority but his coaching wisdom. Deep into the seventies, *Madden* would be inviolate. When Al Davis's eye strayed to lusher financial meadows, it was because he didn't need to keep it trained on the gridiron. That was Madden's domain.

Having mastered life with Al Davis, about the only thing he couldn't conquer was his fear of flying. On plane rides Madden would sit tethered, bolt upright, his face ashen and his palms dewy—a massive American bison as helpless as a bairn. Absurd indeed, the players took to him as a precious mutation.

"One time during John's first year they cut the grass on the field," Keating recalled, "and before practice Ben [Davidson] laid down and covered himself with loose grass, so you couldn't see him. So now it's gettin' close to starting time and Tom Dahms—who was *always* tryin' to change Ben, or somehow discipline him—puts his foot down. He doesn't see Ben and he goes, 'Okay, that's it. Ben's late, he's bein' fined.' And with this, Ben rises out of the grass like a corpse, and Dahms almost has a coronary.

"And Madden's watchin' this and he loves it, *loves* it! In fact, John affectionately called Ben 'Weird Ben.' He'd say, 'Weird Ben, what are you doin'?'—'cause Ben would always be doin' somethin'. And John would be the first guy to laugh about it."

Al was comfortable with his new coach, too. He was on the field more, at almost every practice now, still keeping out of the coach's way but walking about his kingdom easily—though that could be deflating at times, as when he saw Pete Banaszak smoothly spin a football on his index finger like it was a basketball going round and round. "Al would watch you do that," Banaszak said, "and he'd walk down to the other end of the field and pick up a ball and try to do it, and the goddamn ball would roll away from him. He'd go, 'Ah, *shit!*' "

But if Al still rued his failure as a jock, now he had all the means to be an owner of the highest distinction. To do that, his power had to be indivisible, not only in name but in *fact*. His new coach in place, his club's string of success uninterrupted, he made a new commitment to old business—deposing Wayne Valley.

15

I thought he was aggressive, but if I had thought he was a crook, I would never have brought him back.

—Wayne Valley

He's just petty and small and weasely. He's like a rat under your house.

—Gladys Valley

The departure of John Rauch ended the Raiders' classic era of innocent depravity. Only one year remained until the American Football League became the American Football Conference and played in the combined new NFL, and Al—who must have been saddened by another part of his life dying—faced the new era with a hard-eyed lack of joy. If pro football was to be a more corporate game, he would go into it as impiously as any other mercenary, shoring up every loose end of his own power.

While front office staffs all around the league were enlarging to meet the demands and status of the football boom, Al *reduced* his. When Lee Grosscup and Bob Bestor were gone, he wanted to amalgamate their duties and all business, marketing, and public relations matters into one job. For this, he found cause to once again summon the loyal and like-minded leprechaun from Philadelphia, Al Lo-Casale.

In the six years since Davis had arrived in Oakland, LoCasale had broadened his own reputation as a guy who could scout good players, sign them, keep them housed and transported, and count the money they made for their owners. To LoCasale, as to Davis, a player could be both as singular as a son and as faceless as chattel. As testimony to LoCasale's functionary value, when Paul Brown— outmaneuvered by Art Modell into ceding power and then selling out of his namesake Cleveland Browns—returned to football with the expansion Cincinnati Bengals in 1968, the first front office mover Brown hired was a thirty-year-old LoCasale. Within three years, that team would win its division.

LoCasale's loyalties being what they were, an SOS from Al—the man who cushioned him in pro football—sent his tiny feet running to Oakland after only a year in Cincinnati. Fitting right into the Raiders' choleric cabal of Al and Ron Wolf, LoCasale both upgraded the club's business affairs and chilled its relations with the outside world. Routing all contact through him, he hermetically sealed Al inside his mystique.

If Al was suspicious of anything, LoCasale—"Little Al," as he was soon called, as contrasted with the "Big Al" few saw—could be magnificently uncooperative. Since Big Al was suspicious of almost *everything*, Little Al was in no time a heavy. Several years later, *Sports Illustrated*'s Ron Fimrite took a spade to him, writing: "LoCasale's brand of loyalty seldom tolerates criticism, and he has been known to upbraid offending journalists personally. He can be equally abrupt with Raiders employees."

As quoted by Fimrite, one such employee said that "Al Davis wants it that way. He hired himself a fall guy, somebody to yell at secretaries and office workers. LoCasale is a Napoleon." Said another: "He's a little man in a big man's sport. You don't have to be a shrink to see where he derives his bigness."

Even George Ross now had to deal with Al through Little Al, and allowed that LoCasale "is very good at putting into words what Al Davis would've said if Al Davis would deign to say it." But for George this was suggestive of a larger tragedy—on a human level, Al was losing touch with the unique Raider kith and kin.

"At the outset," he said, "Al, Scotty, and I were socially equals. When Scotty went to work for Al, very rarely were the three of us having lunches anymore. Then when Al grew into his ownership role, the original assistant coaches went their way socially and Al went his. Now he moved with owners, that was his new stratum. It was like I didn't know him anymore."

With LoCasale as his proxy, Al didn't have to answer for any ugly business. In the spirit of confederation, NFL and AFL teams began to exchange game films preparatory to the first few interconference games. Al gave not one can of celluloid. There would be no loose lips in the front office and no edges given away on the field.

But while he was now a certified leper in owners' circles, where once other teams made light of his claquelike method, they now began *studying* it for clues to success. Dripping acerbity, Al told *The Sporting News* in September 1971: "A lot of teams have been trying to copy . . . our method of organization. Imagine that? Makes a man feel humble."

John Madden, for one, was rather comfortable in the small, hidebound Raider hierarchy—which, with a deftly ironic touch, Al took to calling "Pro Football's Dynamic Organization" on the press guides. "It was simple," Madden once said. "Al ran the club. I ran the team. Ron Wolf ran the scouting. Al LoCasale ran the office. I didn't even have a secretary. I used Al's. That's how simple it was to work with Al—not for Al, *with* Al."

For all the closeness, though, Madden never really understood Davis. Years later he would tell *Inside Sports*, "Al doesn't have the tools that are visible to people to show [his] feelings. Once we won a big game and my son Mike was in the locker room. He was in fifth or sixth grade. Al said to him, 'What do you want? Name anything. A business? A motorcycle? A store?' That's how he would try to show it." (Eventually, Al found a way to be good to Mike Madden—by putting him on the Raider payroll as an administrative assistant. Just as Al would be good to John Madden, who, when his coaching days were over, would also be placed on the payroll, as a "consultant for special projects.")

Still, Madden was forever fascinated with the incredible, if slightly twisted, obsession that drove all of Al's impulses. Said Madden: "He knows the football, the rules, the ticket situation, the radio contracts, the advertising. He'd have a mood for each one—he would create his own moods. A mood for drafting, a mood for trading, a mood for negotiating. One mood just kicks right into another. You can simplify a simple person. You can't simplify Al Davis."

Comfy as he was, Madden was no luckier than Rauch winning the big one. In 1969, his rookie season at the helm, the Raiders went

12–1–1 and demolished the Oilers 56–7 in the semifinal playoff—
but then broke down against the Chiefs in the last AFL championship game when a hobbled Daryle Lamonica threw three interceptions, George Blanda threw another in relief, and Blanda missed
three field goals. The Chiefs averaged only 2.2 yards per rush and
completed only seven passes, but Len Dawson hit two of those for
long gains on the game's climactic drive and Kansas City won
17–7, for the right to bully the Vikings in the Super Bowl.

The next season, the Raiders lost, tied, and lost again in their
first three games—then lost Lamonica to an injury. Down to cases,
Madden went with Blanda, who was forty-three but still rabid. In
just over a month, the irascible old bushdog won four games and
tied another, most of them in heart-stopping fashion—three last-
second field goals, one of fifty-two yards, another of forty-eight.

Called on again in the AFC title game when Lamonica pulled a
thigh muscle against the realigned Colts, Blanda came in down
10–0. He then kicked a field goal and hit Fred Biletnikoff for a
thirty-eight-yard touchdown to tie the game in the third quarter.
Down 20–10, he hit Warren Wells for a fifteen-yard touchdown.
Here Blanda's luck ran out—in Colt territory twice more, he threw
end-zone interceptions. The Colts, 27–17 winners, then took out
the Cowboys in the Super Bowl.

These and similar losses in the future were so desolating—yet
became so routine—that it seemed as if some great illiberal fist was
punishing them and their Pirandellolike owner for their antiheroic
heathenism. Much like the peace movement—of which they were
the antithesis—the team came close to victory but ultimately suffered in awful frustration. Thus the Raiders were left in the cultural
dust behind the more marketably iconic yet far less enduring Joe
Willie Namath.

But, clearly, in a xenophobic NFL the Raiders were probably
the first team to reflect a changing cultural balance. Certainly they
had more room for outright dissenters, and may have even had pro
football's first hippie—Ralph "Chip" Oliver, a linebacker drafted
out of USC in 1968. Oliver wore his hair long, did yoga, and ingested
all kinds of chemical whoopee. Even Lee Grosscup, in his purple
haze, was amazed by Oliver's capacities. "Here's a guy who played
under the influence of various psychedelics, as well as other things,"
he said. "I can't imagine doing that. When I played I took amphetamines or dexedrines a few times, but I can't imagine playing
on acid."

This was an open secret to Al and the players, and it was tolerated because of Oliver's abilities. Oliver was listed at 220 pounds, but Tom Keating said he was really about 205, "but he'd knock the shit out of people." But *nobody* understood him. Pete Banaszak, whose chiseled chin and bent nose exemplified the Raider profile, said of Oliver, "He didn't even have half of a deck. We called him 'Loose Wire.' "

And then, after the 1969 season, his brains scrambled, Oliver decided it was impossible to reconcile football with peace and love. He dropped out of the game, renounced meat for gerbil food, and went to live in a commune in the northern hills of Oakland—only to decide two years later that football was a vital component in his life after all. Oliver came back to training camp, but his sabbatical had sapped him of twenty-five pounds. Unable to jar people anymore, he again retreated into the hills.

Chip Oliver portended the societal change that became commonplace on the Raiders. By the early seventies, they resembled a traveling freak show. "I always went to the airport early just to see what guys were wearin'," Keating recalled. "Guys were gettin' on the plane with jumpsuits and wearin' granny glasses. George Atkinson had a collection of glasses with little square lenses, one purple, one blue. [Defensive tackle] Art Thoms would get on with a pair of ripped jeans, a T-shirt, and a lunch bucket with Snoopy decorations—it was some kind of fashion statement, I don't know what. And on the same plane you had guys with a suit and a briefcase. That was the Raiders."

More seriously, Oliver's drug dissipation was not isolated. "I'm certain," Keating said, "we had people that did *everything*." Harry Schuh added: "Yeah, we had a couple, and after a while it wasn't hidden. In fact, one guy, a very good ballplayer, became a total vegetable because of it."

The problem was, the transition to spaced-out recreation was so new that no one, not the players, not Al, quite knew of the mortal implications of this feel-good derangement. Having predated the coked-out descendants of the breakthrough potheads and acid freaks, Keating—in Raider tradition—still defends the high principle of hands-off individualism, even having seen the grievous plague that followed.

"I remember the Houston Ridge case," Keating said, referring to the Chargers lineman who in 1971 claimed that team's doctors dispensed amphetamines and muscle relaxers that led to a disabling injury. Ridge sued the Chargers and won a $250,000 settlement. "The next year the league put up signs in the locker rooms saying that you couldn't take amphetamines and all this shit. That was like putting a warning label on a beer can, for Chrissakes. I mean, if there was a pill that made you a player, I'd own a fuckin' pharmacy, but it doesn't work that way; you don't stick your hand in a jar of pills and go out there and be Joe Montana.

"But, hell, who cares what anybody else does? Does the guy play? That's what I care about—is the guy playin' and is he fun to watch? If a guy's playin' on coke and he doesn't play well, well, you get rid of him—I still don't understand why you send him to the clinic and bring him back, like they do now. But this country's not a police station. When a guy's pissin' on the sidewalk, or pickin' his nose in public, *that* should be a crime, not what he does in his sex life or what he puts up his nose.

"That's the way I look at those things—and that was the philosophy of guys that played in Oakland. You *got* there because you were that way. Sometimes other teams didn't like you because you were that way."

Al did not specifically clamp down on the Raider drug-takers, just as he didn't with the boozers. With anyone who went one toke or one shot glass over the line, he kept it under a sealed lid, within the Raider "family." When linebacker Terry Mendenhall took a cue from Houston Ridge and sued the Raiders after a serious injury—he said the trainers and doctors didn't warn him of the dangers of playing tanked up on painkillers—Al settled quickly, out of court and out of the public eye.

Indeed, according to George Ross, Al—out of self-interest—may have had something to do with the Ridge case not going to court as well. During the court proceedings, he said, "A number of depositions were taken from other players, including some who had played in Oakland and who were now playing elsewhere. Those depositions, had they been introduced, might have been extremely damaging. But the Chargers or the league, or both—and Al was a very interested owner—settled and so the thing never blew up."

Before the Mendenhall settlement, Mendenhall's lawyer came to Keating, who as player rep might offer some dirt on the team. Keating reacted as though he was being asked to rat on the Cosa Nostra. "I said, 'Listen, asshole, I'm not testifyin' against [team doctor] George Anderson or against the team.' He said, 'You know, I can subpoena you.' I said, 'Go ahead, put me on the stand and

I'll tell the truth about *everybody*, your guy too.' That was the last I heard from him."

A few years later—as a score of NFL players made headlines in drug cases—life would be simpler to cleanse. High-priced Raiders would have to be wheeled to and from those fancy clinics. But still the public would not hear about anything amiss in Oakland. If depravity wasn't innocent anymore, Al Davis could always pretend it was.

Just how far Al was willing to go with a reprobate—with talent— was shown when the problem of Warren Wells broke open like an ugly pustule. During the off-season in 1969, said George Ross, Wells "went to a party, at which was the wife of one of the prominent black people in town. He offered to drive her home and then climbed all over her. I think she got home with a fat lip and she had to say where she got it, and so the husband pressed charges and wouldn't let up."

That resulted in an attempted rape conviction, and in September Wells was put on probation. He played two more seasons—running from tacklers and the police. He once was nabbed for speeding twice within half an hour, on either side of the Bay Bridge, and violated probation many other times. Only the work of Al's lawyers kept him out of the can.

But, finally, Ross said, "He got too far overboard. If he had one drink he couldn't possibly pass up a second. If he had two drinks he was completely out of it." In February 1971, while home in Texas, Wells was arrested for driving while drunk and for illegal possession of a handgun. Again, Al sent attorneys to help Wells's case, if not his alcoholism, and they were able to get him off. Only months later, he was hauled in again after he beat up a woman in a Beaumont, Texas, bar, who then stabbed him in the chest, missing his heart by inches. Convicted of assault, he served ten months before Al could get him out. But, by now, Wells had lived too hard.

"You could see, watching on the sideline, that this guy was gone," Ross recalled. "There was nothing left."

Al had to cut him in camp, and Wells went back to Texas— where, in 1976, he wound up in the Huntsville State Prison for three years on an attempted robbery rap. In the short term Al helped Wells stay free, but in the end he helped him not at all.

★ ★ ★

By the start of the new decade, the tension between Al and Wayne Valley had flared into a full-blown war of nerves. For a time, as proud and stubborn as both were, neither got in the way of the other's stated function. "I think Wayne respected Al, and I don't think being kept away from the football end bothered him too much," George Ross said.

"At the same time, Wayne recognized that he had a fiduciary responsibility to the limiteds to retain a watchdog position. So at the end of the year he made damn sure the books were audited, and I don't think Al resented that.

"If they had something that had to be talked out, they would. But Al just resented the implications that he had to talk with Wayne about things like the size and shape of the football, how many pounds of air it held, and so on."

As time went on, he was also sickened if he had to appear publicly with Valley. "It happened with quite a bit of stress," Ross said. "If there was a meeting where they had to appear with the Coliseum board or something like that, and there were pictures taken, generally one of them went. Not both." Usually, a petulant Al would be the one to keep away—further driving him into his shell.

"Except if it were a top-level event, he didn't like to speak to crowds," Ross went on. "He would phone me and say, hey, who's gonna introduce me? And I'd divine what he meant—he resented having Wayne on the podium, and Wayne being asked to introduce his managing general partner, because Wayne would say things like, 'We brought the guy here to win and he is, but if he doesn't, he's down the road.' Al just hated being in Wayne Valley's orbit, let alone in his shadow."

One place where Al would not set foot was the Sequoia Country Club, which was Valley's turf. When a dinner in honor of Ross was held there, Al had to decline George's invitation. "He phoned me and made excuses why he couldn't come. And then late in the day, as everyone was arriving, Al drove up and called me over to his car and said, 'I just wanted to explain again, I wanted to come but I can't do it here.' I said, 'Al, I understand it perfectly.' "

Valley, feeling the sting of Al's venom, made a show of *his* independence from *Al*, often with a deplorable lack of couth. Remembered Ross: "On the plane rides once in a while, some of the limiteds—who were almost all Wayne's guys—would get a little bit loaded and after a loss they'd say things across the aisle to Wayne, like, 'Well, where's your genius now?' and they'd all cackle and openly make remarks to Al—sometimes Wayne would tell anti-Semitic jokes, and it would turn quite ugly. It wasn't that Wayne was a Jew-hater. He just wanted to get Al's goat.''

And he did. "Al was sensitive to anti-Semitism," Ross knew. "That was one reason he'd say, 'I hate that son of a bitch,' meaning Valley." His drive to discredit Valley justified, in Al's mind, by Valley's cracks, he decided to use the long-kept secret of Devoir Management—Ralph Wilson's lifesaver investment in the Raiders —against Valley. As Al wanted no part in public criticism of a Raider partner, he turned to George Ross to do the dirty work, by putting it into bold type in the *Oakland Tribune*.

George could see Al's reasoning. "The whole thing was unknown in Oakland," he said. "And if you asked 'em there now, did Ralph Wilson of the Buffalo Bills ever own a piece of the Raiders, they'd say, 'Hell, no, you can't do that.'

"Valley had told Scotty and me about it early on, and if it had ever leaked out, I think he could've bluffed his way along. But Al just wanted to kick Wayne in the nuts with it. It would've been embarrassing to Wayne and the rest of the parties and to the league, and it would've made the Raiders have to fork up the cash to get Wilson out of there, that would've been the only solution.''

But George would not do Al the favor. "He didn't say, 'Will you write this up and give Wayne fits?' But he said, 'Jesus, did you ever know that?' And I said, 'Yeah, Al, I knew about it—and I didn't expose it because I knew, at the time, it was the only viable salvation to the team, to keep it alive.' And as it was, it was then in the process of being liquidated, by the early seventies Wilson was out of it. So I still sat on it.''

Valley had his own financial grievances against Al. Some funny things now began showing up in those books Valley audited. "He had charged dinners in every restaurant on both sides of the Bay," Gladys Valley said. "When we'd go into one of them, the waitress would say, 'Shall we charge this to the Raiders?' Wayne would say, 'I should say not. This has nothing to do with the team.' And they'd say, 'Well, Al Davis has got a big account here.'

"And once I went into a neighborhood pharmacy to get soap or something and the lady at the counter said, 'Oh, Mrs. Valley, do I charge this to the Raiders?' I said, 'For heaven's sakes no, why?'

And she said, 'Well, Mrs. Davis has an account here.' She charged her cosmetics there. And they charged groceries at the grocery store, and so on."

With Al and Valley on an obvious collision course, Al had begun logistical planning for the climactic battle. The arithmetic of the Raiders' partership never having been lost on him, Al had since day one made a notable exception to his insolence about his co-owners. As if by equation, the distaste he saved for Valley was counteracted by the unstinting attention he paid to Ed McGah.

To do this, he had to hide his abiding contempt for McGah. Now an aging cipher, to Al he was less essential to the operation than a hose-spritzing Coliseum groundskeeper. By all rights, McGah shouldn't have even been around the team by then. Before Al came to save the franchise, McGah had wanted out badly. Cowed by Valley into keeping intact his investment, he was rewarded with a prestige he did not rate.

A jowly Irishman with black-rimmed bifocals and a soft, pug-nosed urbanity, McGah was a walking contradiction. "He was a lot of fun," George Ross said, "big, open-faced, relatively naive. You wondered, Christ, if this guy's a millionaire, anybody can be."

But McGah always could count luck as an ally. As a young man, McGah worked in a shipyard, then began a small tile business on the side. By chance, he landed a contract to lay the tile in the tunnel of the Bay Bridge. This earned McGah the resources to go into the building business just as the exodus of returning World War II GIs made that industry boom in northern California. But while McGah made a fortune, he was no match for the bombastic Valley; where Valley ran his own show in business, McGah needed bright men to run his. Brought into the Raiders by Valley, McGah couldn't help but recede before him, in comfort but with a silent, suffering chagrin.

Thus, he was easy meat for Al's patronizing attention. Even if McGah knew what Al was after, the piquant warmth of being massaged by a man like Al Davis was powerfully soothing. For Al, though, it was all work—which included putting up with McGah's diconcerting lack of discretion in his private life. Married for many years, according to Gladys Valley he openly carried on adulterous affairs.

"His wife was a beautiful lady and a wonderful person," she said, "but she was on the ill side and couldn't travel too much, and he always had an extra girlfriend stashed around in apartments. And when we started traveling with the Raiders all across the country, he'd have a girlfriend come on a different plane.

"At owners' meetings the other wives would say, 'Ed just introduced us to his wife.' And we'd say, 'That isn't his wife, it's his girlfriend.' And their mouths would just hang open, and we would be so embarrassed. Hank and Phyllis Stram were very strong Catholics. You should've heard them. They hit the ceiling! Phyllis said, 'That's an insult to the whole league.' "

But not to Al and Carol Davis, at least outwardly. Since Al had elevated McGah to, in George Ross's words, "a traveling companion and an associate," McGah's conduct reflected on the Davises as well as the Valleys. And yet, said Gladys Valley, "Both of them just played up to Ed McGah, no matter what."

Fused into a quilt of acts and intentions, all of this had to disturb Valley for the evidence of Al's separation from him. Looking back some time later at the spiral of their deteriorating relations, Valley remarked: "Within that first year [after becoming managing general partner], he was a different man. He gradually drew away from me. . . . Al does things through other people and he built a wall between us."*

Although Al would claim otherwise, Gladys Valley indicated that by the early seventies, her husband had begun to rethink his grateful commitment to Al Davis. "Wayne admitted it was a mistake to bring him back," she said. If so, the kicker for Valley may have been Al's manipulation of the Warren Wells case for his own use. When Wells's assault rap went to court, the presiding judge happened to be a close friend of Valley's. Reportedly, Al asked Valley to use his influence to ease Wells's sentence. When Wells stayed in jail for ten months, a wrathful Davis was said to have told the players that Valley would have done more about it had Wells been white. At that moment, it has been speculated, an affronted Valley was determined not to renew Al's contract as managing general partner in 1976.†

Given that very real possibility, Al's attack on Valley—based on the precept of hit or be hit—was two-pronged. His preference was

---

*Valley quoted in *The League: The Decline and Fall of the NFL*, by David Harris (New York: Bantam Books, 1988), p. 63.
†*The Rich Who Own Sports*, by Don Kowet (New York: Random House, 1977), pp. 175–176.

to harass Valley right out of the Raider picture; failing that, he would have to *legislate* him out, by validly downgrading him to peon status—which would have to be accomplished well before December 31, 1975. At the *least*, he had to be sure his contract would be renewed, one way or another.

Looking for his opening, Al struck like a gila monster at an early 1970 meeting of the Raiders' general and limited partners. Raising the topic of extending his employment agreement for another ten years, he forced a roll call of all the partners—knowing that everyone but Valley would be in favor. They were, but—refusing to be cowed—Valley stalled the motion, saying it was too early to act on it. Hearing this, the faithful McGah stormed out of the room, screaming, "I want Davis to run the ballclub for life!"

Burned by Valley, it took until 1972 for Al to find a new opening—which he entered with the nerveless audacity of a cat burglar. This time it was a meeting of the general partners on June 6. The meeting was ostensibly called to discuss possible expansion of the Coliseum, but Al would later state for the history books—and court records—that he had previously told Valley he wanted to sign the ten-year contract extension at this meeting, and that Valley had not objected. "Mr. Valley," he said, "went on as to how happy he was with the way things were going and wasn't concerned about it [the contract]." Valley, he went on, "expressed [that he] didn't want any operational control, that he had his own business."

Valley would insist he said no such thing, which made the ultimate ace in Al's hand none other than Ed McGah. Having pumped up McGah to the facsimile of a fully occupational general partner, Al gained all the credibility he needed to safely pull a fast shuffle on Valley.

Under the terms of the Raiders' limited partnership, only two of the three general partners need agree for a piece of business to be put into effect—such as, say, the extension of Al's contract. And so it was on July 10—one month and four days after either acquiring or inventing Valley's tacit blessing—that Al and McGah signed a ten-page agreement that renewed Davis as managing general partner for another ten years (on a revolving plan that could run up to twenty years), effective on January 1, 1976, at a salary of one hundred thousand dollars.

As Al's AFL commissioner severance pay had run out, and his Raiders salary was thirty-three thousand dollars, the raise was well-deserved. However, in a creative rewriting of the contract's language, what Al had done was to devalue the other two general partners to pin money, their duties limited to "consultation" on "policy decisions unrelated to the operation of the [team]."

In sum, said George Ross, Al had "created two kinds of general partners—Al Davis and the other two. They would be reduced to non–decision-making partners, who went along just to watch the games. They had created Al Davis as a club asset, on the same basis that a player or a coach is an asset, and that justified the contract."

Even had Valley gone for the extension, the legality of some of the clauses was deeply suspect. Yet the Raiders team attorney, Herman Cook, routinely rubber-stamped it. "Al was the man who worked with the lawyers in negotiating all contracts, rental agreements, and so on," Ross explained. "So when he went to the lawyers with this new agreement, they just took it on faith that this was the agreement of the owners and wrote it up. Later on, though, Cook told me, 'I would've thought that all three would sign it, but the letter of the law is whether all three *needed* to sign it."

Cook, however, never queried Valley about it. McGah later insisted he had brought up Al's contract with Valley for months before and then twice after the signing—but Valley barely listened to what McGah had to say in the best of times. Whether McGah even *read* the contract himself, though, is not certain. Months later, Ross asked McGah point-blank if he had. "In talking to Ed I realized that he didn't know the substance of the agreement he had signed," Ross recalled. "So I said, 'Ed, you didn't read this thing, did you?' And he said, 'No.' "

When Ross asked if McGah was aware that on January 1, 1976, he and Valley would become "virtually impotent," McGah replied: "No, I wasn't," and then became testy. "It doesn't make any difference," McGah said, "because, what the hell, it's either legal or it isn't."

Al would claim he informed Valley of the deal "one to two weeks" after the signing, and that Valley's response was "dead silence on the phone for thirty seconds," and when Al made no further mention of the contract, Valley "dismissed the matter" until he got more information about it. If that was correct, then Valley made a terrible blunder when, instead of nailing down the Davis matter, he left on an extended vacation to Montreal, to attend the Olympics. Valley didn't return until mid-September, giving Al time to convince people the deal was done. In fact, when Valley finally got back home, he had heard about it in passing conversation with Ralph Wilson.

In late November—during Valley's year-end audit—the Raider bookkeeper forwarded the contract to the team's auditor, who took one look at it and called Valley. "You better do something about this," he told Valley. When Valley saw it, he flipped and called Pete Rozelle. But, even here, Valley never confronted Davis, or McGah, and he never told Rozelle of the contract business or that he wanted the commissioner to mediate the dispute—only that he wanted Rozelle to attend a meeting of the Raiders general partners. In addition, Valley had to put off that meeting because of what he later said was "the press of business."

Valley's widow maintained that an Al Davis power grab could not have caught her husband altogether off-guard. "He knew from the first time we met him," she said. "He expected it at any time, because we knew Al Davis had done that all his life." Yet this seven-month interval of inaction would be devastating to Valley, and key to making Al Davis president for life of the Raiders.

Finally, on February 22, 1973, the three general partners met—although Davis and McGah thought the subject of the meeting was to be a lawsuit brought by one of the limited partners, Lou Barroero, over that sneaker of a clause added to Al's original contract which allowed for the general partners to buy out the limiteds as of January 1, 1976.

The buyout clause too was part of Al's strategy to hang Valley. Hoping to ingratiate himself to the long-ignored limiteds, he had honed in on Valley's own quick shuffle of six years before and the limiteds' discontent with it, encouraging suits of this or any kind against Valley—as they might bloody or preoccupy him and drive a wedge between Valley and at least some of the limiteds. Al, getting the ever-acquiescent McGah to go with him, favored expunging the clause.

But when the parties convened, with Rozelle and the NFL's legal counsel, Jay Moyer, Valley stunned everyone in the room with a wild outburst. Unveiling from his briefcase a copy of *The Sporting News* in which there was an item about Davis's new contract, with a flourish Valley threw the paper on a table and glared at Al.

"Is this true?" he roared at him.

Rozelle and Moyer were so startled that Moyer later spoke of the two of them looking on with "our jaws going slack" as the drama played out. Al, taken aback himself, told Valley it was true, where-upon Valley shouted, "How can you do this without me even being aware of it?"

"I can do any damn thing I want!" Al retorted, raising his voice to meet Valley's. "You knew about it and I don't know what the hell is bugging you."

"I am not going along with this contract," Valley said, then tore into McGah for "taking such a big interest in football all of a sudden." McGah, who rarely challenged Valley, didn't answer the insult. Instead, he asked Valley, "What the hell are you pulling this in front of the commissioner for?"

Valley, his Irish-Portuguese blood swelling his jugular vein, be-gan to yell even louder, at Davis, at McGah, at Herman Cook, and made menacing gestures at them—a scene Al later described as "a little bit of an altercation."

By now, Rozelle, his ears ringing, had had enough. Summarily, he stopped the meeting and—mediation secondary to survival—shooed everybody out of the room. But Valley was still steaming, at McGah in particular, and confronted him in the hallway. "Why the hell did you sign it?" he raged on. "You never signed a fucking contract in your life!"

McGah—using a theory that Al would advance in staking his sincerity in the matter—told him that if he hadn't signed, the Raiders would have lost Al to another team.

Unmollified, Valley then told Rozelle that he didn't want the commissioner to mediate the dispute. "This is between me and Davis," Valley said.

Five weeks later, on April 2, 1973, at an NFL owners meeting in Scottsdale, Arizona, Valley—assured of maximum media exposure—announced by press release that he was filing suit in California superior court against Al Davis, though the suit would in fact name both Davis and McGah. Calling the renewed contract "onerous and unfair," he said—without knowing how prescient he was—that the effect of it would be to turn "over the life and future of the Oakland Raiders to Mr. Davis" and would make Al Davis "synonymous with the Raider franchise, which he is not."

Moving to rescind the contract, Valley also—"in order to pre-serve the integrity of the Oakland Raiders"—asked that Davis be "removed as managing general partner." Said Valley that day: "I want Al Davis out of this organization entirely, because he's not fit to live with."

Al, who even now alone represented the Raiders in executive sessions of league meetings (Valley was allowed to attend only general sessions), came out of conference to learn from reporters that he was being sued for control of the Raiders—that is, for his survival. Smiling serenely in response, he had reason not to fret. As Gladys Valley admitted, "Al Davis can con a rattlesnake." Now, he had only to con a superior court judge.

16

Al Davis returned home late one night after a long session at the Oakland Raiders' office. While he was quickly undressing, he woke up his wife, Carol, an attractive blonde.

"Good God, you're late," she pouted.

"You can call me Al," replied Davis.

—from *The Saturday Evening Post*, November 1975

He doesn't have anything else, you know. His life is entirely the Raiders.

—John Madden

As always, Al was not too absorbed by outside business to keep the Raiders primed. Indeed the most hectic and important period of change in the team's history was the first half of the seventies. By 1975, only Fred Biletnikoff, Pete Banaszak, George Atkinson, and forty-eight-year-old George Blanda remained from the 1967 championship team. Yet only one time in that span did the Raiders miss the playoffs—and that year, 1971, they still went 8–4–2.

In a remarkably successful turnover of talent, key Raiders fell out only to be replaced by equal or greater talent culled from the Davis-Wolf-LoCasale argosy of data. In the early seventies, 260-pound George Buehler moved in at right guard and 280-pound All-Pro Bob "Boomer" Brown was acquired from the Rams to play right tackle. When Brown was hurt, 270-pound Henry Lawrence took that spot in 1974 and didn't leave until 1986. After UCLA's

Dave Dalby replaced Jim Otto in 1974, no other center would be needed until 1985.

While the defensive line lacked the salable, saturnalia-style blood-lust of the Big Ben line, ends Tony Cline and Horace Jones and tackles Art Thoms and Otis Sistrunk held steady through the mid-seventies. Sistrunk in particular became a new-generation Raider homicidal yo-yo. Head shaven and shimmering like nutbrown quartz, with a faceful of hate and a maniacal smile, Sistrunk had played no college ball and no one knew how old he was as a walk-on with the Rams in 1972. Ron Wolf spotted him while watching a Rams practice and knew the Raiders had to force a trade in training camp or Sistrunk would become more valuable. The price was only a fourth-round draft choice and Sistrunk ended up playing eight years with the Raiders.

On both sides of the line came a wealth of talent like that, some blue-chip all the way—USC contributed halfback Clarence Davis and cornerback Skip Thomas in successive years, 1971 and 1972, and Notre Dame's burly All-American tight end Dave Casper came in 1974—but the difference was made by the kind of intuitive hunch playing that Al loved. They drafted Henry Lawrence, for example, after seeing him contain Too Tall Jones—the NFL's top pick in 1974—in practice before the Senior Bowl. Tight end Ray Chester, from Morgan State, wasn't even listed by the scouting combines but was Al's first-round pick in 1970 and made All-Pro his rookie season.

Fullback Marv Hubbard came out of the Atlantic Coast Football League, and was confirmed as a Raider when he was sued after a bar brawl. After each home game Hubbard kept a tradition—he'd break the same window of a dry cleaning store next to Clancy's bar in Jack London Square, with his *fist*, alarming onlookers who had no idea he knew how to pull his hand back before being cut by the glass. Hubbard would walk in every Sunday night and give the bartender fifty dollars. "This is for the window next door," he'd say. Clearly an Al Davis kind of guy, Hubbard played seven years and averaged 4.8 yards a carry, second-best in club history.

Hubbard's successor at fullback, Mark van Eeghen, had also succeeded him at Colgate. Al, knowing what Hubbard had given him, spent a little extra time looking at van Eeghen during a workout before the 1974 East-West All-Star game—even though the workout was indoors in a gym because of rain. Seeing van Eeghen in shorts and sneakers, Al liked something in the way he moved and drafted him on the third round. Van Eeghen played eight years and was, at that time, the Raiders' all-time leading rusher, with 6,651 yards.

If Al wasn't playing a hunch, he was filling a specific need or role—for example, Banaszak for goal-line situations—and often these specialists would bloom in the competitive caldron. Dave Dalby was originally picked because he could snap long on punts. At five-eleven and 190 pounds, Clarence Davis was picked for his blocking in the backfield—a Raider must—but he averaged over five yards a carry his first three years in between obliterating people who dwarfed him.

Colorado All-American Cliff Branch, a feathery football/track man—many scouts saw him as a track/football man, better suited to sprinting on a cinder path—was picked to return punts; in time he became Warren Wells's replacement as the "X" receiver. He played fourteen years, made All-Pro four times, and retired as the team's second all-time leading pass-catcher with 8,685 yards and sixty-seven touchdowns, just behind Biletnikoff's 8,974 and seventy-six.

However, when Al drafted Southern Mississippi's punter, Ray Guy, on the *first* round in 1973, other teams were shocked that a first-round pick was "squandered" on a punter. But Al knew that Guy was a tremendous athlete—when he led the nation in punting in 1972, he also played safety. When Al looked at Guy, he saw him kick balls sixty yards in the air, which was about how long he could *throw* them on the fly. Al loved it that, like Blanda and his place-kicking, Guy was never satisfied only punting, and placated him by also listing him on the depth chart at other positions, but he was *too* valuable to play him elsewhere. Guy—whose gorgeous, booming kicks had a hang time of around a week and a half and were off his foot too quickly to be blocked—as a rookie led the league in punting and was All-Pro for the first of six straight years. Not for fourteen years did the Raiders need another punter.

Appropriately, then, the two megaforces who took the team to their rewards in the 1970s came via distinctly different roads, and could not have been more different as people and players. And yet Ken Stabler and Jack Tatum were equally Raiderish.

Tatum, Ohio State's All-American safety, was the club's first-round pick in 1971, when it was still a rarity for a defensive back to go that high. Just as rare, Tatum was given a three-year, no-cut contract worth nearly half a million dollars. But, as with Ray Guy,

Al had to fill a need and went all the way. Dave Grayson had retired the year before, upsetting the Raiders' defensive fine tuning; if the cornerbacks were to keep giving receivers the middle of the field in order to protect the deep flanks and keep a safety net behind their Bump and Run maneuvers, the same kind of ball-hawking, pulverizing free safety was required.

Tatum, a five-ten, 200-pound high-tension coil of a man, arrived after knocking cold two Baltimore Colt receivers—one being 225-pound John Mackey—in the College All-Star game. Al LoCasale's first press release about Tatum called him an "assassin," and the name stuck to him so tightly that Tatum would write an autobiography titled *They Call Me Assassin*. With his polar eyes and mortuarial air of foreboding, Tatum more than any other Raider before or after gave resonance to that deadly corsair on their helmets— and with him they all played with a heart of darkness.

"Any fool knows that when you hit someone with your best shot and he's still able to think straight, then you're not a hitter," Tatum wrote in that autobiography, and early in his career he was so thirsty for knockouts he dazed receivers *and* other Raider defensive backs in on the tackle. Building up his speed to come at the receiver's chest with maximum impact, Tatum didn't tackle; he defiled. The head or chest, not the ball, was his target, and a pet move was to catch a man's helmet in a headlock between his forearm and biceps—"The Hook," he called it, and his timing was such that he could avoid an illegal forearm-first hit. Tatum often passed up an interception just to make a shattering hit, and with reason. More than interceptions, his knotty elbows and shoulders made receivers timorous when they went across the middle.

"An obstructionist, Jack's the greatest obstructionist there has ever been," was how Al codified Tatum years later. "He put the fear of God in 'em by his location in the middle of the field."

Tatum was taught many of his insidious techniques by the splintery George Atkinson, and it became sport between them to see who could turn out the most lights—two points were given every time a receiver had to be helped off the field, one point if he limped off under his own power. Tatum always won, but in the process Atkinson's own toxicity was pumped up. Along with Skip Thomas, who replaced Nemiah Wilson at right cornerback—the overburdened corner, with Willie Brown still on the other side—and got the nickname "Doctor Death," they were grouped together in a corner of the locker room called "the ghetto," alone in their seething game preparation. Tom Keating half-expected bounty hunters to come after them.

"Especially with Jack standin' back there," Keating said. "Automatically, on his looks alone, you're gonna arrest him."

Stabler's path was far more circuitous. His method haphazard and his mood something less than intense, quarterbacking the Raiders was for Stabler like throwing a few balls between hands in a beery game of five-card stud—yet his best passes were thrown when the weight of all Oakland was hanging over his head. With his yam-soft gut, spindly legs, and pigeon-toed gait, it seemed amazing that "Snake" Stabler was coordinated enough to throw a ball at all, but he had natural gifts few passers ever had.

The son of an alcoholic father who drank himself to death at age forty-seven, Stabler grew up drinking hard himself, and his indifference to discipline and design imperiled those athletic gifts. Succeeding Joe Namath and Steve Sloan as Alabama's quarterback, he led the Crimson Tide to an undefeated season in 1966. But, missing classes and practices, for a time he lost his elgibility and had to grovel before Bear Bryant allowed him to stay on the team. He was drafted in the second round in 1968, but knee surgery killed two years. Stabler came back in 1970 and made the club as a third-string quarterback and holder for George Blanda's placekicks.

Though Stabler played little, he was given a priceless football education when the crotchety Blanda took a liking to him. Trailing Blanda like a stray cur, Stabler began to share the old man's crude conceits. "I remember one time when we came out on the field and it was a game that George and Kenny knew they weren't gonna play in," said Keating. "And George, God, could he get ornery— to him it was a whole plot against him that he wasn't playing quarterback, 'cause he just knew he'd lead the team to the Super Bowl if they'd just give him the chance—and I wasn't the guy who was gonna tell George he's wrong.

"So anyway, I'm walkin' by him and here was George and Snake and they're finishin' their cigarettes and George's helmet has three pieces of fried chicken in it. George is all pissed off, so he's gonna eat on the sideline during the game. And of course Kenny's sittin' on his helmet and he's gonna eat with him."

When Stabler did get into games, his passes—delivered like a spasm, almost without his arm drawn back or his feet planted—

zipped past the unturned heads of defenders and right between the numbers of his receivers. Though Stabler couldn't throw Lamonica's long and beautiful spirals, like Blanda he could hang laundry on the slant-ins and wide-outs, and he could soften the pass and hump-back it like a horseshoe-toss, if he had to drop it in over a big linebacker's head. For Stabler, the *timing* of a pass was the critical element, not its length, and he was made for a time when the NFL was implementing all kinds of flexible zone defenses to stifle the bomb.

Madden became convinced that Stabler would have to run the offense—an opinion that put him at odds with Al, who still thought Lamonica's arm could neutralize any defensive scheme.

This time, Al was wrong. Moreover, he was unresponsive to static on the club about Lamonica, who after seven years had won two MVP awards and thrown for immense yardage, but whose habit of getting hurt and coming out of big games, or making blunders and losing them, led players to question his courage. Never one of the boys, Lamonica had a dismissive, superior air about him. And while he knew the playbook inside out, he was so emotionally wound up that he sometimes got brain-lock—even Al had said after the 1970 playoff loss to the Colts, in which Lamonica kept trying to force bombs into the teeth of double and triple coverage, "Honestly, I don't know what gets into Daryle's head sometimes," although, to be precise, what had gotten into it was the Al Davis philosophy.

Growing ever more in his domain, Madden had bucked Al before the 1973 season when—oveer Madden's strenuous objections—Al traded Ray Chester to the Colts for Bubba Smith, the monstrous defensive end. This was the classic Al Davis, again filling needs. When he'd drafted Gene Upshaw, it was originally to contain one man, the Chiefs' Buck Buchanan. Then, when the six-seven, 280-pound Bubba hurt the Raiders in that 1970 championship game, Al made the trade for Boomer Brown to nullify Bubba. Then he just got Bubba himself. But Madden was right. Bubba, coming off knee surgery, was a dud—after three games he was benched and Tony Cline was restored at left end; in another year, Bubba was gone.

Madden had started Stabler the first game of 1972, but he threw three interceptions in the first half against the Steelers and was benched. Lamonica then had *another* big-game failure, against the same Steelers in the first-round playoff that year. Stabler came in down 6–0 with six minutes left and moved the club fifty yards to the Pitt thirty-yard line. Then, seeing an all-out blitz, he scrambled on his gimpy legs and ran all the way for a touchdown and a 7–6 lead. That's when that nasty rebuking hand smacked the Raiders yet again and now with an ecclesiastical sense of tragedy.

Down to his last play, Steeler quarterback Terry Bradshaw sailed a long pass down the middle to halfback Frenchy Fuqua. Jack Tatum, laying for the hit, hurled himself shoulder-first into the small of Fuqua's back and, like an experiment in matter and motion, the ball came out of the collision with equal force and flew back upfield—a sure incompletion except that fullback Franco Harris, loitering in the area, scooped up the dying ball at his shoetops, threaded traffic, and ran it sixty yards for the game-winning score. Very likely, the catch was not legal—it would have had to touch Tatum to be so—but, in the pandemonium at Three Rivers Stadium, the "Immaculate Reception" stood, a stone-tableted anomaly carved out of Raider frustration.

Still, it did set the table for the Ken Stabler era, though Al had Madden start Lamonica to open the 1973 season. But with Lamonica a real debit now, the Raiders lost two of their first three games and didn't score a touchdown in the last two. Incensed, Stabler then told Madden he "couldn't count on" Stabler to be a mop-up man any longer. Madden recoiled at Stabler's nerve, but he knew he had to go with Stabler now or lose his trust. The next game, against St. Louis, Stabler did start, completing twenty-five of twenty-nine passes for 304 yards and two touchdowns in a 17–10 win.

Now Lamonica was wounded by being benched. Having been closer with John Rauch than Madden, Lamonica had been miffed that Madden was cutting into his and Stabler's authority on the field. "Madden started sendin' a lot of plays in," he recalled. "John had become pretty much independent of Al," and the nature of the new plays—which were right up Stabler's alley, not his—made Lamonica think Al was powerless as the team "changed its thinking quite a bit." Now, with Al silent as Madden went with Stabler, Lamonica decided to sign with the Southern California Sun of the new World Football League, effective in 1975. Up until the end, Al tried to get him not to go, assuring Lamonica of his valued place with the Raiders. But now, not even Al Davis could get his way on the field.

Playing both sides, Al professed his support for Stabler for as long as he won. But the relationship was a distant, often strained one, and Al seemingly blamed—or kept wanting to blame—Stabler for the changes in the game, which he did not fully accept, since it would mean Al Davis and his "vertical game" were becoming dinosaurs. Indeed, Al made sure Madden remembered the crux of the Raider game was still throwing long, and Stabler complied—paradoxically, even with his limitations, he kept the long ball flying enough as a go-for-the-kill weapon to help the bomb survive the zone-induced conservatism of the early seventies.

Besides, even as Stabler was throwing under zones and completing an AFL-high 63 percent of his passes in 1973, Don Shula's Dolphins were far better equipped for low-risk football. Though the Raiders chewed up the Steelers in the semifinal playoff—in which a controlled Stabler hit on fourteen of seventeen passes—in the AFC title game Bob Griese threw only *six* times against them while Larry Csonka and Mercury Morris pounded out over two hundred yards on the ground. Miami won 27–10 and went on to their second straight Super Bowl victory.

In 1974, when Cliff Branch flourished as a deep threat, Stabler threw longer. His completion average fell to 57 percent but he had a league-high twenty-eight touchdown passes—thirteen to Branch. If either Branch or Biletnikoff were double-teamed, the other would romp free; if both were doubled, Stabler found tight end Bob Moore over the middle.

When the Raiders met the Dolphins again, this time in Oakland in the first-round playoff, they didn't try to play it close and got Miami into a raging dogfight. With the Raiders down 19–14 in the fourth quarter, Stabler heaved one to Branch, who caught it, fell down, got up, and *still* blew past the cornerback for a seventy-two-yard touchdown. The Dolphins then pushed it right back down the field to make it 26–21 with two minutes to go. But Stabler hit five straight passes and got to the eight-yard line. Now, with thirty-five seconds left and everyone covered, he ran left and with defensive end Vern Den Herder clutching his ankles, he barely got off a wobbly pass while he was lurching to the turf—and Clarence Davis, between two Dolphins in the end zone, wrestled it into his grasp for the winning score.

This was the *Raiders'* immaculate reception, though it still was not divine enough to deter their taunting fate. Again one step short of the big prize, and on their home turf, they were nonetheless tamed once again by Chuck Noll's Steelers. Rushing for 224 yards, holding the Raiders' ground attack to all of 29 yards, and intercepting three passes, the Steelers won 24–13 and got to do much the same to the Vikings in the Super Bowl.

By now, however, Ken Stabler had become immaculate. He won the AFC Player of the Year award and was a unanimous All-Pro in 1974. But, all the while, there was something in Stabler's unkempt style, his lack of a game face—unlike Blanda, his bloodshot eyes didn't turn into fiery nibs when he took the field—that rankled Al Davis. To Al, some guys were not Raider stock, and he never believed Stabler was. For all the hooliganism and general nuttiness inimical to the team, the military poseur in Al always craved a steel-gray, expeditious approach on the field. Lamonica's huddle was like a General Motors board meeting—if *anyone* else spoke, Lamonica would back out until there was quiet. Stabler's huddle was more like a hoedown, with *everybody* talking at once and offering play suggestions. But Stabler was immune to pressure and while his heroics were an affront to game plans they were unbelievable theater.

"Oh, he was great," said Keating. "He'd come over to the sideline and lift up his helmet, and John would be standin' there and there'd be people all around him for these big discussions—and Snake would just be kinda lookin' up in the stands, totally unconcerned, like, "Hey, we got 'em where we want 'em, John.' And he'd trot back out on the field and he'd stop at the hash mark and go, 'Hey, what was the play?'

"Fuckin' great. I loved it. As soon as he'd go out there I'd get up off the bench. I didn't get up for much when I was restin', but with Snake I always knew somethin' was gonna happen, it was just pure entertainment. I mean, if he'd throw four interceptions in the first half, you *knew* he'd throw four touchdowns in the second."

The odd thing was that Madden, high-strung as *he* was, loved Stabler's maddeningly phlegmatic style, believing that it complemented his own. "The hotter it got, the cooler he got," Madden once said. "Which made for a good mesh. The hotter it got, the hotter I got. Everything he was, I wasn't." But not for a minute could Al stomach the notion that Stabler complemented *him*.

Or maybe it was just that Stabler was Madden's boy, not his. Both of them had shown Al to be on the wrong side of the Lamonica issue, and if he could not hold that against the coach he could hold it against the player.

For his part, Stabler was wary of Al, and every time he picked up a paper and read Al praising him, he would cringe at the hy-

Branded "a criminal" by Steelers coach Chuck Noll, Atkinson—prodded by Davis—sued for libel. Here, he waits outside the courtroom with teammate Gene Upshaw (*right*). But Atkinson lost that argument, too. *AP/Wide World Photos*

Freeze-frame of a tragedy: Jack Tatum moves in to make the hit that paralyzed Darryl Stingley and sickened the nation in 1978. *AP/Wide World Photos*

A handshake was about all that Dan Pastorini got from Al after a 1980 injury ended his Raider career after four games. Pastorini had to sue Davis to get paid in full. *AP/Wide World Photos*

As the Raiders' head coach, Tom Flores always knew his place—behind Al. *AP/Wide World Photos*

No doubt choosing his words carefully, Flores discourses for the media as Raiders executive assistant Al LoCasale grimly takes notes. *AP/Wide World Photos*

Al and Carol—showing no signs of her near-fatal heart attack in 1979—stroll through the Oakland airport en route to the AFC championship game in 1981. Al had declared his intention to leave Oakland for Los Angeles the year before; police protection was a good idea. *AP/Wide World Photos*

Bitter enemies Davis and Commissioner Pete Rozelle avoid eye contact as Rozelle presents the Vince Lombardi Trophy after the Raiders' Super Bowl XV victory over the Eagles on January 25, 1981. *AP/Wide World Photos*

As always, a salute to his players. *AP/Wide World Photos*

May 7, 1982: Davis and his attorney, Joseph Alioto, flash million-dollar smiles outside the Los Angeles federal courthouse where Davis won his biggest victory—the antitrust lawsuit against the NFL that freed him to move the Raiders to L.A. *AP/Wide World Photos*

One coat or two? Lester Hayes glops on the stickum during
Super Bowl XV. *AP/Wide World Photos*

Plucked from the scrap
heap by Davis, Jim Plunkett
cranked up and passed the
Raiders to two Super Bowl
wins. *AP/Wide World
Photos*

The new Raider era began with home-town hero Marcus Allen . . . *AP/Wide World Photos*

. . . but Bo Jackson came out of left to steal Allen's yardage and headlines. *AP/Wide World Photos*

Entrepreneur Davis had lost none of his bite or fight in 1981 . . . *AP/Wide World Photos*

. . . but he spent too much time away from the fie
pleading his case. Here he does so before a U
Senate committee in 1982, Joe Alioto at his si
AP/Wide World Photos

Waiting to do battle in the courtroom in 1983, Al whi
away the time with the sports section. His son Ma
in background, tries to get on the same page. *AP/W
World Photos*

A natty Davis descends yet more courthouse steps, with old friend Jimmy the Greek; no odds were too long for Al. *AP/Wide World Photos*

'88 Raider head coach Mike Shanahan, Al's biggest [mi]stake. *AP/Wide World Photos*

Hall of Famer Art Shell restored the old Raider pride in 1989. *AP/Wide World Photos*

Even good Raiders die: Al pays his last respects at the funeral of strong safety Stacey Toran—killed while driving drunk in 1989. *AP/Wide World Photos*

John Matuszak takes it all off for *Playgirl* magazine in 1982: vodka and valium, and a premature death. No other player more typified the mystique of Al Davis's Raiders. *AP/Wide World Photos*

pocrisy. In 1975, Davis publicly called Stabler "the most accurate passer in football today . . . the only thing I can say about him is that he is a winner."

However, as Stabler would later recall, "He never said anything like that to me. Al didn't say much of anything to the players. What he did say was rarely a compliment. No matter how well anyone performed, Al's words always seemed designed to motivate us to do better. In one game I hit Freddy [Biletnikoff] with a touchdown pass. Afterward Al said, 'You know, Clifford [Branch] was wide open on that play, nobody near him.'

"I couldn't see what difference it made if I'd had three other receivers open. You can only score one touchdown per pass. But Al liked to nudge you."

Stabler told of the time he remarked to Al how nice it was to be putting a lot of points on the board.

"Well, you should," Al replied. "You're driving a Cadillac."

"Al," Stabler said, "even a Cadillac needs somebody to steer it in the right direction."

In 1974, Stabler had also signed with the WFL, one of a rockslide of NFL stars who inked big deals with the new league—including the Dolphin trio of Larry Csonka, Jim Kiick, and Paul Warfield, who all jumped to the Memphis club in 1975. Stabler, who'd just signed a new Raider contract for $37,500, covering the 1974 season and an option year afterward, went for a seven-year, $825,000 offer—plus a percentage of the gate—from the Birmingham Americans, to take effect in 1976. When he signed, he never bothered to tell Al. "I knew he'd be upset with me," he said. "Maybe that's why I didn't get in touch with him. Like everyone else, I was always a little afraid of the man."

The problem for Al was that he could find no suitable quarterback who could replace Stabler. And when the Americans defaulted on payments to Stabler and the courts ruled his WFL contract void in 1975 (the league went under in October of 1975), Al decided to be big about forgiving and gave him a new three-year, $600,000 contract with the Raiders. The only thing that mattered now was that Stabler was an essential on a team peaking in hunger and experience. At least for the time being he was.

Wayne Valley v. *Al Davis, Ed McGah, et al.* was heard by Judge Redmond C. Staats, Jr., in Alameda County, California, Superior

Court during May and June of 1975. Even before its adjudication, however, Al's war against Valley had—sadly but perhaps inevitably—claimed the long and once-so-important union between Al and George Ross. This was by Al's choice, on the simple basis that Ross had the temerity to do his job as a reporter, even if it meant Al would be sullied.

"Right after I spoke with McGah [about Davis's new contract] in Scottsdale," Ross recalled, "I phoned Al and told him I was going to print McGah's quotes. And he said, 'I can't trust you anymore.' Al's sense of loyalty is absolute. You're either on the team burning down the enemy fort, or *you* are the enemy."

Any chance of reconciliation vanished when George was called by Valley's lawyers to attest that McGah had not seen the contract he had signed. On the stand, George knew he was now a pariah by Al's hard, accusing stare.

For Al, the demotion of Ross from malleable ally to quisling was no more than a minor matter now that the Raiders were a thriving, multimillion-dollar concern and Al no longer cared about favors from the local press; it was Al LoCasale's job to deal with them anyway. George knew this as well, and the unhappy lessons of compromising his integrity at the beginning with Al made *him* feel sullied. But none of this troubled him as much as the human tragedy Al could not see. When Ross says, "I haven't spoken to Al since that phone call," there is hurt in his voice.

All that the loss of George apparently meant to Al was that he had to prepare for the legal consequences of Ross's testimony. Accordingly, when Ed McGah took the stand he insisted that he had "misunderstood" Ross's questions in Scottsdale. But Valley had to do some backtracking of his own, explaining that when Al mentioned the contract extension right after it was signed, Valley believed it to be a "trial balloon" designed to "apply pressure" for a new contract—not evidence of the contract itself. When Ralph Wilson mentioned it, Valley testified, he told Wilson he didn't believe it was true.

Then it was Al's turn in the dock. Almost jovially relaxed, he captivated Judge Staats with his easy recollection of details and smooth plausibility. The defense also pulled out an ace card when it called to the stand Leonard Tose, the Philadelphia Eagles' owner. Tose said that *he*, at least, had made employment offers to Al that would have given Davis "10 to 15 percent of the club"—thus backing up McGah's contention that he felt he had to sign Davis or lose him.

On June 18, Judge Staats rendered his decision—with a palpably Solomonlike compromise that in effect gave Al a smashing victory. The judge said that "the Court feels Mr. Davis' testimony [is] more creditable," and that "it was incumbent upon [Valley] to take some action [earlier than he did]." Therefore, Valley, "by his conduct of silence or acquiescence had ratified the . . . contract." Seemingly starry-eyed, the judge concluded:

> The evidence is uncontradicted that Mr. Davis is reputed to be one of the top men in the trade . . . and was sought by other teams . . . because of his ability and performance. [Valley's] contention as to the agreement being onerous can not be sustained.

Judge Staats did find that "several provisions" of the contract, covering Al's expanded powers, were "in conflict" with the laws of limited partnership and "are therefore invalid" unless the partnership was expressly altered with the consent of all parties. But this was a sop to Valley, for while illegality by itself might have been Al's undoing, it was now meaningless in light of the upholding of the contract.

This was no accident. For the judge, the real issue all along was the perpetuation of a successful franchise. "He was a very good judge," said George Ross, "and his concern, even in his remarks from the bench, was in preserving the Raiders as they were, and this looked like the best solution"—because it left the lifeblood of the Raiders intact and in his black-and-silver-appointed office.

For a time, Valley believed he could still hang Al with the albatross of the invalidated clauses. His lawyer, Robert C. Burnstein, entering into a second war with Al and his mouthpieces over who had won in court, declared that the ruling "cut the guts out" of Davis's role and that "It is not a victory for him." But in the cold daylight, Valley could plainly see that Al was cemented in his command—the court prohibited Valley from firing Davis—and had taken Valley's best shot without flinching.

Critically, Valley also knew he had lost his political base on the Raiders—in a double blow, Lou Barroero won *his* suit against Valley, and Barroero had paid a dividend to Al by testifying in his favor. Stalemated with Al, Valley's only hope was to appeal, and for months, during the 1975 season, he weighed his course. Al, meanwhile, went back to psychological in-fighting, now with implied impunity.

"That's when he got so mean," recalled Gladys Valley. "Oh, he was so nasty. He couldn't seriously hurt us, but we'd be in a hotel and he'd tell one of his gofers to order the buses to come an hour earlier, 'but don't bother the Valleys.' And the players could hardly wait until they could find a phone and they'd call us and say, 'Al's ordering the buses early.' So we'd go down to the lobby and Al would be furious that we wouldn't be stranded.

"You know, any man that could stoop that low, you can't be bothered with him. And he was just getting so disgusting, he took the fun out of the team. So we decided one night, let's get out of it."

One other factor in that decision was that Robert Burnstein died before appeal papers could be filed, and Valley didn't care to start fresh with a new lawyer. And, by then, Valley had plenty of pressing business. The massive Singer Corporation was in the process of procuring Valley's building enterprises for a staggering $83 million. Creating the Singer Housing Subsidiary, they wanted Valley to serve as president—and made it clear they preferred Valley's attention to be undivided by his sporting quagmire. With Valley now Singer's single largest stockholder and charged with lining up other major builders across the country for acquisition, the Raiders and Al Davis were just too small a deal for Valley to continue working himself into a snit.

Quietly, in January of 1976, Valley began to divest his Raider ownership shares, which by then stood at 15.2 percent to Al's 16.1 percent. (Ed McGah, who had already transferred almost all of his holdings to his son, E. J., now held around 1 percent.) Apprised of Valley's decision to sell, most of the old Valley bloc of limited partners got out in sympathy with him—an important exception being John Brooks, who had been Valley's lobbyist and liaison with California politicians, and as such a valuable man for Al to keep around.

With Valley's and the others' shares all on the table, Al—who by law could buy no more shares than those proportionate to what he already owned—beefed up to 28 percent; those who came in through McGah also solidified by carving up the leftovers. With McGah now the only other general partner, it really was Al Davis's club, to run as he pleased and for as long as he wanted.

Following as soon as it did on the court ruling, Valley's departure made for an easy induction, running precisely along the tracks of what was said by Davis's cronies after the lawsuit, that Al "kicked Wayne Valley's ass." Perhaps more than anything else about Al Davis, that inference—which long ago hardened into fact—irked Gladys Valley many years later.

"Everybody thinks that Al won, and that he forced us out," she acknowledged with great exasperation. "He didn't win anything. It was such a relief to us to get out of it because he had made it disgusting and we thought we could have fun with other teams."

At the time, in fact, it seemed that Valley's exit from the Raiders was expediently fateful. Not long before, the 49ers—the team Valley had first dreamed of buying into—were put up for sale. As soon as Valley was free of the Raiders, Pete Rozelle asked him if he'd like to bid on the team across the Bay. Valley was at once receptive and soon came to an agreement with 49ers president Lou Spadia to buy the club for $11.3 million. It was then that Valley found out how long Al Davis's claws of vindictiveness could be.

Though the outgoing owners, the sisters of the two Morabito brothers who had founded the team in the late forties, wanted to sell to Valley, the club's minority owner—Franklin Meuli, who also owned the NBA Warriors—had a first-refusal right. Meuli was also a friend of Al Davis, and Al Davis didn't care to see his wealthy enemy in a position to hurt the Raiders and its new majority owner with the NFC's Bay Area franchise.

Reportedly "convinced" by Al Davis, Franklin Meuli vetoed the sale to Wayne Valley, and blunted further attempts by Rozelle to work out a deal with Valley. For over a year longer, the 49ers lay in limbo, unsold, its interests managed by the bumptious Meuli. By midseason 1976, Meuli didn't have enough capital to run the team—which couldn't have disturbed Al Davis either. Thoroughly disgusted and embarrassed by Meuli, Rozelle gave him a December 1 deadline to find a new owner—and Meuli, incredibly, called Wayne Valley, who now wanted nothing to do with it. Then, rather than fight Davis, the Morabito sisters came *to* him, for aid in finding a buyer—which may have been the first time in history that a team asked its main rival to do its business for it.

Al, of course, loved being at the epicenter of this bizarre scenario—and, in Davis style, operating behind the scenes and crunching details as though civilization depended on it, approved and practically contracted the deal that brought to the 49ers Edward

DeBartolo, Sr., as a financial angel and his puckish thirty-year-old son, Eddie, in whose name the team was placed. DeBartolo Senior, whose Ohio construction company was one of the largest land developers in the country, had first been solicited by a former Baltimore Colts executive, Joe Thomas, who became the 49ers' general manager. But Al had to act as "a consultant and conduit," as he later said, "and we brought the transaction to fruition."

The DeBartolos' price tag turned out to be $18 million—a stunning windfall for the Morabito sisters—out of which Al was paid a hefty "consultant's fee." Since by league law no owner could profit from another franchise (Ralph Wilson notwithstanding), this payoff horrified most of the other owners—Cleveland's Art Modell called it "appalling" and "outrageous." For these owners, many of whom already had a problem with his ethics, Al stated the fee to be one hundred thousand dollars. Then a reporter noted to him that a normal finder's fee—10 percent—would work out to $1.8 million.

Caught in his fib, Al snorted in laughter. "I didn't receive anything like that," he said. Then he added: "But it was a lot more than one hundred thousand dollars."

"That's just like Al," one of the owners shrugged. "After himself, there's not much more Al cares about."★

Much the same thing would be said later about Eddie DeBartolo, who learned what he knew about football from Al Davis.

As for the Valleys, they showed up infrequently at the Coliseum, the house that Wayne Valley built but now needed a ticket to get into. A decade and a half later, Gladys Valley would try to put a hundred years more distance between her and a football team she once loved as much as a child, but not without a painful hint of sorrow.

"I still go to some of the Raiders' games," she said, "like when they play up in Seattle. The [Chuck] Knoxes are good friends and I'll go up there and visit with them and cheer for the Seahawks."

Then, softly, "They're not our Raiders anymore."

★*The League: The Decline and Fall of the NFL*, by David Harris (New York: Bantam Books, 1988), p. 281.

17

In my mind Al was the biggest thing in football. And as a guy who played for him, I kept wishing he would loosen up a bit and be more like John Madden.

—Ken Stabler

This is magnificent. I said we'd get it someday and we have.

—Al Davis, accepting the Vince Lombardi trophy, January 9, 1977

If Al wasn't able to run roughshod over John Madden, neither did Madden ever feel emboldened to publicly differ with Al. In fact, for all of the sway Madden earned, team insiders never doubted that Pinky knew his place in the Raider bigtop.

"You very seldom saw a strong coach with the Raiders. You're not gonna ever find a Chuck Noll type guy there," said Marv Marinovich, a Raiders assistant coach from 1968 to 1970 who then continued as an ad-hoc conditioning coach into the eighties.

"To the players the coaches were good people, but the guy makin' the decisions was Al Davis, even if they didn't see it. John's biggest talent was being able to prosper within that system. Al didn't embarrass him in front of the assistant coaches but you knew that Madden had to go into Al's office and defend himself.

"See, the whole thing was the 'Raider line.' If you're there, you gotta do everything with the press by what Al wants to be said. This isn't America; this is the Raiders."

By 1975, a gaggle of assistant coaches had come and gone—the current crop included, since 1972, Tom Flores, Al's old gutty quarterback—and Davis loved to reinforce his authority by making them quake.

"He would just toy with the assistants," Marinovich recalled. "He had 'em all flustered. The coaches would be breaking down film and Al would say something like, 'They'll run such-and-such a play when we're in such-and-such a defensive front.' And he'd just wait to see how everyone responded. What he said might've been bullshit; he just wanted to see who had any balls to say so—and very few did.

"You could have a mind of your own, you could be vocal, if you knew what you were talking about. But because he'd wait in the weeds for you to say something, these guys would just bow and scrape. Ollie Spencer and Tom Dahms would do that. Whatever he said, they'd go, 'Oh, yeah, right.' And Al would keep those guys around, as yes men, because they were loyal to him.

"But he'd really like the ones who *couldn't* have gone on that long with him. Guys like Richie McCabe [an assistant coach in the late sixties]—now *there* was a guy who was a helluva coach and he argued with Al tooth and nail. He even erased Al's x's and o's and *nobody* did that. But guys like that weren't around long. They loved and respected Al but they'd move on because they wanted more freedom.

"In that light, you know what type of person gets to be head coach of the Raiders."

More important to Marinovich than Al's ego games was the Raiders' paleontologist-eyed notion of the perfect football animal. Being outside the scouting mainstream, Al approached player drafting not just with intuition. Long ago he had inspected the anatomy of his prospects' *mothers*; he now wanted to build that kind of thinking into an Al Davis branch of anatomical science.

"He wanted an advantage from the physical standpoint," said Marinovich. "He wanted numbers to look at, prototypes, and that was way ahead of its time. It's damn near what they're doin' now in Russia and East Germany.

"For instance, offensive linemen had to have larger hips than what most scouts looked for, defensive linemen bigger hands and *slimmer* hips, receivers longer arms. I'd have to go check guys and he'd always wait until the last possible minute to send me 'cause he thought people were watchin' where I was goin' and would know who he wanted. With Ray Chester, I went on draft day."

But even Al could not read a man's mind, or gauge his courage under fire. His top draft pick in 1975, defensive back Neal Colzie, may have followed Jack Tatum at Ohio State but he was a pussycat by comparison. The number-one pick in 1976, six-eight, 285-pound defensive end Charles Philyaw, had a slight problem: he had a hard time staying on his feet—or thinking on them. Philyaw kept blowing in, only to be submarine-blocked at the knees. Never did he adjust. One day Philyaw mistakenly went into a meeting with the *offensive* linemen. "Good," said Tom Dahms. "Let him stay there."

Refusing to admit he'd made a mistake with them, Al kept Philyaw and Colzie around for four seasons. Still, blind as he was to the failure of some of his top picks, he never was wedded to building via the draft. Always, draft choices could be leveraged to obtain a key veteran. When All-Pro linebacker Ted Hendricks became a free agent in 1975, Al promptly gave up *two* number-one picks as compensation for signing him. Hendricks was one of those endpieces of life so matched to the Raiders—no one ever knew what went on in his head. The only NFL player to be born in Guatemala (his father worked for an airline that made stops there), Hendricks grew up in Miami but his head was always south of the equator.

A walking riddle, Ted Hendricks more than fit the description of his nickname as a six-seven, 215-pound All-American defensive end at Miami—"The Mad Stork." A wild loon indeed, he went to the Pro Bowl four times as a boisterous outside linebacker with the Colts and Packers but he was easily disgruntled; with Green Bay he fell into what he recalled as "the Valley of Fatigue." At his best as a loose wheel on and off the field, when the Pack wouldn't give him a guaranteed contract, he rolled away.

Al, his linebacking now thin, called Hendricks directly but he did have reservations about the Stork's downy frame and told him he should gain weight. "Al," Hendricks assured him, "when I grab 'em, they're grabbed. Don't worry about it." Bramble-haired and endomorphic, Hendricks—who compiled a record twenty-six blocked kicks in his career—could practically step over people with his long legs; routinely hurdling over a pile of bodies at one practice, his knee caught Pete Banaszak on the helmet, knocking him out. From then on, the Stork became "Kick-'em-in-the-head-Ted" as a four-time Raider Pro Bowler.

Hendricks, who drank beer from a pitcher, *never* from a glass, and often recited poems by William Blake, could not have been better situated to play his best football. Legend now is his talent for broad farce—riding onto the practice field on a horse, wearing a pumpkin instead of a helmet, his "barbells," which were actually empty cans—yet he readily admitted that once he came to the Raiders he was "just another guy." But, clearly, he wasn't just another linebacker. Playing on pure instinct, Hendricks seemed to divine where the ball was going and his educated recklessness wired up a front seven that had begun to sag.

With Hendricks standing upright behind the right end, the Raiders now had enforcement behind *both* sides of the line—the left side was already well tended by Phil Villapiano, a square-jawed, undersized throwaway draft pick from Bowling Green in 1971 who felt no pain outside or between yard lines. Villapiano, who once took on a biker gang in a bar fight—and lost—played ball the same way, rarely losing. Absolutely fearless, Villapiano threw himself into every play, only egged on by his own pain. Once, after taking a huge hit, Villapiano, blood gushing, was stumbling back to the huddle, and had to be dragged off the field.

Teams had begun to dent the Raiders with the pass, but Hendricks, looming like the Chrysler Building—and blitzing if he saw an alley—caused such disarray that *every* Raider defensive back on the roster and all but two linebackers had at least one interception in 1975, an NFL-high thirty-five in all. They also led the league with fifty-five quarterback sacks, up from thirty-six in 1974. But dominant as the defense was, they had to bail out a late-jelling offense. Snake Stabler had hurt his right knee in an exhibition game, and though he numbed up on Darvon and codeine he could barely move, much less pass; favoring the right knee, he also damaged the left one. Not until two straight late-season overtime wins over the Redskins and Falcons—the old goat, George Blanda, in his final season, won both with field goals—did Stabler literally hit his stride.

Washington's great receiver, Charlie Taylor, had said before the Redskin game that the Raider defense hadn't seen receivers such as himself—but Taylor could catch just one pass, while Fred Biletnikoff caught nine. Winning a challenge like that in RFK Stadium was really the Raiders' best medicine. Flying to the division title again, they beat the Bengals in the first playoff game with a mashing ground attack and *four* sacks by Hendricks. Now having to get by the Steelers still once more for a Super Bowl berth, cruel Destiny this time threw them into a turbid Pittsburgh winter.

Framed by symbolic natural manacles, the ice and snow that garnished the field brought the offense to a halt. But so did the

Steelers stall. With both defenses aided by the elements, there were eight fumbles and five interceptions. Frozen pads smashed into each other, exacting a painful toll—a George Atkinson forearm "knock-out" of slinky receiver Lynn Swann would later send Swann to the hospital with a concussion. That might have been worth three points in the Atkinson–Jack Tatum side game, inasmuch as the Raiders believed that for all his vanity Swann had a deep fear of contact and for that reason could be intimidated when he came across the middle.

The Raiders, though, cracked first, falling behind 10–0 in the fourth quarter. They cut it to 16–10 with seconds left, and kismet tantalized—but ultimately mocked them when they recovered an onside kick and Stabler heaved one that Cliff Branch caught at the fifteen just as time ran out.

Although the Steelers went on to another Super Bowl win, the Raiders would take much out of this game that profited them. To their good fortune, Opening Day in 1976 brought them none other than the Steelers, now on the sloshy turf of the Coliseum, and the result was an epic bloodbath that rearranged faces and the balance of power in the AFC. The Raiders had to believe they were hip to the Steelers by now. Right guard George Buehler, for example, came out on the field with Vaseline all over his jersey, having had to contend too long with the grabbing tactics of All-Pro defensive tackle Joe Greene.

More ominously, the Raider safeties were laying for anything that moved across the middle. Fights broke out all over on this day, but the ugliest moment came late in the first half when Atkinson sprang at Swann—even though the ball wasn't thrown to Swann but fifteen yards away from him. As he had done in Pittsburgh, Atkinson leveled a roundhouse forearm smack at the base of Swann's helmet, a sickening atrocity Swann could not have antic-ipated. Completely unsuspecting, he crumpled to the ground, in-stantly unconscious with a second concussion that sidelined him for two games—though, ironically, because the hit was away from the play, no official saw it and no penalty was called. And, scoring seventeen points in the last three minutes, the Raiders won 31–28.

But the end of the game only began the perverted circus that the hit set off. Replays of the villainy were shown endlessly on television—as it had occurred during a nationally televised game —and fans nationwide were horrified. Chuck Noll percolated in rage. The next day, Noll—who had almost fought with several

Raiders under the stands after the game—said he believed the hit was no accident and was *intended* to injure. "You have a criminal element in all aspects of society," he stated, calling for players like Atkinson to be "kicked out of the league."

For years, of course, people had harbored such thoughts about the Raiders. Now Chuck Noll was on the record at the same time that even the *Oakland Tribune* called the play "dirty football." The truest Raiders had no beef with that—"Oh, that was great, 'criminal element,' " said Pete Banaszak. "We loved it." Still, they were astonished that Noll was playing the good-citizen role. "Mean Joe's nickname wasn't 'Cupcake' or 'Poopsie Flower,' " Banaszak pointed out. "Those guys didn't play with featherdusters."

Tom Keating, having by then been around both teams, had to laugh about Noll's presumption of innocence. "I can't think of two more opposite guys than Chuck Noll and Al," he said. "But, again, their teams are *so* alike. I mean, [cornerback] Mel Blount is a first-class guy but he liked to hurt you on the field. You tell me Joe Greene spittin' in guys' faces wasn't disgusting? But, hey, it *worked*."

In fact, as time went on, George Atkinson was really lost in the burning issue of which was dirtier, the Raiders or the Steelers—and, by implication, which team was more effective; and by further implication, who was pro football's prime flume of wisdom, Noll or Al Davis. "That was an organization cold war," Banaszak put it. That was true enough, as far as it went, but the ensuing tornado actually had little to do with the teams, per se.

Fearing a fan backlash against player violence if he did nothing, Pete Rozelle within a week fined Atkinson fifteen hundred dollars for committing "as flagrant a foul as I have seen in sixteen years in this office"—and fined Noll one thousand dollars for his intemperate remarks. But Steelers' president Dan Rooney, son of the Steelers' aging owner Art Rooney, escalated the verbal war, charging that the Raiders' "efforts . . . to seriously injure Lynn Swann" carried back to "the Raiders' coaching staff"—which everyone took to include Al, who, in trying to downplay Raider culpability, became a little irrational.

"No one got killed," he protested with a remarkable lack of sensitivity. "Why get excited?"

Outwardly, Al blamed not Rooney but the press he loved to caress when it served him. The media, he said, "treated the game like the

My Lai massacre." Said Davis: "You guys are the problem. You want us to win. You want us to be tough. But when we're in a vicious game with the Steelers, a team that is notorious for busting up opponents, you seize on an incident . . . and you hammer away."

But he was more than willing to support, and encourage, Atkinson's next move—a $2 million slander suit against Noll for branding him as a criminal. For Atkinson, this was a matter of honor. The year before, he had stood trial in San Francisco on federal embezzlement and larceny charges after purportedly getting two female bank tellers to steal $3,200 from two Alameda County banks; after a mistrial, a second trial acquitted him. Atkinson had also once been arrested (and cleared) for carrying a concealed weapon and threatening to castrate a man. Being called a criminal obviously struck a raw nerve.

Al, who'd paid Atkinson's other legal tab, now did the same as the slander suit was filed on October 6 and heard in San Francisco's Federal Building the following July. While Atkinson hired his own lawyer, a Raider attorney conducted the examination of witnesses and often posed questions after being handed notes by Al.

This showed more than a commitment to one of his players. In truth, both Al and Dan Rooney had deeper motives and strategies in this legal tussle than the obvious ones, and they had been building to a collision for months. The Raiders and Steelers really represented polar ends of the NFL spectrum. The Steelers, forty-two years old and still owned by their founder, had suffered and then grown rich with the NFL; in so doing the team had long ago become entombed within the league's inner councils, its WASP and old Irish aristocracy, and its dense tenets of "league think." Comfortable with their own and the league's power, few owners were more offended by against-the-grain Al Davis than the Rooneys.

Living in uneasy symbiosis since the hard feelings of the 1966 merger, the Rooney side of the football culture had clashed again with the minority-of-one Davis side only recently over Al's apparent empathy with the players' union in its burgeoning strife with NFL owners. Al's stated sympathy to player issues was bad enough to baronial owners unwilling to pry open their eyes to modern free market realities; worse, many of the old-line owners believed Al's posturing went no further than the mileage he could get out of it *personally*. During the players' aborted strike during training camp in 1974, for example, important Raiders crossed picket lines without objection through an eye-wink deal between Al and player rep Gene Upshaw—a man otherwise so vociferous in the cause that he later became president, then executive director, of the union.

Then, late in 1975, a Minneapolis federal district court ruled in favor of John Mackey's antitrust suit against the NFL and over-turned the league's so-called "Rozelle Rule"—which by requiring compensation for a player signing with another team after his con-tract expired had effectively restrained any manner of free agency. In order to chart how to get around that ruling, Pete Rozelle named a planning committee composed of five of the biggest-name exec-utives in the NFL—the Cowboys' Tex Schramm, Paul Brown, Art Modell, Lamar Hunt, and Al Davis. Only Al among them did not seek to avoid the inevitable. The owners, he said at the committee's first meeting, should "just cut all the players and make everybody a free agent."

Rather than bother themselves with this issue, he suggested that the committee should be a "council" with broad powers—or as one observer construed it, a "junta" that would "run the league," which would have placed Al Davis closer to the seat of NFL power than ever before. Not by coincidence, that was also the committee's last meeting.

But Al was not through. While Rozelle was making the point that free agency would be the death of the NFL, Al predicted it would happen and—in a profound harbinger of his own course of action—averred that "wealth will be the prerequisite for greatness in the eighties."

Only weeks later, in the summer of 1976, the league and the players' union drafted an agreement negotiated by Dan Rooney and union president Dick Anderson. But Al felt the pact had circum-vented, and was designed to get rid of, the union's strong-willed executive director, Ed Garvey. Again, Gene Upshaw—this time correctly—went along with his boss and not the rank and file; Upshaw was on the union's executive committee and his nay vote helped kill the Anderson-Rooney agreement.

This of course enraged Dan Rooney, who with many of his breth-ren now believed Al was "playing commissioner" and that his hid-den agenda in these intraleague affairs was to embarrass Pete Rozelle—who held the office Al had lost and a good many assumed he still wanted—and thus weaken Rozelle to the point where Al *did* run the NFL, with or without Pete Rozelle.

Whatever his intentions, Al could feel walls of resentment closing in on him. When the George Atkinson lawsuit was filed on October 6, Atkinson's lawyer stated that one of the suit's aims was to prove "a conspiracy on the part of the Rooney-Rozelle establishment to get the upstart Oakland crowd led by Al Davis." With this gauntlet thrown down, Rozelle had no choice but to actively line up behind Dan Rooney, pitting Rozelle and Davis against each other in court for the first time. Eschewing neutrality, the commissioner would take the stand to deny any such collusion and to defend his honor—and his league, as he was fully convinced Al was out to destroy it as it now stood. In pushing the lawsuit, Rozelle said later about Al Davis, "hurting the league didn't bother him at all."

Rooney too was worried about that. The lawsuit, he told other owners, was only a first hint of insurrection; the precedent of one NFL team suing another had potential shattering implications for the grand old league. Whatever the outcome, he knew Al Davis would be around to survey the damage.

The Raiders used the courtroom confrontation to their advantage. They came away from the Steeler game shored up in the "us-against-them" mindset that had flagged as the team melded into the new, diluted NFL. The problem now wasn't mental but physical—three defensive linemen were injured in exhibition games and lost for the season. As famous a win as the Steelers battle was, needing bodies, Al went out on a limb again and signed his biggest problem child yet: six-eight, 280-pound John Matuszak.

Matuszak was the NFL's top draft pick in 1973, but his career had taken a downhill slide into a sludge pile. Unhappy under Sid Gillman while with the Oilers, Matuszak—a ticking time bomb of a man who in college once punched and nearly killed a guy he thought was messing with his girlfriend—walked out on the team. He signed with the WFL's Houston club and was playing with them when a twenty-five-man sheriff's posse came *onto the field* to serve him with a court order Gillman had obtained. He was traded to the Chiefs in 1974, his wife tried to run him over in a car, he was arrested for marijuana possession, and then hospitalized when he overdosed on alcohol and sleeping pills. Hooked on booze, cocaine, and Lord knows what else, he was traded to George Allen's Redskins in 1976. That lasted only through the exhibition season, and when Allen was asked why he cut Matuszak he quipped, "Vodka and Valium, the Breakfast of Champions."

Even Al wasn't sure about this one. On the practice field he asked Ted Hendricks if a loose screw like the Tooz would fit in. "Al," Hendricks said, "what difference will one more make?"—a comment that should be a Raider epitaph.

Before Matuszak arrived, John Madden had decided that he had only enough intact bodies up front to play three of them and thus began the season playing the 3-4 defensive alignment portended way back with the Dan Birdwell "Rover" days but long resisted by Al. Now, instead of using Matuszak in a 4-3, he permanently benched the lamentable Charles Philyaw after he was hurt in the season's fourth game and went with Matuszak in his place at left end.

And, in fact, Matuszak was the perfect 3-4 lineman. In this scheme the three down linemen must be big, mobile, and immovable; able to occupy two or three blockers at a time so that the four linebackers can go right to the ball unmolested. Matuszak, who took up roughly the space of a Buick *and* could mount a pass rush, cleared the field for Phil Villapiano—and both of them, along with Hendricks, made so much mayhem that teams had to be scared to death, not knowing what any of them would do if they snapped and went haywire. As usual, Matuszak was also a pain to his own employers—Madden once had to order off the team plane two bimbos who were brought on by a boozy Tooz—but the man played big and played hurt.

Ken Stabler, meanwhile, his throbbing knees anesthetized by an endless stream of Darvon and codeine, had a storied year in 1976 —2,737 yards passing, twenty-seven touchdowns, *and* a completion rate of 67 percent. In the ninth game of the season, the Bears knocked him cold, but when he came to, he went back out in a daze and threw a forty-nine-yard touchdown to Cliff Branch that won it 28–27.

With a 13–1 record, the Raiders faced the only team to beat them, the Patriots, and were losing again, 21–10, with sixteen minutes to go. Even though George Atkinson had broken the nose of Russ Francis, the Patriots' huge tight end, with another vicious forearm, Francis came back and caught a touchdown on him. But—in a wondrous irony—an official's call against an *opponent's* use of excessive force saved them. On fourth and eighteen, down 21–17 with a minute to go, Stabler misfired—but defensive tackle Sugar Bear Hamilton was flagged for roughing the passer, keeping alive the drive that Stabler capped with a one-yard touchdown run to win the game 24–21.

That drive was what finally got the Raiders back to the Super Bowl. For although the Steelers were in their way again in the AFC title game, now the winds of misfortune were busy on the *other* sideline—with running backs Franco Harris and Rocky Bleier out injured, the Steelers didn't make a first down until mid–second quarter against the hellish Raider defense. On the field all day, the Steel Curtain eventually cracked like dry bamboo as the Raiders ran the ball fifty-one times in the 24–7 win.

The next stop—glory hallelujah!—was Super Bowl XI in Pasadena's cavernous Rose Bowl, against the Minnesota Vikings, and the Raiders considered this game to be a gimme. Indeed, coming up one short all those previous years was very hard to take, given that in the eight years since they'd bowed to Vince Lombardi's legacy, NFL/NFC teams had taken the pipe in the big game seven times. No dark Raider fate could possibly obscure AFC superiority—nor the vital statistics of the Vikings' defensive front four.

These supposed "Purple People Eaters" were more like purple onions, made to *be* eaten. Of the four, tackle Doug Sutherland was the heftiest at 250; the bigger names, if not bodies, were tackle Alan Page and ends Carl Eller and Jim Marshall—all light and quick men who ran well-coordinated stunts and cross-rushes. But they had been minced by the Chiefs' big and quick offensive line in Super Bowl IV, and the Raiders' line was bigger and quicker.

Most of the Vikings, in fact, were fossils from the NFL's ice age. Their timid zone defenses were a cover for some very weak sisters in the secondary, and their dump-off passes compensated both for a porous offensive line and for weak-armed quarterback Fran Tarkenton, whose crazy-legged scrambles filled reels of NFL "follies" films but who had already lost two Super Bowls. Madden, seeing his team fire on all cylinders in practice the week before the game, called off further workouts on Wednesday, knowing they were ready to roll.

Al, who was so tangible in making the Super Bowl a reality, saw his Raiders trot onto the field on January 9, 1977, before 100,421 spectators and 100 *million* television viewers and rip the gizzards out of this last remaining ghost of the old NFL. Offensively and defensively, they held the line of scrimmage in a tight fist. On one side of the line, Art Shell all but erased All-Pro Jim Marshall, who had *no* tackles in the game. On the other side, they destroyed the timing of the Vikings' passes and held fullback Chuck Foreman— a thousand-yard rusher during the season—to forty-four yards on seventeen carries, and forced him to fumble on the goal line. Ted Hendricks, blowing through the line, deflected one pass into line-backer Willie Hall's hands for a key interception.

Once more needing to throw only sparingly, Stabler handed off fifty-two times in a 266-yard ground stampede—Clarence Davis, profiting the most, ran for 137 yards. Fred Biletnikoff, fourteen years removed from taking Al's pen in hand under the goalpost, caught four passes for seventy-nine yards and won the game's MVP award, mostly for his Raider symbolism; afterward, he cried like a baby. Pete Banaszak, the old warrior, scored twice. Finally, in a moment of sublime symmetry, thirty-six-year-old Willie Brown iced the game almost exactly the way Herb Adderley had done in reverse nine years before—cutting in front of a sideline pass, intercepting, and running a straight dash seventy-five yards for a touchdown.

And yet most of the attention at the end of the 32–14 rout was focused on Al Davis and the personal vindication of his wrathful genius. In the fourth quarter, a mob of well-wishers and reporters began to gather behind him in the press box, both congratulating him and trying to get him to answer questions. Biting his fingernails and keeping his sunglasses-shielded eyes fixed on the field, he ig-nored the commotion, not even looking up when somebody knocked over a cup of coffee in front of him.

"Hey, Al, congratulations," one of them yelled to him. "Your team's playing great. Really super."

"What bullshit," he growled, still not diverting his gaze.

If Al was unresponsive, perhaps it was because he was preoc-cupied with his private war with Pete Rozelle, which was most conspicuous in the pending George Atkinson lawsuit. When the final gun sounded, Al made haste to get down to the locker room, not only to drink in the nectar of triumph at long last but mindful that, in a sense, his team's victory was a defeat for Rozelle—who likely would rather have been anywhere else on that day than under hot klieg lights right next to Al Davis presenting him with the Vince Lombardi trophy.

Al approached this incredibly satisfying moment on the heels of another run-in with Rozelle that almost no one knew about but that in the mind of Al Davis was a seed to be nurtured until it could do him the most good. The week before the game, Al had requested from Rozelle more than the 15,000 tickets allotted that year to the Raiders as a Super Bowl finalist. As Pasadena was so near to Oakland, he wanted to accommodate many more Raiders fans who could easily attend the game. Al had in mind three or four more thousand tickets—but all Rozelle provided was 200.

"As commissioner," he told Rozelle, "you do an awful lot of things for the 'good of the league.' You should get us more tickets."

Rozelle again offered 200, and Al took them—but in his hands this small issue had the makings of an atomic bomb; not only did he think the league offices' requisition of 10,000 tickets and the host city team's (in this case, the L.A. Rams) share of 30,000 were unfair, but Al had reason to believe that many teams around the league—and the league office—were *selling* blocks of these coveted tickets through associated travel agencies, with the consent and even the participation of Rozelle.

Al was hardly prepared to go public with this potentially volatile issue and he had played it cool and was coyly nasty about Rozelle during Super Bowl week. Asked at one point why he had been keeping mostly out of sight, he cooed, "You know me. If I come around, I say something controversial and the commissioner doesn't get the headlines." But it was squarely on his mind as he stepped on the stage of his greatest victory.

Rozelle was ever gracious and dignified. Handing Al the two-foot-high trophy adorned with a silver football, he said affably, "I'm sorry it's not silver and black, but it's close. Al, your victory was one of the most impressive in football history."

Barely looking at Rozelle, Al clutched the trophy, squinted into the lights, and chirped about keeping his covenant of winning it all. Then he slipped in a disjointed complaint about "the season ticket holders we had to leave home." He added, "That we upset some of our loyal fans is the only negative part of this whole thing. I hope the fans will forgive us."

Rozelle, of course, knew what Al was talking about, but only to the extent that it affected him during this one Super Bowl. Besides, it was so nebulous a spew that almost no one understood it, or cared to press it. Because Al Davis said nothing *else* noxious, Rozelle went home happy. As did Al, with the Super Bowl trophy in his hands. But, all the while, his mind was churning, already carving out battles that for Pete Rozelle were still no more than frightening fantasies.

18

Let me tell you something about Al. He scares 'em. It's the fear he strikes in the players that makes everyone act right. He knows how to do it. You don't want Al Davis pissed off at you.

—Gene Upshaw

Al is a guy capable of bringing the roof down around his own head.

—New York Giants owner Wellington Mara

When George Atkinson's slander lawsuit came to trial in July of 1977, John Madden took the stand and offered a unique character reference for Atkinson. Within the Raiders' defensive concept, Atkinson's gratuitous hit on Lynn Swann was, Madden said, "an instinctive reaction by a safety, not a premeditated cheap shot. . . . With a cornerback, a forearm is more likely to be premeditated because he's covering [a] wide receiver. With a safety, who usually covers a tight end, that wide receiver is suddenly in his area and he reacts." At that point, Madden could have interjected the trademark exclamation he now uses covering football games on television—*boom*.

Ken Stabler had another possible explanation. Raider defenders were so aggressive, he recalled, because "they tended to take speed. By the handful." On the sideline, Stabler said, these men's eyes "would get real big and they'd have a kind of wild, distant look in them. They would be so wired they couldn't stop moving their jaws and grinding their teeth." Even with the supposed crackdown on speed after the Houston Ridge case, "the stuff was always readily available" and the defensive guys took it "for that extra jolt."*

Despite Madden's defense, or perhaps *because* of it, Atkinson himself was not a very convincing martyr—and, surprisingly, neither was Al, who might have been more at ease if he'd been there to argue Pete Rozelle's fitness for office. Instead, almost seeming distracted by the actual case, he tepidly decried "the hypocritical thing that there are some [hits] that are more malevolent than [those] that are legal. Our problem is to confront this."

After the plaintiffs ran film clips of ugly hits by Steelers players—with accompanying groans and wincing looks by Al, who sat by the jury box—Chuck Noll indeed admitted that many of his own players qualified as members of the "criminal element." But Noll was rescued by Pete Rozelle at his most regal. Not mentioning that offending term, he surely described the Swann hit as one "calculated to disable." Snide remarks by Atkinson's lawyer—for example, comments about the commissioner's rich suntan—only won Rozelle sympathy. Pushing Davis's conspiracy theory, the lawyer asked Rozelle if it was true that he had spoken with Dan Rooney before the trial but not once with Davis.

That was true, Rozelle said, adding slyly, "because I get the impression [Davis] isn't interested in having much contact with the league."

Even the attorney had to admit in summation that Rozelle was "very smooth and very clear" but the attorney's plaint that Rozelle "brainwashed the truth" and that George Atkinson was a "pawn" because "he wore a Raider helmet" didn't go down well in the jury box. After four hours of deliberation, they cleared Noll—no slander, no malice, no damages. Rozelle again went home happy, though seething at Davis for tarring and feathering the league as he had.

Al said nothing about the verdict, but it might have been Atkinson who paid for it. Now disposable as a *Davis* pawn, he was released after the upcoming 1977 season, sentenced to live with the "criminal element" label evermore. Al also took his lumps. In retreat, the other owners celebrated his defeat while Rozelle considered *his* means of payback.

Expecting retribution, Al and the Raider players now saw all

Snake, by Ken Stabler and Berry Stainback (New York: Doubleday, 1986), pp. 76–77.

kinds of nefarious forces at work on the field. Having benefited so handsomely from an official's call only a year before, it seemed to them an overly stark coincidence when calls now went against them. Suddenly, Jack Tatum swore, "Some fines were issued, which I refused to pay, and . . . every official in the NFL is throwing quick flags in my general direction."

Still, the Raiders went 11–3 and made the playoffs. In the opening round they trailed the Colts by three with a minute left. Stabler then flung one deep into the Baltimore mist and Dave Casper—who was called "Ghost"—emerged wraithlike with the ball in his hands forty-two yards downfield. A field goal sent it into sudden-death overtime, which lasted until Casper caught a ten-yard touchdown forty-three seconds into the second overtime period.

But then in the championship game in Denver, cruel fate didn't just mock them; it channeled all of Al Davis's karmic debts and paranoiac fears into one play. Down 7–3 in the third quarter, they fumbled away the ball on their own seventeen and the Broncos moved it to the two. Halfback Rob Lytle then took the handoff and tried to dive over the pile into the end zone, but he was met in midair by a Tatum hit. The ball popped loose and was picked up by defensive tackle Mike McCoy, who ran all the way downfield. At first, this play seemed to make amends for Daryle Lamonica's stray lateral against the Jets in 1968—only this time the whistle blew as McCoy took off. Never seeing the ball come loose, the officials gave it back to the Broncos, who took it in on the next play and won 20–17. A day later, while the Broncos were on their way to the Super Bowl, the league admitted the error.

"We got fucked!" declared a still-truculent Pete Banaszak over a decade later. "And I felt we got screwed by the Immaculate Reception, too."

The Raiders' suspicions cemented Al's now-open opposition to Pete Rozelle. When league owners met in May of 1977 to approve a new ten-year contract for the commissioner, Al cast the lone nay vote. Indeed, if Rozelle's prestige was at stake Al could victimize any innocent bystander—even the needy. At Rozelle's prodding, the owners agreed to donate profits from the league's marketing and promotion division—which licensed team T-shirts, souvenirs, and the like—to noble causes under the name of NFL Charities. Only

Al demurred, refusing to join NFL Charities and asking for "receipt of royalties" due the Raiders.

As the Chargers' Gene Klein recalled it years later, when Al did this "I stood up and verbally attacked him. I called him every name I could think of. . . . But nothing I said seemed to bother him. He just sat there impassively. I realized then that Al Davis is the kind of man who if you spit in his face looks up at the sky and says it must be raining. . . .

"Davis contended that the Raiders preferred to spend their money in local charities. That was the first time I'd ever heard of an office claiming that it gave at home."

Perhaps not incidentally, when the Chargers and Raiders played an exhibition game in Oakland that year, Al wouldn't pay Klein his cut of the gate until Rozelle intervened and ordered it done. Klein said of Davis at the time, "He's an asshole and he wants to run the whole league. Rozelle had no choice about dealing with him. If you don't put a guy like Davis in his place, pretty soon you've got no league left."

And, in fact, it was *Rozelle* who was on the offensive, and with a cunning that went over even Al's wary head. At that same May meeting Rozelle quietly asked for authority to make owners' committee assignments. Al—who was on the powerful Competition Committee, he thought beyond recall—joined in a unanimous vote.

Only at another meeting in October did Al learn the import of this seemingly routine piece of business. There, at the end of a long day of mundane affairs, Rozelle doled out new assignments—without a single mention of Al Davis. While he did not actually say so, this meant that Rozelle had kicked Al off the Competition Committee. As the committee was in charge of such matters as scheduling and game rules, the NFL had only gained by having a man of Davis's expertise on the committee. By all accounts, he had worked well with its chairman, the Cowboys' GM Tex Schramm. Yet, without even consulting Schramm, Rozelle acted on the grounds that, as he later said, Davis had given "validity to positions contrary to league policy."

When the deed was done, Schramm—the man who gave Pete Rozelle his first NFL job, and who was sometimes called "Mr. Vice-Commissioner" for his close alliance with Rozelle—branded the move "a disservice" to the league. As for Al, he seemed to use it to slap himself back into his former state of caffeine-edgy awareness. Rozelle, he growled, "Never faced me man to man . . . [he] just did it and then leaked it to the press so it would be a big story, make him strong." If the Davis-Rozelle matchup wasn't manifestly a personal thing before, it was now nakedly so. And if Pete Rozelle wanted to play hardball, Al would not be caught with his guard down again.

However, into the late seventies, Rozelle was transcendent in his league, braced in his power as Al Davis seemed to decay in his. In 1978, the *new* Competition Committee—trying to save the passing game from extinction in the strangling hands of modern zone defenses—changed the rules to allow offensive linemen freer use of hands on pass blocking and to restrict pass defenders to *one* hit within *five* yards of the line. The latter was especially injurious to the Raiders; no other team used the Bump and Run style as heavily, and now their cornerbacks would have to lay off receivers all the way downfield. Under the circumstances, Al was thankful the league still let them bump at *all*.

That season, during a game with the Chargers, they *won* on a mondo bizarro play—down by six with ten seconds left, Stabler, hit by a blitzing linebacker, intentionally fumbled the ball forward; as it spun crazily on the ground, Pete Banaszak batted it farther forward and Dave Casper first tried to pick it up, then dribbled it like a basketball, and finally fell on it in the end zone. In the Raiders' litany of weirdness, this Immaculate *De*ception may have won a game but when the NFL shortly thereafter changed the rules and made intentional fumbling illegal (appropriately, only the Raiders had ever done anything like that), it seemed like a kind of *retroactive* crack on the knuckles.

Worst of all for Al, the first serious problems in a decade were severing the team's stable tethers. The 1978 season was the last for Fred Biletnikoff, Willie Brown, George Buehler, and Clarence Davis; John Vella missed the season with a chest injury and Phil Villapiano had a bad knee. Taking a beating on both sides of the line, their quarterback sacks were way down, while Stabler's touchdown passes fell to sixteen and his interceptions rose to thirty.

Stabler's numbers were cause for concern. While his pass blocking was damaged without Vella and Davis, his left arm was getting rickety and his mobility was almost nil. Gray-haired and corroded looking at thirty-two, Stabler threw a lot but was unable to deliver the ball deep, often stranding Cliff Branch—who caught just *one* touchdown all season. The Raider "vertical" game was now Dave

Casper going ten to fifteen yards over the middle, which confused
and troubled Branch. Losing confidence, he missed a practice and
players began to worry about him.

Actually, the face of the offense had been regressing for some
time; perhaps *too* comfy with the winning ball-control attack of
1976, Stabler and Madden seemed to lose their nerve. Only when
they fell behind did they go for the big, killing plays. In 1978, with
the playoffs in the balance, Oakland lost three of its last four games
and missed going for the first time since 1971.

This was Al's cue to stop holding his tongue about Stabler. His
reservations having been held hostage by winning, he now allowed
himself to be interviewed by several Bay Area newspapers. Stabler
bore the brunt of his remarks. Of the past season Davis said,
"You've got to point to someone, so blame Stabler. He makes the
most money. . . . If you can't get the ball to your wide receivers,
you can't win. It all starts with the lefthander." He also faulted
Stabler for not being in shape, noting that "he doesn't do any work
in the off-season."

Weeks later, a sportswriter for the *Sacramento Bee*, Bob Padecky,
went to Stabler's Alabama hometown and elicited some uncompli-
mentary statements about Stabler's lifestyle from several people
around town. Stabler, who was infuriated by Davis's comments,
came unstrung when the Padecky interviews ran as part of a three-
part series. "I may have become a little paranoid," he later admitted,
"wondering if Al Davis had sent Padecky to dig up dirt on me."

Stabler then called the writer and invited him back to Alabama
and Padecky came all the way from Sacramento to be greeted by
Stabler maniacally screaming at him for "writing that crap." Before
he left town, Padecky was arrested when police searched his car
and found a small amount of cocaine. Even by backwoods standards,
this was a clumsily obvious setup, and the charges were dropped.
If Stabler or his buddies had anything to do with it—which he
denied, though he later said he knew who planted the stuff—it
backfired on him. Suddenly, Al's criticism of Stabler had a broader
context, placing Stabler in a germ culture of rednecks with cocaine
and no sense.

Al kept jabbing at Stabler. During the summer he had Al
LoCasale send releases to the press that raved about the talents of
other quarterbacks on the roster, including the much-traveled Jim
Plunkett. Stabler's response was to enlist the press himself. After
publicly demanding to be traded he was asked by *Sport* magazine

if he and Al would bury the hatchet. "I'd like to bury the hatchet—right between Al Davis's shoulder blades," he said.

The 1978 season had also been the last for John Madden. Ten seasons on the razor's edge had left Madden with 103 victories—which he racked up faster than any other coach in NFL history—but also an ulcer. His diet had become mostly antacid pills and all the plane rides, hotels, and third-down plays gave him raging head-aches. Always a sensitive soul beneath the frantically jiggling love handles, his last drop of innocence drained in an August exhibition game that year when Jack Tatum—in what seemed written on the wind for him—brought about one of the blackest of Raider fates. It happened when the Patriots' receiver Darryl Stingley ran a slant pattern over the middle, leaped for a too-high pass, and was rammed head-on by Tatum—a normal, "legal" Tatum hit that in this case did so much damage that Stingley, lying crumpled on the ground with a broken neck, could not move. Taken off on a stretcher, he came out of the hospital a quadriplegic.

The Raiders of the day, men who lived in the killing fields every Sunday, quickly discarded the memory of this unspeakable horror. They had to, especially Tatum, or perish from the game. Accordingly, Pete Banaszak recalls the hit today etherized by cold football law. "It was a stupid call to send the receiver over the middle," he said, "when you got a head-hunter back there. To do that, you're lookin' for trouble."

But Madden—who had defended George Atkinson's profligacy as an "instinctive reaction"—was unable to stomach football violence at this price. Feeling somehow responsible, he went to the hospital after the game and demanded to be in the operating room while doctors worked on Stingley, whispering "You're gonna be all right" in his ear. When Stingley's wife flew to Oakland, she stayed in Madden's home. Convinced he had to get out of the game, Madden was gone at season's end.

Tatum too had gone to the hospital, but couldn't get in to see Stingley. Thinking, incorrectly, that he was being turned away by Stingley's family, he stole away and held to a pitiless silence when-ever Stingley was mentioned—a reaction that made Tatum, like Stingley, a victim of himself, and like Atkinson a dark echo of one single play among hundreds. His knees worn and his body old at thirty-one, even this wrought-iron Raider was traded after one more season.

Madden's retirement was a propitious moment for Al to try to repeal the stagnation of the offense. Pointedly turning back the clock even as time marched on, he named forty-one-year-old Tom Flores as the top man. This was a move with obvious symmetry; not only did it complete the orbit that Flores began as an original Raider in 1960, but by Raider criteria Flores was *the* realization of an Al Davis head coach—a player and coach for Davis, an offensive-minded guy, he was a quiet company man seemingly certain to breed ideological compliance.

Not everyone was sure about Flores. A slim, darkly handsome man with a bent nose and a tuft of soap-pad hair, he could appear like a Galician sphinx. With his arms folded serenely around his middle on the sideline, swaying slightly from side to side, his round face unfretted, if it were not for his small, diligent eyes the temptation would be to hold a mirror under his nose. After the typhoon of John Madden, Flores's phlegmatic, even timorous exterior was freaky and inaccessible to the players. Though he knew more football than Madden had, he had none of Pinky's motivational skills or *mensch* qualities.

Early in his first season at the helm, trying to show his authority, Flores raged at a verbally enthusiastic John Matuszak to shut up, an outburst so out of character that the players didn't buy it for a minute—and it made Matuszak sulk for a long time. Even Al would have to get on Flores about his coolness. When a newspaper ran a photo of a calm Flores near the end of a loss, with a caption that said Flores "takes things as they come," Al took it into the coach's office.

"I said, 'Bullshit!' " Davis told *Inside Sports*. "You've got to dominate to get things done. Not let them happen. . . . He said, 'I didn't sleep last night after losing.' Damn, you better *not* sleep. I wouldn't sleep for two weeks. If you want to be head coach, be what it is—be a fucking head coach."

But Flores was able to establish a magisterial presence, driving hard from within—though it could be argued that his greatest challenges had already been met years before. The son of itinerant Mexican farm workers, Flores at five years of age was in the orchards of the San Joaquin Valley picking fruit for three cents a tray. Later, he put himself through the University of the Pacific and graduated summa cum laude. When his tuberculosislike lung ailment arose in 1962, he allowed himself to miss only one season and wound up playing twelve years. His first year as the Raiders' head coach, he lost three of his first four games and thirteen players to injury—and still finished 9–7, though in third place and out of the playoffs.

By way of explaining a second straight year out of the money, Al was willing to advance the narcissistic mea culpa that his attention had been consumed elsewhere and was not on team matters. "I let Tom down because of a misfortune," Davis said.

It sounded as though he could have been talking about his stocks taking a dip instead of the near death of his wife.

As with other dictators, little was known about Al Davis's home life. As Al didn't generally patronize social events and often flew it alone at the football convocations he did attend, the cliff-dwelling Piedmont home with its indoor swimming pool and bomb-shelter-turned-weight-room was his latter-day citadel. Few *Raider* people saw Carol and the now twenty-three-year-old Mark Davis—including, much of the time, Al.

"I sort of felt that Al had a relationship with Mark sort of like Al's father had with him," said George Ross, who'd spent enough time near the family to know. "It was adversarial, with Al putting all of his interest in football and Mark probably waiting for the time to play catch on the front lawn. I don't think Al ever held a fishing line, let alone took the kid fishing."

Red-haired and small, Mark Davis did go into sports, but not as an athlete or as a budding Raider heir. Upon graduating from Chico State College, he worked briefly as a player agent—Cliff Branch was one of his clients—then began marketing a line of thermal athletic gloves. For Al, it had to be a let-down that his own blood did not necessarily carry the tonic of greatness.

Bob Wallach, the college chum to whom Al still confided, told of a conversation he had with Al on the subject. "He once told me that his son is a nice boy, but hasn't got the hundred percent commitment that Al has to the Raiders," Wallach said. "He would have loved his son to be with him but he said he'd never take Mark in until he showed he had that commitment. Al's disappointed, but I guess the boy just doesn't want to live in Al's shadow."

Nobody ever said that "Carolee" Davis lacked such a commitment, or the power to daunt even a man like Al Davis. Through the years, Al had described her—in terms that for him were like vespers—as "a big-time New York girl" and "a wild woman, a good-looking woman, my kind of woman," and that was how almost everyone thought of her. Beautiful, but hard, loyal to the end with him, right or wrong.

But marrying a man like Al Davis can sap the strength of the strongest of humans. And Al's football obsessions finally took a toll on her. While Al could always find a world of occupation in game films and personnel moves, Carol could only wait and shop at those drug store counters. "I'm sure there were times," said George Ross, "when she would've liked a closer relationship."

Already smoking four packs of cigarettes a day, something inside her body made her heart stop beating in the early morning of October 19, 1979. Jolted out of sleep by a surge of pain, she tumbled out of their bed and onto the floor. Al, awakened by the noise, found her lying there, eyes glazed, unable to speak, and barely breathing. Because her jaws were tightly clenched, he tried to pry her mouth open, cutting his finger on her teeth, and then blew his breath into her lungs. Breathing a little more easily, while Al called a doctor she struggled to her feet and walked into the bathroom, where she collapsed again on the cold tile floor.

By the time the Davises' physician, Dr. Robert Albo, got to the house, Carol's breath and her heartbeat had ceased. Albo tried pumping her heart as a frantic Al kept asking, "How is she? How is she?" The answer, as Albo recalled later, was that she was "essentially dead."

Stricken with a heart attack *and* a stroke, she was taken to Oakland's Merritt Hospital, placed motionless and in a coma on a respirator in the coronary care unit. For days, doctors would walk into her room, glance at her, and walk out with grave looks. But for every one of those days, Al sat beside her bed, and he slept beside her when his eyes couldn't stay open anymore. The 1979 season went on without him, and for once in his life he had no hunger for football. Instead, living out of a storage room on the same floor, he diverted his jingly nerves into positive energy for Carol—and calling old friends across the country to locate heart specialists; the ones who told him they could help he flew in and brought to her bedside.

But every day began to look more hopeless. The Raiders' orthopedic specialist, Dr. Robert Rosenfeld, didn't want to give Al his diagnosis. "I'd have given thousand-to-one odds against that woman coming back as anything but a vegetable," he said. That was *if* she came out of it. Al, though, wouldn't hear of such talk, and wouldn't let Carol hear it either. No one knew if she could hear anything, but with the two of them there in the darkened room, Al would talk to her, squeeze her hand, speak of things only the two of them knew about.

"I talked about our dreams," the rarely seen softie in Al Davis said, looking back later. "I might have made some promises, too."

Mostly, he told her she *had* to live, and he'd look hard for any signs of response. Once, during a sleepless night, he thought he saw her open her eyes and screamed for a doctor, who told him he was seeing things. "Fuck you," came his reply. The doctor's opinion was widespread, and Al heard hushed talk about "pulling the plug." And then, after seventeen days in hell, Al was out in the corridor stretching his legs when nurses inside the room squealed. Minutes later, one of the nurses came over to him. "Mr. Davis," she asked, "do you want to talk to your wife?"

When he got to her bed, Carol was awake and—to the astonishment of the doctors—only slightly less coherent than she would have been after waking up groggy from a good night's sleep. Her first words to Al were, "What happened?"

"You were sick, baby," he said.

Doctors still knitted their brows, concerned about brain damage since she had breathed no oxygen for five minutes during the attack. But Carol came through therapy without obstacle, learning to reorient her slowed motor responses and slurred speech. A year later, Al pronounced her "97 percent recovered." Today, the recovery is full.

"He brought her back from the dead," marveled Harry Schuh.

Indeed, Al had reason to believe that he might even have this death thing licked. Eight years before, a Davis office crony named Del Courtney had contracted a rare muscle disease and lay paralyzed for three months; as with Carol, doctors were almost certain he'd die. But then, too, Al stood beside him, constantly reassuring Courtney he would not die, that he had to fight. Finally, Courtney too made a complete recovery. Today, he clearly remembers one thing Al kept telling him while he lay in a death pose—"He said, 'Del, you're a Raider. Raiders don't die.' "

While Al presented televisions to the Merritt doctors and nurses in gratitude, he firmly believed *he* had been the best medicine for Carol. And for anyone who believed something as cloyingly ineffectual as human love had played a part in the miracle recovery, he wanted to straighten *that* out flat away. "Everyone thinks it was based on love," he said. "It wasn't. I just had to get it done. I'd do it for anyone I knew or was close to."

Not for a moment did anyone who knew Al believe this. "It wasn't like that," said Pat Sarnese, who had watched the newlywed Davises bill and coo on the Fort Belvoir army base almost three decades before, and knew how lovesick they still were. "It was a front. He always wants the tough-ass image to supersede everything else. But he'd do anything for her."

Still, as close as he had come to losing this part of himself, he may have resented that which had frightened him so. Despite the outpouring of sympathy from people all over the country who responded to his hospital pleas, he now seemed to pity them for getting so emotionally attached. A year later, he told *Inside Sports*: "I only want to be loved by certain people—my players, the people I live with. No, not by humanity. I push it away because I don't need it. Maybe everyone else should work at it, but we need a few people to lead and dominate and get things done. I feel the role of love belongs to other people."

If Al wasn't in the mood for love, it may have been partly because he was preparing to end an old love affair—the one the "loyal fans" in Oakland had with the Raiders.

Though he spoke with few people about football business during his wife's coma, and for several more weeks tending to her after the crisis passed, he did have several important phone conversations with a man whose name wasn't known to football fans but who would help Al Davis change the NFL map. This was Bill Robertson, the president and chief negotiator of the Los Angeles Memorial Coliseum Commission, which operated the famous old stadium that for thirty-three years housed the Rams. Beginning in 1980, that team was going to play its home games in fresher surroundings in Anaheim Stadium across the street from Disneyland, and the LAMCC—which was suing the league for allowing the defection —was actively wooing other teams to play in the musty, one-hundred-thousand-seat Coliseum.

The first time Al Davis *officially* entered into this maelstrom-to-be was just two weeks before Carol took ill. It came at an owners meeting in Chicago called to approve the Rams' move and discuss the L.A. Coliseum lawsuit—which specifically challenged the league constitution's Article IV, Section 4.3, requiring unanimous consent by club owners for the transfer of any franchise into the home territory of another franchise, and a three-quarter vote for any other shift.

This headlock of a bylaw was anathema to the LAMCC since it would have killed any bid by another team to move to the Coliseum; and the commission's suit to annul Section 4.3 as a violation of the Sherman Antitrust Act opened up a tempest of worry for a league operating on thin antitrust exemptions. Consequently, Pete Rozelle proposed in Chicago that Section 4.3 be amended to a three-quarters vote in all team shifts. By this Rozelle and the league's attorneys hoped to remove the oppressive and probably illegal clause as an issue.

At first some owners doubted the action would make the LAMCC capitulate—and this was where Al put himself on record as being interested in a possible move to Los Angeles. With the Raiders' lease in Oakland due to expire at the end of the 1979 season, he told the group "I may want to move" and that he didn't think he *needed* a vote to move. Instead, he urged the owners to consider the use of "outside forces" or "neutral bodies" to oversee franchise shifts.

Eventually, all of the other owners voted aye on the Rozelle proposal—while Al "passed," believing a nonunanimous vote would defeat it. However, creating a new kind of parliamentary democracy, Rozelle ruled the vote to be unanimous *anyway*.

"If you are going to consider that unanimous," an angry Davis told him, "and it isn't, then I reserve the right to move the Oakland Raiders as I see fit."

With these words Al Davis was either citing or inventing legal precedent. But, for now, Rozelle and the other owners couldn't imagine that Al was anywhere near serious about moving a thriving team away from its rabid fans—partly because Al was so coy, his reasoning about "reserved rights" so ambiguous. To them, it was just another case of Al Davis trying to twist Pete Rozelle's nose out of joint. "That's the way Al likes to be," Rozelle later said. "He has done it before."

The year before, in fact, the two of them had locked horns when Al supposedly pondered buying the Oakland A's baseball team from Charlie Finley—an odd desire given that Al had once opposed the A's coming to Oakland at all. Told by the commissioner that this

would be against the league's ban on cross-ownership, Al railed
that Rozelle was being unfair with him, since at least six NFL
owners at the time had an interest in other teams, and the Browns'
Art Modell was on the board of the Cleveland Indians.

But this may have been nothing more than Al picking a small,
losing fight in order to smudge Rozelle and his "running dog"—
as Al called Modell—at an owners meeting that year.

Although Rozelle and the owners didn't know it, Chicago was
different. In truth, Al *had* to get the L.A. thing on record when
he did, and his stridency was more than a rude floor show.

Only Al Davis knew how serious he was about jilting the "loyal
fans" of Oakland.

Al Davis's vote in Chicago had been plotted on an invisible graph
in Al's head dating back years—maybe as far back as that pipsqueak
parade in downtown Oakland honoring Al Davis's first year of
Raider deliverance. With all of the team's success since then, by
the mid-seventies Al believed he personally had more grandeur than
Oakland could fit between its borders.

"By 1976, he had already become disenchanted with Oakland,"
George Ross said. "Al was a New York guy, he knew that sports
heroes back there were given ticker-tape parades, they were quoted,
they got endorsements. In Oakland there was no mountain named
for him, they didn't change Lake Merritt to Lake Davis. And I
think that was a deficiency on the part of the town; it took him for
granted. He was never the Lombardi of Oakland.

"And yet, at the same time, Al resisted going out in front, didn't
like to go speak to crowds. He and the town really were two separate
trucks going past each other."

But Al only blamed the town—especially after Wayne Valley's
exit and a Super Bowl victory sent his Napoleonic quotient clear
through the roof. The active agents in this combustion were his
instincts about player free agency and spiraling salaries; Al already
owned one of the highest payrolls in the game, and his fears about
survival in a new, mercantile NFL altered his old Darwinism. Davis
once said, "There are three alternatives in a changing environment.
One, you adapt your activities to it. Two, you migrate. Three,
survival of the fittest. I decided on number three." But that was
before. Now, it was possible to combine two and three.

In the new spirit of survival of the richest, his gaze was that of a bear roaming over the football landscape—to be sated only by the victuals of abundance. Not long before, Al had buffed his image with the gloss of money that didn't exist. Now, with the ghost of his childhood bugaboo buried completely, his aim *was* money.

Money, as factored by venue. Only two global poles now mattered to him—the markets of New York and Los Angeles. The Rams, he pointed out, made $5 million more in profit than he did most years. How did he know that kind of privileged information? "I know," he said. "I know professional football. It's my business." To be sure. As early as 1975, Davis asked a network television executive about the economic possibilities of two NFL teams playing in L.A. He had also discussed this with the Rams' owner, Carroll Rosenbloom—a man Al admired for his gifts of connivance and his many feuds with Pete Rozelle—including the potential of local and pay television in the area. Though Rosenbloom was not eager to cut up the territory, Al would half-joke that he would be there someday.

"There was no reason Los Angeles shouldn't have a franchise," he said after Rosenbloom made his deal with Anaheim. "You take weather, gate attraction, stadium size, TV . . . there's no way that franchise doesn't come out as the flag-bearer of the NFL."

New York also beckoned him, but not with the Raiders. In 1979, at the funeral of former Jets owner Phil Iselin, the current team owner Leon Hess made Al an extemporaneous and possibly facetious offer to take over operating control of the franchise. "Keep me out of it," Hess said. "Just call me when it's time to go to the Super Bowl." Al, who always took such flippancies seriously, told Hess he couldn't leave Oakland for "deeply personal" reasons. At the time, those reasons included Bill Robertson and his LAMCC, and the Raiders' lease with the Oakland–Alameda County Coliseum.

That lease was due to expire after the 1979 season, and had the extent of Al's L.A. fascination been known, his increasingly hesitant and bitter negotiations with the Oakland Coliseum's board of directors, which began in January of 1979, might have been seen as a masquerade. As it was, Al was able to act as the aggrieved party being screwed *by* the Coliseum board.

In truth, Al had legitimate gripes with the Coliseum. In its twelve years this concrete slabhouse had eroded as quickly as it had been made obsolete by the more modern superstadiums it had helped to inspire. While it had been intended as a convertible football/baseball field, it took two days to rearrange the stands from one configuration to the other; since the baseball A's played regularly in the World Series, the Raiders had to play nearly all their September and October games on the road. The stadium's biggest defect, though, was that it was built before the era of private luxury boxes, which were sold generally to corporate sponsors. The profit from those expensive suites with bars and televisions went to the home team in full, and not a penny went to the league or the visiting team.

When Al began negotiating with the Oakland Coliseum board, he asked for a remodeling of the stadium that would accommodate the construction of luxury boxes. Architects were called in and plans drawn for sixty-four boxes, at an estimated cost of $4 million. This the Coliseum board said it could handle, by issuing new bonds in the same way it had when the Coliseum was erected—but only if Al committed to a ten-year lease so as to assure repayment. As that kind of permanence was the last thing Al wanted at the moment, he walked away from the discussions and left a stone-faced Al LoCasale in his place, to agree to nothing as each month drew nearer to the end of the lease.

Al had first made contact with Bill Robertson just after the boisterous Chicago owners meeting the previous October. At that juncture, two other owners—the Colts' Robert Irsay and the Vikings' Max Winter—also made noises about taking the Rams' place in the L.A. Coliseum, but they backed off after their threats bartered them a better deal at home, in Winters's case a new domed stadium. Pete Rozelle, the other owners, and the Oakland Coliseum people all assumed Al's recalcitrance in Oakland was also a negotiating ploy. But the *Oakland Tribune* sounded a prophetic warning. Davis, said the paper, "really might be hungering for appreciation from the glittering star colony in the southland where he has many friends and where . . . the weather suits him better."

With the LAMCC facing insolvency if a deal wasn't clinched, Robertson turned up his pitch to Davis. By February—when Al stopped talking to the Oakland people—Al was flying to L.A. a number of times to put together a package; in his room in the Beverly Hilton Hotel the raw numbers were hashed out. What Al wanted from the LAMCC was much like what he wanted in Oakland—luxury boxes. Other needs would be office and training facilities near the Coliseum and a reduction of thirty thousand seats so as to get the place sold out and not have to black out television games to a populace that would need to be force-fed a new team.

Bill Robertson, who had rejected the building of luxury boxes when Carroll Rosenbloom wanted them in return for staying put, now saw things differently. Plans were made for ninety-nine double-deck boxes to rim the perimeter of the one-tier stadium. But Al was no easy sell for Robertson. Though Robertson was a dogged labor leader by trade, Al's manner of negotiation, busting his nuts over every dollar, was trying. As with the Oakland Coliseum, Al was talking about a total package of around $15 million in stadium improvements, yet he would not sign a lease as long as ten years in duration. Because Al had huge risks in taking the long step to L.A.—not only going against the NFL but running out on Oakland—Robertson was unable himself to know how serious Al was. *Neither* side could decipher his motives, and both were kept dangling like fish bait.

In September, after nine months of Al's foot dragging, the frustrated Oakland Coliseum board announced that an impasse had been reached after Al refused its offer to build the luxury boxes *if* their income was used to defray construction costs. Then, in November, the board tried hardballing it with Davis—and played right into his hands. When board member Jack Maltester claimed that Al had new demands totaling over $8 million, he told the press that the Raiders "owe the people of this area something."

Laying indignation on thick as treacle, Al fired back, "To hell with the Coliseum and the Coliseum board. They've been sold out for years. Don't they owe anything to these people?"

Soon after, in late December, Al rushed to give verbal assent to an agreement with the LAMCC, even though the money figures and term of the contract were not yet specific. While this was kept from the public, a week later he dished dirt on the Oakland Coliseum with his own bravado as his defense. "We never got any of the things we deserved," he said with finality. "You know who built the Coliseum. They can talk about this guy and that guy, but you know. You know who's had a commitment to excellence."

This, of course, was to be the "Raider Line," and it played well because the Coliseum indeed gave Al's threats no urgency, assuming that Section 4.3 would keep Davis right where he was no matter what. But, by now, Pete Rozelle did take the threat to move seriously, and summoned Al in early January to the league office in New York. There, Al admitted he was "strongly thinking" of moving, and, for now, put aside his war cudgels and asked for Rozelle's *help* in doing it. The commissioner was terse. "You'll have to put it to a vote," he said, and subsequently sent Al a letter saying Davis would be "extremely ill-advised" to try a move without "complying with the league's charter."

But that only juiced up Al more. Without delay, he moved closer to closing a deal with the LAMCC, which had pieced together a $17 million package—$7 million from the city of Los Angeles, a $5 million loan by the county of Los Angeles, and a $5 million advance on rent to be paid the Coliseum for the 1984 Olympics.

Now Oakland finally woke up to a ringing alarm—or, more precisely, Oakland Mayor Lionel Wilson did. In his first term as the city's first black mayor, Wilson understood the political and socioeconomic implications of a town with much blight losing not only a revenue-maker but a unifier of all classes. Inserting himself into the negotiations, Wilson, with Cornell Maier, the head of Kaiser Industries, the city's largest employer, romanced Davis with money figures that Al said "greatly encouraged" him.

When Jack Maltester heard of these figures, however, he had a fit. The package called for $8 million, a two-hundred-thousand-dollar-a-year rent reduction, and a five-year lease—*and* a $5 million loan to stretch over thirty years but for which Al was held accountable just for those five years. Withdrawing that offer, and repudiating Wilson and Maier, the Coliseum board substituted a watered-down offer with a ten-year lease. In response, Al LoCasale walked out of the meeting and threw the lease into a mud puddle on the street. Scoring the "lousy way we've been treated," LoCasale accused the board of "arrogance, procrastination, deceit, and misrepresentation."

These terms actually might have been used in reference to Al Davis's behavior over that past year. Indeed, if Al could play the offended party, it may have been *because* he had played those gambits well. George Ross, for one, believes that when Al entertained the entrance of political concerns into the game, he fully knew it would doom Oakland *and* give him yet another straw man.

"Had he wanted it badly enough, Al had all the stature he needed in Oakland to bring the Coliseum board around," Ross said. "All it would've taken to fix up the stadium was money, and all it took to get the money was to go to the bonding house and show them a valid long-term lease.

"The fact was, the Coliseum board was empowered by the city

and the county to negotiate. The mayor and Cornell Maier weren't. Al knew this. He didn't have to bring politicians into it to muck things up, but he still stroked them. It was divide and conquer."

Things happened quickly now. On February 21, acting on the LAMCC–L.A. Rams lawsuit—to which Al was now a party—a federal district court in L.A. granted an injunction against Section 4.3, clearing the way for Al to move. But the NFL then obtained a stay from a federal circuit court in San Francisco, meaning Section 4.3 was still on the books. The next day, Oakland filed a cuckoo lawsuit in California superior court to have the Raiders condemned, as if they were a piece of swampland, and run the team by eminent domain. Amazingly, the city won a temporary restraining order. Al, calling it "sham litigation" by the politicians that did him in, ignored it.

On March 1, 1980, Al Davis went to the office of Los Angeles Mayor Tom Bradley and signed a "memorandum of agreement" with the LAMCC—*not* a lease; Al, getting the jump on Pete Rozelle, had moved so quickly that this came *before* approval from the Los Angeles Board of Supervisors—for an $18 million package covering seven years, with five-year options thereafter. When Davis gave his marker, Bill Robertson compared it to the crossing of the Rubicon.

Rozelle thought so too. On March 3 he called a special owners meeting in Dallas on the subject. Since he surely didn't expect Al to change his mind, the meeting was really to set in motion the league's response via Section 4.3 and the roll call vote that Al was still insisting he did not need to move. Though Al claimed that many owners were "receptive" to his rationale for moving—and they should have been, jumping cities being such a profitable option—he would have nothing to do with a vote. Now officially, Rozelle posed two questions to him.

"Do you intend to move to Los Angeles?" came the first.

"Yes, of course," Al said.

"Do you intend to come to the league for a vote?"

"No."

On March 8, at the annual owners meeting in Palm Springs, the vote would be taken. Knowing the outcome, Al didn't wait. Several days before, when Alameda County sheriffs came to the Raiders' offices to enforce the restraining order, they found the building empty and dark, the contents of the team's business having already been taken by vans to Los Angeles, to the University Hilton Hotel, where Al had set up temporary offices. Working out of there, Raiders staffers had sold thirty thousand season tickets and seventy of the not-yet-built luxury boxes in five days.

Personally supervising the transit of the innards of his empire, Al was the last thing to leave the old offices. Found there by an *Oakland Tribune* reporter who described him as "bleary-eyed, his tousled hair flopped over his forehead, and . . . [with] several days' growth of beard," Al looked genuinely heartbroken that this sad day had come.

"I feel a lot of nostalgia about it," he said gently. "I've lived here for eighteen years. I love Oakland and the fans, I really do. I just think that you take a certain direction in life and you make things happen and you hope it all works out for the best."

From then on, his public utterances on the matter of Oakland and its fans would be considerably less sentimental, and coated with Al Davis brine.

If there were other owners "receptive" to what Al had done, by Palm Springs they had heard enough about the need for "league stability" from Pete Rozelle to go almost down the line against the Raiders' move: twenty-two to none, with five abstentions and one —Al Davis—absent. Al, who sat out the vote on the veranda of his room at the Marriott's Rancho Las Palmas resort, offered a succinct and angry rejoinder. Saying the owners were "not men" and that they acted with neither courage nor truth, he concluded: "We'll see what happens when this thing gets down to punitive damages. You'll see how many guys will back down rather than fight."

On March 25, Al Davis made good on that threat. He filed a $160 million antitrust suit against the NFL. Though the plaintiff would be the Oakland Raiders, much could be ascertained from the fact that Pete Rozelle was listed by name as a specific defendant. By the nature of the issues involved, and the pent-up loathing of the two main contestants, there now was going to be a war like no other ever witnessed in sports.

19

Al says he's not for anarchy, and I'm sure he wants a stable league. He just wants anarchy for himself.

—Pete Rozelle

When you're dealing with Machiavelli, you don't know what his motives ever are.

—George Ross

By the eighties, fifty-year-old Al Davis's transformation from waif to wealth could be gleaned from this old Brooklyn boy's neocapitalist reverence for the devil of Flatbush Avenue himself, Walter O'Malley. This shame-faced nabob of yore, Davis said in 1980, "told me many years ago, 'The city that gets you doesn't win you. It's the city that has you that loses you.' They think they own you in perpetuity. . . .

"What people are saying about me, I'll have to live with the rest of my life. They said that about O'Malley at the beginning, but when he died, God bless him, he was considered the greatest entrepreneur ever in professional sports."

His parallel with O'Malley now drawn, Al faced a queer irony, and a danger. In terms of public theater, Rozelle—even with *his* patrician hubris and petty spitefulness—might now have been seen in the way Al always was, as champion of the plebeian interests in sports; increasingly, that included sports fans such as those in Oakland. At the same time that Al was disenfranchising them, winning the hearts and minds of the public at large—from whom would come the jurors that decided his future—was pivotal.

To do that, Rozelle had to be smeared, vilified, provoked into losing his cool, analytical balance. If Al had ever really wanted to be commissioner, the point was moot now; but if he could beat Rozelle now, the world would know who was the better man. And though Rozelle himself was *legally* a sideshow here, it would be easy for Al to turn this lawsuit into a personal grudge fight; for Rozelle, Davis knew, not so easy. Last time out, Al had had to defend a barbaric player. This time, it would be life, liberty, and the pursuit of the city of his choice.

Going in, Al had the satisfaction of knowing that he actually had done well, overall, in his waltzes with Rozelle—and that when he had looked to be far out on a limb, Rozelle could do nothing about sawing it off. There were, for example, the friends he had made in his late-coming mania for money making.

"Al is an extremely able man with dollars and cents," George Ross noted. "He's made a lot of money in investments since he came to the Raiders wholly aside from the Raiders." In Davis style, these investments were made under the cloak of secrecy. In the sixties he quietly became a business partner with an Oakland Buick dealer named Andy Herrera in several profitable Bay Area apartment complexes; concurrently, Herrera's son John was employed as a Raiders ballboy, then a PR man and a scout, and today is listed as the team's "senior executive."

He branched out, boldly, in 1972 after Ron Mix, his old USC and Chargers lineman who'd finished his career with the Raiders in 1971, turned him on to a San Diego developer, Allen Glick. Barely thirty, Glick was on the verge of big doings, though his brief past was already quite intriguing—a decorated Vietnam hero, he was a licensed lawyer friendly with certain alleged organized crime figures in the Midwest. Working for a San Diego realty developing company that found tax-sheltered land investments for many NFL players and coaches, in just a year Glick suddenly owned a 45 percent interest in the firm. With Glick and a Glick partner named Dennis Wittman, Al invested several million dollars in projects, one with football cohorts he had solicited, including Carroll Rosenbloom, Ralph Wilson, and Don Shula. Davis also went in with Glick and Wittman alone on another partnership.

Two years later, Glick had built or bought into four Las Vegas hotels, including the famous Stardust—with almost $63 million in financing through the Teamsters Union's Central States, Southeast, and Southwest pension fund. Only Howard Hughes owned more Vegas casinos than did Glick at the time, and the Teamsters' generosity to him prompted his investigation by the Justice Department, the state of Nevada, the SEC, and the IRS. By this time as well, Dennis Wittman had been sent to prison for fraud, and another Glick associate who had filed fraud charges against him would soon be murdered, gangland style. Glick also had employed as his chief assistant a Vegas bookmaker tied to the Chicago Mafia who was once convicted for fixing football and basketball games.

Given this sordid tableau, the football executives Al had brought into Glick investments pulled out of the partnership—but not Davis. Admiring Glick, not fearing him, Al—who later said he saw "nothing wrong" with Glick's friends—loaned Glick $250,000 to help liquidate the others' investments and repay them in full. He then went in on another deal with Glick late in 1974 after Glick took over the payments on the giant Eastmont shopping mall in east Oakland not far from the Coliseum. Again, Glick had pulled this off through his friends at the Teamsters, out of whose pension funds came a $25 million loan to originally finance the mall when it was built in 1966.

For Al's loyalty, and his value to the property, Glick offered him a sweetheart deal not unlike Al's initial managing general partner steal: to become a limited partner at Eastmont, he had only to kick in five thousand dollars to gain a one-quarter interest in the mall. Al's function was, he said later, to "bring image and stature" to the shopping center in the mostly black area, and through him current and former Raiders Gene Upshaw and Clem Daniels came to own taverns there.

The image and stature of Al Davis, however, were not openly seen at Eastmont. Al was not prone to publicizing his new property, and it is debatable just how eager he was to see it prosper; as a tax writeoff, he had to be content with the $1 million he was said to have saved in taxes while the mall operated in the red over the next decade. One former manager of the mall even claimed that Glick and Davis fired him for making the place "too successful."

The public might have never known any of this had not an *Oakland Tribune* reporter, Jeff Morgan, been researching Allen Glick's links to the Teamsters and found Davis's name among his investment partners. Morgan's ensuing stories about Al's curious ties to Glick, and about Glick's alleged ties to Mob wiseguys, ran through the summer of 1975. Yet instead of being forthcoming about it, Al looked like a man hiding something by clamming up. Later on, admitting that some things about Glick made him "squeamish," he would insist he hardly knew Glick and vaguely hint at divestment of his partnerships with him at some time in the future.

More important to Al at the time was that the stories had broken during his courtroom battle with Wayne Valley. If he felt any need to address the issue, he submerged it in hatred for George Ross—who by then had become the *Trib*'s assistant managing editor—mistakenly believing George was out to embarrass him.

"Al passed the word that he would be in touch with my publisher and that I'd be hearing from his lawyer," Ross recalled. "Apparently he was just blowing steam because he did neither."

What is revealed by the sooty light of Allen Glick is Davis's apparently shameless pride in being enriched in these murky ways. With no overt sense of abhorrence, he once said that bookmakers "had contacts with every owner in the league." Carroll Rosenbloom, in fact, had counted Dennis Wittman as a "financial adviser"—and Rosenbloom's involvement with people of that ilk was a rumor mill staple for years up to and including his mysterious drowning death in June 1979.

Al Davis's feeling seemed to be that if other owners profited from such associations, so must he. Testing the waters early on this, Al had struck up a friendship with Las Vegas bookmaker Jimmy "The Greek" Snyder. This was before the Greek became an inane wind-bag on CBS's NFL telecasts and Pete Rozelle thought it serious enough to fine Al one thousand dollars for the fraternization. Al, though, did not disavow Snyder and for years he showily wore a gift from the Greek, an onyx bracelet with tiny diamonds spelling out "Al." At times, Davis joked that it was once worn by Al Capone.

In the wake of the Allen Glick revelations, it was left to others to see any tinctured morality in Al's capital ventures. But—and this was the part that swelled Al's chest—Pete Rozelle, the Saint Augustine of the NFL, could not enforce any moral imperative, not with the labyrinth of gambling ties that would need to be dealt with if Davis were to be made an example. Better still, beyond the moral haze, Al had left himself open to no hard counterstrokes—although, strangely, the NFL's only public comment on the matter was simply that Al's Eastmont investment was "too small" to be indecent, and that Glick (who has never been indicted on any charge) was legally licensed to own casinos.

This circuitous, largely irrelevant response ignored a multitude of circumstances. Said George Ross; "When a guy's offered 25 percent of something for five thousand dollars and then it's refinanced for millions, you know, it raises questions. I would've thought that any owner being in business with a man who owned casinos in Las Vegas, with or without Allen Glick's reputation, would've been censured."

But the league's timid exculpation was heavenly hash to Al, which he could then sling back at Rozelle. "As much as they [the NFL] have investigated me," he said in 1981, "I'd have capitulated long ago if I had anything to hide. Rozelle has two, three ex-FBI agents in every city and keeps a dossier on everything."

Al would get further mileage out of this supposed "secret police" force in going head to head with Rozelle, trying to prove his immolation at the hands of the league. Now grandly paranoid—and not without reason—while the Allen Glick matter would fade away, every time the subject was raised Al had the feeling it was the work of Rozelle and his army. When the Los Angeles Board of Supervisors began deliberating on the Raiders' move, one of the five supervisors objected, after, he said, he "became aware" of the Davis-Glick business. That was when Davis, through Al LoCasale, suggested that association with Glick was "winding down," but that "any implications of wrongdoing would be totally irresponsible."

Prodded by the supervisor, the L.A. district attorney's office opened an investigation and asked Al to furnish certain data from his past tax returns. He refused. Both the DA and the Los Angeles Organized Crime Intelligence Division probed Davis. Both cleared him. By now as well, the NFL—in preparation for its defense of Al's lawsuit—had finally gotten one of its internal security men on the case, and Al later disclosed that the guy "found that all it was was a business deal [with Glick]." But this did not stop Al from thinking that the league had at least one real use for the Glick matter, and that was "to try to hurt me publicly."

A much bigger problem for Al than Allen Glick was that Rozelle was indeed seeking to undo the LAMCC agreement. Several votes on approval by the increasingly nervous board of supervisors were put off, and one board member voiced concern that the league was trying to intimidate them. Meanwhile, major banks in L.A. had received letters from the league office urging them not to finance the deal. Whatever Al had signed, went the league's explanation, the Raiders by law would be playing in Oakland come the 1980 season—and to underline this, Rozelle announced that the NFL would not schedule Raiders home games in L.A.

Facing these obstacles—and another in a preliminary injunction won by the league against selling any more tickets outside of Oakland—Al took one step back in retreat until the courts ruled. The Raiders would have to play the 1980 season in Oakland. But he would give in no more. As awkward as it would be, the offices and training grounds would stay in L.A. The team would commute four hundred miles for practices, then *back* to Oakland for games. At the expense of his players' nerves, he was going to show Pete Rozelle the will of a winner.

At the start, however, it was hard to see that Rozelle wasn't holding all the cards. Certainly his logic was impeccable, his digs at Al on the mark. "There are ways of working these things [franchise problems] out, and if you can't, then you go to the owners," the commissioner pointed out. "Al chose to do things his own way. I guess the carrot was just too big down in L.A."

This was the one bit of truth that Al couldn't avoid—his surface rationale for moving was the stadium issue, but the fact was that no team with so much support in its city had ever moved as much as four hundred miles away. "I've got problems, too," said the Browns' Art Modell. "Does that mean I move to Phoenix?"

As it was, Rozelle didn't have to rally the other owners in a stand against Al. Although there were many internecine schisms and hatreds among them, never had one offended so many as did Davis. At owners meetings his balkiness was a given. Al, the same man who had wanted to fight the NFL-AFL merger all the way, drove his peers up the wall when he proposed that the merged NFL merge *again*, with the World Football League in the seventies, his aim being multimillion-dollar franchise fees in league coffers. The Chargers' Gene Klein, with almost everyone else, was aghast at the idea, knowing the division of television revenues this would cause.

"Davis didn't care," Klein later said. "I suspect he also wanted to be a hero to the WFL owners, who would eventually be entitled to vote for NFL commissioner."

Al also had something to say about such television money. When

Klein, Rozelle, and Modell negotiated the NFL's five-year, $2.1 billion TV deal in 1980—a 250 percent increase from the previous TV contract and the largest in sports history up to then—Al was *against* the deal, saying the contract should be shorter in duration. Explaining his reasoning, he was cut off by the Eagles' Leonard Tose.

"Hey, wait a second, Al," Tose said. "Are you saying we can't take the fucking money?"

Later, even Al admitted his target wasn't wholly the contract but also Rozelle. "It was a victory [for Rozelle] . . . and he watches his life very carefully on victories," Davis said, adding that the contract gave Rozelle "a power base with the networks. . . . The league probably has the most massive media control of any entity in America other than the president."

Said Gene Klein: "At league meetings Davis would sit directly in front of Pete Rozelle, whom he hated . . . a copy of the league constitution on his desk, constantly biting his fingernails, brushing back his hair, waiting to find something to complain about. Whatever we were discussing, he would find something to complain about."

The funny thing was that Al *still* believed other owners were dying to support him, but that Rozelle was cracking the whip, aided by Art Modell and, now, the same man whom he'd thought wanted him only a year ago, the Jets' Leon Hess. Hess, in fact, succeeded in playing with Davis's hidden insecurities and guilts, much more so than Rozelle could. After one owners meeting, Davis called ABC's Howard Cosell and asked him, "Am I hurting the Jews by moving to Los Angeles?" When Cosell asked him what he could possibly be talking about, Al went on to relate that Hess, who is Jewish, told him he couldn't move because "It'll cause a wave of anti-Semitism in northern California."

By playing on Al's lapsed religious faith, in fact, Hess may have caused Al's only real qualm about jumping from Oakland—but it actually may have aggravated the uncomfortable sense that the league was singling him out for punishment *because* he was Jewish. If so, he may have resented Modell and Hess all the more, for coming to an accommodation with covert bigotry.

In any case, on Cosell's *SportsBeat* show, Al maintained that both Leonard Tose and the Vikings' Max Winter wanted Rozelle to settle the lawsuit. "But Hess is the key," he said. "He's in Rozelle's pocket. . . . For one reason or another, Hess is in bed with a group of owners who listen to him and always back Rozelle." Accordingly, Al maintained his public stance that the owners were a pitiful lot. "Not all of them are the brightest of human beings," he told *The New York Times* in 1981.

Still, knowing that much of his position *was* at least morally indefensible, Al was thankful to have Rozelle as a foil. While the lawsuit awaited a trial date, he again made himself available to the press, to mount a public relations offensive. In these rambling conversations, his jabs at Rozelle fell along the following lines.

Rozelle's greed: Rozelle wanted him out of L.A. to keep it open for a franchise headed by Rozelle after he retired as commissioner.

Rozelle's fascism: Other owners were "threatened" not to side with him by the "personal gestapo for the commissioner." Said Davis: "Rozelle's the most important man in professional sports and he doesn't want to give up his power base." And: "It's the old fear package, something that's typical of Rozelle. He had a nickname for a while, Sneaky Pete . . . that's the way he operates."

Rozelle's stunted vision: Rozelle's "stupid" and "ridiculous" judgment had hurt the league. "Every time one of our illegal rules was struck from our constitution," he said, "it's meant 'doom' for the league [according to Rozelle]. But in reality it's always been a new beginning, and the NFL has become better for it."

Rozelle's hypocrisy: Rozelle blew it for the Raiders in Oakland, not Al Davis. "He destroyed my negotiations. . . . He told them that I was locked in and therefore they repudiated their own negotiators."

While this artillery barrage went on, Rozelle tried to remain above the fray, brusquely denying the Davis allegations. But, clearly, he was *getting* frayed. "He's trying to make it 'him against me' for the purpose of the case," Rozelle lamented to *Inside Sports*. "It's easier for him to say 'I'm fighting Rozelle than 'I'm fighting my twenty-seven partners.' He's trying to make it look like I'm silver-spoon—fed Madison Avenue and he's the kid from the streets when our backgrounds are actually somewhat the opposite. My father lost his grocery store during the Depression and we were middle or lower-middle class."

Al had to be pleased that Rozelle had taken the bait, and he turned up the heat. "I'm going to take Rozelle on the streets," he promised. "He can't take it there. He's never been in the theater." Rozelle could weather that kind of blather. But when Al made use of pretrial depositions to turn the seed of the two-year-old ticket-scalping charges into a fully grown mushroom cloud, it hit Rozelle's nerves like a tripwire.

Explaining how Carroll Rosenbloom first revealed to him the alleged leaguewide ticket reselling scams, he told of one ticket agent who offered to buy his Super Bowl tickets. The agent, Al claimed, "said that [he] had the full approval of the commissioner" and that "he gets his Super Bowl tickets from Pete Rozelle." What made this relevant to the case—at least to Al—was that the Super Bowl was played so often in L.A. and Pasadena and "Rozelle certainly didn't want me in Los Angeles as the host team," which was entitled to a bigger share of tickets.

Having no hint that Al would drop this incendiary bomb on the trial, Rozelle was stunned and quickly labeled the charges "cocktail party gossip, without substance." But that he had to answer them and defend his honor knocked him off the moral high ground. And with the details Rosenbloom had told Davis, he was prepared to use the same inference to cry conspiracy against Rosenbloom's widow, the now-remarried Georgia Frontiere—whom he had named, with Rozelle and Gene Klein, as specific codefendants.

In a year when winning should have been an afterthought, seeing Pete Rozelle's face between the numbers of opposing players may have been the little extra juice that made the 1980 season seem like the benediction of Al's newest crusade.

These were now the third-generation Raiders, soon to be the first-generation Los Angeles Raiders, who now were innocent bystanders in the strangest fan/home team conjugation of all time. Though most Raiders wanted the team to stay in Oakland, and lived out of suitcases in L.A., they were lame ducks playing before fans torn between loyalty and anger. As these fans had never sanctified Al Davis, and were maybe the only people in the country who could separate him from the substance of the team, many could live with the fact that they would retain the Raiders' legacy only if Pete Rozelle beat Al in court. Still, living on the edge of rejection, attendance for most home games was off by as much as fifteen thousand after many years of sellouts, and, but for the shepherding presence of Davis, some of the players might have been similarly torn themselves.

This was Tom Flores's team now, for better or worse, since there were so many new people—apart from the draftees, more than twenty players had experience with other NFL teams. After keeping Ken Stabler to help cushion Flores's transition, Al had finally done the inevitable and traded the rickety quarterback to Houston, following the 1979 season. When he made the deal, Al tried to ease the bitterness between them with Al Davis–style levity, telling Stabler's attorney, Henry Pitts, "Sorry, Henry. The deal's off. He's going to Green Bay."

Pitts's reply, while jocular, was truly icy. "He's changed his mind," the attorney said. "He wants to die a Raider. I hear that when somebody tells you that, it's an automatic raise for him."

For Stabler, Al got a quarterback right off the Al Davis drawing board—sleek, trim, hot-headed Dan Pastorini. Now thirty-one, Pastorini got along with very few people and he too had the wear and tear of a fast life—he was damn near killed once when his speedboat disintegrated during a race, and as a Raider he was arrested (but never convicted) on cocaine-possession charges—but he could throw the ball farther than Stabler could drive it in a pickup truck. But Pastorini threw as recklessly as he piloted speedboats. He tossed eight interceptions in the first four games of 1980, and the fans grew to detest him as the Raiders lost two of those games. Then, against the Chiefs, a hard hit broke Pastorini's leg. When he was carried off the field in agony, the fans cheered.

That game was also a loss, and with chaos all around the players called a team meeting that almost turned brutal. After Gene Upshaw urged greater team unity, Dave Casper—whose moods nobody could ever figure out—told them they should just go out and play for themselves. Told to sit down and shut up by Upshaw and Art Shell, he called them both "assholes." A week later Casper was gone, also to Houston, for three draft choices—a trade Al later said he made with tears in his eyes. Once in Houston, Casper continued the argument, blasting Upshaw—ludicrously—as "the Michelin Man in his white suit. He never falls down and never gets his uniform dirty."

With the season looking grim, Jim Plunkett at long last found his overdue NFL birthright. At thirty-two, Plunkett had to climb out of the football graveyard, in which were buried the remnants of the Rose Bowl and Heisman Trophy he won while at Stanford and the career that he began in neon as the top pick in the 1971 NFL draft. Reared to throw the ball deep, Plunkett became a lost soul running Chuck Fairbanks's option-play ground game with the Patriots. Often injured and always frustrated, he demanded a trade to the 49ers in 1976 but was shunted aside; in 1978, he was cut, and unclaimed even at a hundred-dollar waiver price. When Al signed him as a free agent, it was strictly as a backup guy.

But when Plunkett took over the Raiders offense, he finally had pass protection and an offense suited to his strong arm. He also had Flores, with whom he had so much in common that it was scary. Like Flores, Plunkett's dark Latin calm was a mask for pain suffered much earlier, as the son of blind Mexican parents in San José. Plunkett's grit overcame poverty, a bone disease, and a tumor on his neck that caused *him* to miss a year of football.

On unique terms with Flores, Plunkett excelled in a way unseen in the days of wine and Stabler. The Flores-Plunkett style almost completely changed the nature of the team—at least with the offense. The huddle was again hushed and orderly, dependent on the communication between coach and quarterback.

The defense was where the characters were, held in tow by stern old Charlie Sumner, who'd returned to Oakland after ten years coaching elsewhere. The newest odd bird was Willie Brown's successor at right cornerback, Lester Hayes. Typically, Al had looked beyond the pale in drafting him on the fifth round in 1977. A six-foot, 200-pounder built like a small tank, Hayes was a linebacker and then a safety at Texas A&M, and Al projected him to play Bump and Run because he could sprint even with his bulk.

Hayes also had a Raider kind of lip—even though with a stutter that many scouts mistook as a sign of a slow wit. The key to playing man-to-man coverage, he said, was "to put yourself on a plateau where you say you can't be beat. . . . There's no mere mortal I fear—I am auspiciously euphoric." In 1980, Hayes intercepted thirteen passes, one off the NFL record, and went to the Pro Bowl for the first of six straight seasons.

Some fine tuning on defense made Hayes unbeatable. One move was Ted Hendricks's shift to left linebacker. He was now a step slower at age thirty-two, and more ground could be covered by Rod Martin—a one-time Raider reject but now a holy terror at only 210 pounds—behind pass-rushing right end Dave Browning. With Hendricks behind John Matuszak, passers couldn't throw away from Hayes, as they'd been doing, without facing the two left-side monsters.

Likewise, with nose tackle Reggie Kinlaw—a number-twelve draft pick—on the light side, 230-pound free agent Bob Nelson anchored the linebacking inside with the number-two draft choice,

Penn State's 250-pound workhorse Matt Millen, allowing Hendricks and Martin freer latitude outside. The final adjustment came when the number-two draft choice of 1977, Mike Davis, an agile former high school hurdler, was inserted at strong safety.

Still, it was Hayes who now defined the new class of Raider reprobates. Lining up inches from the receiver, daring him from the get-go, Hayes's compulsiveness was seen in his unbelievable burst to the ball and the muck all over his body—a compost of dirt and stickum, which Hayes applied to places Fred Biletnikoff never heard of. Not only did Hayes dig his hands into big jars of the goo, he *sprayed* it onto his uniform and exposed skin using areosol cans filled with it. With Lester looking like a human gravy boat, the NFL decided in 1981 to ban the use of unsightly "slippery substances"—which the Raiders, of course, saw as further deliberate castigation of Al Davis's team.

Jelling in one great heave, the Raiders won six straight games and nine of their last eleven. Most were crazy, some nail-biters. They won one game on a club record eighty-two-yard run by spare halfback Arthur Whittington, another on an inhuman, falling-down touchdown catch by thirty-two-year-old tradee Bob Chandler. Two other games featured a ninety-yard kickoff return by Whittington and a bootleg touchdown by Plunkett.

"Never was the adage more apropos about being better lucky than good than it was that season," said Todd Christensen, who signed as a backup tight end in 1979 after being cut by two NFL teams. "You had all these castoffs winning all these crazy games. I remember Lester intercepting one pass when the ball stuck to his *helmet*. He reached up and peeled it off. Lester really had twenty-three interceptions that year, counting ones that were called back on other guys' penalties. That's like hitting seventy-five home runs."

In the playoffs as an 11–5 wild-card team, they were now a steamroller, crushing the Oilers in the first round 27–7, besieging Stabler with a flood of blitzing that had even the defensive backs coming in after the Snake. Next came the Browns, on a Siberian early January day in Cleveland. Anticipating the flesh-lacerating wind and subzero cold, Al pulled a variation of the Shea Stadium shelter caper of 1968. This time, he came in with thermal, fanny-warming benches—not to be rebuffed by the home team again, when the Browns wouldn't erect the benches on their sideline, he paid for *theirs* as well, at a total cost of $3,700.

This game was one for the psychiatrists, who probably are still trying to figure out the Browns' quarterback, Brian Sipe. Down 14–12 with under a minute to go and on the Raiders' thirteen, a game-winning field goal only a couple of safe runs away, Sipe *passed* into the end zone for tight end Ozzie Newsome—but, unfooled, Mike Davis sliced in front of Newsome and intercepted. Sipe, the league's MVP that season, was never whole again.

As fate would have it, to get to the Super Bowl as a wild-card team the Raiders had to beat the two teams with the most vehement anti-Davis owners, first Art Modell and then Gene Klein, aka Gene Klein, *codefendant*. San Diego was balmy for the AFC title game, but Klein was balmier. Three days before, he read a column by *Los Angeles Herald Examiner* columnist Mel Durslag—who had pushed hard for the Raiders to come to L.A. and was close to Al —which suggested facetiously that given Al's challenge to the league the Raiders might get a fairer shake from the officials playing the game in Canada. Missing the levity, Klein ranted that the column was "a devious plot to undermine and intimidate the officials." On a one-to-ten scale, Klein said, Davis "has a character of zero."

Klein must have needed sedation when the Raiders, needing no aid from the officials, blew out to a 28–7 lead and won the game 34–27 to go to their third Super Bowl. While Al decided not to make the game symbolic of anyone or anything else, his players did, and even gave him the game ball.

"One thing that gave me great pleasure," said Gene Upshaw afterward, "was coming down here and sticking it to Gene Klein. The only thing that's left is to win the Super Bowl and stick it to our commissioner. I'm waiting for him to come into our locker room to present the trophy to us and find out what it's like to be booed."

For Al Davis, Super Bowl XV was the ultimate. No other Super Bowl before or since hung as heavily with pungent drama as the one on January 25, 1981, in New Orleans. Knowing the implications of the Raiders' winning truly as outsiders, Pete Rozelle—who had a hard enough time with Al in Super Bowl XI—had to look upon this growing Raider beast with foreboding.

Almost everyone had picked up on Gene Upshaw's stated threat to boo Rozelle in the postgame locker room—and now there was talk that the Raider players would even throw Rozelle out. "I may not give Rozelle a chance to present the trophy," Upshaw cautioned. "I may snatch it away from him. Rozelle sees me as the right arm of Al Davis and if he can slap that arm, he will."

Rozelle's only hope of avoiding humiliation lay with the NFC champion Philadelphia Eagles—which only further piqued the contrast between rogue and reactionary. The Eagles were the most tight-assed team in the league. Their coach, Dick Vermeil—a small, tense, agitated man—ran them like a hot-wired scoutmaster, all cleats and chains. The Eagles arrived in New Orleans clad in matching green and white jogging suits, and during Super Bowl week Vermeil kept them caged; they watched films of the Raiders, had all meals together, and held meetings each night. On Tuesday, picture day—when the players usually mill around and goof off— Vermeil put the the Eagles through *two* practices, in full pads.

The Raiders, naturally, were running wild on Bourbon Street. When their first Super Bowl week practice began, all of twenty-six players showed up. There were fistfights in ensuing practices, and by week's end fines for curfew breaking had reached fifteen thousand dollars. One rumor went around that a certain Raider was in Peru that week scoring some dope. Of them all, Matuszak's publicized excesses offended Vermeil the most. If he was coaching a player like Matuszak, he said, the guy would be sent home. Hearing this, Upshaw said that if Flores took that approach with the Raiders, he'd be the only one left on the sideline.

What should have worried Vermeil was the Eagles' regular season 10–7 win over the Raiders on November 23 in Philadelphia. In that one, the Eagles sacked Plunkett eight times. It might have seemed to Vermeil that the Raiders could again be exploited in the trenches. But all it took were a few corrections for the Raiders to wrap this one up early. By rigging their blocking to jam the Eagles' defensive stunting and running shorter pass routes, the Raiders gave Plunkett time to do some carving. Late in the first quarter, up 7–0, he scrambled left and threw a short sideline pass to halfback Kenny King, who was covered by cornerback Herman Edwards. Edwards leaped for the ball, missed, and King took it eighty yards to make it 14–0.

On defense, the new Raider wrinkle was *not* playing Bump and Run; falling back in a zone instead, they forced a lot of time-eating, short-play drives that didn't add up to points—in large part because of linebacker Rod Martin. A man many teams thought they could pick on because of his size, he had three interceptions, scavenged the Superdome turf, and was the game's MVP.

By the time Plunkett hit Cliff Branch with a twenty-nine-yard TD in the third quarter, the game was out of reach—27–10 was the final score—and thoughts turned to the postgame encounter Pete Rozelle had dreaded, which the Raiders had hyped all during the week. As soon as they reached the locker room they pulled cameras out of their bags and massed at the foot of the makeshift wooden stage on which the commissioner would present the Lombardi Trophy, straining in their damp uniforms to capture the moment that Al Davis would dress down his archfoe. When Al appeared in the room, they chanted "Genius! Genius!" and waited to get obnoxious.

Instead, seeing Rozelle manage to assume the affable and dignified Rozelle posture, Al decided he could do more damage on the high road.

"We had a code worked out with Al," Upshaw said later. "If Al's first words were, 'We'd like to thank the commissioner,' that meant he didn't want us to do anything."

Taking his second world championship trophy in his hands, Al, dressed in white slacks and a white cardigan—the good guy, for 100 million television viewers to see—looked straight ahead and began, "Thanks very much, Commissioner. . . ."

Only the chilled air of edgy politeness told the story on this day of football worlds in collision. Al had proven he could play Rozelle's game and win. Now Rozelle would have to prove he could do the same playing Al's game.

Al's choice of a hired gun in legal warfare was rife with irony. Delegated in early 1980 to advise Davis during the coming avalanche of infighting with the league was Joseph Alioto, the former Democratic mayor of San Francisco. A bald, nasal-voiced man with the peckish eyes of a vulture, he was as carnivorous in the courtroom as he'd been in political back rooms. Yet while nominally a liberal as mayor, after Alioto lost a bid to become California's governor in 1970 he became an antitrust lawyer in service to some very well-heeled clients—most notably the National Football League and one of its owners, the Eagles' Leonard Tose.

These alliances were a natural for Alioto, since he had recently married the daughter of Patriots' owner Billy Sullivan. In 1974, Alioto had come to Sullivan's defense when one of the Patriots' players sued the league for $12 million, claiming the standard player contract violated antitrust laws.

The real irony was in Alioto's words to the court back then that the league's rules had generated "the greatest mass entertainment . . . in the history of the world." All of that would be lost, he pleaded, "if we let the prima donnas in this game have their way, and if this thing turns out to be a lawyers' paradise instead of a spectator's delight."

By 1980, Joe Alioto found sufficient cause to defend a prima donna owner as an antitrust victim—even at the price of friction within his family. It was Alioto's idea that Al send the ticket-scalping allegations flying against the fan. When the NFL's lawyers had introduced the matter of Allen Glick early in the trial, Alioto warned them that two could play the same game. The NFL shrugged off the warning, then suffered a serious blow—though it was to have no effect legally, this was when Pete Rozelle had taken the bait and subordinated the league's case to volleyballing enmity back at Al. Although Rozelle proclaimed in the face of the charges, "I've been in the fish bowl for twenty-one years, I can take it," he had to admit, "I have strong personal feelings against him after what he's accused me of."

As a result, Rozelle's gifts of mediation and acute sense of reasonable and *winnable* expectations went out his Park Avenue window. What was left was an obsession to annihilate Al Davis. After Al won a key victory in March 1981—a ruling by Judge Harry Pregerson that the trial could be held in Los Angeles—some owners believed the league couldn't win and should settle the case then. Instead, the trial went forward, commencing on May 13 in Los Angeles federal court before a ten-person jury. And in the first few weeks, the toll in human pain was a measure of unconditional war.

One of the first in the witness box was Gene Klein, who was grilled for four hours. Klein was as feisty as ever, but toward the end he began sweating heavily. When he climbed down from the stand, pain shot down his arm and shoulder, he slumped to the floor in a side room, and was rushed to the hospital with a massive heart attack. He'd remain hospitalized for four months.

Georgia Frontiere took the stand soon after and she was bewildered by Davis's sudden turn from apparent family friend to hostile accuser of conspiracy to block the Raiders' move to her team's territory. She did catch a break on Al's ticket-scalping charges. After her lawyers moved to bar these allegations as "sensational, inflammatory, and fundamentally irrelevant," Judge Pregerson sustained them and ruled the subject inadmissible (although five years later her husband, Dominic Frontiere, was given an eighteen-year prison term and a twenty-thousand-dollar fine on charges brought by the IRS—including failure to report the resale of Super Bowl tickets). Even so, anguished that Al "was rejecting me . . . maybe [because] he couldn't see a woman as being equal as an owner," she left the stand in tears.

Al had by now refined the original vague position he had staked out in Chicago about "reserving my rights" to move his team. As it turned out, he had some serious legal ammunition behind it, which compressed into four major points of argument:

- Section 4.3 was illegal and "anticompetitive."
- Section 4.3 could only have been altered by unanimous vote; his abstention voided the rule and was his ticket to ride.
- He had given an "oral contract" to move in Chicago and Rozelle had, in effect, endorsed it by not saying he *couldn't* move.
- Even if Section 4.3 were legal, the league was using it illegally to prevent competition in Los Angeles and thus was acting in bad faith.

Much of this arid legal dissertation, however, was lost in the main event—Davis versus Rozelle—and in contrast to their performances on the stand in the George Atkinson case, this time Al made Rozelle look bad. While Rozelle was staunch that he never countenanced a Raider exodus—"Absolutely not," he said—Alioto got him to admit to league inequities that made some teams more competitive than others, as well as Rozelle's own legal omissions in Chicago. Though many of the points were of the fine-print variety, Alioto hammered away at him, and Rozelle grew visibly tired and short-tempered, not at all the sunny patrician, and there were lapses in his memory.

"I watched him on the witness stand and I'm just not impressed with him when he's under pressure," Al gloated. "He's good at a press conference when he can control the situation. He looks very smooth . . . unflappable. [But] I think he's very flappable."

While Al had said he was nervous about taking the stand, when he mounted those steps in early June he performed with the aplomb of Olivier in rising to the watershed moment of his life. In past courtroom spectacles, Al had looked as if he came straight from having espresso with Carlo Gambino, in a black suit and silver tie, with Jimmy the Greek's onyx trinket dangling from his wrist. Now, at Alioto's command, he wore the muted blues and grays of a commoner, and liberally sprinkled his cocky brio with deferential politeness to the judge and the lawyers. He had a firm grasp of legal minutiae. But, as ever, he was the fighter.

When an NFL lawyer cited a mass of testimony that differed with his version of what had transpired in Chicago, Al made a vital point—that the league's own attorneys had found Section 4.3 to be illegal.

"I don't know that, sir," the lawyer said snidely.

"Oh, you don't," Al retorted, his shoulders hunching. "Well, I'll tell you."

As with Al's association with Allen Glick, the league did not help itself by trying to skewer Al with his own intemperate words. During the trial, a Davis profile ran in *Inside Sports*, quoting his logistical fascinations with Adolf Hitler, the most provocative of which was his admission that "I didn't hate Hitler. He captivated me." On Al's last day on the stand, the league's lawyer arranged to have the quotations projected onto a huge screen as he queried Al about them. That had Alioto on his feet screaming his objection, calling it "a cheap shot" and "a stab in the back." Judge Pregerson not only agreed, instructing the jury to ignore the Hitler quotations, but when Al stepped down the judge couldn't resist saying a fond farewell to a splendid witness.

"I sort of hate to see you leave," he said.

"I'll see you around," a jaunty Al told him.

And yet Judge Pregerson soon after issued a ruling that went against Al. After Alioto rested the plaintiffs' case on June 26, the league made a motion to drop all charges—and though the trial would go on, the judge did just that, with the charges against the *individual* defendants, Gene Klein, Georgia Frontiere, and Rozelle. "Reasonable jurors," said the judge, "would not find that [they] conspired." While Al angrily fled the courtroom, Rozelle rejoiced. "I feel like $160 million," he cackled, flashing the old Rozelle smile.

But, again, he couldn't see the overall situation. In truth, Al had gained crucial ground. He'd introduced evidence that, as far back as 1966, NFL attorneys *had* stated doubts about Section 4.3. During the trial, Davis said later, the NFL's counsel had signed a stipulation that they had frequently advised the league of this. "Rozelle knew it," he said, "but decided to go ahead with it because they thought they could get away with a court case . . . because of their power, their law firms, and their large amounts of money."

Rozelle had scant time to savor the partial victory. On July 24, Judge Pregerson made another ruling—barring the jury from considering the league's claim that it operated as a single enterprise composed of twenty-eight members. This had been the gantry of the league's case, and it would have made it most difficult for Al to prove restraint of trade. But Pregerson hacked it down, calling the NFL "an association of separate business entities."

Still, when the jury was given the case on August 11, the outcome was hardly open and shut. For two weeks they deliberated. And then Rozelle was again handed a reprieve. When a juror was revealed to be the cousin of a team owner in the defunct World Football League—and apparently more familiar with the sport than he had let on during jury selection—Pregerson declared a mistrial. Because a poll of the jury showed an eight-to-two split for the plaintiffs, Al and Joe Alioto were infuriated, blasting the juror as a "plant" by the NFL. "I anticipated this type of thing," Davis said. "It's the law of the jungle." Al could be pleased that he was two votes shy of winning, but the mistrial also allowed the other side of the room to posture, though Art Modell was seriously deranged in saying it was a "total vindication of Pete Rozelle."

After eighty-four days and more than one hundred witnesses, the case would have to be retried. What that meant for Al was that the Raiders were trapped in Oakland for at least another season. Appropriately, and as though in a postcoital languor, that season was a dreary let-down. Injury-riddled, undermanned, and aging in spots, they finished fourth in 1981, going 7–9, their first sub–five-hundred season since 1964.

As the year expired, Pete Rozelle—not eagerly awaiting a retrial in which the judge's "single-entity" ruling would stand—wasted no time in running a thinly veiled end run designed to make the court case irrelevant. Gearing up the league's lawyers once more, he pushed for an act of Congress to exempt the NFL from the Sherman Act altogether. For Rozelle this was a far more pleasant task than being pounded by Joe Alioto, a return to the days when he built his league and his reputation in the cloakrooms of the Congress.

Rozelle, whose skill in the art of "persuasion" was seen back then in the none-too-subtle granting of the New Orleans franchise when he needed the support of a powerful Louisiana senator, met now with Howard Baker of Tennessee, the Republican Senate minority leader. Baker had been actively petitioning for an NFL franchise in Memphis and came away after conferring with Rozelle saying the town had "the best chance of any city in the country" to get a new team.

Rozelle discoursed before the House Judiciary Committee that the NFL was "unique" among American businesses in that its teams were "coproducers and cosellers, not competitors." Antitrust courts, he said, were rendering his league "powerless," by allowing teams to "second-guess every league operating principle."

But his real message was aimed at politicians from nonleague cities. No exemption, he warned, "risks foreclosing further expansion of the NFL," since this was the kind of decision that could be "challenged as a conspiracy with antitrust consequences." Aspiring franchise-hunters in Congress could do well by him if they gave him his exemption, *and* if they made it retroactive to include any current court cases in litigation. This codicil might as well have been named for Al Davis, and not without reason did Joe Alioto say that, in calling for it, the NFL was "giving even arrogance a bad name." As Al saw it, the league was "desperate now," and "the dangling of franchises makes ABSCAM look like penny-ante stuff."

Cynical as Rozelle's methods were, he went ahead full blast, assured by the league's new chief counsel, Paul Tagliabue, that while controversial, retroactivity had been applied before. "The Civil Rights Act was retroactive," he said, leaving no doubt that the NFL considered this legislation to be just as urgent. In the spring of 1982, two bills were being readied—one in the House entitled The Major League Sports Community Protection Act, the other Senate bill S.2784. Both, in the language of the former, forbade "a franchise from using antitrust laws to attack a sports league."

Before these bills could be introduced, however, the Davis lawsuit had been retried before a six-woman jury in Los Angeles Federal District Court. Though the trial this time spanned only five weeks over March and early April, Rozelle—looking greatly aged after more than two years of insane warfare—did just as much harm to himself. While Rozelle steadfastly denied that he personally had an interest in owning an expansion team in L.A., he admitted that the *league* had plenty of interest in such a franchise, since all of its teams were "entitled to share" in entrance fees. And a Los Angeles franchise, he remarked under questioning, was worth "considerably more" than an Oakland franchise.

In Joe Alioto's hands this became pure TNT. Twisting Rozelle's simple declarative sentences into knots of opportunity, Alioto was able to extract from the tired commissioner an admission that, by strained logic, the league could impel Davis to stay "where a franchise is worth less money."

Alioto then asked if owners who wanted a franchise for themselves, to "divvy up" the profits, could "vote their pocketbook against Mr. Davis."

"Yes," Rozelle said, hastening to add, "but Mr. Davis would share equally."

The jury, as Alioto hoped, heard the "yes" loud and clear. Getting the case on May 7, it took them only six hours to give Al Davis and the LAMCC a victory on grounds that Section 4.3 violated the Sherman Antitrust Act, and that the NFL had not dealt in good faith with Davis. Damages were to be awarded later.

"It's an injustice that has been rectified," a jubilant Davis told a brace of reporters outside the courthouse. But what gave him the biggest kick was not clarification of antitrust law. It was that "We showed Mr. Rozelle that he can't treat people like that. He can't push people around like that."

Looking ashen, Pete Rozelle vowed that the league would appeal, but while some league stalwarts wanted Rozelle to fight to keep the Raiders in Oakland until the appeals process played out, when the 1982 NFL schedule was released, it listed the games of the "Los Angeles Raiders."

Rozelle's only immediate recourse was to press on in Congress for his antitrust exemption. But, now, with an NFL players' strike looming for the 1982 season, union executive director Ed Garvey, bolstered by union president Gene Upshaw, testified against the legislation before the Senate Judiciary Committee. "To just trust [a] monopoly," Garvey said, "I think is folly." Al also came to Washington, D.C.—and, with his recent triumph, was able to embellish, Davis style, on the meaning of that victory to turn off the committee to Rozelle's aims.

"Pete Rozelle admitted under oath," he said, "that the reason they did not want me to move to Los Angeles was that . . . I would get a valuable piece of property that the other owners thought they should . . . divvy up amongst themselves." This, of course, was a stretch, but such scare-off talk contributed to Rozelle's problems in selling the bills. Congressmen not eager to butt into a labor dispute made the legislation a terminal case.

On a monumental high now, Al also used the court win to make Rozelle the villain in Oakland, not incidentally trying to get that monkey off his back and out of his guilts. Still clearly touchy about leaving that city in the lurch, when he was asked about it he snapped, "Let me tell you something. When people get into the guts of this case, I think Oakland can sue Rozelle's ass. When they discover all the things he did behind my back, they're going to be awfully upset."

Here, though, he was groping in the dark. Though he had caught much of the public's fancy in his fight with the powers that be, Oakland would not forgive him.

20

You can't get away from yourself by moving from one place to another.

—Jake Barnes in *The Sun Also Rises*, by Ernest Hemingway

I think I am the establishment, I always have been.

—Al Davis, 1982

That Al was still contemptuous of him made Pete Rozelle no more amenable to Davis and no closer to clear thinking in dealing with him. Rather than revising Section 4.3 to make it enforceable before the courts, Rozelle sought to *restore* it, intact. He implied to the Congress and to the media that it was all or nothing, when in fact the NFL still retained the power to prevent moves—*if* Section 4.3 could be modified.

Even Al wanted that. "I am willing to do anything that is reasonable," he said. Instead of a continuing blood feud with Rozelle, he added, "I am willing to let him win in some way, if he needs a victory."

The solution, as he had said way back in Chicago, was "objective standards or guidelines" that included attendance, stadium conditions, and so on. This, said Al Davis, would prevent moves based on the "whim or caprice of individual owners."

That was not so in *his* case, naturally, but with further self-absolution, Al would take up the cause of abandoned cities such as

Oakland when Leon Hess moved the Jets to the New Jersey Mead-owlands in 1984. At the owners meeting that year, Al verbally mugged Rozelle with the issue. "Should we allow the Jets to leave New York City without a team?" he asked, even though he had *supported* Hess's move.

Wearily, Rozelle told him, "The point is moot, based on your courtroom victory."

"That's wrong!" Al bellowed. "Why do you keep dancing around the truth? My courtroom victory was based on [the phrasing of] your lousy rule. . . . That's why you can't stop the Jets from mov-ing, even if you want to."

By then, Al could afford to be big-hearted toward cities left high and dry by sheer greed, since his team was untouchable. On No-vember 5, 1983, the United States Supreme Court had refused to hear the NFL's appeal of the Davis jury verdict. And while Rozelle fought on in Congress, his doomed battle was framed by the words of one ranking senator that "the NFL ought to put its own house in order."

In full retreat now, other owners were turning on their intrepid leader and his counsel. When Paul Tagliabue told an ensuing owners meeting that he had *thought* the Supreme Court would hear the appeal, Buffalo's Ralph Wilson got up and roared, "Don't give me any of that shit! You told us they'd hear it!"

While Rozelle kept fighting for total victory from *some* court or *any* congressional committee, with no modification of Section 4.3 the Colts picked up and moved from Baltimore to Indianapolis in 1984 without so much as notifying the league. Finally, late that year, Rozelle set forth a list of guidelines for franchise shifts—and, damned either way now—the league was sued by the Cardinals' Bill Bidwill to *stop* it from enforcing the guidelines.

Clearly, things had come full circle. Bidwill, Al noted with high satisfaction, had only a few years ago "said I shouldn't move but in recent weeks he has come up to me and said he shouldn't have done what he did. Now he realizes what I went through." In his gloating, Al neglected to mention the fans of St. Louis. Despite his team playing to near-capacity houses when he sued, Bidwill would soon enough jump to sunny Phoenix.

Staying L.A.-ready, as Al had for two years, did not prevent the problems of a late and hurried start-up of the 1982 season. With the first exhibition games due only two months after the court victory, the tiny Raider staff, which was stationed at the suddenly hectic University Hilton Hotel, was no match for the inundation of business that now greeted the city's new team.

Dealing with a new wave of ticket requests, Al LoCasale worked himself into exhaustion and finally had to be hospitalized with pneumonia. What he left behind was a mess he'd made out of the first batch of tickets that went to "preferred" fans—clients, longtime Oakland fans, LAMCC members, politicians, and movie stars—and many of them displaced Coliseum ticket-holders who'd had the same seats for decades. With only thirty thousand choice seats between the goal lines, people who had had fifty-yard-line seats now were given locations behind the end zones.

And yet, for all their discomfort, what the L.A. fans were getting was their first dose of what Al Davis can breed. Along with end-zone seats, the *Los Angeles Times* noticed, many fans had gotten "rude talk and the runaround from the Raiders."

Most significantly, among the people Al was failing to charm were those on the Los Angeles Board of Supervisors, and even some on the Coliseum board. Balky before the court victory, the latter seemed *less* into finalizing a binding, long-term lease with the Raiders now. LAMCC personnel had changed in the two years since the initial fervor of the move. Bill Robertson, the key man, had retired, and his and other replacements weren't happy with the terms of the package. In a grim Catch-22, millions of dollars in promised guarantees were not paid because Al hadn't signed a lease, and Al wouldn't sign without the money.

But this was okay by Al. Working on the memorandum of agreement, he was getting a $675,000 annual rent credit at the Coliseum—also a bone of contention with the city—and while that cost the Coliseum an $84,000 deficit in 1982, it was a boon to Al. He also knew he had leverage now in L.A.—to do what with, only he could know—not unlike the kind he'd had in Oakland. Here, as there, he had all the politicians he wanted to blame for anything.

The real downside was that, for the foreseeable future, he wouldn't be getting the luxury boxes, the creature that began this whole cataclysm. Still, Al was in no rush to sign, and the thick L.A. smog became metaphoric of the city's diffidence about the Raiders.

Another debit of the dormant deal was not having that nice office and practice site beside the Coliseum—miles away, mostly symbolically, Al broke ground for such a complex on an eight-acre plot around an abandoned junior high school in El Segundo. But for the 1982 season, the team, which had resumed practicing in Oakland the year before, would do a reversal of 1980: they'd work out up north and commute to *Los Angeles* for games. In effect, all their games would be road games, especially since the players and coaches—and Al—kept their homes in the Bay Area, where their mortgages were.

For fans and football people alike, it would be hard to break the habit of calling them the *Oakland* Raiders; many still do today. What's more, adding to the lack of a new identity at the outset— and this time because of unrelated factors—Al would have to wait yet longer to see his team play in L.A. The Raiders did play their first exhibition games in the Coliseum on time. On August 29, they beat the Packers before a modest crowd of 40,096; six days later, they lost to the Browns. But the first regular-season home game wouldn't be played for another three months while the NFL went dark and players walked picket lines after the season's second game.

Called to force owners to pay salaries out of a collective fund based on a percentage of gross revenue, the strike was a fiasco and nearly a total loss for the players when rank-and-file support collapsed under league unity—excluding Al, who insisted that, for his part, "the idea should not be to defeat the players . . . [they] are the game. We own it, they play it." And, in a way, Al won on both sides. He benefited with the rest of the owners; and when the futile strike hastened the departure of Ed Garvey, Gene Upshaw would retire to become the union's new executive director. An avowed Al Davis man, Upshaw—who, like Garvey, had once believed free agency was impractical in football—would gradually begin reconsidering the issue, just as Al was looking to go after big-name free agents in the "buy-me" eighties.

The shortened 1982 schedule—nine games—resumed with the Raiders at 2–0 and in the Coliseum against the Chargers. Al could hardly have gotten a better script for this one on the Paramount back lot. Down by twenty-four to Gene Klein's defending division champs, they rallied to win 28–24 on *Monday Night Football*. Four weeks later the Rams came back to their old home field; another biggie for Al, which his boys won 37–31, and the game did over sixty thousand at the gate.

That whole season, in fact, was a progression of proof levels, and Al had prepared his team for that. Disgusted by the jowly indifference of 1981, he ordered Jim Plunkett and Lester Hayes to come to camp without the post–Super Bowl banquet circuit flab of the year before—and Plunkett was again to be pressed by Al's quarterback of the future, 1981 BYU draftee Marc Wilson. Stocking up more and more on the short-term gains of proven veterans, he gave up draft choices to the Browns for thirty-three-year-old one-time Broncos All-Pro Lyle Alzado, who became the new sacker at right end, and thirty-one-year-old halfback Greg Pruitt.

And, once more, he went against the prevailing winds to get a guy he wanted in the draft—USC tailback Marcus Allen. The Heisman Trophy winner in 1981, Allen had rushed for a record 2,342 yards and had eight two-hundred-yard games, but he fell on scouts' lists when he fumbled twice and ran poorly in the Fiesta Bowl. For Al, Allen was a box-office must, an L.A. hero to play in the same stadium where he had starred—even though this was a radical change in Raider thinking. Never before had Al cared about a breakaway runner, as he felt most of them didn't care about blocking. The fullback always got the crucial Raider yards on the ground, off tackle or on a sweep.

Al knew the pick would look like hype. He also knew Allen didn't only block, he *crushed*. This was the type of tailback Al could go for. As a rookie, he ran for 697 yards and eleven touchdowns, earning every yard now that the huge left-side convoy on the offensive line—Upshaw and Art Shell, both in their last season—was suddenly assailable.

At 8–1, the Raiders won the division, clocked the Browns in the first playoff round, then had the Jets in the semifinals. For this game, L.A. came out in numbers—90,037. But the ride ended here in a nostalgic time warp.

These teams had not met in postseason since 1968, and Heidi and Ben Davidson and Joe Namath lived again, through a game filled with fistfights, dumb mistakes, and a reminder of Al Davis folklore. The last came during a nutty halftime interlude. Up 10–0, Jets coach Walt Michaels, an old AFL guy, took a phone call in the locker room and heard someone on the other end tell him to keep kicking tail. Michaels couldn't help but think it was Al doing the old psych-out *shtick*, and laced into him after the game—until a tavern owner in Queens, New York, who had a bet on the game, came forward and admitted he'd made the call.

In the second half, the game turned even nuttier. After the Raiders surged into a 14–10 fourth-quarter lead, there was a Raider fumble and a Jet interception. The Jets went ahead 17–14, then Plunkett threw an interception, the Jets fumbled, and Plunkett threw another interception to end the burlesque and send the Jets to the AFC title game.

It was in 1983 that Davis was rewarded for his endurance. He already had two large victories in his pocket before the season began. On April 13, the jury in his antitrust suit against the NFL assessed damages of $11.5 million, with $4.9 million more to the LAMCC. According to antitrust law, these amounts were tripled to a combined $49.2 million. The league would also have to pay the plaintiffs' legal fees of $10 million. Pete Rozelle was again reduced to wanly announcing an appeal, now on damages.

Three months later, Oakland's eminent domain suit was heard in Salinas. Now a defendant, Al rested his case on pure gall—and, as usual, won with it. Although Al had dealt with a public authority in the Los Angeles Coliseum—prohibited to spend money on anything but a public use—he now claimed the Raiders were *not* a public use in Oakland. More nervy still, he used in his defense none other than the dreaded NFL constitution, which stated that a city cannot own a team. Livid, but turned inside out, legally, the NFL couldn't explain its way out of its own conflicts with eminent domain laws, and lost.

"The American flag flies proudly over Salinas today," Joe Alioto crowed when the judge rendered his verdict. "It's a great day not only for the Raiders, but for the American dream and free enterprise."

For the 1983 season, key changes made a world of difference on the Raiders. With Gene Upshaw now at the players' union full-time and Art Shell on the sideline as a line coach, the Raiders' ground game—that is, Marcus Allen, who had the first of three straight thousand-yard seasons—went *right*, with the burden on tackle Henry Lawrence and guard Mickey Marvin. Another of Al's draft plums, Marvin too had turned off scouts, in 1977, by eating his way to over 300 pounds after an injury; now a hard 270, he was clearing out bodies like brushwood. And in waiting was the number-one draft pick out of USC, 280-pound Don Mosebar, a future Pro Bowl center.

The big switch on the defensive line was the new left end—six-five, 270-pound Howie Long, a number-two draft pick in 1981 who replaced John Matuszak when big Tooz's body finally broke down. Yet another one downgraded by scouts—too much body fat, they said—Long looked soft and could do only two pull-ups, but he could tear holes in blockers; always double-teamed, he opened up freeways for the linebackers, forced holding penalties, and *still* had thirteen sacks in 1983, the first of five straight Pro Bowl years.

Said Long: "[Other] teams make you do dips, bench presses, and aerobics, they drop you into a sensory-deprivation tank to test your body fat. You think Al would go for that?"

However he judged his players, by 1983 Al had again built a team with astounding variety, experience, and depth. During the season, Lyle Alzado alternated at right end with 265-pound rookie Greg Townsend—a third-down demon, with tremendous speed and mobility—and the two combined for seventeen sacks; Townsend also ran a fumble back sixty-six yards. And another rookie end, Bill Pickel—a future All-Pro nose tackle—waited *his* turn.

At tight end was Todd Christensen, the old failed running back and a self-described "slow white guy" who could also read a zone defense at one hundred paces and maneuver into the clear under the deep coverage. Christensen caught ninety-two passes in 1983, then an NFL record, with twelve touchdowns. In that and each of the three following years, all Pro Bowl years, he caught at least eighty—the first time in history *that* had been done.

The defensive secondary was a scale model of this duality of new talent and old-shoe savvy. The 1982 draft had yielded the newest "killer" free safety, Baylor's Vann McElroy, an instant starter and a future Pro Bowler. But when the number-one pick of 1981, cornerback Ted Watts, didn't pan out, Al looked at his roster early in the 1983 season and saw he had to go still another route—right to the top of the line in cornerbacks: six-time All-Pro Mike Haynes.

A contract holdout since before the season, Haynes was demanding big numbers, $1.5 million over three years. When the Patriots sought to trade him—asking for first- and third-round draft picks in 1984—only Davis was willing to pick up that size tab to help his team, though he was still dickering with Haynes's agent as the trade deadline neared. Agreement wasn't reached until thirty-five minutes after the deadline, and the trade was then made. This detail became cause for one of the last fleeting skirmishes in the fading Davis-NFL war. When Gene Klein heard of the late consummation, he egged on Pete Rozelle to void the trade and, regrettably, Rozelle did so.

"Even though that little fellow up there doesn't like to play by the rules," Klein said, "he's going to have to learn that he must."

Al was furious, and his backlash could be felt in another legal action, this one Haynes's $5 million lawsuit against the league for "arbitrary and capricious" interference. Even the individual co-defendants were familiar ones—Rozelle and Klein—and part of the suit's language decried the alleged NFL vendetta against Al Davis. But, now, fresh from being handed their heads by Davis, Rozelle and the NFL didn't chance fighting again, and within two weeks the trade was allowed to go through.

At this moment in his life, Al Davis's power was supreme, and as if to emblazon the hologram of an NFL backing down from his threats, his team—6–3 through October—tore off five straight wins and six in the last seven games to finish at 12–4. And while Mike Haynes typified the catalytic effect of the Raiders melting pot, a sidebar of the Haynes trade may have been the big spark of 1983. Haynes's agent, Howard Slusher, also happened to represent Marc Wilson, the backup Raiders quarterback. When Wilson complained early in the season about not playing and considered jumping to the new United States Football League, Al changed Wilson's mind by abruptly starting him and bumping him up to a new five-year, $4 million contract—dashing the hopes of one Donald Trump, to whose New Jersey USFL team both Haynes and Wilson had appeared headed.

Wilson threw for 318 yards in his first start, against the Cowboys—which also had the desired effect of goosing Jim Plunkett. When Wilson hurt his shoulder three games later, Plunkett came in, beat the Chiefs, and was sizzling the rest of the way. In the playoffs, the Raiders blasted through the Steelers 38–10 and then the Seahawks 31–14 in the AFC title game.

Super Bowl XVIII, pitting the Raiders against the Washington Redskins on January 22, 1984, in Tampa, was a self-testimonial to Al Davis. Just so the nation's assembled media would know it, thousands were spent to buy billboard ads all around Tampa on which were the Raiders' logo and Al's new apothegm, "Commitment to Excellence"—which unlike "Pride and Poise" made more room for him to jam in on the team's charge, since the commitment began with him. To Al, toppling the NFL's Ming Dynasty and being here again attested to the unwithered greatness of man and team.

Yet, as he sensed, others had to be reminded of this. The end of the Davis-Rozelle war and the club's still-lukewarm cheer in its new home—as with the Jets game a year before, only the playoffs had lured big crowds to fill that huge gaping tureen in south central Los Angeles—seemed to make people consider them nearly without emotion; frothing vagabonds still, they now hailed from a Coliseum less Roman than avocado.

For this Super Bowl, then, Al cast out the old rules of gamesmanship. Where always he had built up his opponents, now he spoke of the victory—*big* victory—he expected was at hand. And where he never consented to hype marketing before, he took not only his new slogan to Tampa but his new fans from the rabid dens of Bel Air and Malibu; on his private plane were Frank Sinatra, Jane Fonda, and James Garner. Although there was something wrong about this forced mating of lunchpail and sushi bar—something Al either didn't realize or had forgotten somewhere between Oakland and Hollywood—for now he didn't need to remember. The 1983 team was his cushion.

And the Redskins, the defending NFL champs, were his kind of foil. While this prehistoric franchise could hardly be damned as old NFL anymore, these 'Skins were a new sort of enemy for Al —by being *too* modern, with their encyclopedic playbook and exercise of the "in" offense of the eighties: one back, four receivers, and players in motion all over the place. This was another reach by Al. The 'Skins were driven more by their "Hogs," the old-fashioned bulldozers on the offensive line, than anything else; what is more, the Raiders, with their tailback offense, were close to being newfangled themselves, though Al was loath to admit it.

"Look, we play a two-back offense," he humphed, "we play man-to-man, bump-and-run pass defense. Our quarterbacks call their own plays—we don't have coordinators. Some of the other teams, well, all the technical stuff they use is getting so technical I don't think they understand it themselves."

For now, Al could get away with that kind of facile coda. Soon enough, much of what his own team did would be out of his hands, and at the mercy of football's technocratic evolution. Super Bowl XVIII, in fact, was the last hurrah for the kind of football that had spawned Al Davis. And, fittingly, the Raiders laid on a hell of an exclamation point. Although the Redskins had beaten the Raiders during the regular season, even that game showed how easily the Washington dam could break—L.A., playing without an injured Marcus Allen, went on a twenty-eight-point rampage to take the lead, only to lose 37–35.

This time, the favored 'Skins went under early. Five minutes into the game, L.A.'s Derrick Jensen blocked a punt and fell on it in the end zone for a 7–0 lead. Sensing an early kill, the Raider defense went after the Hogs, putting their two big inside linebackers right up at the line of scrimmage and daring the blockers to open holes for fullback John Riggins; they tried, and failed, and when Plunkett threw a thirteen-yard touchdown pass to Cliff Branch to make it 14–0, the 'Skins quarterback Joe Theismann went to the air—with disastrous results.

The Raider secondary had counted on this. Unfazed by Theismann's arm, and with the warm Tampa winds swirling hard that day, Mike Haynes and Lester Hayes played way up on the receivers, taking away the short passes. Looking long, Theismann either threw errantly into the wind or was buried by the pass rush, being sacked six times. All that abuse must have turned Theismann's brain to tapioca. Deep in his own territory with twelve seconds to go in the half, he threw a *screen pass* from his own end zone. Even this the Raiders smelled out—or at least linebacker coach Charlie Sumner did. Before the play, he yanked Matt Millen and put in Jack Squirek, a better pass-defending linebacker. Squirek intercepted at the five and took it in for a touchdown that devastated the 'Skins.

Up 21–3, L.A. then pounded it out in the second half, which was a showcase for Marcus Allen—who had two touchdown runs that pumped the final score to 38–9. On his second TD, he swept left, then broke it back to the inside, and streaked past two linebackers and a cornerback on a breathtaking seventy-four-yard jag. Allen's 191 rushing yards won him the game's MVP award.

As a sequel to the avidly awaited postgame locker-room scene of three years before in New Orleans, Pete Rozelle's presentation of the Lombardi Trophy to Al Davis this year was a dud. Their private war might as well have been in the Dardanelles for all it mattered now to most people. Rozelle congratulated Al for "putting this cast together." Al said, "Thank you, Commissioner," took the trophy, shook Rozelle's hand, and in the course of a rambling speech only briefly referred to overcoming "all the outrageous things the league has done" to his team. Hearing that, the Raider players cheered and Al responded by raising a fist. "Just win, baby," he screamed in communal beatification. "Just win."

That, as Al had stressed all during the week, was what this Super Bowl was about—winning not to beat the league but for history's chalice of greatness. That state of grace was all that was on Al Davis's mind as the locker room emptied. Sitting alone on top of a bin of dirty towels, refusing to let the taste and smell of this one go just yet, he was approached by a lone reporter.

"We could have scored fifty today," Al said, "but we shut it down in the third quarter. This is the greatest win we've ever had, one of the greatest in history, hell, one of the greatest of all time in any professional sport. Next year, God, wait till next year, the depth we have on this team. . . ."

On February 28, 1984, just over a month after Al Davis's greatest win on the field, the Ninth Circuit Court of Appeals by a two-to-one vote upheld his greatest victory off it, the antitrust verdict against the NFL. Similar rulings would trickle in through the decade, in state appeals courts and in the United States Supreme Court.

In March 1985, Al strode into the annual NFL owners meeting in Phoenix prepared to exert his new sway. Part of the league's business there was to broach a settlement with Davis on the damages he had won. "So what's the bottom line, Al?" one owner asked during a discussion that could best be called frigid. The owners got their answer after Davis met with Pete Rozelle and demanded to settle at no less than ninety-two cents on the dollar. "That's not settlement," said Rozelle, "that's capitulation."

The NFL again took its chances in court—and this time it actually won one when the federal appeals court ruled in June 1985 that his original damages of $34.5 million were excessive in view of what it called Davis's "windfall" in Los Angeles. Stung by that defeat, Al went back to the owners, though hardly with hat in hand. The settlement finally reached on March 4, 1989, netted him $18 million.

In the end, that may have been the ultimate cost of not making Al Davis NFL commissioner in 1966.

There were other scores to settle now, personal ones. Eight days after Super Bowl XVIII, Gene Klein filed a $33 million federal damages suit against Davis in state superior court in San Diego, charging malicious prosecution in being named as a defendant in Al's suit against the NFL. With typical Klein run-on bombast, his suit labeled Davis's acts as "willful, wanton, vexatious, and oppressive," and alleged that they caused Klein "loss of goodwill, loss of reputation, humiliation, injury to his health, strength, activity [and] great mental, physical, and nervous pain and suffering"—

which included, he maintained, the heart attack he suffered while testifying at the trial.

Since Al had won that trial, he had a ready defense for the Klein suit, which he called "frivolous and a sham." Filing a countersuit against Klein for malicious abuse of the court process, he suggested that if Klein's health was in decline it wasn't due to Al but rather because Klein's team and his league were found liable in a $50 million jury verdict. Al also took great comfort in listing for the court other Klein woes within the league—including "a large fine for drug-related activities" in connection with the Houston Ridge scandal—and without the league, an eight-hundred-thousand-dollar fine in a civil case that found Klein guilty of malicious prosecution.

Al might have thought he had Klein dead to rights, but he took the first blow when his countersuit was dismissed. Klein's suit was then heard before Judge Gilbert Harelson in September 1986, and the tone of the trial was established when Al's lawyer asked the plaintiff, "Isn't it true that you dislike Mr. Davis?"

"Dislike?" Gene Klein bellowed. "I hate the son of a bitch!"

Evidently, so did the San Diego jury. On December 10, after two days of deliberation, they returned a verdict for Klein and awarded him $5 million in compensatory damages, $5 million in punitive damages, and $48,606.82 in medical costs. Recalling the verdict, Al's San Diego attorney, Bob Baxley, was blunt. "Let's face it," he said, "I think the jury trial boiled it down to the Chargers against the Raiders. I don't think the jury ever understood the legal principle; obviously the judge didn't."

That principle had to do with "probable cause" in Al naming Klein as a defendant, Judge Pregerson's severing of the individual suits notwithstanding. Said Baxley: "I kept trying to tell Judge Harelson, look, the Pregerson ruling didn't make sense, he did it in the interest of compromise and brevity. The judgment against the league meant he had probable cause." But if the jury was kindly disposed to Klein, his sullen recitation of his witness stand heart attack convinced them.

Baxley was well aware that Pete Rozelle had made exactly the same surmise when he had lost to Al—that he fell victim to a hometown decision. "But, in that one," Baxley said saliently, "the decision held up on appeal." Which was why Al practically leaped into his appeal of the Klein verdict. On law, the no longer legal neophyte knew he'd prevail. At least partly, the trial judge beat him to it, by quickly reducing the $10 million award to $2 million. Then, on May 31, 1989, the California appellate court went down the line, on law, for Al: verdict overturned, judgment entered for Davis.

As Klein saw it then, "The game is tied 1–1 and we go into overtime," meaning he would appeal the ruling to the California supreme court.

Gene Klein was long gone from the league by then, having sold the Chargers in 1984—he had better luck with the ponies than with Davis, owning the 1988 Kentucky Derby champion Winning Colors—and it was a telling sign of the NFL's mid-eighties realignment that the new Chargers owner was an Al Davis man. Alex Spanos, a Stockton, California, developer, had known Al for over a decade, and he was front man for an emerging, and vocal, pro-Davis axis. Urging peace with Davis, Spanos called him "a great football man. . . . [T]he man is outstanding in this business. I think he's the best there is. Just look at what he has said and look at what has happened. He's been right all along in many cases."

Sounding a clarion call for the rest of the league, Spanos said, "I, for one, would prefer to be his ally rather than his adversary. It's hard enough to beat him on the field."

And while this avowal was still in the minority, what was shocking about the gradual tilt toward a Davis consensus now under way was the genus of his new friends. Al Davis, a football man who never could get along with the old-world football men who built their franchises as the preoccupation of their lives, was thick with Reagan-age entrepreneur/marketeers, men whose Super Bowl was the junk bond market. To these men, Al was not a threat but an icon—or *Icahn*, literally a corporate Raider, busting trusts to begin his own.

The old-guard holdouts, pinched by rising salaries and crowded out by rapacious buyers, could only rue that the new order had been partially created by another football man. "When the NFL lived by the constitution, it prospered," bemoaned the Steelers' Art Rooney, the NFL patriarch, shortly before his death. "We never sued each other. But that's the whole world now. What Davis did won't make it easier. A lot of new people haven't lived with the constitution. It's a wholly different game now."

The Patriots' Billy Sullivan was a bit more direct. "Guys like Davis," he hissed, "I don't want any part of them. I like the term

'Fighting Irish.' If you fight one of us, you fight us all. . . . Commitment to Excellence? I like Commitment to Integrity better."

In fact, Al wasn't through yet in his dissidence. If the old brigade couldn't understand Al suing his own league, they couldn't *believe* he would actually help another league sue his own league. This he did when the United States Football League filed a multibillion-dollar lawsuit in 1985, charging that the NFL was a monopoly that had conspired to put the USFL out of business.

Though he'd had to fight Donald Trump for Marc Wilson, Al wanted not to destroy the USFL but—as he'd wanted with the old World Football League—to merge with it. Thus, he wanted nothing to do with the NFL's legal defense. The Raiders, he said in a letter to Pete Rozelle, were not "liable for contributions to any judgment or litigation expense. We are not a defendant in this case. If you again violated the antitrust laws we were not a party to it."

With the NFL facing a jury verdict, he wrote, "only because of [its] gross mismanagement and malpractice, exhibiting a reckless disregard for the rights of others and the economic welfare of NFL members," he proposed that the NFL settle the suit by taking in four USFL teams, at $90 million per franchise, and form its own spring development league.

"To Al, there's no magic in the NFL that he cannot reproduce and do better himself," observed George Ross. "He saw a new league in that way."

Threatening to testify against the NFL, Al had warned Gene Klein in the middle of their private court battle, "I'm gonna bury you"—using Klein as a stand-in for the league. He went on: "You can try to cross-examine me, but if you do you'll be sorry. This case should be settled, [otherwise] you're gonna get tagged for a big number."

As promised, Al did testify. But when the verdict was returned in June 1986—technically for the USFL—the "big number" reached by the jury was exactly one dollar in damages, upon which the USFL promptly closed shop. Clearly, Al Davis had enjoyed better moments.

Al finally had gotten down to hard negotiations with the Los Angeles Coliseum board. Reappointed to the LAMCC for that purpose by Mayor Tom Bradley, Bill Robertson obtained for Al his long overdue $6.7 million loan—$4 million of it in cash toward the construction of luxury boxes and stadium renovation and the rest applied as a continuation of the $625,000 a year rent credit at the Coliseum. On December 9, 1984, Davis and the LAMCC entered into a retroactive ten-year lease to run through the 1991 season and with three five-year options thereafter.

Hardly by coincidence, the negotiations leading to the agreement ran far more smoothly once the Raiders had won the Super Bowl and become less of a risk. As defending champions, they drew an attendance of over 70,000 a game, and on October 28 against the Broncos 92,456 jammed the august old park to establish a record NFL gross of $1,596,000; and the $10 million gross over the season was another record.

Two seasons later, when one quarter of the league's twenty-eight teams lost money, the Raiders averaged 73,000 a game, and with a top ticket of twenty-five dollars took in revenues of $40 million. Even with the league's highest payroll—over $15 million—the club made a $5 million profit, and the revenue and profit numbers doubled the league average. These figures not only warmed Al. The twenty-seven other teams that had tried to keep him in Oakland were suddenly overjoyed that the Raiders *weren't* up there; provided that Al could get those smaller stadium renovations that would lift the home blackout, a second L.A. franchise was far more attractive to the television networks than the Oakland market.

In 1986, the franchise that had once played in a stadium named for an undertaker was worth around $80 million.

But maybe Al Davis was a too-comfortable capitalist. As he edged more and more into the power elite, his team began to ebb on the field, drifting further from his active touch. Al was wrong when he talked big in the aftermath of Super Bowl XVIII. There was no Raiders dynasty, not with all that age and physical uncertainty.

For a couple of seasons they held together, but were dragged down by—and this had to kill Al—their quarterbacking. In 1984, the year Ted Hendricks retired, they started out 7–1, but when Jim Plunkett was hurt the offense collapsed around an inadequate Marc Wilson. Finishing a third-place 11–5, they lost with Plunkett to the Seahawks in the wild-card playoff, 13–7. The following season they won the division at 12–4, Marcus Allen won the conference MVP with an NFL high 1,759 rushing yards, and the defense led the league with sixty-five quarterback sacks—but Wilson completed only eleven of twenty-seven passes and threw three interceptions in the 27–20 playoff loss to the Patriots.

That was the last time the Raiders made the playoffs in the eighties, and as they sank—8–8 in 1986, 5–10 in 1987—the quarterback problem became a running joke in the league. A serpentine six-six and 205 pounds, Marc Wilson was a deferential Mormon who by admission had "anxieties" about coming to the Raiders straight from BYU. During these trying seasons, his worst fears were met as he became Al Davis's eighties' folly; clinging to the dream of a revived dynasty, Al would pin his hopes each season on a maturing Wilson, only to see him fail under the pressure and be sent back to the bench in favor of the aging Jim Plunkett.

Though trade rumors constantly encircled Wilson—at times floated by the Raiders front office—Al kept him, seemingly the only observer around the league not alarmed by this stagnation. No trades were made for a capable arm, no draft choices bartered—rather, his top picks were expended on drawing board Gorgons such as three-hundred-pound tackle John Clay in 1987, most of whom were stiffs. Wilson, meanwhile, his head and mechanics screwed up and his body beaten pulpy each week, somehow endured until his release after the 1987 season.

The NFL was hit by another player strike in 1987—now fought over the issue of unrestricted free agency—and this development made evident the paradoxes of Al's serrated brand of ownership. With the rest of the league he fielded a scab team during the three-week union walkout, and when the players returned—without a new collective bargaining agreement, as is still the case today, but granted a limited number of free agents per team whose loss required no compensation—the union filed an antitrust suit against the NFL of Pete Rozelle and Al Davis.

And yet this was entirely appropriate, since Al's dualism wasn't so apparent anymore. Not since his embarrassing USFL escapade had Davis clashed with the NFL as a whole. Indeed, with the bloodshed of the early eighties seeming more like the Book of Deuteronomy with each passing year, when Pete Rozelle listened to his tired body and retired in March 1989, Al Davis—only four years Rozelle's junior and about to reach his sixtieth birthday—realized how mortally locked in history they really were. Rozelle had just announced his resignation at the owners meeting in Palm Springs and was walking toward the door when Al got up and embraced him—a vignette that needed no words.

Thus did Al Davis suddenly become establishment. It wasn't a lack of fight, only of wars, and by the turn of the nineties even Art Modell was unresistant to him. "I'd rather have Al Davis inside the league than outside," Modell said, a left-handed compliment that left unsaid the obvious reason why—the fans of Oakland notwithstanding—the owners could now get behind Al Davis. For all the caviling about his moving, "now they think it's a great idea," said Ron Mix, the Hall of Famer who has known Davis for over thirty years. "He did them the biggest favor they could ever imagine.

"Listen, Al Davis quadrupled the value of their franchises. He showed 'em the way. Now, all of 'em get concessions from their cities, 'cause the cities are afraid to lose them. Not only did he win this for them, he became the drum major, he led them into the real future. He became establishment because *they* joined *him*."

Certainly they did in the making of Rozelle's successor. The favorite candidate for the job had been Saints president Jim Finks, a longtime NFL functionary, but Rozelle asked for trouble when he named a search committee of six old-guard owners who would rubber-stamp Finks. Unhappy being shoved out of the way, eleven new-guard owners united to block his election at the July 1989 owners meeting.

Desperate to end the unsightly deadlock, Rozelle called on Al Davis in his new life as an elder statesman. He named Davis to a new search committee as a dog bone to the new guard, two of whom were also named. It was the first time Al had sat on a committee since Rozelle so cheesily ousted him from the Competition Committee twelve years before, and his work as a *healer* helped join all sides and bring Paul Tagliabue the job. As *Sports Illustrated* noted, "One of Rozelle's last acts [was] putting Davis on the committee to select the man to lead the league into the next century."

21

Know, then, that for you is neither surfeit nor content. In your rocking-chair, by your widow dreaming, shall you long, alone. In your rocking-chair, by your window, shall you dream such happiness as you may never feel.

—Theodore Dreiser, *Sister Carrie*

I've been a winner my whole life and will be the rest of my life.

—Al Davis

But what was all that goodwill worth now? Al had once told this story: "In 1969, when Vince Lombardi left Green Bay to go to Washington, Vincent said: 'The greatest thing in our country is to rebuild.' I sent him a telegram the next day that said, 'No, Vince, the toughest thing to do is to maintain excellence.' So the next day in the papers he told the reporters, 'And when we rebuild, the toughest thing to do is to maintain excellence.' "

He could tell this tale with great smugness, as long as the winning droned on. And never did he think it would stop. As late as 1985, still holding to his dynastic fancies, Al said, "I just hope that someday this team [will] be recognized, if it isn't already, as the greatest team of all time in any sport."

But, by 1988, the Los Angeles Raiders were simply a mediocre bunch with waning pretensions of Raider greatness and tradition, playing again in a half-filled stadium not one rivet closer to renovation—a stadium the *Los Angeles Times* described as "an aging monolithic structure assaulted on three sides by what socioeconomists would call urban blight."

Now, the other owners weren't nearly as thrilled with a second team in the L.A. market—in 1989, the NFL would have to sign a network television deal for reduced money because of recent low ratings, in large part caused by blacked-out games in the Coliseum. Not long before, the owners had feared Al might try to cut his own pay-TV deal on the same antitrust basis as before. To their relief he did not, but it may have been less a matter of his league conscience than dwindling local interest in the Raiders.

The whole situation in L.A. was hitting the rocks now. Construction was due to begin on luxury boxes in 1987, as part of an overall $9 million Coliseum renovation that would lower the field six feet to bring the stands closer to the sidelines—seeing a game at the Coliseum, Al said, was like "looking at a parade from a helicopter"—reduce its seating capacity to seventy thousand, and eliminate the running track around the edge of the field. However, even now, the LAMCC had still only made *verbal* assurances that it would go through with the improvements; no more money had been delivered, and with the team losing the politicians were edgy again.

Al began work on the luxury boxes in the spring of 1987, but then the Coliseum board asked that he file plans and building permits before they moved on the rest of the deal. Al took that as an obstacle for obstacle's sake; furious that the board might be running from its agreement, he opened talks with developers and civic leaders in the industrial suburb of Irwindale, just southwest of L.A. According to details leaked during the 1987 training camp, the Irwindale package called for a $115 million loan with which to erect a sixty-five-thousand-seat stadium; as a good-faith gesture, $10 million would be released to Al immediately, just for considering the offer, which looked can't-miss to that city.

When the first Irwindale stories began to appear in the papers, the Coliseum board insisted that they intended to renovate their stadium *next* year, but that they hadn't been able to get Davis on the phone to set negotiations. Al, of course, felt there was nothing to negotiate, that he'd been betrayed, and suddenly the whole mess was an eerie echo. It was the stand-off in Oakland all over again, with heated accusations and threats—but with a few twists. First of all, Al was indisputably in the right now. And if there was duplicity in his method, it would be felt this time by the suitors.

For while Al formally entered into a deal with Irwindale to begin play there in 1991, he would be bound legally to the agreement only until February 1989, by which time the city government had to approve the terms. The $10 million, however, was nonrefundable.

The LAMCC reacted to this news by filing a $58 million breach of contract suit against Al Davis, the real aim of which was to take back their $6.7 million loan.

In turn, Al filed a breach-of-contract suit against the LAMCC.

For Al Davis, it was all very old hat.

The 1987 season was significant only in terms of transition. It was Tom Flores's last with the Raiders and Bo Jackson's first. And Lester Hayes never made it to the starting gate. For the blathering Hayes this was the completion of a shocking free fall begun in the early eighties. He was still an All-Pro then, but his weight gains and mental lapses grew from concerning to alarming. While drugs were suspected, Al could still put a lid on in-house imbibing. Some, though, got tired of shielding Lester. According to Joe Madro, the old Chargers assistant who was the Raiders' line coach from 1977 to 1982 and is now a team consultant, Hayes was "on the shit"— cocaine.

"Al took good care of Lester Hayes," Madro said. "We had some drug problems and he was one of 'em." With Hayes, and others, Al took steps he had not with the lamentable Warren Wells. As Madro recalled, these players were "put away for a while and sent to funny farms for help."

Yet, by 1987, Lester was out of it, and when he hurt his foot in camp he was put on injured reserve and never brought back, as Lionel Washington, whom Al had traded for to replace Hayes, moved in at left cornerback.

Tom Flores, as had John Madden, lost *his* stomach for coaching. Victimized by Al's bad drafting and his misplaced faith in Marc Wilson, Flores grew irritable playing Tonto to Al's Lone Ranger. "That had been Tom's strength," said Todd Christensen, "that he could defer his ego for the good of the team. And, believe me, in this age of Mike Ditkas and Jerry Glanvilles and Buddy Ryans, that takes something to do. Flores never had a problem that people gave credit to Al Davis.

"But it had to be taxing to have this guy over your shoulder constantly, especially when the guy is drafting Jessie Hester and Bob Buczkowski. I mean, what's the point, right? Tom couldn't have done any worse on his own. So he was on the downside of it. Tom's goal was to match Madden's one hundred wins in ten years. But when he realized that was unrealistic, then it was time to go."

After Flores bailed out and went to a nice desk job in Seattle as team president of the Seahawks in January 1988, Al looked at his coaching staff—from where all of his previous head coaches had come, as brahmins of Raider Football. Among others, he saw Art Shell and Willie Brown, erudite football men who were also wonderful candidates to become the first black NFL head coach in sixty-six years. But instead of going in that bold yet logical direction—his kind of direction—Al outsmarted himself. Reaching to the *Denver* coaching staff, he hired the Broncos' thirty-five-year-old offensive coordinator, Mike Shanahan.

The choice was a daffy one for a number of reasons, even apart from a violation of Raider continuity. For one thing, all of Davis's coaches had been the likeness of what Al Davis would have loved to be: football men, *real* men. Shanahan, a spare wafer of a man who could have come right out of *Les Miserables*, had played quarterback briefly at Eastern Illinois but his entire adult life had been spent on sidelines in Ban-Lon slacks, as an assistant coach, at Florida and Oklahoma and for four years in Denver.

Though Al called his new man "an outstanding young football coach," what Al saw in Shanahan was really not Shanahan but John Elway and the Broncos. Essentially, this was an update of the old Al Davis arithmetic of filling needs—if possible, do it by subtracting from the enemy. In his years at Denver, working closely with Elway first as quarterback coach, the Broncos had won three divisional and two AFC titles. Al, absolutely desperate for better quarterbacking, hoped to lift the Raiders' passing game and debilitate the Broncos'. "One of the best things you can do if you wanna get picked up by the Raiders," Christensen confirmed, "is to have good games against them."

Yet what Al failed to see here was that overwriting a different operating system onto the Raiders memory was not only unworkable—on its face alone, it was a freakish deviation from the Raider identity he still blew tributes to all the time, and which existed in at least one important respect: perhaps only a Raider mentality could mate all of the team's past rituals and make it plausible that there *was* such a thing as Raider Football, even if the team didn't technically play it anymore.

Al's thinking on Shanahan, then, was too linear. He was just a football man, the choice a bow to the pragmatic, and you don't suspend reality with a dose of reality. Which was why, almost at once, there was culture clash.

Said Todd Christensen: "We were coming off the worst record a Raider team had in over twenty years. And so Al was looking for some apocalyptic change. So the thinking was skewed. I mean, Al had talked to John Elway and Elway said, yes, this guy would make a great head coach. Well, if I'm the owner of the team, I'm not sure that I'd put that much stock in a player who was intimately involved with somebody over a period of time.

"And so now Shanahan comes in and I'm sure Al is thinking, okay, I'll mold this guy in my image, to do what I wanna do. Well this guy's background, his philosophy, was totally the antithesis of what Al wanted to do. Not only is Shanahan here but he brings two Denver assistant coaches with him, and the Denver terminology.

"Sitting in the team meeting the first time with them, they showed me film, they said, 'We want you to watch [Broncos tight end] Clarence Kay run this route.' And for me it's like, 'Yeah, right. Just kneel down, I got your Clarence Kay right here.' After ten years in the league and five All-Pro seasons, I don't want you telling me how to run a route, especially not with somebody like Clarence Kay."

As the press tore into Al and his new marionette, Shanahan tried to stand tough. Early curfews and a code of discipline the likes of which had never been seen around the club were invoked—and there was nearly a mutiny when Shanahan told them helmets had to be on all heads at all times; no more of that squatting on helmets. Looks like loafing, said the coach. "For years, sitting on helmets was a Raider staple," Christensen said, quite seriously. "And he took it away."

No wonder Shanahan's larger ideas did not catch on. And if Al expected Shanahan to adapt to the yellowed precepts of Raider Football, part of Shanahan's quest for his own Raider identity took the vertical game very far afield. "Sure he believed in the deep throw," said Christensen, "but he believed in getting to it in a different way. From my standpoint, and you'll have to take this as objectively as possible, he wasn't a big believer in throwing to the tight end. He was used to 250-pound tight ends blocking like tackles and here I am 225 pounds and six-three—that's not my thing.''

At times during the 1988 season, Shanahan seemed to kiss off the passing game altogether, even though Al had purposefully used his number-one draft pick in 1988 to get Notre Dame's Heisman Trophy receiver Tim Brown and traded his 1989 number one to land the Bears' disaffected deep threat Willie Gault, a gold medalist on the 1980 Olympic four-hundred-meter relay team and a former NCAA indoor champion sprinter and hurdler. Brown did make it to the Pro Bowl, but as a spectacular kick returner. Gault, who was also slowed by injuries, caught only sixteen balls.

Like no other Raiders team, this one was dependent on the runners—and, in this, Shanahan was playing on his strengths: Marcus Allen and Bo Jackson. Bo had come in another coup for Al, though at the time it looked as if it could be another Davis folly.

The 1985 Heisman winner at Auburn, Jackson was drafted by three big league baseball teams and set Alabama state records in sprints, hurdles, long jump, high jump, and decathlon. Chosen by Tampa Bay as the top NFL draft pick that year, he instead signed to play baseball with the Kansas City Royals; a year later, when he was available to any team in the draft, only Al gambled a pick— all of a seventh-rounder—on Bo playing football.

The pick was a small price, but when Bo tried it as a two-sport man he became surely the only number-seven draft pick in creation to score a five-year, $7.5 million contract—and for part-time work yet, only after the baseball season ended in October. "Bo's Hobby," skeptics took to calling Jackson's new football career, yet in 1987 he ran for 580 yards and seven touchdowns in nine games. He also set a club record with 225 yards against Seattle, which featured a ninety-one-yard run.

With Bo around, meanwhile, Marcus Allen's carries fell. Worse, he started five games as fullback, while the 230-pound Bo ran out of the I as the tailback, with more room to run wide. While Marcus again went to the Pro Bowl in 1987, he ran for only 754 yards, the second-lowest total of his career.

But Shanahan, who had a middling running game in Denver and thus let loose Elway, went the other way now. He geared everything around the backs in 1988, Marcus carrying the load early in the season, Bo taking it later on—facilitating this, Al had drafted in the second round 285-pound Penn State guard Steve Wisniewski.

But this only further bared the continuing vacuum at quarterback. The new big hope, Notre Dame All-American Steve Beuerlein, the number-four draft pick, was on the bench by the season's fourth game. It was then that the void seemed to be filled. Early in the season, Al had traded for Redskins quarterback Jay Schroeder. A bomb-happy All-Pro in 1986, Schroeder had fallen out of favor, was labeled a malcontent, and was benched for Doug Williams in the 'Skins 1987 championship year. Now, starting for the Raiders against the Broncos, he rallied them from twenty-four points down to a 30–27 win.

Schroeder looked to be the perfect guy for the job. Having given up veteran tackle Jim Lachey to get Schroeder, Al's attachment to him was strong, and Schroeder—an L.A. boy who went to UCLA—had appropriate blond hair and the look of a winner, dude. But Schroeder was out of place in the binding Shanahan system, and neither he nor Beuerlein could hold the job; each man started eight games, and—a little frighteningly—each had the same ghastly completion rate of 44.4 percent.

Almost all on legs—Allen and Jackson combined for over fourteen hundred yards and ten touchdowns—the Raiders crept up to 7–9 in 1988. But what to make of a Raider team on which a 230-pound back with blinding speed like Bo Jackson could catch just nine passes out of the backfield all season? Marcus Allen, who caught forty-eight passes in the Raiders' 1984 Super Bowl season, now had thirty-four. Shanahan's offense, as it had been in Denver, had a lot of people in motion, a lot of deception—the offense of the eighties that Al openly loathed at Super Bowl XVIII. The quarterbacks took quick drops and threw short. Sometimes they took the snap out of the shotgun formation. Were these not the Raiders?

Al had to be dying on the vine at this metamorphosis. Asked in 1982 if he considered changing the Raider style, he had said: "No. We are the pressure game, the deep throw, the attack. The philosophy of this team should always be—and will always be, as long as I'm connected with it—not to make opponents respect us, but to put the fear into them." He adhered to that sentiment now as then. But this was one of those wistful Raider rituals, since as long ago as the mid-seventies the Al Davis vertical game had become more a secondary option, a quick-kill strike still, but usually after the running game had numbed defenses. Jim Plunkett, for example, was a conservative thirteen for twenty-one in Super Bowl XV; sixteen for twenty-five in Super Bowl XVIII. From John Madden on, it was really overpowering defense that did it for them when they won.

So then just what was the on-field influence of Al Davis now? Christensen had to wonder himself.

"I remember before the playoff game in 1985 I was running my routes in practice," he recalled, "and Al comes over and says, 'I want you to run that deeper.' And I said to him, 'It's a 94-short corner and a cover-three defense. If I run the route deeper, I'm gonna run into the cornerback.' Now that's fairly standard football conversation. What I was saying was nothing brilliant, nothing too intricate—and it was the terminology he gave to the Raiders.

"And he just had a blank look on his face. He says, 'Well, I don't know what the route is, I don't know what you're talking about, but just run the route deeper.' And I thought, now wait a minute. My silent response was, 'This is the football genius?' So you're talking to somebody that never thought he was a football genius. And he now had made the biggest mistake he ever made, organizationally, in hiring Shanahan."

Although Al Davis had elevated his title to Raiders president (Ed McGah, the only other remaining general partner, had died in 1983), the Davis illusion of power was splintering. In the span of one month there was tragedy, the kind that always made him feel vulnerable and small. First, on June 18, 1989, the bomb finally exploded in John Matuszak and he dropped dead of an apparent heart attack at age thirty-eight. Retirement had not mellowed the Tooz. Working as an actor in recent years, he had at different times been arrested for drunken driving, carrying a concealed weapon, and driving with a suspended license. An early death, Matuszak had often pointed out, would not necessarily be premature in his case.

Then, just before 1989 camp opened, twenty-seven-year-old Stacey Toran—a six-year strong safety fast approaching Pro Bowl status—was killed when his car smashed into a utility pole in Marina Del Rey. An autopsy showed that Toran had been legally drunk.

Del Courtney was wrong. Raiders *did* die.

Al himself seemed to be somewhat battle-fatigued, and not eager to come to grips with another new generation of football players that included mutations like Brian Bosworth, men who wore a crewcut and an earring.

"I've lost track of our culture, I really have," he admitted to *Sport* in late 1986. "I've spent the last six years in courtrooms . . . so don't ask me about 'modern parents' or the kids of today. All I know is these kids on the football field. I know about them, what are their needs, their expectations. I know you gotta teach them to win."

At least he thought he knew them. When the 1989 camp opened in Oxnard, California, Marcus Allen was a high-profile contract holdout, and would remain so until the season's first game. Each day of stalemate ate deeper into both Al's pride and the old Raider Line about Al's abiding benevolence to his players—although, in truth, Al could be penurious or worse, most so with rookies and guys on the outs with him.

"I know certain players have had to sue him," Tom Keating, the ex-Raider, said. "I know Dan Pastorini did [after being released in 1980]. In fact, on that one I think he lost $1.2 million to Pastorini on an unpaid contract."

Keating, reading Al's mind, laughed. "He didn't get his million-two out of Pastorini, I tell you that. You can't really blame him for not wanting to pay a guy if he stinks."

Allen's holdout, though, was not as it seemed. "I don't think that's money," said Christensen. "That's a matter of respect, that's the 1985 season." That season, Marcus ran for a career-high 1,759 yards, but Al—upset by an Allen tirade the previous year about not being used enough in a late-season loss to the Steelers—didn't reward him. In mutual pique, the two barely spoke that year, and the hard feelings didn't completely subside. And now, Bo Jackson was making big money as Al's frontpiece.

"Here is a guy who bleeds silver and black, a great, tough, proud back who has given his all to the club and is still a fine player," wrote *Sports Illustrated*'s Paul Zimmerman last year. "Then Bo comes waltzing in from a baseball field and Allen is forgotten. It ain't right. It ain't the old Raider way."

Bo may have been Al's boy, but Marcus would not be used. Christensen knew how he felt. Though a perennial All-Pro, he called his relationship with Davis "functional," no more. "I was grateful that he gave me an opportunity but, in retrospect, he got a lot of good football out of me." Coming off knee and gall bladder surgery in 1988, Christensen went to Al.

"I asked him, I said, 'Look, I'm thirty-three, tell me what my situation is. I'm a big boy, I can handle it.' And he said, 'Oh, no, no, don't worry.' He could've just pulled me aside and said, look, you're thirty-three, we're goin' in a different direction. But he never did that and I worked extremely hard to get back in shape.

"Then, when it was too late for me to be picked up by anybody else, he called me in and said, 'You're not in our plans.' I felt that my career had warranted his being a little more honest with me."

Al eventually appeased Marcus Allen—making the pertinent names in the Raider backfield Dun and Bradstreet—and he wasn't the only one who needed to be appeased that season. Mike Shanahan, seemingly testing Al's éclat, had crossed the line of sanity by firing two long-time assistant coaches and Davis favorites, Willie Brown and Charlie Sumner, during the off-season. Sputtering mad, Al hired Brown as an administrative assistant, though a bitter Sumner went to the Patriots.

There were other ruptures between the Davis and Shanahan factions. When a Shanahan coach, Nick Nicolau, insulted Art Shell, maliciously asking him, "Why are you hanging around in this job?" Davis fired Nicolau. Shanahan then tried to fire two other Davis coaches, but Al overruled him. That led Shanahan to put himself on the gallows—he disregarded Al's football advice. Amazingly, Shanahan actually made it through four games in 1989 before Al —who *must* have hated firing people to have waited this long in the face of such defiance—sent Shanahan and his men walking back to Denver, and then only because the club had lost three straight.

At this stage, the Raiders were 1–3, and when Al named Art Shell as head coach on October 3, the honor was dubious. And yet for Shell it was a moment of supreme achievement. As a player, this large and quietly ferocious man was also probably the best student of the game on the team; if anyone had questions about formations and tendencies, he came to the big man. Back then, Shell and his running mate on the line, Gene Upshaw, would kid each other about their future. The outspoken Upshaw would be a politician, and the practical Shell would be a head coach. Now Upshaw was head of a union and Shell was the first black head coach in the modern NFL.

For those who knew Shell, he wore that circlet with stately dignity. And while almost everyone in the media gave the race angle heavy, even hysterical play, Davis and Shell admirably refused to magnify the obvious into a vulgar spectacle. For Shell, that source of pride was self-evident, but he was far more emotional that in the year he was elected to the Hall of Fame and elevated to head coach, his father, Arthur Senior, had a stroke and died before he could see his son inducted in Canton, Ohio, in August.

"I didn't get to see him before he closed his eyes," he said.

recalling how he flew home to South Carolina to be at the deathbed. "I went straight to the hospital and sat in the room with him by myself. I reflected on my life. I knew I had made him happy."

Hardly unmindful of the plaudits he was receiving for the move, Al demurred that Shell wasn't hired because he was black but because he was *silver and black*, an effective one-liner that made both men look good. Besides, the fact was that Al never really had a choice.

"That's Al Davis for you," marveled Christensen. "He had to go to Art, he had no place else to go. But he also knows how to make headlines and he knows the timing of things. And he comes out smelling like a rose because, of course, Al Davis is the one who's going to integrate the league, what a terrific guy."

As a primordial silver and black man, the underspoken, softie-at-heart Shell was precisely the man to replace Shanahan. While Al rode hard on the theme that there was going to be a "return to Raider Football," for Shell the task was more fundamental. "They need to think positively and relax," he said. "I need to bring the closeness back." Liberating the helmets as a sideline settee, easing curfew, and taking an "Uncle Art" approach, Shell coaxed the team into winning seven of the next ten games—and all six at home—before road losses in the last two games killed their improbable playoff drive.

Even at 8–8, the season was a tribute to Shell. It happened with Marcus Allen injured for almost the entire season, the quarterback situation still unresolved, Mike Haynes a thirty-six-year-old substitute, Rod Martin retired, and Matt Millen starting for the Super Bowl–bound 49ers after Al deemed him washed up and let him go. But it was not Raider Football. Indeed, it looked more like Shanahan Football. Under Shanahan, the Raiders threw about thirty times a game; under Shell, whose lack of natural flamboyance—and a decent quarterback—likely were factors, it was down to around twenty. And the receiver who profited the most was not Willie Gault but Mervyn Fernandez, a nimble medium-yardage "possession" receiver Al had signed out of the Canadian League. Fernandez caught fifty-seven passes for nine touchdowns. Gault, starting all sixteen games, caught twenty-one. Bo Jackson, who rushed for 950 yards, again caught nine out of the backfield.

Still, there were signs of regenerated Raider character. In other words, they were repellent to many around the league. In Philadelphia, Jay Schroeder threw a late touchdown pass to cut the score to 10–7, then yelled at an Eagles lineman, "We're gonna score one more on you!" He didn't, and they lost. In Buffalo, they went macho and wore short sleeves in the biting cold. They lost. Against Phoenix, Greg Townsend kicked the ball away from the Cardinals' center with the clock running out and the Cards driving for a win. That one they won, because the officials didn't see the infraction.

For Al, though, the most important game of 1989 may have occurred *before* the season. This was an August 27 exhibition game with the Oilers—in the Oakland Coliseum. The outcome of the game was inconsequential; the site of the game was not, as it emerged as the core of yet another Al Davis capital venture—and *ad*venture.

While it appealed immensely to Al to ease his conscience about Oakland in this way, and it later aided him for people to think it was his idea, this was an opportune football that bounced into his lap. The Oakland Coliseum Commission had for years tried to promote an exhibition game, so as to credibly petition the NFL for an expansion team. The Coliseum's interest was not the Raiders, per se, but to pack the stadium, and that's where Davis fit in.

Al was free of the Irwindale commitment now, the February deadline having passed—predictably—with no deal. At first the city council there backed off the original $115 million loan package as a fiscal risk. Then, in the summer of 1989, came another offer of $155 million, but now the city seemingly had outlived its usefulness in Al's plans; by then, with things griddling in Oakland, he had given Irwindale enough attention for its $10 million.

Al took the game in Oakland at first to pressure the LAMCC into moving. Then, seeing the game sell out a month in advance —50,642 would cram the Coliseum and cheer the Raiders—Al waded deeper into the plot. That spring, negotiations began between the Oakland Coliseum board and Davis to once and for all effect the agreement that might have kept Al Davis from sticking the NFL for $18 million and gaining $6.7 million from the LAMCC. This *really* was suspending reality. Believing that Al would actually, and *in good faith*, make a deal to bring the Raiders *back* in 1992 to the city he had rejected required belief in an irony knowing no shame. But it played, to bureaucrats in Oakland and Los Angeles, with no further explanation, simply because it came from a man knowing no shame.

The Oakland fans, Al knew, would be a tougher sell. The Coliseum might be packed for one game, but out there in the Bay Area was a cuckolded populace just now getting over the old hurt. For legions, Al Davis wasn't a hero in exile, just a weasel.

"It's like the guy that goes and has an affair with the sexy blond, then wants to go back with his wife," Tom Keating sensed as he watched the scenario unfolding in Oakland. "He's cheated publicly. But Al, not being one to take a slap in the face, you tell him he can't have it and he wants it more.

"It was also like the movie *The Bad and the Beautiful*. Kirk Douglas is Jonathan Shields, this Hollywood producer, and he'll do anything to win. Well now, in the end, everything's gone. He's kinda lost in Europe and wants to come back and make the big production. And all the people he's used and hurt before, they're all sittin' in the room and Shields is on the line. He wants them all to work with him again, he's givin' 'em the same pitch: I'm comin' back, it's gonna be great.

"And nobody wants to talk to him. But then they gather around the phone and they're listenin' as the credits roll. *Great!* That's Al Davis. That's what he is! And Oakland listened, because they also used him, to become a sports town. And he gave people a chance nobody else would. It's the classic of that team. I mean, it's from Ben Davidson on. And if he got back here, he'd do it all again."

Keating believed it would happen, that L.A. just was no place for that ethic. "I think Al thought it was, or could be. And he couldn't. They're always gonna be front-runners. There are certain places that you're comfortable. Al's wife never left here. She never moved down there." Then, chortling, "Don't forget, she met him in the movie theater. She knows."

But was this the Davis of the old theater? Or was it the Davis who had mastered the art of hidden agendas? Certainly his credibility was enhanced when he chose John Brooks, the long-time Raiders limited partner, as his point man in the negotiations with Oakland. Brooks—once a prominent lobbyist for Wayne Valley's building firms and an influential fund-raiser for the California Democratic party—was now the state party chairman, and his smooth, agreeable manner was a welcome change from Al LoCasale's narrow-eyed surliness. And his counterpart across the table, Don Perata, the chairman of the Alameda County Board of Supervisors, was an old political ally.

However, like a bad rerun, the negotiations stalled, dragged past numerous deadlines, and became subject to the intervention once again of Mayor Lionel Wilson—whose involvement the first time had turned out to be Al's ticket *out* of Oakland. Wilson was so hot to make amends for losing the Raiders that—just as before—his generosity went haywire.

Not incidental to this was Al's sudden interest in yet another city, the state capital, Sacramento, familiar turf for John Brooks. A $50 million offer had been made there after voters in the fall of 1989 approved a bond issue to build a $100 million stadium adjacent to the ARCO Arena. But this offer would take on a semicomical quality when the City Council voted to take Davis's $50 million from the city's hotel tax and the hotels sued to stop them. Al was to give an answer to Sacramento by the time the bonds were due to expire in February 1990. When the deadline passed, so did he, as now he and Oakland were closing in on a blockbuster deal.

Before Sacramento joined the game, Lionel Wilson had vetoed as too much a prospective $50 million revenue bond package worked out by Brooks and Perata. Now, Wilson committed to a truly hare-brained deal far riskier to his city—a staggering, fifteen-year, $602 million package that shivered even Al Davis. On March 13, 1990, while at the NFL owners meeting in Orlando, Florida, Davis announced the fabled return of the Raiders to Oakland.

As if it was written in the sky how much of life is one great absurd irony, it was on that day that Gene Klein—whose life became so miserable the day Al Davis left Oakland—finally found peace, in death.

On that day, too, Al was asked if he now regretted moving to Los Angeles. "I regret that it has affected the team, it's affected my life, and it's affected a lot of people here unnecessarily," he said uneasily. "If you mean that kind of regret, yes." He concluded: "I expect great things are on the horizon for the Oakland Raiders."

Lionel Wilson, however, must have been suffering from hallucinations. Davis's announcement was actually nothing more than an oral agreement in response to a deadline by the Oakland City Council and the Alameda County Board of Supervisors; they had not yet discussed the offer and had no intention of doing so until Al gave his word. Now, the recrimination was immediate.

The linchpin of the deal was the unheard-of provision that the city would *guarantee* Davis fifteen years of sellout crowds at the Coliseum. This meant that, as guarantors, if the crowds ever fell short, the taxpayers would foot the difference. Only politicians could have dreamed this one up, and what made it seem even more idiotic was that it coincided with the massive economic rehabilitation following the Bay Area earthquake that fall. With a city pared to the bone—in no small part due to the Raiders' desertion—few saw the need to invite bankruptcy by *subsidizing* them now.

"If the fans don't support this team, I'm looking at living in a city with less fire and police protection," complained Wes Risedorph, a sixty-eight-year-old dentist, at a public hearing on the matter. His concern was heard again and again by the city's politicians, many of whom began campaigning *against* the Raider deal.

"*Give* Al Davis $602 million to come back?" remarked Gladys Valley. "If Al Davis will *pay* $602 million to come back, then I'd go for it."

George Ross, now in retirement in Oakland, could not believe that a sincere Al Davis could have run into this wall of opposition. In fact, much of what he was seeing was disturbingly familiar.

"It was the same as in 1979," Ross said. "Al needed another revenue bonding, but instead he brought it back into the political realm where everybody on the city council and the board of supervisors had to answer to their constituents—very few of whom are ticket buyers. He didn't need the ticket guarantee and he didn't need to open a Pandora's box."

Possibly, he didn't need Oakland, either.

Ross wasn't as sure about that now as he had been the last time around. "Unless there's something more to it, you'd think a detail guy like Al would know what would fly. But I think Al puts together some outlandish-sounding things and if they score, great. So if he could have gotten that guarantee, hell, he could sit back and watch the money pour in.

"Maybe he thought, Christ, if Oakland wants me back so badly they'll go down and lick my boots and pay me for the privilege. And if not, I've lost nothing, I've still got L.A."

Indeed, it seems more than a minor detail that at the time Al complied with the Oakland deadline, the LAMCC was working on, but not yet done, putting some important internal business in order. The Los Angeles Coliseum was now being operated by the giant MCA entertainment combine, through its Spectacor sports management firm of Philadelphia. Early in 1990, the LAMCC was bargaining with Spectacor's Ed Snider for a twenty-year lease extension. Not until then could it offer Davis a competing bid. Now, as the arguing went on up north, Snider okayed the extension as a way to finally deal with Al Davis.

"What Al needed was to find a sure-handed dictator in L.A.," Ross said, "to tell him, yes, we can do this and we will do it. The people he'd talked to down there were not the people who could deliver, they didn't have the power of the city or the county. So he got led down the primrose path by promises that weren't kept."

Ed Snider's clout made L.A. a lock. Not for a minute did Davis need to engage politicians in his talks with Spectacor, and Don Perata pointed out the difference that made. "Public agencies like ours have a standard of perfection and scrutiny beyond what Spectacor has," Perata said. "They were able to put down a deal and formalize it much more quickly than we could." The deal that was mounted left L.A. politicians gasping but helpless—$145 million over twenty years, solely secured and warranted by Spectacor.

The agreement hinged on Ed Snider settling old complications on conditions extremely favorable to Davis. The LAMCC's breach-of-contract suit against the Raiders was withdrawn, the legal meaning of which was that the Coliseum Commission now forfeited any claim on the $6.7 million loan it had given Al in 1985. Only with this provision would Davis commit himself to a twenty-year lease.

The Raiders began the 1990 season with Al's plans still up in the air and their residency in the Los Angeles Coliseum seeming like a forced stay in a halfway house. This did nothing for Al's already-tattered prestige—"The image was that of Al Davis tilting at windmills, and the windmills winning," George Ross thought. Then, on September 11, 1990, two days after a season-opening win over the Broncos, Al signed the new LAMCC agreement. On *that* day, nothing was said of his six-month-old repudiation of Los Angeles. Also on that day, he was given a $10 million advance on the new deal.

In Oakland, Mayor Wilson took the news hard. His city's revised offer of $127 million—with *no* ticket-sale guarantee—had been presented to Davis weeks before, and on the eve of the L.A. announcement, Al, playing it coy to the end, asked for an immediate $5 million advance. When no positive word came the next morning, Al could sign in L.A. with the fact, or pretense, that he had at least given Oakland a last chance.

"Had it not been for the unfortunate fact that politics took the negotiation hostage," Lionel Wilson said bitterly, "the original deal would still be in place and the Raiders would once again be playing in Oakland." Though Wilson of course meant *other* politicians, whose opposition to the Raider deal he made so easy—this was not the brightest stand that a mayor running for reelection could take. But with Wilson having to defend himself to his political enemies, he had no time to malign Al Davis—who, said George Ross, had "sucked up and used" Wilson. But then, Al's finese was such that he could be held blameless. In Oakland, where the public reception of his return had always been cool, to many he was nearly irrelevant to the whole fiasco.

"He didn't lead Oakland down the garden path," Don Perata explained. "We started it."

Lionel Wilson—widely seen as a "Davis dupe"—would pay dearly for that. In the political wreckage, Wilson failed to win re-election, taking down with him many of the office-holders who had gone for that demented deal. Al Davis, who had never actually set foot in Oakland during these negotiations, left bodies, careers, and acrimony strewn with the autumn leaves.

Al did take some lumps, though, and not just from the again-spurned Oakland faithful, who held public burnings of Raiders memorabilia. The nation's sporting press now bared the long knives. "Once upon a time, Davis's motto for the Raiders was 'Just win, baby.' But now it's 'Just give me $10 million, baby,' " wrote *The New York Times*'s Dave Anderson. "[And] when the NFL owners vote next year on expansion cities for 1993, don't expect Al Davis to vote for Oakland. . . . If his latest deal with Los Angeles starts to get lost in the smog, he'll still want Oakland for himself. Just give me $10 million, baby. Or if it's Oakland, $5 million."

Los Angeles fans, those who cared, did have to be cautious. The deal, it was pointed out, was contingent on Spectacor raising private financing; it also had to get clearance to renovate the Coliseum, which now had landmark status and would need to be remodeled without disturbing the stadium's historic exterior. Yet, according to the terms, construction had to begin within twenty-one months; then, Davis's $10 million advance became nonrefundable, no matter what course Al took.

Asked whether he'd be uncomfortable with hitches down the line, Al admitted, "I'm not comfortable right now."

It did not make him any less so that he now had to repeat the cycle of the Raider genesis in L.A. Attendance at the Coliseum had fallen to 423,000 in 1989, the lowest in six seasons. Now, he had to lure back people he'd kissed off. Getting the ball rolling, the team announced a two-thousand increase in the number of season tickets, and Al's catchphrase was that "the greatness of the Raiders is in their future." For better or worse, at least twenty-one months of that future belonged to Los Angeles.

As luck and the charmed nature of Al Davis would have it, the 1990 season was when the tumblers of his team began to click into place. On the field now was the old eclectic Al Davis mix: a handful of homegrowns (Howie Long, Marcus Allen, Bo Jackson, Don Mosebar, tackle Bruce Wilkerson, defensive tackle Scott Davis, cornerback Terry McDaniel) and past free agents (defensive tackle Bob Golic, tackle Steve Wright) sprinkled among a football Ellis Island of new arrivals. The Raiders' linebacking corps alone boasted three past free agents (Linden King, Tom Benson, Ricky Hunley) and a thirty-four-year-old tradee from 1985, Jerry Robinson.

Now, Al had given up a draft choice for the Rams' top rusher, Greg Bell, and signed as free agents three-time Bengal Pro Bowl guard Max Montoya, the Rams' kick returner Ron Brown—another former Olympic gold medal sprinter—and 49ers linebacker Riki Ellison.

Beset with more holdout problems before the season began, Al dealt with them harshly. Steve Beuerlein, who'd finished 1989 as the first-string quarterback, had been making just $140,000. But Al stonewalled, and when Beuerlein sat out the whole exhibition season, Jay Schroeder became Al's man for 1990. But then, Schroeder had *given back* $100,000 of *his* salary. Still on his old Redskins contract and due to make $1 million in 1990, he told Al, "I'm not a million-dollar quarterback. Take something back." Those were terms of endearment to Al Davis.

The other holdout was free safety Vann McElroy. At thirty and on the downside, he was forced to take a pay *cut*, then traded to the Seahawks for an eighth-round draft choice.

Said McElroy: "If you're a player he likes, he'll take care of you. Some of [those] are great players and some aren't worth shit. Unfortunately, I wasn't one of those guys, and I got used as a whipping post."

(This would later ease the way for Al's biggest free agent plum —the signing of 49ers All-Pro free safety Ronnie Lott before the 1991 season, restoring the killer safety quotient to the defense.)

When the season began, attendance at the Coliseum idled at around fifty thousand a game as the Raiders won their first four. Then the Bears came in, the Raiders won 24–10, and the crowd was 80,156. And, with the team racing toward the playoffs, the indicators suddenly were pointing upward, the Irwindale-Oakland-Sacramento charade seemingly long distant. Art Shell wasn't defeated at home until the eleventh try, by the Packers in mid-November. The week after that loss, his team went on the road to play the 8–1 Dolphins and won a taut defensive struggle 13–10, limiting Miami to fourteen yards rushing on twelve carries.

At that point the Raider defense—back in the old 4–3 set up front and the secondary still straight-up, Bump and Run, man-to-man—had given up an average of nine points a game and had an absolute monster in right end Greg Townsend. Suspended for twenty-six days in 1988 for chronic marijuana use, Townsend had lost excess weight and gained mobility. Among the league leaders in sacks, against the Bears he picked up a fumble and rolled into the end zone for a key touchdown.

And while they won both, Jay Schroeder's performance in the critical Chicago and Miami games attested to the death of the vertical game. Against the Bears he completed eight of fifteen for 178 yards; against the Dolphins, ten of nineteen, for 116 yards. The Raiders had entered the nineties winning with a lot of ball control (Allen and Jackson alternating at halfback behind 235-pound blocking fullback Steve Smith), a lot of defense (the 1990 draft having brought three beauties, defensive end Anthony Smith, linebacker Aaron Wallace, and cornerback Garry Lewis), and the occasional long heave. There were not a lot of points.

And Al Davis was still talking about Raider Football.

"He's still talkin' about how, hell, we don't believe in a tailback-oriented offense because it's never won a Super Bowl," said Todd Christensen. "Well, look at John Riggins with the Redskins, look at Joe Morris with the Giants, look at Walter Payton with the Bears. And now look at the Raiders. What are Marcus Allen and Bo Jackson? They're runnin' the ball almost two-to-one to passing plays.

"Again, let's see things as they really are. Raider Football—in the technical sense—doesn't exist anymore. If it exists, it exists in their character."

As the season lengthened, the team's capacity for resilience became thematic. A thirteenth-week loss to the surging Chiefs at home (tied for first place and having swept the Raiders, Kansas City now had an inside lane to the division title) was followed by tidy victories over the Lions, Bengals, and Chargers. The last, combined with a Chiefs loss on the final weekend, gave the Raiders the AFC West and a first-round playoff bye.

From the convulsions of 1989 had emerged a solid if limited 12–4 club (Al confided to people that the team was still a year away from Super Bowl level) with the single most combustible weapon in the game. Bo Jackson's legs were really the Raiders' vertical game now. Those last few games had featured one breakaway run after another by Bo; on one, against the Bengals, he went left, cut back across the field, hurdled a fallen Jay Schroeder, and blew 88 yards before being caught from behind at the one-yard-line.

The semifinal playoff, which brought in the Bengals again, was another study in resilience. Up 10–3, Greg Townsend, closing in on a sack, let quarterback Boomer Esiason dance away from him and throw the tying touchdown with 11 minutes left. But they broke it open on the next series, when Schroeder caught the Bengals safeties doubling on the wideouts and zipped a 41-yard touchdown pass to tight end Ethan Horton (who'd been coaxed out of a two-year retirement by Al before the season) who was covered by an overmatched linebacker. Townsend then wrote a personal postscript by hunting down Boomer with a 15-yard sack, preserving the 20–10 win.

However, even in victory, the fragile equilibrium that held together this team's many loose ends was severed. Though the Raiders rushed for 235 yards, Bo Jackson, after a 34-yard run, was pulled to the hard turf, injured his hip, and was lost for the upcoming AFC title game in Buffalo. In fact, the injury was far more serious than it appeared, and threatened his career.

While the Raiders were fortunate that they could give the ball back to Marcus Allen (in Jackson's absence, Marcus found his youth, going for 140 yards on an array of sleek, slicing moves against the Bengals) the severed bow of stability was fatal against the Bills, a team closing fast on perfection after years of fusing. In the fifth game of 1990, they'd turned a 24–14 deficit against the Raiders to a 38–24 win with a late-game avalanche of big, crushing plays to hand L.A. its first loss. That victory, in effect, gave the Bills the home field for this game—for which they prepped by decimating the Dolphins the week before, racking up 300 yards in the first half alone.

In the corrosive Buffalo winter, Raider instability became frozen-over death. Manhandled on either side of the ball, the defensive line took most of the punishment. Seeming to be manacled at hand and foot, they ceded huge yardage as the Bills' linemen spread wide and their runners charged through the gaps; lack of a pass rush sprouted acres of open space downfield. The Raiders tried a 3–4 defense, a nickel back, two nickel backs. The Bills covered all the angles.

The Raiders' last gasp was in the *first* quarter. Down 14–3, Garry Lewis intercepted a Jim Kelly pass to stop the Bills' thresher-like attack. But Schroeder, perhaps demonstrating why Shell didn't have him pass more all year, was rushed and threw over the middle—right into linebacker Darryl Talley's hands. Talley's 27-yard touchdown return made it 21–3. There would be four more Schroeder interceptions. By the half it was 41–3, and the Bills had gained almost *400* yards, both the score and the yardage playoff records. The final was 51–3.

"They were very efficient today," Art Shell felt he had to say of the other team.

Except for a 55–0 loss in 1961—the lost life of the pre-Davis era—the Raiders had never lost like this.

So now January 20, 1991 had entered the liturgy of Raider glory/tragedy. Indeed, in the long view of history, this mortifying defeat was not so hard to understand. For the Raiders, there is always a familiar, connecting bridge between humiliation and redemption. In 1990, Shell was AFC Coach of the Year, and the team had moved from one victory short of the playoffs to one victory short of the Super Bowl—but it wasn't going to be *that* easy a jump, not with this team.

Once again, fate was seemingly the real opponent in Buffalo, swatting them for rushing too fast toward success. If Al Davis and the Raiders were going to be resurrected in the nineties, indignity would again be a prelude. On January 20, there was enough indignity for a new Raider generation to feed off of for the rest of the century.

At age sixty-one, Al Davis is an odd, melancholy man for whom losing is a kind of death, and vice versa. He lives for the Raiders, *his* Raiders, *his* guys.

He takes care of them with a parochial sense of obligation.

Former Raiders are always on his staff, as assistant coaches, in player personnel, as administrative assistants with unclear functions. Dick Romanski, from the Fort Belvoir football team, has been the Raiders' team trainer for twenty-eight seasons. When Angelo Coia needed a job after a seven-year NFL career, he got one from the man who had recruited him for The Citadel thirty-five years ago.

Loyalty. He retains an amazing familiarity with and fondness for men he matured with in the streets of Brooklyn and on the campus in Syracuse; game tickets are theirs for the asking, though if they come they will not get to see him. He will go to great lengths to attend funerals for men he has not seen in decades. When Al Badain, the basketball coach he revered at Erasmus Hall High School, died in 1987, Davis flew all the way to Florida for the funeral, and then financed the building of a new gymnasium in Badain's name at the old school.

But, even here, he will breed contempt among the old enemies.

"I don't consider doing favors for people making friends," sneered the crustaceous John Sauer, the crisp army gentleman who gave him his first big coaching job and lived to regret it. "You can always buy 'em with anything. You can buy 'em with jobs, you can give people tickets, make 'em scouts. All you have to do is know what they want. But if you have to buy your friends and you have to buy respect, you're not gaining either."

Some enemies hate him, always will hate him. When Wayne Valley died on October 2, 1986, his pallbearers included Jim Otto, Fred Biletnikoff, Tony Cline, and Tom Keating. The managing general partner was forbidden to attend.

"The police were watching for him," Gladys Valley remembered, with a certain delight. "They had orders to throw him out on the street if he came near the church. His wife came, not him. When I was sitting in the limousine to go to the funeral, she came out and threw her arms around me and I stood like a pole until she got away from me.

"I run into him at Super Bowls and Hall of Fame games, and he's always there blubbering on the same speech over and over again, how great it is to have Raiders go into the Hall of Fame, nothing about the Raiders but all about how great he is.

"But if he's so great, why isn't *he* in the Hall of Fame? He's cried about it for five years. The sportswriters call me every year and say, 'He didn't get in again,' and we laugh about him. The sportswriters can't stand him either and they vote on that."

He has his own little ways to get under the skin. In the Raiders media guide, Ed McGah is listed "In Memoriam" and eulogized as a man "who added stability and credibility to the franchise for three decades." Nowhere in the book can be found the name of Wayne Valley.

There are old enemies who have let grudges die, some because of a gesture on his part.

"About ten years after he fired me," said Lee Grosscup, who'd lost his job as PR director because of his drinking, "I got a phone call out of the blue and it was Al Davis. He was asking me for an opinion about a couple of players who had alcohol and drug problems. That was sort of his way of saying that it's over, that ten years was too long to go on not speaking."

"When I got in trouble [fired] as general manager of the New York Knicks," recalled Scotty Stirling, once his right-hand man and then written out, "Al was the first guy to offer me a job. He heard about it and he tracked me down. I was on the road scouting somewhere, and it must've taken a dozen calls to find me, but he called me and made the offer."

The problem, of course, is that he can establish *new* grudges so easily. Like other great men in history, he has left indelible marks, some scars. But those he has touched are never at a loss for encomiums.

"You know what it is for me?" said Ron Mix, now an attorney in San Diego. "I'm on the executive committee of the players' union, the retired players section, and I've heard players in substantial positions within the union indicate that they would feel fairly comfortable to trust Al Davis to work out a collective bargaining agreement.

"Now that's probably naive, but Al's a realist, he can see the direction things are going in. I think he would understand that football players are destined to obtain free agency and destined to win an antitrust lawsuit against the current compensation system that restricts free agency. Look, seven players have chosen him to introduce them at the Hall of Fame ceremonies. Can you say that about any other owner?"

"He's not a simple guy, let me tell you something," laughed Tom Keating. "Did he make the fuckin' world go around the rest of those nitwits or what? Hey, Eddie DeBartolo gives the 49ers their Super Bowl rings in Hawaii. Think Al would ever do that? We got 'em here in Oakland, with the people that brought us to the dance. They didn't come in from Youngstown, Ohio, on a fuckin' plane.

"There's nothin' like him, man. Is he a piece of work? I mean, we would not refer to Al as a social animal, would we? I could go to a cocktail party and meet everybody and have a nice time. Al would be miserable, because somebody might be out there out-workin' him."

Keating is right about Al Davis being like Jonathan Shields in *The Bad and the Beautiful*. There is a scene in that movie in which Shields, the producer, has a blowup with a director he has made famous though Shields has used him. "It was my idea, you stole it from me!" the director rages.

"Without me," replies Shields calmly, "it would've stayed an idea."

If you can understand that about Al Davis, you know why Raider Football *has* to exist—for him, for his team, so that the idea can move mountains. If it exists, it makes Al Davis dangerous. And Al Davis is dangerous.

"Like him or hate him," said Todd Christensen, "you have to respect the fact that he always does seem to succeed."

There's nothing more dangerous than that.

INDEX